Hazardous Materials for Industrial Technicians: A Definitive Guide

First Edition

Barton E. Taylor B.Sc.

Dedication

This book has been developed from the cumulative years of collective wisdom and experience that I have gained from seasoned colleagues, and the hands-on experience I have had that has helped me define my own understanding of what is needed in a book such as this. I originally started the process of writing all of this information in early 2005, developing an extensive series of training modules for hazardous materials, emergency response and regulatory compliance that I could use to help train employees and clients, but also as a means of creating corporate safety programs for various employers I have had. As the training modules evolved over the years and my work expanded into the United States and beyond, each section became more pertinent and refined for people like me who went back and forth across international borders for work. By 2016 when I made the decision to incorporate HAZ-MATTERS Emergency Management, the information I am presenting in this book was the core of all my training sessions that I provide throughout North America. My process has always been to start with understanding the regulations and standards that we use within this industry and then move through a step-by-step process that allows me to abide by my own personal Number One Rule: ***If you don't know what you are getting into, how could you possibly know how to get out.***

Many have contributed countless years of advice, support, and opinion, and several of the ideas presented in this book come from a life time of learning I have gained from each of them. To recognize each individual would be impossible, and I'm thankful to each for the years of friendship and support, and carry you with me every day. The information in this book belongs to all of us, and if this book in any way helps others find a safer way to make things easier every day, then we've all done something special.

It is deeply personal to me in extending my deepest thank you to Randy Soley who took me under his charge at the University of Saskatchewan so many years ago, and helped me become who I am today. Randy took a chance on me, sharing his wealth of knowledge and ideas while letting me loose in a transfer station to hone my skills into what would help forge who I am today. We lost Randy in 1992 to a confined space accident that changed how I saw the industry every day since, but his advice, friendship, and often off-side humour have been with me every day. For all of that Randy, I am truly grateful.

Without question, the greatest thank you goes to my family who have endured decades of me travelling the world doing what I do at the expense of moments missed by not being home. The life associated with this industry is never easy for anyone, often cluttered with always waiting for the phone to ring and then calling home from hotels, and I want to thank my son Griffin and my daughter Brighton for being the light in the darkness that always showed me the way home. We are the Musketeers, and I love you both very much, prouder of you than any words could ever say.

To my partner in life, Angela, who found me when the stars finally aligned. You always make me want to be the very best version of me even when that is hard, always right beside me through all of it. For that, I can only say thank you. You are my best friend, my muse, my calm, and my greatest love, You always will be the best part of my day.

    -Bart

Contents

Preface

Barton Evan Taylor began actively working as a HazMat Specialist in 1991. By 2005, the foundation of all of Bart's work was to help serve as a training platform to assist other hazardous material industrial technicians and employees in understanding all aspects of the work, learning how chemicals operate, and finding safe protocols in the handling of hazardous waste. Throughout his extensive career, Bart focused on providing real-life protocols gained from hands-on experience through highly specialized educational seminars to a very diverse international group. This aimed to assist them in achieving a higher understanding in the field of hazardous materials handling while creating dependable work procedures for all levels of response to incorporate into their work environments.

The purpose of Bart's courses over the years was to deliver unique skills and knowledge that significantly increase each worker's workplace safety and productivity, even if those workers have no prior hazardous materials or industry experience. To achieve this, Bart believes that every worker has the right to reach their full potential in a safe, secure, and successful manner, and we do this by empowering them with technical knowledge and techniques in a way that makes sense to them.

"Hazardous Materials For Industrial Technicians: A Definitive Guide," First Edition, is the product that comes from a combination of years of field experience, development of hundreds of written manuals and protocols, thousands of hands-on chemical identifications, and hundreds of responses to chemical spills. It is an encompassing product of all of our training presentations and experiences and is a comprehensive roadmap that is the result of our years of writing protocols for ourselves and others as we developed them along the way.

While the "Hazardous Materials For Industrial Technicians: A Definitive Guide" is robust and comprehensive in scope, it is by no means a complete guide. The author has made every effort to ensure that all information is accurate at the time of publishing and there are no representations or warranties, expressed or implied, about the completeness, accuracy, reliability, suitability, or availability with respect to the information, products, services, or related graphics contained in this book for any purpose. The author does not assume and hereby disclaims any liability to any party for loss, damage, or disruption caused by errors or omissions, whether such errors or omissions result from accident, negligence, or any other cause.

The information in this book is for general informational purposes only. This book does not replace any governing regulation that is Federal, Provincial, or State, and does not relieve any person from their responsibility or accountability under regulation. Any person that applies the ideas within this book takes full responsibility for their own actions. Each person is responsible to use all aspects of "Due Diligence" to adhere to the integrity of the information, and each person using this book as reference agrees to and accepts all conditions associated with this book as stated within.

This book is developed with the understanding that the author is supplying information but not attempting to render engineering or other professional services. If such services are required, the assistance of an appropriate professional should be further sought. No part of this book may be reproduced by any mechanical, photographic, or electronic process, or in any form of a photographic recording, nor may it be stored in a retrieval system, transmitted or otherwise copied for public or private use, without written permission from the author.

Chapter 1: Laws, Regulations and Standards

Introduction To Tort Law

Tort law deals with the laws regarding civil wrong-doing that deal with a ***"Tort"***, which is an act or omission that gives rise to injury or harm. Generally, this wrong-doing allows the injured person to sue for some form of damages and compensation, and Tort law decides if another person is held legally responsible for that injury. It also stipulates what type of financial compensation the injured person is entitled to.

Tort law is difficult and robust in nature and is often difficult to clearly define. This chapter will assist in understanding how individual behaviours and actions are accountable in everything each one of us does.

Intentional Torts

Intentional torts are the most serious torts and deal with civil wrongs that are committed with a deliberate action and often are dealt with through the Criminal Code. Intentional torts are actions implemented with malice to cause injury. These include:

- assault

- battery

- slander and libel

- false imprisonment

- intentional infliction of emotional distress

- sexual and workplace harassment

Under tort law there are two (2) primary areas that are considered, these being Personal torts and Property Torts.

Personal

Personal torts are defined as actions that are a wrongdoing toward or against a person. In general, personal tor deals with injury to one's reputation, feelings or legally protected interests. Often personal injury is incorrectly included in personal tort: personal injury arises as a *result* of the violation of personal tort law and deals with the consequences of when a party is injured either physically or psychologically from this breach.

Property

Property torts are defined as actions that pose an unlawful interference by a person with the enjoyment by another of their private property. Essentially property torts deal with rights that are invaded from a property right rather than a personal right. Property tort includes:

- trespass – the entry onto/into another person's property without permission

- chattel trespass – the handling of another person's property other than real estate without permission

- conversion and detinue – the taking of another person's property with the intent of not returning it

Negligence

Negligent tort is defined as an act that causes damage based on actions that lack due care and often are dealt with through the Civil Code. These torts are based on the premise that individuals have the duty to observe proper diligence and use reasonable care and skill to avoid the causation of injury to other people.

Negligence arises from careless or thoughtless actions or, when the lack of action occurs in a situation that a reasonable person would have acted. Even without the intent to harm others or the inclusion of malice, behaviour is deemed "negligent" if it falls below what is generally accepted as a legally recognized standard of care. Within negligence, tort law has established the principle that each person is legally obligated to take "reasonable care" to ensure that others will not be injured due to careless conduct and behaviour.

Duty Of Care

Duty is defined as a legal obligation that is owed, or due, to another and that needs to be satisfied. It is the obligation for which someone else has a corresponding right. An easy example of this is if you drive a car, you have the duty to obey the rules of the road. Subsequently, each of us has a duty to act responsibly with those around us and is referred to as Duty of Care.

Duty of care is established under one core principle when evaluating personal conduct: the question becomes would a reasonable person exhibiting ordinary levels of cautiousness have acted the same way in the same situation. This question forms the basis of how a court rules on Duty of Care. A reasonable person obviously is a relative term that each of us may view differently, so the law identifies that a reasonable person considers:

- the likelihood of a certain harm to occur

- the seriousness of that harm

- the burden involved in avoiding that harm

Clearly, certain factors need to be weighed in on this when evaluating a person, including physical abilities and disabilities, age, actions during an emergency and competency.

Breach Of Duty

Once the appropriate Duty of Care is established, a person's action(s) that fail to act as the law obligates a person to is termed Breach of Duty. Breach of Duty is proven in court by determining whether a person's action met or violated the legal obligation of duty and if, in fact, there was a presence of duty to be breached. Duty is a relationship between the offender and the victim and needs to be both identified and recognized as being present by a court. The extent of degree that this duty is breached determines the extent of damages awarded to the victim. Again using the example of driving, if a person exceeds the speed limit and in turn causes an accident that causes injury, the speeder is deemed to be in breach of duty of the standards of driving.

The Reasonable Person

A reasonable person obviously is a relative term that each of us may view differently, so the law identifies that a reasonable person considers:

- the likelihood of a certain harm to occur

- the seriousness of that harm

- the burden involved in avoiding that harm

Clearly certain factors need to be weighed in on this when evaluating a person including physical abilities and disabilities, age, actions during an emergency and competency.

The question in Breach of Duty often deals with the individual's competency and experience.

Therefore, a person who is held within the industry as a specialist, a subject matter expert, or a skilled professional will be more accountable for actions with that industry than a person of no skill. A person with specialized training will inherently be held closer to a standard within that industry than an individual with no training.

Foreseeability

One of the core elements of Breach of Duty is if the person could foresee the risk of harm and then failed to prevent that harm. Actions, alternate safer actions and appropriate adjustments are all taken into consideration to see if other options would have been safer or in fact, implausible.

When determining whether a defendant breached his duty of care by acting below the standard of care, the court first determines whether the risk was foreseeable. Obviously, if it is unreasonable to foresee that a risk exists, the defendant will not be required to take measures to prevent it. Therefore, a person is only liable for damages that were foreseeable and not too remote.

Causation

Causation provides the connection between an action and the resulting effect. In layman terms, causation is known as cause and effect and is premised on the concept that even as children, people are inherently aware that consequences result from both physical actions and omissions. As such, the more predictable the outcome, the greater the intention was to cause some form of injury.

Causation is extremely broad and subject to interpretation and is generally broken into two (2) core steps:

- factual causation – referred to as cause-in-fact, factual causation relates to what actually happened and whether or not a person's action or omission, referred to as conduct, was the cause of a particular harm. Many references call factual causation the "but-for" test: *if it was not but for the person's conduct, would the harm have occurred?*

- legal causation – referred to as proximate causation, legal causation assesses whether the harm that occurred was in fact imminent, natural and foreseeable from the conduct and not too remote in nature to have been reasonably foreseen: *is the outcome in the bundle of risks created by the persons conduct?*

Liability

In general, a liability represents an obligation that is owed to somebody else and within tort law, is very extensive and complex. However, with liability, fault does not always need to be proven for a person to be liable for the action.

Strict Liability

Strict liability occurs when an individual is responsible for the consequences of an action even when they are not at fault or negligent, and intent cannot be shown. The tort must only be proven to have occurred that in some form, the individual was responsible for this to occur. Strict liability is used specifically to hold people responsible for their actions and products without the need to prove fault. Often, strict liability is found in situations that are considered to be inherently dangerous. The presumption of strict liability is that due to the nature of the activity, the person should be able to foresee that others could be hurt by it.

There are three (3) primary categories within strict liability:

- the keeping of wild animals: the keeping of wild animals that may by nature harm other people

- ***inherently hazardous activities: activities in this include the use of explosives and the handling of hazardous and volatile chemicals***

- consumer product: defective products that cause injury

Each of these categories is dangerous and requires a high degree of responsibility on the part of the individual. As you can see within the hazardous waste management industry, the activities many of you have fallen directly within strict liability areas that not only pose concerns but require people to be deemed as professionals or subject matter experts who have had to take specialized training to handle these items.

Product Liability

As noted above, product liability deals with manufacturers, distributors, suppliers, retailers, and others who produce or make products available to the public. A product represents something that is a tangible form of personal property.

As noted, strict liability does not need to prove fault or intent. Therefore, with product liability, the manufacturer et al. is expected to anticipate hazards to life and health that would be inherent in the defective product since the public cannot be expected to know this. Even if the manufacturer et al. is not negligent, they are still responsible for the defective product reaching the public market.

Product liability has three (3) main types of liability associated with it that you will be familiar with:

- **Manufacturing defect**: defects that occur in the manufacturing process and involve either substandard materials or workmanship

- **Design defect**: defects that occur when a product is inherently dangerous or defective regardless of how carefully manufactured and fails ordinary customer expectations.

- **Failure to warn**: defects that occur that carry nonobvious dangers and can be mitigated by user warnings or relevant product instructions.

Regulatory Agencies

The hazardous materials industry is under the diligent scrutiny of a multitude of regulatory authorities and industry standards organizations on municipal, provincial, and federal levels. Each body has jurisdiction over legislated regulations, codes, standards, guidelines and other forms of rules for all areas of an organization's operations, including transportation, health and safety, environment, zoning, labour, emergency response, as well as a host of others.

The most significant authorities and organizations will be discussed in this module. Each has jurisdiction over various regulations and standards, all of which are itemized with links in Section 10. For now, all that is important is to become familiar with the backgrounds and mandates of each organization and to learn how each might impact your company.

Canada

Environment and climate change Canada

Environment and Climate Change Canada, also commonly referred to as Environment Canada, is a federal agency that assists in preserving and enhancing the quality of the natural environment, including water, air, and soil quality, and conserving Canada's renewable resources, including migratory birds, and water resources. Environment Canada also carries out meteorology; enforces rules made by the Canada – United States International Joint Commission relating to boundary waters, and coordinates environmental policies and programs for the federal government.

Environment Canada responds to the needs of Canadians by undertaking the following mandates:

- controlling and preventing pollution in order to secure a clean environment for Canadians

- conserving Canada's rich legacy of nature

- providing weather and environmental predictions that enable Canadians to adapt to changing weather and related environmental influences and impacts

Environment Canada has five (5) administrative regions and one national office:

- National Office Ottawa

- Atlantic Region New Brunswick, Nova Scotia, Newfoundland and Labrador, PEI

- Quebec Region Quebec

- Ontario Region Ontario

- Prairie and Northern Region Saskatchewan, Manitoba, Alberta, Northwest Territories, Nunavut

- Pacific and Yukon Region British Columbia and Yukon

Environment Canada is further departmentalized into the following distinct business lines.

Nature

The objective of the Nature business line is to conserve biological diversity in health ecosystems. This business lines leads in building shared sustainability strategies for Canada's wildlife and ecosystems. It contributes to scientific understanding of ecosystem functioning, develops partnerships to improve the health of nationally significant ecosystems, and discharges federal responsibilities for managing wildlife, water and wetland resources.

Specifically, Environment Canada's roles in achieving its objective are:

- developing scientific knowledge and tools needed to understand and respond to the effects of human activities on ecosystems

- managing migratory birds and nationally significant migratory bird habitat

- collaborating with provinces and other partners, developing and implementing recovery plans for endangered species

- providing leadership on the implementation of the Convention of Biological Diversity

- partnering with others, applying the integrated approach to conserving and restoring significant ecosystems, and providing tools to build local capacity to continue this work

This group represents Canada's interests in international arenas dealing with wildlife, ecosystem health, and biodiversity.

Weather and Environmental Predictions

The objective of the Weather and Environmental Predictions business line is to help Canadians adapt to their environment in ways that safeguard their health and safety, optimize economic activity, and enhance environmental quality. Through this business line, Environment Canada provides meteorological and hydrological warnings and forecasts, develops information on weather, air quality, ice and hydrology, and contributes to the understanding of the impacts of human activity on the atmospheric environment.

Specifically, Environment Canada's roles in achieving its objectives are:

- monitoring the state of the atmosphere (weather, climate, air quality and ultraviolet radiation), hydrosphere (water) and cryosphere (ice and snow)

- providing information on the past, present and future states of the physical environment

- issuing warnings of severe weather and environmental hazards

- engaging in scientific research on the causes of severe weather, the mechanisms that transport chemicals and weather through the atmosphere and around the world, and the impacts of human activity on the atmospheric environment

This group provides advice on the adaptation to changing weather and climate.

Clean Environment

The objective of the Clean Environment business line is to protect Canadians from domestic and global source of pollution. Emphasizing a preventative approach, this business line leads in the development of shared, long-term strategies to reduce human impacts on the atmosphere and air quality (including climate change, smog, and depletion of the stratospheric ozone layer) and to reduce the threat posed by toxic substances.

Specifically, Environment Canada's roles in achieving its objectives are:

- identifying threats from pollutants, their sources and means of controlling them through the application of sound science

- developing standards, guidelines and codes of practice to ensure adequate levels of protection of environmental quality

- collaborating with provinces, industry and non-governmental organizations, identifying and implementing appropriate strategies for preventing or reducing pollution

- administering and enforcing regulations for pollution prevention and control within areas of federal jurisdiction

- monitoring levels of contaminants in air, water, and soil

- representing Canada's interest in the development of international agreements and accords to reduce pollution

This group provides advice and tools for preventing pollution and supports the development and deployment of green technologies.

Enforcement

In addition to informing those who must comply with the laws and encouraging voluntary efforts of Canadians to achieve compliance, Environment Canada's enforcement personnel conduct formal inspections to verify compliance with laws and regulations, direct or take correction actions if needed, investigate alleged violations of the laws that department administers, and recommend to the Department of Justice to prosecute alleged offenders. Measures to deal with violations include warnings, orders of various types, tickets, seizure, detention, arrest, and prosecution.

CANADIAN CENTRE FOR OCCUPATIONAL HEALTH AND SAFETY, CCOHS

The Canadian Centre for Occupational Health and Safety, CCOHS, is a federal government agency that serves to support the vision of eliminating all Canadian work-related illnesses and injuries. The mandate for CCOHS is to provide work-related injury illness prevention initiatives and occupational health and safety information. This includes providing consulting among federal, provincial and territorial jurisdictions and participation in labour and management. CCOHS's mandate is to also assist in the development and maintenance of policies and programs as well as to serve as a national centre for information related to occupational health and safety.

CCOHS is a federal departmental corporation reporting to the Parliament of Canada through the federal Minister of Labour. CCOHS is governed by a council representing three stakeholder groups in a structure that mandates that CCOHS is impartial in the approach to information dissemination:

- government: federal, provincial and territorial

- employers

- workers

Occupational health and safety is enforced by jurisdictional authorities for each province and territory (i.e., Saskatchewan Occupational Health and Safety). CCOHS has no jurisdictional authority but rather consults and provides information, policies and programs to each jurisdictional authority in Canada.

TRANSPORT CANADA

Canadians need a reliable, safe, and sustainable transportation system to connect communities and trading partners. Transport Canada works to help ensure that Canadians have the best transportation by developing and administering policies, regulations and programs for a safe, efficient and environmentally friendly transportation system; contributing to Canada's economic growth and social development; and protecting the physical environment. They do this by:

- setting policies, regulations and standards to protect the safety, security and efficiency of Canada's rail, marine, road and air transportation systems, including the transportation of dangerous goods and sustainable development

- working in partnership with other federal, provincial, territorial and municipal departments and organizations, the Transportation Safety Board, the Canadian Transportation Agency, NAV Canada, other private organizations, stakeholders, and members of the transportation industry

- promoting and enforcing departmental policies, regulations and standards through inspection, education and consultation

- monitoring and assessing the performance of the transportation system

- administering the transfer of ports, harbours and airports to communities and other interests and operate the facilities not yet divested

Transport Canada offices are divided into five (5) regional sites across Canada:

- Head Office Ottawa, Ontario

- Pacific Region Vancouver, British Columbia

- Prairie and Northern Region Winnipeg, Manitoba

- Ontario Region North York, Ontario

- Quebec Region Dorval, Quebec

- Atlantic Region Moncton, New Brunswick

There are five (5) designated branches of Transport Canada:

Air

Transport Canada maintains safety and security of air transportation – for pilots, flight instructors, maintenance technicians and passengers. Transport Canada also plays a significant role relating to commercial airlines and security.

Marine

Transport Canada maintains the safety and security of maritime transportation – for operators and passengers of small commercial vessels, large commercial vessels and pleasure craft. Transport Canada also plays a role in marine security and marine infrastructure.

Rail

Transport Canada works to improve safety at railway crossings and monitors Canada's rail infrastructure in areas such as its impact on the environment and sustainable transportation, safety and accessibility.

Road

Transport Canada assists with the improvement of safety of drivers and their passengers. Transport Canada also plays a leadership role in the development of the national motor carrier transportation system, and it plays a partnership role in ensuring Canada's highway infrastructure is safe and efficient.

Transportation of Dangerous Goods

The Transport of Dangerous Goods (TDG) Directorate is the focal point for the national program to promote public safety during the transportation of dangerous goods. The TDG Directorate serves as the major source of regulatory development, information and guidance on dangerous goods transport for the public, industry and government employees.

The transportation of dangerous goods by air, marine, rail and road is regulated under the federal Transportation of Dangerous Goods Act 1992. The Transportation of Dangerous Goods Regulations, adopted by all provinces and territories, establishes the safety requirements for the transportation of dangerous goods.

Regulatory Support Agencies

Transport Canada works with various federal and provincial agencies to ensure the safe and compliant transportation of materials. These governmental agencies focus on the research, development, administration, and adherence to the standards they are responsible for. These agencies include:

- Regulatory Affairs Branch
- Research, Evaluation and Systems Branch
- Compliance and Response Branch

Regulatory Affairs Branch

The Regulatory Affairs Branch is responsible for the administration, development and amendment of the TDG Regulations. Personnel represent Canada on international organizations responsible for establishing uniform international requirements for classification, labeling and marking of means of containment, transport documentation and safety marks for vehicles carrying dangerous goods. These organizations include:

- United Nations Committee of Experts on the Transportation of Dangerous Goods

- Association of American Railroads (AAR)

- International Civil Aviation Organization (ICAO) – Dangerous Goods Panel

This group has initiated the development of standards for all types of means of containment used in the transportation of dangerous goods. They also issue permits when exceptions to the regulations are warranted.

Research, Evaluation and Systems Branch

The Research, Evaluation and Systems Branch makes recommendations and implements decisions and directives to minimize the adverse effects of accidental losses to people, property and the environment associated with the transportation of dangerous goods. They apply risk management techniques in a regulatory framework targeted toward highly diverse and competitive sector of the Canadian transportation system. These techniques reduce the uncertainty surrounding the potential for accident-related losses by estimating the likelihood and severity of losses and by taking action to reduce the probability and severity of these losses.

Policy Group

The role of the Policy Group is to develop, recommend and coordinate modal and multi-modal policies. Essentially, the group offers advice, analysis and data on transportation issues, system performance and stakeholder positions. Advice on policy options is based on efficiency, competitiveness, safety and security, environmental sustainability, and inter-modal integration.

The Technology Research and Development Group undertakes R&D to enhance the efficiency and sustainability of the transportation system and to improve the safe, secure, efficient, and environmentally responsible movement of people and goods in Canada.

Research priorities are established by a senior management committee that reviews proposals and establishes funding priorities based on the Department's strategic objectives.

An intradepartmental working group develops selection and evaluation criteria as well as performance metrics and documentation. It identifies opportunities for integrated and shared R&D

projects for better management of resources, and it identifies and shares best practices for R&D program delivery and monitoring, as well as assessing effectiveness and measuring outcomes.

Compliance and Response Branch

The Compliance and Response Branch, with the assistance of five regional offices across Canada, ensures that consignors, federal carriers and consignees are complying with the regulations through a national inspection, investigation and enforcement program and coordinates the activities of all dangerous goods inspection agencies. The regional offices also provide information and advisory services to industry and the public.

There are Remedial Measure Specialists within the agency who review industry emergency response assistance plans registered with Transport Canada to ensure these can be activated to respond effectively to dangerous goods transportation accidents.

This agency is also responsible for the development of training programs for all federal and some provincial inspectors. They provide general education and awareness programs for industry and the public and manage the explosives vehicle certificate program on behalf of the Explosives Branch of National Resources Canada.

Canadian Transport Emergency Centre, CANUTEC

CANUTEC is the Canadian Transport Emergency Centre operated by Transport Canada to assist emergency response personnel in handling dangerous goods emergencies. This national bilingual advisory centre was established in 1979 and is part of the Transportation of Dangerous Goods Directorate. It has the mandate to regulate the handling, offering for transport and transport of dangerous goods by all modes, ensuring public safety. CANUTEC is one of the major programs instituted by Transport Canada to promote public safety during the movement of people and goods in Canada.

CANUTEC has set up a scientific data bank on chemicals manufactured, stored and transported in Canada and is staffed by professional scientists specialized in emergency response and experienced in interpreting technical information and providing advice. CANUTEC deals with some 30,000 telephone calls per year with approximately 1,000 of these that require emergency reports.

CANUTEC's data bank consists of information on more than 750,000 commercial products. The data bank is computerized with easy access to comprehensive information on individual product properties. CANUTEC also has access to a large number of industry data banks and has communication links with their emergency response centres. CANUTEC has also established communication links with emergency response centres in other countries and has access to various international organizations' data banks. This provides CANUTEC scientists with quick access to a vast national and international resource network.

In addition to these data banks, CANUTEC has access to, among others, the following resources:

- an extensive emergency response reference library

- directories of Canadian and foreign chemical manufacturers, shippers and transporters

- directories of emergency response groups across the country including public agencies both federal and provincial, medical facilities and health specialists

- list of specialized equipment suppliers

Taking into consideration the characteristics of the dangerous goods involved and the particular conditions at the emergency site, CANUTEC's staff can provide immediate advice on:

- chemical, physical and toxicological properties and incompatibilities of the dangerous goods

- health hazards and first aid

- fire, explosion, spill or leak hazards

- remedial actions for the protection of life, property and the environment

- evacuation distances

- personal protective clothing and decontamination

CANUTEC staff do not go to the site of an incident. Advice and information are provided by telephone. In some instances, standard information and data can be transmitted in printed copies to the site. This complements the verbal advice and recommendations given by CANUTEC staff members. CANUTEC can also provide communication links with the appropriate industry, government or medical specialists. The shipper of the dangerous goods involved can also be linked to the site to deal with instructions on cleanup, disposal and/or recovery.

Should on-site assistance be required, CANUTEC can assist in the activation of industry emergency response plans such as TEAP, the Transportation Emergency Assistance Plan, operation by the Canadian Chemical Producers' Association or on-site assistance from other industry or government specialists.

A team of Transport Canada inspectors enforces the Transportation of Dangerous Goods Act, by ensuring that shippers, carriers and recipients comply with the Transportation of Dangerous Goods Regulations concerning classification, documentation, indication of hazards, and safety standards and rules.

A Transport Canada inspector has the right to:

- inspect computer, digital and electronic records

- seize any item

- search vehicles, aircraft, buildings and boats

- issue fines, penalties, and criminal and civil charges

Transport Canada inspectors provide services including:

- education, information and advice to the public and industry

- inspection and investigation with respect to handling, transport demand and transport of dangerous goods through the entire chain from manufacturer to recipient.

- review plans for emergencies involving dangerous goods, and application of corrective measures.

- act as emergency consultants regarding chemicals, emergency measures and regulatory requirements through CANUTEC.

FISHERIES AND OCEANS CANADA, DFO

Fisheries and Oceans Canada is the lead federal government department responsible for developing and implementing policies and programs in support of Canada's economic, ecological and scientific interests in oceans and inland waters. Fisheries and Oceans Canada is responsible for conserving and sustaining use of Canada's fishery resources while continuing to provide safe, effective and environmentally sound marine services that are responsive to the needs of Canadians in a global economy.

They have the mandate to:

- manage and protect the fisheries resource

- manage and protect the marine and freshwater environments

- understand the oceans and aquatic resources

- maintain marine safety

- facilitate Maritime trade, commerce and ocean development

DFO has six (6) administrative regions:

- Pacific Region Vancouver, British Columbia

- Central and Artic Region Winnipeg, Manitoba

- Quebec Region Montreal, Quebec

- Laurentian Region Quebec, Quebec

- Maritimes Region Dartmouth, Nova Scotia

- Gulf Region Moncton, New Brunswick

- Newfoundland Region St. John's Newfoundland

Additionally, there are three (3) focus groups within Fisheries and Oceans Canada:

Conservation and Sustainable Resource Use

DFO protects and conserves marine and freshwater habitat, establishes fishery management plans, develops conservation and protection policies and implements programs to provide for sustainable use of Canada's marine resources. DFO provides leadership on the development and implementation of an Oceans Management Strategy and a national system of marine protected areas, integrated coastal zone management and marine environmental programs.

Scientific Research

DFO provides sound scientific basis for the conservation and sustainable development of fishery resources, fish habitat management, defense and shipping, as well as studying the influences of climate variations and aquatic ecosystems.

Marine Safety and Environmental Protection

DFO is responsible for safe harbours, waters and waterways, producing reliable navigational charts and maintaining and extensive system of navigational aids and marine communication. DFO fleets provide icebreaking aids to navigation, rescue, safety and environmental response services.

Statues and their regulations provide the framework and authority that Fishery Officers and other staff work under to implement fishing plans and provide protection for fish and fish habitats. The legislation lays out the framework in which Fisheries Officers can open and close fisheries, issue licenses and attach conditions, and gather biological and statistical information.

Fishery Officers use a variety of legislation that can vary for each location. Fishery Officers, while working in Saskatchewan, are Ex Officio Conservation Officers, as well as Peace Officers under the Criminal Code of Canada, regardless of location. Fishery Officers work closely with other government agencies, including Environment Canada and Saskatchewan Environment and therefore must have a working knowledge of local statutes and regulations not directly related to fish and fisheries.

DFO's Habitat and Enhancement Branch (HEB) serves for habitat enforcement. Many HEB staff have legal designations as habitat inspectors and fishery guardians, conferring specific powers of investigation. Fishery Officers team up with HEB biologists and technicians, who are needed to:

- collect specialized technical evidence (from mining sites, pulp mills, construction zones, and forestry harvest areas

- prove habitat charges in court. They give their expert opinion on how the alteration was harmful or that a deposited substance was "deleterious."

- help assess possible defenses of the accused

- help design sentencing options that can restore or prevent further damage to fish habitat

PROVINCIAL AGENCIES

Under Canada's federal system, the powers of government are shared between the federal government and 10 provincial governments. The provinces are responsible for public schooling, health and social services, highways, the administration of justice, and local government.

However, overlapping and conflicting interests have stretched provincial concerns across virtually every area of Canadian life. Provinces are free to determine their own levels of public services, and each province has been true to its economic and cultural interests in its own fashion.

Regulatory activity and programs for economic development conducted by a variety of provincial government agencies and Crown Corporations play an important role in provincial life. Workers' compensation, labour relations, agricultural marketing, liquor sales, energy and public utilities are all, for example, regulated by provincial agencies.

Provinces have publicly owned development corporations or other agencies which provide assistance, loans and other incentives for the expansion and diversification of their economies, and often compete with each other, with varying degrees of success. Other provincial crown corporations, particularly those responsible for the generation of electrical power, are also important in provincial economics. The contraction of provincial government services and activities since the late 1990s has, however, led to a re-examination of the role of some provincial crown corporations and agencies and to their privatization.

United States

Environmental Protection Agency, EPA

The United States Environmental Protection Agency (EPA) employs 18,000 people across the United States, including its headquarters in Washington D.C, 10 regional offices and more than a dozen labs. The EPA leads the United States' environmental science, research, education and assessment efforts.

EPA responds to the needs of Americans by undertaking the following mandates:

- developing and enforcing Regulations
- performing environmental research
- sponsoring voluntary partnerships and programs
- furthering environmental education.

The EPA works to develop and enforce regulations that implement environmental laws enacted by Congress. EPA is responsible for researching and setting national standards for a variety of environment programs, and delegates to states and tribes the responsibility for issuing permits and for monitoring and enforcing compliance. Where national standards are not met, EPA can issue sanctions and take other steps to assist the states in reaching the desired levels of environmental quality.

The EPA works to assess environmental conditions and to identify, understand, and solve current and future environmental problems: integrate the work for scientific partners such as nations, private sector organizations, academia and other agencies; and provide leadership in addressing emerging environmental issues and in advancing the science and technology of risk management.

The EPA works with industry, business and government on voluntary pollution prevention programs and energy conservation efforts. Partners set voluntary pollution-management goals; examples include conserving water and energy, minimizing greenhouse gases, slashing toxic emissions, re-using solid waste, controlling indoor air pollution, and managing pesticide risks.

The EPA is organized into offices within ten (10) regions across the United States. The offices are:

- Office of Administration and Resources Management
- Office of Air and Radiation
- American Indian Environmental Office
- Office of Enforcement and Compliance Assurance
- Office of Environmental Justice
- Office of Environmental Information
- History Office

The Regions are:

- Region 1 – New England
- Region 2 – New York, New Jersey
- Region 3 – Mid-Atlantic
- Region 4 – Southeast
- Region 5 – Northeast
- Region 6 – South Central
- Region 7 – Central
- Region 8 – Mountains and Plains
- Region 9 – Pacific Southwest

- Region 10 – Pacific Northwest

EPA's civil enforcement program helps protect the environment and human health by assuring compliance with federal environmental laws. Civil enforcement encompasses the investigations and cases brought to address the most significant violations and includes EPA administrative actions and judicial cases referred to the Department of Justice. EPA works closely with states, which bear the lion's share of responsibility for implementing federal programs, as well as with tribes and federal agencies. Civil enforcement actions serve a number of important goals, such as returning violators to compliance, eliminating or preventing environmental harm, deterring others from misconduct, and preserving a level playing field for responsible companies that work hard to abide by the law. The Agency emphasizes those actions that reduce the most significant risks to human health or the environment and consults extensively with states and other stakeholders in determining risk-based priorities. For over two decades, EPA's enforcement program has made a measurable contribution to reducing the amount of pollution that goes into the air and water, and by encouraging safer handling of hazardous waste and toxic materials.

Occupational Safety And Health Administration, OSHA

The Occupational Safety and Health Administration (OSHA) is administered under the United States Department of Labour. Congress created OSJA under the Occupational Safety and Health Act in 1970. Trade and professional organizations, businesses, labour organizations, educational institutions, and government agencies share an interest in workplace safety and health to collaborate with OSHA to prevent injuries and illnesses in the workplace. OSHA works with these entities to achieve goals that address training and education, outreach and communication, and promoting a national dialogue on workplace safety and health.

Many OSHA regulations and methodologies have been adopted in Canada where no Canadian regulation or standard exists. For example, the HAZWOPER (Hazardous Waste Operations and Emergency Response) training requirements for hazardous waste and emergency response workers has been adopted as a guideline for training.

The mandate of the Occupational Safety and Health Administration (OSHA) is to prevent injuries and protect the health of America's workers. Federal and state governments work in partnership with more than 100 million working men and women and six and a half million employers who are covered by the Occupational Safety and Health Act.

OSHA's mandate is to:

- reduce occupational hazards through direct intervention
- promote a safety and health culture through compliance assistance, cooperative programs, and strong leadership
- maximize its effectiveness and efficiency by strengthening its capabilities and infrastructure

OSHA is comprised of eleven (11) regional offices throughout the United States. OSHA is organized under a directorate system. Offices under each directorate focus on key areas of workplace safety and health.

- Directorate of Administrative Programs
- Directorate of Cooperative and State Programs
- Directorate of Enforcement Programs
- Directorate of Evaluation and Analysis
- Directorate of Information Technology
- Directorate of Science, Technology and Medicine
- Directorate of Standards and Guidance

OSHA is committed to strong, fair and effective enforcement of safety and health requirements in the workplace. OSHA inspectors, called compliance safety and health officers, are industrial hygienists and safety professionals whose goal is to assure compliance with OSHA requirements and helps employers and workers reduce on-the-job hazards and prevent injuries, illnesses and deaths in the workplace.

OSHA can issue citations for violations and impose deadlines for correcting hazards.

State agencies

State governments of the United States are institutional units in the United States exercising some of the functions of government at a level below that of the federal government. Each state's government holds legislative, executive, and judicial authority over a defined geographic territory.

State and local administrative agencies often mirror federal agencies. As such, individual states have agencies that control sections including transportation, public health and assistance, education, natural resources, labor, law enforcement, agriculture, commerce, and revenue.

Any regulation established by agencies that may conflict with federal regulations are not legally valid, but states are allowed to create some regulations that may differ from those promulgated by their federal counterparts. State agencies are often empowered to hold their own series of hearings that can be conducted by their administrative boards which are mandated to represent the public interest.

Links to all State Regulations can be found in Section 10.1.4, State Regulations United States.

Acts And Regulations

Canada

Canadian Environmental Protection Act, CEPA 1999

The goal of CEPA 1999 is to contribute to sustainable development that meets the needs of the present generation without compromising the ability of future generations to meet their own needs. CEPA 1999 came into force on March 31, 2000 following an extensive Parliamentary review of the former CEPA. As of June 13, 2023, Bill S-5, *Strengthening Environmental Protection for a Healthier Canada Act* has been introduced to modernize the Act as well as help strengthen chemical management in Canada.

In Canada, each level of government has powers to protect the environment. This shared nature of environmental jurisdiction makes close cooperation among the federal, provincial, territorial and Aboriginal governments important to Canada's environmental well-being. CEPA 1999 is the primary element of the federal legislative framework for protecting the Canadian environment and human health. A key aspect of CEPA 1999 is the prevention and management of risks posed by toxic and other harmful substances. CEPA 1999 also manages environmental and human health impacts of products of biotechnology, marine pollution, disposal at sea, vehicle, engine and equipment emissions, fuels, hazardous wastes, environmental emergencies, and other sources of pollution. The Minister of the Environment is accountable to Parliament for the administration of all of CEPA 1999. Both the Minister of the Environment and the Minister of Health jointly administer the task of assessing and managing the risks associated with toxic substances.

CEPA 1999 contains significant improvements for the protection of the environment over the former Act and

- makes pollution prevention the cornerstone of national efforts to reduce toxic substances in the environment;
- sets out processes to assess the risks to the environment and human health posed by substances in commerce;
- imposes timeframes for managing toxic substances;
- provides a wide range of tools to manage toxic substances, other pollution and wastes;
- ensures the most harmful substances are phased out, or not released into the environment in any measurable quantity;
- includes new provisions to regulate vehicle, engine and equipment emissions;
- strengthens enforcement of the Act and its regulations;
- encourages greater citizen input into decision-making; and
- allows for more effective cooperation and partnership with other governments and Aboriginal peoples.

Canadian Centre For Occupational Health And Safety, CCOHS

Occupational health and safety (OH&S) legislation in Canada outlines the general rights and responsibilities of the employer, the supervisor and the worker through an Act or statute and related regulations. Regulations made under an Act define the application and enforcement of an Act. CCOHS was established in 1978 by the Canadian Centre for Occupational Health and Safety Act, which was passed by unanimous vote in the Canadian Parliament. CCOHS promotes the total well-being – physical, psychosocial and mental health – of working Canadians by providing information, training, education, management systems and solutions that support health, safety and wellness programs.

A federal department corporation, CCOHS is governed by a tripartite Council - representing government, employers and labour - to ensure a balanced, approach to workplace health and safety issues. They offer a range of workplace health and safety services to help organizations raise awareness, assess risks, implement prevention programs, and improve health, safety and well-being.

Each of the ten provinces, three territories and the federal government has its own OH&S legislation. There is special "right-to-know" legislation that applies to hazardous products. It actually comprises a series of complimentary federal, provincial and territorial laws and regulations collectively called WHMIS - the Workplace Hazardous Materials Information System. It is a comprehensive plan for providing information on hazardous products intended for use in workplaces. WHMIS applies in all Canadian workplaces which are covered by occupational health and safety legislation and where WHMIS regulated hazardous products are used.

Hazardous Products Regulations, HPR (WHMIS 2015)

Canada has aligned the Workplace Hazardous Materials Information System (WHMIS) with the Globally Harmonized System of Classification and Labelling of Chemicals (GHS). WHMIS 2015 legislation is currently in force which means that suppliers may begin to use and follow the new requirements for labels and safety data sheets (SDSs) for hazardous products sold, distributed, or imported into Canada. However, there is a transition period with various stages. At the outset of the transition period, the supplier must fully comply with either the repealed *Controlled Products Regulations* (WHMIS 1988) or the HPR (WHMIS 2015) for a specific controlled or hazardous product. The classification, label and (material) SDS must comply fully with the specific regulation chosen by the supplier, and not be a combination of the two.

WHMIS stands for the Workplace Hazardous Materials Information System. It is a comprehensive system for providing health and safety information on hazardous products intended for use, handling, or storage in Canadian workplaces. Health Canada is the government body responsible for making the required changes to the overall federal WHMIS related laws.

WHMIS has aligned with the worldwide hazard communication system known as GHS – the Globally Harmonized System of Classification and Labelling of Chemicals.

Aligning with GHS provides many benefits, including:

- Hazard classification criteria are more comprehensive which improves ability to indicate severity of hazards.
- New hazard classes are included.
- Physical hazard criteria are consistent with the Transport of Dangerous Goods (TDG

regulations).

- Standardized language (hazard and precautionary statements).

- Standardized SDS format and more comprehensive requirements.

Exploding bomb (for explosion or reactivity hazards)	Flame (for fire hazards)	Flame over circle (for oxidizing hazards)
Gas cylinder (for gases under pressure)	Corrosion (for corrosive damage to metals, as well as skin, eyes)	Skull and Crossbones (can cause death or toxicity with short exposure to small amounts)
Health hazard (may cause or suspected of causing serious health effects)	Exclamation mark (may cause less serious health effects or damage the ozone layer*)	Environment* (may cause damage to the aquatic environment)

Biohazardous Infectious Materials
(for organisms or toxins that can cause diseases in people or animals)

Controlled Products Regulations, CPR (WHMIS, 1988)

Prior to the implementation of WHMIS 2015, Canada used WHMIS 1988 which was known as the Controlled Products Regulations. Even though Canada repealed the CPR as of December 2018, many waste products that will be encountered will still have former WHMIS 1988 labels and Material Safety Data Sheets, MSDS, associated with them.

WHMIS 1988 It was created in response to the Canadian workers' right to know about the safety and health hazards that may be associated with the materials or chemicals they use at work. Exposure to hazardous materials can cause or contribute to many serious health effects such as effects on the nervous system, kidney or lung damage, sterility, cancer, burns and rashes. Some hazardous materials are safety hazards and can cause fires or explosions. WHMIS was created to help stop the injuries, illnesses, deaths, medical costs, and fires caused by hazardous materials.

Under WHMIS 1988, there were three (3) main components:

- identification
- Material Safety Data Sheets, MSDS
- training and education

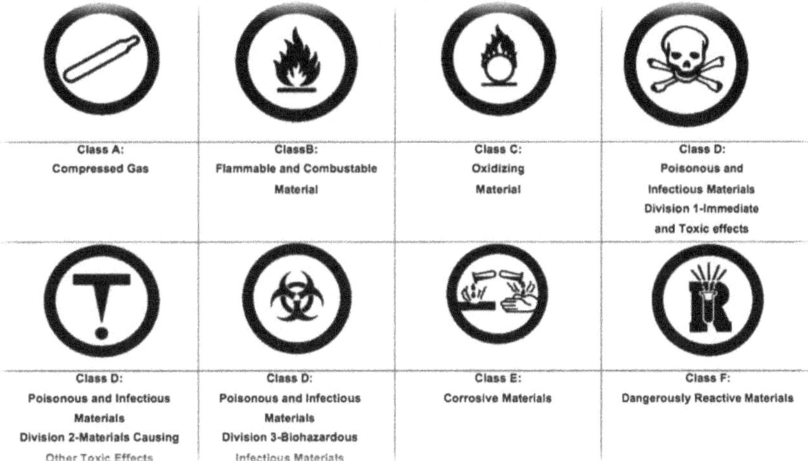

Transportation Of Dangerous Goods Act, SOR/2001-286

The purpose of the Transportation of Dangerous Goods (TDG) Act and Regulations is to promote public safety when dangerous goods are being handled, offered for transport or transported by road, rail, air, or water (marine). TDG also establishes safety requirements.

A product is considered to be a dangerous good when one of the following conditions is met:

- it is listed in Schedule 1 or Schedule 3 of the TDG Regulations,
- or if it is not listed in Schedule 1 or 3, it may still be considered to be a dangerous good if it meets classification criteria outlined in Part 2 of the TDG Regulations.

The TDG Regulations are a set of rules that prescribe safety standards and shipping requirements for thousands of different dangerous goods. The Regulations also provide a means of communicating the nature and level of hazard and risk associated with these dangerous goods. The key elements of TDG Regulations are:

- training
- classification
- preparation of documents such as shipping papers
- using dangerous goods safety marks to communicate hazards that the product may pose to public or environment
- selection of appropriate containment (packaging)
- emergency response assistance plans (ERAP) if required
- reporting incidents

Training is the most important element. Employees must receive training before they handle dangerous goods.

There are both federal and provincial TDG Regulations. Provincial and territorial requirements typically parallel the federal regulations. Generally, the provincial TDG Regulations apply to the handling and transportation of dangerous goods within the Province on highways, as defined in the Motor Vehicle Act and on rail vehicles that are within the provincial jurisdiction.

When the following three conditions are met, the TDG Regulations will apply:

- the product meets the definition for a dangerous good, and
- if the product does not meet any of the exemptions (see below) in the TDG Regulations, and
- if the product is being transported outside the boundaries of a facility.

When the above conditions are met, all of the steps in transportation must be done in compliance with the TDG Regulations, including those segments taking place within a facility (e.g., loading, unloading, labelling, placarding, etc.). Note that TDG Regulations generally do not apply when dangerous goods are moved only within the company's building, facility or private property.

Controlled Drugs And Substances Act, S/C/ 1996, c.19

The Controlled Drugs and Substances Act is Canada's federal drug control statute. Passed in 1996, it repeals the Narcotic Control Act and Parts III and IV of the Food and Drugs Act. The CDSA and its regulations provide a framework for the control of substances that can alter mental processes and that may produce harm to an individual or to society when diverted to an illicit market.

Scheduling substances under the CDSA provides law enforcement agencies with the authority to take action against illicit activities with those substances. It provides that "The Governor in Council may, by order, amend any of Schedules I to VIII by adding to them or deleting from them any item or portion of an item, where the Governor in Council deems the amendment to be necessary in the public interest."

The Act serves as the implementing legislation for the Single Convention on Narcotic Drugs, the Convention on Psychotropic Substances, and the United Nations Convention Against Illicit Traffic in Narcotic Drugs and Psychotropic Substances. Compliance with the Regulations is monitored by Health Canada and authorized places such as licensed businesses and pharmacies may be subject to on-site inspections.

Examples of controlled substances and precursors include substances explicitly listed in the Controlled Drugs and Substances Act (CDSA) such as:

- cocaine
- fentanyl
- morphine
- methamphetamine
- ephedrine

Many other substances are also captured under the CDSA as analogues, derivatives, isomers and salts of listed substances. Health Canada provides a public service to stakeholders to confirm the control status of substances. The status confirmation process includes a scientific review with respect to the heading in the Act for the relevant CDSA Schedule entry.

Controlled substances can be used improperly, resulting in harm to public health or safety. Precursors are chemicals that can be used to make controlled substances. That is why CDSA regulates the substances and precursors listed in the CDSA.

BILL C-45 WESTRAY BILL

On May 9, 1992, 26 miners lost their lives in the Westray Mine located in Pictou County, Nova Scotia, when a buildup of methane gas and coal dust ignited and caused an explosion. Prior to the explosion, several safety concerns had been raised by employees, union officials and government inspectors. This incident resulted in changes to legislation regarding how to establish the criminal liability of corporations for workplace deaths and injuries.

Commonly referred to as the Westray Law, former Bill C-45, An Act to amend the Criminal Code (criminal liability of organizations), came into force on March 31, 2004. It modernized the criminal law's approach for establishing the criminal liability of corporations for workplace deaths and injuries. Specifically, it:

- established rules for attributing criminal liability to organizations, including corporations, for the acts of their representatives
- established a legal duty for all persons directing the work of others to take reasonable steps to ensure the safety of workers and the public
- set out factors that a court must consider when sentencing an organization
- provided conditions of probation that a court may impose on an organization

The Criminal Code requires various elements to be proven before a person can be convicted of a crime. The commission of a prohibited act by the accused – for example, causing bodily harm, counselling a person to commit an offence, driving while impaired, or touching a person for a sexual purpose, must first be proven.

The Crown must also prove that the accused had the requisite guilty state of mind in committing the offence. A person cannot be found guilty of a crime if, for example, the court concludes that the person was suffering from a mental disorder at the time the act was committed or did not know of certain facts that give the act its criminal quality. Depending on the offence, that state of mind can differ. For example, the accused must:

- know a fact (e.g. that goods are stolen), or
- have a specified intent, either to achieve a certain outcome (e.g. to mislead) or to do a certain act (e.g. to intentionally apply force to another person).

Some offences, however, are based on negligence and judged "objectively" so that the person's conduct is itself proof of the necessary "criminal" fault. Some examples, as defined in the law, include:

- storing a firearm "in a careless manner";

- operating a motor vehicle "in a manner that is dangerous to the public"; and
- showing "wanton and reckless disregard" for the lives or safety of others.

United States

Environmental Protection Agency Title 40 Federal Regulations

The Environmental Protection Agency (EPA) was established in December 1970 and is an agency of the United States federal government whose mission is to protect human and environmental health. Headquartered in Washington, D.C., the EPA is responsible for creating standards and laws promoting the health of individuals and the environment.

Regulations are codified annually in the *U.S. Code of Federal Regulations* (CFR). Title 40: Protection of Environment is the section of the CFR that deals with EPA's mission of protecting human health and the environment.

The EPA regulates the management of hazardous waste through Title 40 of the Code of Federal Regulations (40 CFR) Part 266, under the authority of the Resource Conservation and Recovery Act (RCRA).

COMPREHENSIVE ENVIRONMENTAL RESPONSE, COMPENSATION AND LIABILITY ACT, CERCLA (Superfund)

The Comprehensive Environmental Response, Compensation, and Liability Act -- otherwise known as CERCLA or Superfund -- provides a Federal "Superfund" to clean up uncontrolled or abandoned hazardous-waste sites as well as accidents, spills, and other emergency releases of pollutants and contaminants into the environment. Through CERCLA, EPA was given power to seek out those parties responsible for any release and assure their cooperation in the cleanup.

EPA cleans up orphan sites when potentially responsible parties cannot be identified or located, or when they fail to act. Through various enforcement tools, EPA obtains private party cleanup through orders, consent decrees, and other small party settlements. EPA also recovers costs from financially viable individuals and companies once a response action has been completed.

EPA is authorized to implement the Act in all 50 states and U.S. territories. Superfund site identification, monitoring, and response activities in states are coordinated through the state environmental protection or waste management agencies.

The Superfund Amendments and Reauthorization Act (SARA) of 1986 reauthorized CERCLA to continue cleanup activities around the country. Several site-specific amendments, definitions clarifications, and technical requirements were added to the legislation, including additional enforcement authorities. Also, Title III of SARA authorized the Emergency Planning and Community Right-to-Know Act (EPCRA).

Resource Conservation And Recovery Act, RCRA

The Resource Conservation and Recovery Act (RCRA) gives EPA the authority to control hazardous waste from the "cradle-to-grave." This includes the generation, transportation, treatment, storage, and disposal of hazardous waste. RCRA also set forth a framework for the management of non-hazardous solid wastes. The 1986 amendments to RCRA enabled EPA to address environmental problems that could result from underground tanks storing petroleum and other hazardous substances.

The Federal Hazardous and Solid Waste Amendments, HSWA, are the 1984 amendments to RCRA that focused on waste minimization and phasing out land disposal of hazardous waste as well as corrective action for releases. Some of the other mandates of this law include increased enforcement authority for EPA, more stringent hazardous waste management standards, and a comprehensive underground storage tank program.

The Office of Resource Conservation and Recovery (ORCR) implements RCRA. ORCR's mission is to protect human health and the environment by ensuring responsible national management of hazardous and nonhazardous waste.

Toxic Substance Control Act, TSCA

The Toxic Substances Control Act (TSCA) is a United States law passed by the Environmental Protection Agency that regulates the introduction of new or already existing chemicals. When the TSCA was put into place, all existing chemicals were considered to be safe for use and grandfathered in.

Its three main objectives are to

- assess and regulate new commercial chemicals before they enter the market,

- regulate chemicals already existing in 1976 that posed an "unreasonable risk to health or to the environment", as for example PCBs, lead, mercury and radon,

- regulate these chemicals' distribution and use.

TSCA does not separate chemicals into categories of toxic and non-toxic. Rather it prohibits the manufacture or importation of chemicals that are not on the TSCA Inventory or subject to one of many exemptions. Chemicals listed on the TSCA inventory are referred to as "existing chemicals", while chemicals not listed are referred to as new chemicals.

The TSCA defines the term "chemical substance" as "any organic or inorganic substance of a particular molecular identity, including any combination of these substances occurring in whole or in part as a result of a chemical reaction or occurring in nature, and any element or uncombined radical". Generally, manufacturers must submit premanufacturing notification to the EPA prior to manufacturing or importing new chemicals for commerce.

Oil Pollution Act, OPA

The Oil Pollution Act (OPA) of 1990 streamlined and strengthened EPA's ability to prevent and respond to catastrophic oil spills. A trust fund financed by a tax on oil is available to clean up spills when the responsible party is incapable or unwilling to do so. The OPA requires oil storage facilities and vessels to submit to the Federal government plans detailing how they will respond to large discharges. EPA has published regulations for aboveground storage facilities; the Coast Guard has done so for oil tankers. The OPA also requires the development of Area Contingency Plans to prepare and plan for oil spill response on a regional scale. The Office of Emergency Management (OEM) works with other federal partners to prevent accidents as well as to maintain superior response capabilities.

Occupational Safety And Health Administration, OSHA, 1970

Congress passed the Occupational and Safety Health Act to ensure worker and workplace safety. Their goal was to make sure employers provide their workers a place of employment free from recognized hazards to safety and health, such as exposure to toxic chemicals, excessive noise levels, mechanical dangers, heat or cold stress, or unsanitary conditions.

In order to establish standards for workplace health and safety, the Act also created the National Institute for Occupational Safety and Health (NIOSH) as the research institution for the Occupational Safety and Health Administration (OSHA).

OSHA is a division of the U.S. Department of Labor that oversees the administration of the Act and enforces standards in all 50 states.

Hazardous Waste Operations And Emergency Response

Hazardous Waste Operations and Emergency Response, HAZWOPER, is a set of guidelines produced and maintained by the Occupational Safety and Health Administration which regulates hazardous waste operations and emergency services in the United States and its territories.

With these guidelines, the U.S. government regulates hazardous wastes and dangerous goods from inception to disposal.

HAZWOPER applies to five groups of employers and their employees. This includes employees who are exposed or potentially exposed to hazardous substances including hazardous waste, and who are engaged in one of the following operations as specified by OSHA regulations 1910.120:

- cleanup operations required by a governmental body (federal, state, local or other) involving hazardous substances conducted at uncontrolled hazardous-waste sites
- corrective actions involving clean-up operations at sites covered by the Resource Conservation and Recovery Act of 1976 (RCRA) as amended (42 U.S.C. 6901 *et seq.*)
- voluntary cleanup operations at sites recognized by a federal, state, local, or other governmental body as uncontrolled hazardous-waste sites
- operations involving hazardous waste which are conducted at treatment, storage and disposal facilities regulated by Title 40 of the Code of Federal Regulations, parts 264 and 265 pursuant to the RCRA, or by agencies under agreement with the EPA to implement RCRA regulations
- emergency response operations for releases of, or substantial threats of release of, hazardous substances (regardless of the hazard's location).

OSHA recognizes several levels of training, based on the work the employee performs and the degree of hazard faced. Each level requires a training program, with OSHA-specified topics and minimum training time.

- general site workers initially require 40 hours of instruction, three days of supervised hands-on training and eight hours of refresher training annually

- workers limited to a specific task, or workers on fully characterized sites with no hazards above acceptable levels, require 24 hours of initial training, one day of supervised hands-on training and eight hours of refresher training annually

- managers and supervisors require the same level of training as those they supervise, plus eight hours

- workers at a treatment, storage or disposal facility handling RCRA waste require 24 hours of initial training, best practice two days of supervised hands-on training and eight hours of refresher training annually. Employees of TSD facility emergency response organizations shall be trained to a level of competence in the recognition of health and safety hazards to protect themselves and other employees. This would include training in the methods used to minimize the risk from safety and health hazards; in the safe use of control equipment; in the selection and use of appropriate personal protective equipment; in the safe operating procedures to be used at the incident scene; in the techniques of coordination with other employees to minimize risks; in the appropriate response to over exposure from health hazards or injury to themselves and other employees; and in the recognition of subsequent symptoms which may result from over exposures

- the First Responder Awareness Level requires sufficient training to demonstrate competence in assigned duties

- the First Responder Operations Level requires Awareness-Level training plus eight hours

- the Hazardous Materials Technicians require 24 hours training plus additional training to achieve competence in specialized areas

- the Hazardous Materials Specialists require 24 hours training at the Technician level, plus additional specialized training

- the On-scene Incident Commanders require 24 hours training plus additional training to achieve competence in designated areas.

National Insitute For Occupational Safety And Health, NIOSH

The National Institute for Occupational Safety and Health, NIOSH is responsible for conducting research and making recommendations for the prevention of work-related injury and illness. NIOSH is part of the Centers for Disease Control and Prevention (CDC) within the U.S. Department of Health and Human Services. NIOSH is a professionally diverse organization with a staff of 1,200 people representing a wide range of disciplines including epidemiology, medicine, industrial hygiene, safety, psychology, engineering, chemistry, and statistics.

Unlike its counterpart, the Occupational Safety and Health Administration, NIOSH is not a regulatory agency. It does not issue safety and health standards that are enforceable under U.S. law. Rather, NIOSH's authority under the Occupational Safety and Health Act [29 CFR § 671] is to "develop recommendations for health and safety standards", to "develop information on safe levels of exposure to toxic materials and harmful physical agents and substances", and to "conduct research on new safety and health problems".

NIOSH may also "conduct on-site investigations (Health Hazard Evaluations) to determine the toxicity of materials used in workplaces" and "fund research by other agencies or private organizations through grants, contracts, and other arrangements".

NIOSH was intended to function as an agency at the same level as, and independent from, the Centers for Disease Control. NIOSH was initially placed within the Centers for Disease Control in order to obtain administrative support from the Centers until NIOSH was ready to assume those responsibilities for itself; the Centers, however, never relinquished control and the original intent of the Act never came to pass.

Also, pursuant to its authority granted to it by the Mine Safety and Health Act of 1977, NIOSH may "develop recommendations for mine health standards for the Mine Safety and Health Administration", "administer a medical surveillance program for miners, including chest X-rays to detect pneumoconiosis (black lung disease) in coal miners", "conduct on-site investigations in mines similar to those authorized for general industry under the Occupational Safety and Health Act; and "test and certify personal protective equipment and hazard-measurement instruments".

DEPARTMENT OF TRANSPORTATION, 49 CFR PARTS 171-177 HAZARDOUS MATERIALS REGULATIONS

The U.S. Department of Transportation Pipeline and Hazardous Materials Safety Administration regulates the transport of hazardous materials through Title 49 of the Code of Federal Regulations (49 CFR), Subchapter C, "Hazardous Materials Regulations." Parts 171-177 provide general information on hazardous materials and regulation for their packaging and their shipment by rail, air, vessel, and public highway.

The Act was passed as a means to improve the uniformity of existing regulations for transporting hazardous materials and to prevent spills and illegal dumping endangering the public and the environment, a problem exacerbated by uncoordinated and fragmented regulations. Regulations are enforced through four key provisions encompassing federal standards under Title 49 of the United States Code:

- Procedures and Policies
- Material Designations & Labeling
- Packaging Requirements
- Operational Rules

The Department of Transportation consists of the Office of the Secretary and eleven individual operating administrations:

- Federal Highway Administration
- Federal Aviation Administration
- Federal Motor Carrier Safety Administration
- Federal Railroad Administration
- National Highway Traffic Safety Administration
- Federal Transit Administration
- Maritime Administration
- Saint Lawrence Seaway Development Corporation
- Research and Special Programs Administration
- Bureau of Transportation Statistics
- Surface Transportation Board

The Homeland Security Act of 2002 authorized the establishment of the Department of Homeland Security, which, on March 1, 2003, assumed management of the United States Coast Guard and the Transportation Security Administration, formerly DOT operating administrations.

There are many regulations in which DOT enforces. The most relevant regulation in 49 CFR – Occupational Safety and Health Standards. 49 CFR is broken down into three sub-chapters:

- Sub-Chapter A: Hazardous Materials and Oil Transportation
- Sub-Chapter B: Oil Transportation
- Sub-Chapter C: Hazardous Materials Regulations

Sub-Chapter C is the most relevant chapter to 49 CFR (Code of Federal Regulations):

Part 171: <u>General Information, Regulations and Definitions</u>

Part 172: <u>Hazardous Materials Table, Special Provisions, Hazardous Materials Communications, Emergency Response Information, and Training Requirements.</u>

Subpart A – General

      Subpart B – Table of Hazardous Materials and Special Provisions

Subpart C – Shipping Papers

Subpart D – Markings

Subpart E – Labeling

Subpart F – Placards

Subpart G – Emergency Response Information

Subpart H – Training

Subpart I – Security Plans

Part 173: <u>General Requirements for Shipments and Packaging</u>

Subpart A – General

      Subpart B – Preparation of Hazardous Materials for Transportation

      Subparts C to I – Definitions, Classification and Packaging for Class 1 to 9

Part 174: <u>Carriage by Rail</u>

Part 175: <u>Carriage by Aircraft</u>

Part 176: <u>Carriage By Vessel</u>

Part 177: <u>Carriage By Public Highway</u>

Subpart A – General Information and Regulations

DANGEROUS GOODS PLACARDS

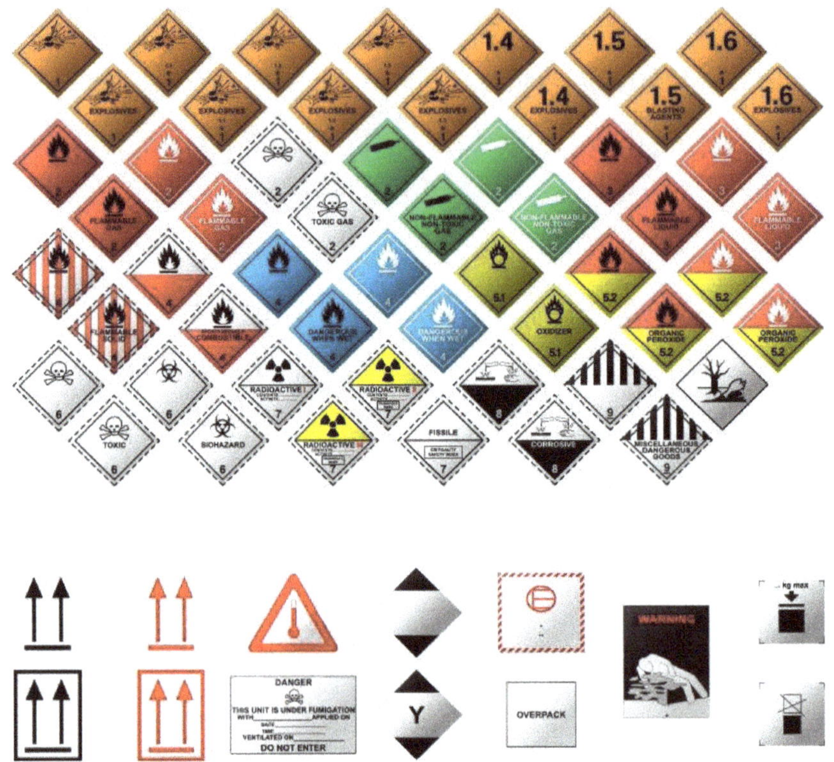

DEPARTMENT OF LABOUR

The United States Department of Labor (DOL) is a cabinet-level department of theU.S. federal government responsible for occupational safety, wage and hour standards,unemployment insurance benefits, reemployment services, and some economic statistics; many U.S. states also have such departments. The department is headed by the U.S. Secretary of Labor.

The purpose of the Department of Labor is:

- to foster, promote, and develop the wellbeing of the wage earners, job seekers, and retirees of the United States
- improve working conditions
- advance opportunities for profitable employment
- assure work-related benefits and rights.

In carrying out this mission, the Department of Labor administers and enforces more than 180 federal laws and thousands of federal regulations. These mandates and the regulations that implement them cover many workplace activities for about 10 million employers and 125 million workers. The DOL has 28 agencies within it, all with the mandate to provide a productive workforce throughout the United States by protecting the rights of workers.

Federal Mines Safety And Health Act Of 1977

The Mine Safety and Health Act of 1977 provides the framework for the actions of the Mine Safety and Health Administration (MSHA). The act amended the 1969 Coal Act in a number of significant ways and consolidated all federal health and safety regulations of the mining industry, coal as well as non-coal mining, under a single statutory scheme.

The Mine Act strengthened and expanded the rights of miners and enhanced the protection of miners from retaliation for exercising such rights. The Mine Act also transferred responsibility for carrying out its mandates from the Department of the Interior to the Department of Labor and named the new agency the Mine Safety and Health Administration (MSHA). Additionally, the Mine Act established the independent Federal Mine Safety and Health Review Commission to provide for independent review of the majority of MSHA's enforcement actions.

Underground mining in the United States is regulated by the Mine Safety and Health Administration, which employs nearly one safety inspector for every four coal mines. Underground coal mines are inspected at least four times annually by MSHA inspectors. In addition, miners can report violations, and request additional inspections. Miners with such concerns for their work safety cannot be penalized with any threat to the loss of employment. Key components of the Mine Act include:

- four (4) annual inspections required at all underground mines
- two (2) annual inspections required at all surface mines
- strengthened and expanded rights of miners
- enhance protection of miners from retaliation for exercising their rights
- mandatory miner training provisions established
- mine rescue teams required at all underground mines.

Standards Organization

National Fire Protection Association, NFPA

NFPA is an international non-profit membership organization founded in 1896 as the National Association. Today, with more than 75,000 members representing nearly 100 nations and 320 employees around the world, NFPA serves as the world's leading advocate of fire prevention and is an authoritative source of public safety. NFPA's 300 codes and standard influent every building process, service, design, and installation in the United States, as well as many of those used in other countries such as Canada.

NFPA codes and standard have helped save lives and protect property around the world. NFPA encourages the broadest possible participation in code development. The process is driven by more than 6,000 volunteers from diverse professional background who serve on 230 technical codes and standards committees. Throughout the entire process, interested parties are encouraged to provide NFPA technical committees with input. All NFPA members then have the opportunity to vote on proposed and revised codes and standard.

NFPA's focus on true consensus has helped the association's code development process to earn accreditation from the American National Standards Institute (ANSI). Aside from vast development of fire and property standards, NFPA has been seriously involved in the development of codes of competency for hazardous materials emergency response.

Some of the codes and standards relevant to are as follows:

- NFPA 10 – Standard for Portable Fire Extinguishers
- NFPA 30 – Flammable and Combustible Liquids Code
- NFPA 77 – Recommended Practice on Static Electricity
- NFPA 326 – Standard for Safeguarding of Tanks and Containers for Entry, Cleaning and Repair
- NFPA 329 – Recommended Practice for Handling Releases of Flammable and Combustible Liquids and Gases
- NFPA 385 – Standard for Tank Vehicles for Flammable and Combustible Liquids
- NFPA 434 – Code for Storage of Pesticides
- NFPA 471 – Recommended Practice for Responding to Hazardous Materials Incidents

- NFPA 472 – Standard of Professional Competence of Responders to Hazardous Materials Incidents
- NFPA 704 – Standard System for the Identification of the Hazards of Materials for Emergency Response
- NFPA 1001 – Standard for Fire Fighter Professional Qualifications
- NFPA 1006 – Standard for Rescue Technician Professional Qualifications
- NFPA 1561 – Standard for Emergency Services Incident Management System
- NFPA 1620 – Recommended Practice for Pre-Incident Planning
- NFPA 1670 – Standard on Operations and Training for Technical Search and Rescue Incidents
- NFPA 1852 – Standard on Selection, Care, and Maintenance of Open Circuit SCBA
- NFPA 1992 – Standard on Liquid Splash-Protective Ensembles and Clothing for Hazardous Materials Emergencies
- NFPA 1994 – Standard on Protective Ensembles for Chemical / Biological Terrorism Incidents

NFPA 471 is an adopted standard. Outlines the minimum requirements that should be considered when dealing with responses to hazardous materials incidents and to specify operating guidelines for responding to hazardous materials incidents.

NFPA 472 is an adopted standard. NFPA 472 covers the requirements of the first responder, hazardous materials technician and hazardous materials specialist.

NFPA 1001 LEVEL 1 AND 2

The National Fire Protection Association, NFPA, has developed training standards for those working in the fire service, and issues certificates for firefighters who pass the training. The Firefighter 1 and Firefighter 2 Certifications use job performance requirements to measure the knowledge and skills needed as a firefighter. The Firefighter 1 Certificate covers basic fire service qualifications, while the Firefighter 2 Certificate involves more specialized areas and command.

Level 1

The firefighter must know the organization of the fire department, how the department works with other agencies and all standard operating procedures. They must demonstrate the ability to don and remove protective clothing quickly, tie knots, mount/dismount fire apparatus. The firefighter must demonstrate ability to use telecommunications equipment including telephones and radios to receive emergency calls and take and relay information accurately.

The firefighter must know how to use Self-Contained Breathing Apparatus (SCBA) and the conditions when it is required. They must know how to force entry into a building, set-up ground ladders, and attack a vehicle fire. The firefighter must demonstrate an understanding of fire streams, including water flow from various sizes of hoses and nozzles. They must also know how to conduct search and rescue inside a building, ventilate a building, and connect a pumper or tanker truck to a water supply.

Level 2

The firefighter must know how to assume and transfer command at a scene using the incident management system. They must demonstrate the ability to complete an incident report and communicate the needs of his team to command authority using the department's standard operating procedures.

The firefighter must demonstrate the ability to extinguish an ignitable liquid fire using foam and ensure that the fire does not reignite. They must show the ability to assemble a team and devise the attack technique for fighting various kinds of fires. The firefighter must be able to select tools to force entry into a building and how to provide proper ventilation in a building based on the structure and nature of the fire. They must know how to protect evidence in cases of arson and demonstrate the ability to rescue victims of motor vehicle accidents using extrication tools. The firefighter must also know how to conduct hazard inspections and how to properly document any hazards found.

NFPA 1081 industrial

NFPA 1081 establishes minimum job performance requirements necessary to perform the duties as a member of an organized industrial fire brigade providing services at a specific facility or site. NFPA 1081 is advanced exterior and interior structural firefighting as well as Brigade Leader level competencies.

NFPA 1072 HAZARDOUS MATERIALS

NFPA 1072 establishes minimum job performance requirements necessary to perform the duties for responding to hazardous material situations. The firefighter must demonstrate ability to offensively mitigate chemical based emergencies by at a minimum:

- interpreting hazard information, hazard symbols, SDS information, charts and response literature
- interpreting information regarding specific containers, both large means and small means, and transportation containment systems
- being versed in chemistry and toxicology
- operating within the Incident Command System, ICS, and understanding roles and framework
- identifying and selecting appropriate chemical personal protective equipment
- performing offensive measures
- performing air monitoring
- identifying and understanding proper decontamination methods

Canadian Standards Association Group

CSA Group is a non-profit membership-based standards organization which develops standards in 57 areas. CSA Group publishes standards in print and electronic form and provides training and advisory services. CSA Group is composed of representatives from industry, government, and consumer groups.

As a solutions-orientated organization, CSA works in Canada and around the world to develop standards that address the public safety and health. CSA has developed standards for safety and environmental management for Canadian business including but not limited to:

- CAN/CSA – B335 Safety Standards for Lift Trucks
- CAN/CSA – Z321 Signs and Symbols for the Workplace
- CAN/CSA – Z259.1 Safety Belts and Lanyards
- CAN/CSA – Z259.10 Full Body Harnesses
- CAN/CSA – Z94.1 Industrial Protective Headgear
- CAN/CSA – Z94.2 Hearing Protection Devices – Performance, Selection, Care, and Use
- CAN/CSA – Z94.3 Eye and Face Protectors
- CAN/CSA – Z94.4 Selection, Care, and Use of Respirators

- CAN/CSA – Z96-02 High Visibility Safety Apparel
- CAN/CSA – Z195 Protective Footwear
- CAN/CSA – B339 Cylinders, spheres and tubes for the transport of dangerous goods
- CAN/CSA – B620 Highway and portable tanks for the transport of dangerous goods
- CAN/CSA – Z731 Emergency Planning for Industry

International Organization For Standarization, ISO

ISO is a non-governmental organization. Its members are not, as is the case in the United Nations System, delegations of national governments. Nevertheless, ISO occupies a special position between the public and private sectors. ISO is a bridging organization in which consensus can be reached on solutions that meet both the requirements of business and the broader needs of society, such as the needs of stakeholder groups like consumers and users.

Since 1947 to present day, ISO has published over 13,700 international standards. ISO's work program ranges from standard for traditional activities, such as agriculture and construction through to engineering and environmental.

The ISO 9000 and ISO 14000 families are among ISO's most widely known standards. ISO 9000 and 14000 are implemented by over 164,000 organizations in 152 countries. ISO 9000 has become an international reference for quality management requirements in business and ISO 14000 is designed to help meet companies with environmental challenges.

ISO 14000 is primarily concerned with environmental management. This means what the organization does to: 1) minimize harmful effects to the environment caused by its activities; and, 2) achieve continual improvement of its environmental performance.

American Conference Of Governmental Industrial Hygienists, ACGIH

ACGIH is a member-based organization and community of professionals that advances worker health and safety through education and the development and dissemination of scientific and technical knowledge. Examples of this include the annual editions of TLVs are work practices guides in ACGIH publications.

ACGIH is a respect organization for its dedication to industrial hygiene and occupational health and safety industries. The board of directors and committees consist of members who strive to provide essential, cutting edge information to government, academia, and corporate facilities throughout the United States, Canada and countries abroad.

The information provided to members and others in the industry through ACGIH include the Journal of Occupational and Environment Hygiene (JOEH) in addition to approximately 400 technical and scientific publications.

United Nations

The United Nations Transport of Dangerous Goods Sub-Committee provides leadership in internationally harmonizing regulations on the transportation of hazardous materials (dangerous goods) by developing an internationally agreed regulatory framework set out in the United Nations Recommendations on the Transportation of Dangerous Goods (UN Recommendations). The UN Recommendations are used are the basis of developed of regional and national transport regulations, including the Canadian Transportation of Dangerous Goods Regulations.

The UN Recommendations cover all aspects of transportation necessary to provide international uniformity. They include comprehensive criteria-based classification system for substances that pose a significant hazard in transportation including a global product identification numbering system (UN Number – UN 1993). They prescribe standards for packaging and multi-modal tanks used to transport hazardous materials (UN Standardized Means of Containment). They also include a system of communicating the hazards of substances in transport through hazard communication requirements which cover labeling and marking of packages, placards, and documentation and emergency response information that is required to accompany each shipment.

Railway Association Of Canada, RAC

RAC was established in 1917 and represents approximately 60 freight and passenger railway companies throughout Canada. The mission of RAC is to work with both government and communities nationwide to ensure that the Canadian railroad network remains sustainable and most importantly, safe. RAC also provides research and public education to ensure that as part of the fifth largest rail network in the world, Canadians are aware of the vital role railroads play in our economy.

American Association Of Railroads, AAR

AAR includes members from United States, Canada and Mexico. The mandate of the AAR is to keep the railroads of North America safe, fast, efficient, clean and technologically advanced.

The AAR is also involved in programs to improve the efficiency, safety and service of the railroad industry. Two AAR subsidiaries – the Transportation Technology Centre (TTCI) and Railing – ensure that railroads remain on the cutting edge of transportation and information technology.

Bureau Of Explosives

Following a growing number of accidents involving explosives which raised the cost to the railroads of transporting explosives, the BOE was created under the American Association of Railroads (AAR). The BOE is responsible for inspecting shipments, encouraging improvements in shipping techniques, and developing rules that formed the basis of all modern regulations of hazardous materials shipments. The BOE's pioneering developments have also extended beyond railroads; the BOE's regulations were applied to highway transportation in the 1930s, and the Coast Guard and Civil Aeronautics Board adapted them for marine and air transport as well.

When the U.S. Department of Transportation was formed in the late 1960s, the regulations were eventually transferred. Today there is little reference to the BOE in the DOT's hazardous materials regulations in 49 CFR, but the BOE, with its inspector force and publications, remains a major and vital force in the safe transportation of hazardous materials by all modes of transportation.

United States Coast Guard

Decades ago the United States Coast Guard realized that the marine industry was expanding into chemical cargoes that were far different and potentially more dangerous than traditional cargoes – and that someday they would have to deal with cargo spills of hazardous materials and crude oil. The Coast Guard began taking step for preparedness for such an occurrence. The Coast Guard created CHRIS (Chemical Hazardous Response Information System) and HACS (Hazardous Assessment Computer System) to predict what would happen if a cargo spilled.

The U.S. Coast Guard and since then become an internationally pioneer for assisting in the preparedness and response to marine incidents involving hazardous materials.

International Air Transport Association, IATA

IATA strives to lead industry efforts to ensure the safe handling of dangerous goods in air transport, by providing a broad array of technical knowledge, products, services, and training solutions tailored to meet industry needs.

Ensuring that undeclared dangerous goods do not get on board an aircraft is one of the many key objectives of IATA's dangerous goods program. By defining standards for documentation, handling, training, and by the air cargo industry, a very high degree of safety has been achieved in dangerous goods transport.

Working closely with governments in the development of regulations, including ICAO (International Civil Aviation Organization) and other national authorities, IATA ensures that the rules and regulations governing dangerous goods transport are both effective and efficient.

Canadian Chemical Producers Association, CCPA

CCPA represents over 65 member-companies and partners with chemical and resin manufacturing sites across Canada, accounting for more than 90 percent of basic chemical and resin manufacturing operations in Canada.

Responsible Care an initiative undertaken by the CCPA members. Responsible Care is a Canadian creation. It is a new ethic for the safe and environmentally sound management of chemicals throughout their life cycle.

The CEO or most senior executive of every member must commit to implement the guiding principles and codes of practice for Responsible Care within three years of joining the association and to be publicly verified as having done so. All companies are re-verified every three years. The expectations of members are partners in the Responsible Care program go beyond the required implementation of codes of practice. Expectation include members networking via leadership groups, public input through an advisory panel, and mutual assistance through sharing of successful practices.

TEAP was established by the Canadian Chemical Producers' Association (CCPA) to provide technical information to emergency teams at the site of transportation incidents involving dangerous goods and alert shippers to the emergency situation.

Under the Transportation of Dangerous Goods Act, every owner-shipper of commodities on a special list of dangerous goods must have an approved emergency response assistance plan (ERAP) as a condition to the right to ship. TEAP meets this requirement on behalf of its members.

TEAP Regional Response Centres (RRC's) are located across Canada along main transportation routes. Additionally, CCPA member companies cooperating under the TEAP umbrella are responsible for equipping and training their own emergency response teams to provide assistance when needed. The types of equipment are outlined in the TEAP manual. Training is at a level such that those people on the RRC teams are generally familiar in handling all chemicals. When a member company's product is involved in an incident, the company can request a response from the closest RRC. The requesting company must immediately dispatch a technical advisor to the scene and make provisions to have their own team at the accident site as soon as possible.

Canadian Emergency Response Contractors Alliance, CERCA

Under the auspicious of the Emergency Response Committee of the Canadian Chemical Producers' Association (CCPA), an emergency response contractor task force was formed in 1992. The task force was comprised of members from CCPA, Transport Canada, railway carriers and emergency response contractors. In the 1997, the task force was re-developed into the Canadian Emergency Response Contractor's Alliance (CERCA) with a mandate to provide and promote a sound dangerous goods emergency response contractor network in Canada.

The mandates of CERCA are to:

- develop standards and verification (on a three-year cycle) process for emergency response contractor sites
- communicate CERCA activities to all stakeholders in land transport emergency response involving dangerous goods
- promote the advantages of membership and communicate to all carriers, manufacturers, industry associations and government.

Transportation Community Awareness And Emergency Response

TRANSCAER

TRANSCAER is an initiative that was started in 1985 by the Chemical Industry Association of

Canada (CIAC) and the Railway Association of Canada (RAC). The program exists to ensure that communities are informed and aware of materials being moved through their community and the associated emergency measures that are in place in the event of an incident. TRANSCAER work with various members of the municipality, emergency responders and residents to help them develop and evaluate community response plans. TRANSCAER is an outreach program that now covers all of North America as of 1986, and is led by industry professionals that are supported by a variety of partner agencies throughout North America. The mandate of TRANSCAER is:

- Provide awareness of the safe transportation and handling of hazardous materials;
- Conduct training for communities and emergency responders on how to safely respond to incidents involving hazardous materials during transportation;
- Assist communities with emergency response planning, training and exercises for hazardous materials transportation incidents.

The Responsible Care program is a program that covers all aspects of a chemical company's business and the lifecycle of the products it creates. By implementing the environmental, social and governance pillars (ESG) since 1985, Responsible Care is now practiced in 73 countries and by 96 of the 100 largest chemical producers in the world. Through TRANSCAER, members engage with communities and various stakeholders to advance laws and regulations that support sustainability.

Chapter 2:

Hazardous Materials Chemistry

States Of Matter

Matter is described as anything that occupies or takes up space and is composed of minute particles termed atoms. For matter to be considered tangible, it must exhibit the properties of both mass and volume.

- **Mass** is the "amount or quantity of matter" in an object. Mass is different than weight which is the measurement of the gravitational pull on mass. Mass is also not a measurement of size: for example, you may have a small object with extremely heavy mass such as an object made of lead. Conversely, you may also have a large item such as a large balloon filled with helium that has very little mass.

- **Volume** is the "amount of space" an object occupies. For example, a pebble occupies a small space whereas a boulder occupies a large space.

The form that matter takes is referred to as the state of matter which is also often referred to as a phase. There are five (5) primary states of matter that we currently know of that occur in non-extreme environments, with the top three (3) being our primary concern in this industry:

- **Solids**

Solids are objects that hold their shape and do not flow in any manner. The molecules within a solid have no translational freedom and are packed tightly together and set in a specific structure that does not allow them to move around like they can in liquids and gases. The atoms within a solid still vibrate with the electrons moving in their respective orbitals, but the atom itself will not change its position.

Solids encompass a wide array of things and can be comprised of a pure element like gold or have a variety of compounds such as granite which has quartz, mica and feldspar. A solid can also have atoms arranged in a very specific order which is commonly referred to as a crystal, such as common sodium chloride table salt, NaCl. Some crystals which are comprised of a specific element only such as carbon, can exist in two or more forms within the same physical state with the atoms being bonded in a different way. As example, a diamond which is made of pure carbon is very different to graphite which is also pure carbon. These elemental crystals are referred to as allotropes.

- **Liquids**

Liquids exists between the solid and gaseous states with water being the most common liquid on earth. Unlike solids that hold their shape, liquids are malleable and have some translational freedom, filling or taking on the shape of any container they are in. When a liquid fills a container, it settles with a flat surface. The molecules within a liquid are held together by the process of cohesion which is essentially the force that "sticks" the molecules together. This can be seen every day with water that drips from a faucet. The cohesive force continues to keep the water droplet together until the weight of the droplet exceeds the cohesive force holding that drop together.

Liquids are not easily compressed and maintain a constant volume over a wide pressure range. When placed in a sealed container, liquids will not expand to fill that space. However, when compressed in a container such as a hydraulic hose, liquids will distribute applied pressure evenly to the surface of the container.

Since the molecules of a liquid have some translational movement, an increase in temperature will increase the vibration of the molecules which in turn causes an increase in distance between the molecules. As this distance increases, eventually the liquid turns to a gas and is called evaporation.

- **Gases**

Gases exist when molecules are spread out over a wide area with atoms that are separate. Unlike a solid or liquid, a gas has no fixed shape or volume and will expand to evenly fill a container since they have very little gravitational force exerted on them and have the translational freedom to move. Gases that are generally liquid at room temperature are often referred to as vapours.

The molecules in a gas are vibrating very fast and therefore have a large amount of energy within them. By compressing the gas and decreasing the temperature, gases can be easily compressed into smaller containers which we are familiar with in every day. Upon release, a gas with move from an area of high pressure to an area of low pressure.

- **Plasma**

Plasma is considered the fourth state of matter is a unique state which is similar to a gas but with a different atomic structure. Plasma is made up of positively and negatively charged particles called ions that unlike gases, are not bound to the nucleus and are therefore free to move around. This allows the plasma to act as a cloud instead of as a bunch of atoms bound together. Plasma is difficult to understand and even though acting similar to a gas, is different than a gas in structure. Plasma can also flow like a liquid.

Natural plasma is not very common and is most frequently experienced when simply looking at the light from stars or with the phenomena known as the Northern Lights. Man-made plasma however is everywhere and include common fluorescent light bulbs and neon signs. In these units, inert gases known as the Noble Gases. are exposed to an electrical current which charge the gas and releases the electrons which subsequently creates a plasma cloud. Noble or inert gases used for these are helium, neon, argon and xenon, but also include krypton and radon.

- **Condensate**

The fifth state of matter was only created in 1995 and is formally known as Bose-Einstein Condensate. Unlike plasma, which is both extremely hot and extremely excited, condensate is extremely cold and extremely unexcited. Bose-Einstein Condensate forms at extremely low temperatures known as absolute zero (-273.15^0C or -460^0F) where the molecules are at their very minimum movement to an extent that movement is considered non-existent. At this point, every atom is exactly equal in energy, so they do not act independently and in turn "clump" together to create one massive atom which is referred to as a "super atom".

Periodic Table of Elements

The Periodic Table of Elements, or Periodic Table, was created in 1869 by Dmitri Mendeleev who at that time identified 69 known elements and arranged them by atomic number which is the number of protons in the atomic nucleus.

The Periodic Table is a tabular chart of the 118 known chemical elements (2019) which are arranged by atomic number, electron configuration, and recurring chemical properties. These properties known in chemistry as periodic trends, are specific patterns in the properties of chemical elements. An online interactive periodic table can be found at https://www.ptable.com/.

OVERVIEW

Groups or Families – Columns 1 through 18

The columns of the table represent groups or families of elements that have similar chemical or physical properties based on the outermost electron shells or orbits of their atoms. In total there are eighteen (18) columns which are generally identified by their top element. All elements in a family have the same number of valence electrons which is discussed later in this module.

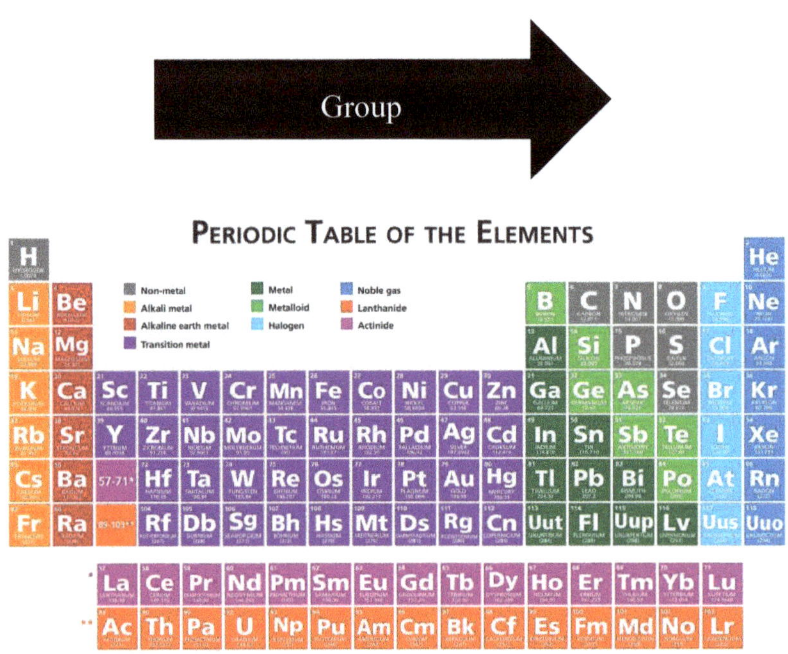

- Group 1: Lithium Family

- Group 2: Beryllium Family

- Group 3: Scandium Family

- Group 4: Titanium Family

- Group 5: Vanadium Family

- Group 6: Chromium Family

- Group 7: Manganese Family

- Group 8: Iron Family

- Group 9: Cobalt Family

- Group 10: Nickel Family

- Group 11: Copper Family

- Group 12: Zinc Family

- Group 13: Boron Family

- Group 14: Carbon Family

- Group 15: Nitrogen Family

- Group 16: Oxygen Family

- Group 17: Fluorine Family

- Group 18: Helium Family

Periods – Rows 1 through 7

The rows of the Periodic Table represent periods of elements that increase in atomic number from the far left (1) to right (7). Each row represents elements that have the same number of electron shells - electron shells can be thought of as the orbit an electron follows around the nucleus in the same manner that a planet follows the orbit around the sun. The difference however is that unlike planetary orbits, electron shells can hold more than just one electron in the same orbit. As the elements progress from left to right, each consecutive element has one more proton (positive charge) and is less metallic. The first element in a period is always an extremely active solid. The last element in the period is always an inactive gas.

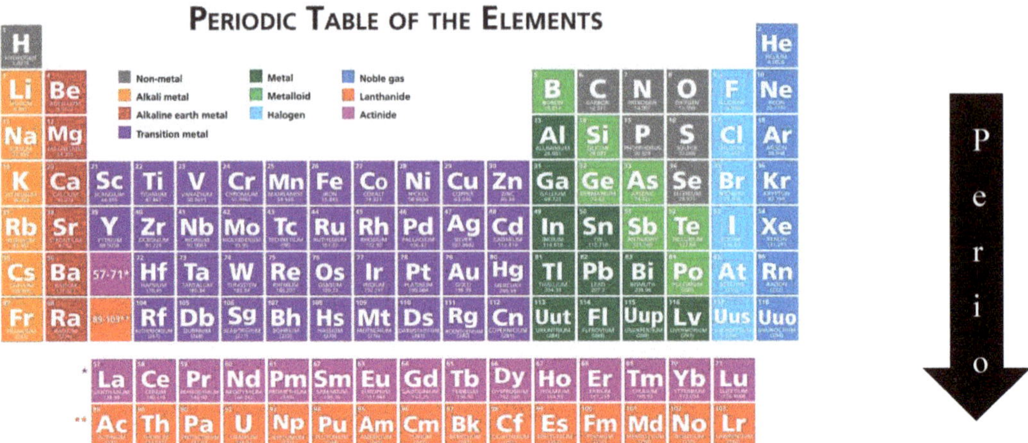

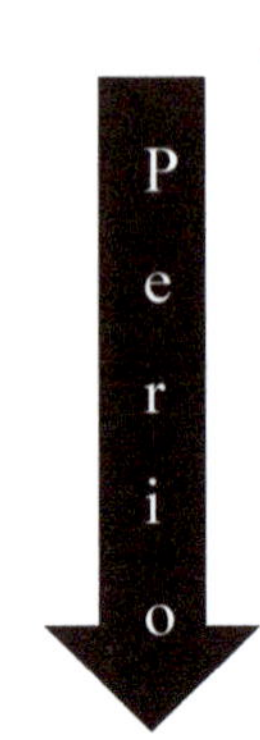

- **Period 1:**

Contains only hydrogen which is the most abundant element and helium which only exists as a gas. Follows the 1s orbital.

- **Period 2:**

Include 8 elements which form the basis of the most essential biological elements aside from oxygen, nitrogen, carbon and hydrogen. Follows the 2s and 2p orbitals.

- **Period 3:**

All period 3 elements occur in nature and have at least one stable isotope. With the exception of argon, all elements in period 3 are essential for basic biology and geology. Follows the 3s and 3p orbitals.

- **Period 4:**

Contains the lighter transitional metals including iron. Elements in period 4 are stable, usually very strong and extremely common in the Earth's crust. Follows the 4s, 3d and 4p orbitals.

- **Period 5:**

Contains 18 elements that fall into alkali metal, transition metals, metalloid and post-transition metals. the lighter transitional metals including iron. Elements in period 4 are stable, usually very strong and extremely common in the Earth's crust. Follows the 5s orbital first, and then the 4d and 5p orbitals.

- **Period 6:**

Contains 32 elements including the Lanthanides. Lanthanides are a series of 15 chemical elements that are generally referred to as rare earth elements and exhibit similar chemical properties to lanthanum. As a rule, period 6 fill the 6s orbitals first, then the 4f, 5d and 6p orbitals.

- **Period 7:**

Contains 32 elements including the Actinides. Actinides are a series of 15 chemical elements that are exhibit similar chemical properties to actinium. All period 7 elements are radioactive. As a rule, period 7 fill the 7s orbitals first, then the 5f, 6d and 7p orbitals.

Hazardous Materials Considerations

- **Group 1 Alkali metals** begin with lithium and move down through items including sodium and potassium. In all cases Group 1 Alkali metals are water reactive to various degrees. They all react violently and not only produce flammable hydrogen gas but enough heat to ignite the gas.

- **Group 2 Alkaline Earth Metals** are less reactive than their Group 1 counterparts and with the exception of beryllium, are still water reactive. Group 2 elements are all solids and need to either be burning or in fine powder form to be water reactive.

- **Group 7 Halogens** are all toxic and strong oxidizers. As elements they do not burn themselves but will strongly enhance fires due to their oxidizing nature.

- **Group 8 Noble gases** are all in gas form and are non-flammable, non-toxic and non-reactive.

Electron Shells and Orbitals

In order to understand electron shells and orbitals as earlier discussed in this section, it is important to understand the concept behind the theory that was presented by Danish scientist Niels Bohr. The Bohr Model describes the atomic structure of an atom and then explains the energy level of that atom by calculating the distance an electron is from the nucleus.

Bohr's model defines an atom as having a central nucleus that contains both protons which are positively charged, and neutrons which are neutral in charge. Orbiting around the nucleus are the negatively charged electrons which are responsible for deciding how much energy that atom has. Comparatively speaking, the model of the atom is similar to how the planets orbit around the sun. As with each planet, every electron has a specific place in orbit, and around each nucleus there may be several specific orbits for an electron to go into as seen below. However unlike planets, two electrons can share an individual orbit. Every atom is defined by where these electrons are and form a strong basis of understanding molecular chemistry.

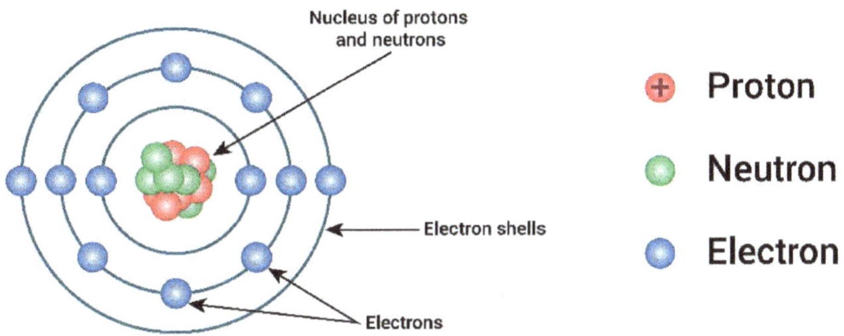

To summarize how this works:

- electrons orbit the nucleus at varying distances depending on what the atom is with each different orbit operating within four (4) primary energy levels referred to as Quantum Levels (n)

- each quantum level is then broken into various Sublevels (s,p,d,f)

- each sublevel has a varying number of orbits determined by $(n)^2$

- each orbital can contain 2 electrons and is determined by $2(n)^2$

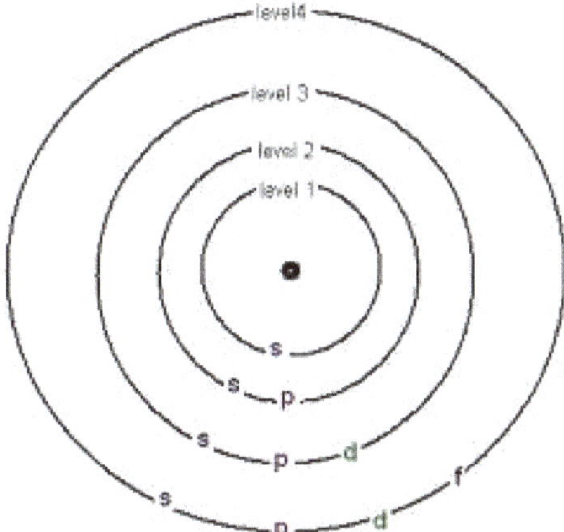

Each orbit within a specific quantum level has a different amount of energy associated with it, with the orbits closest to the nucleus having less energy than those orbits further out - the greater the distance from the nucleus, the greater the energy required to get the electron out that far. The less energy the electron has, the closer it stays to the nucleus.

To help put this into perspective, visualize a steep flight of stairs with each stair representing an increased quantum level. The higher the stair, the higher the quantum level and the more energy it takes to get higher and higher. However, when you are at the top of the stairs, it takes very little energy to fall backwards down the stairs. Electrons work in a similar way - when an electron "falls" back toward the nucleus, it releases the energy it has stored up in the form of light. The wavelength or colour of this light is directly relatable to the amount of energy the electron has and the energy is released at different frequencies which we see in the colour spectrum. It is important to also understand that electrons can only exist at each specific energy levels and can not exist between two orbitals anymore than you can hover between two stairs.

Valence Electrons

Once we understand how an atom is put together and where the electrons of each atom sit as previously discussed, it helps us understand two (2) fundamental cores of chemistry: (1) how elements correlate to each other and why they are placed where they are on the Periodic Table and (2) how atoms are built and how that design allows them to merge together to form chemical bonds.

The question that needs to be answered at this point is how different elements combine with each other to form all the chemicals compounds that we know. This is done through the combination of the most energized and outermost orbital that each atom has in the highest quantum level. Remember, the orbital that is farthest away from the nucleus holds the electrons with the highest energy. Each of these electrons are moving at very high rates and are the ones that we need to focus on when understanding how chemical compounds are formed. The electrons in the outermost orbit are the ones that merge with other atoms in a chemical reaction and are referred to in chemistry as Valence Electrons. In turn, the orbit that the valence electrons are in are called Valence Shells.

The number of electrons in an atom's valence shell decides how that atom will bond with others since bonding can either create energy or required energy. The elements are listed on the periodic table based on their valence electrons in a manner that groups similar atoms with each other as noted below.

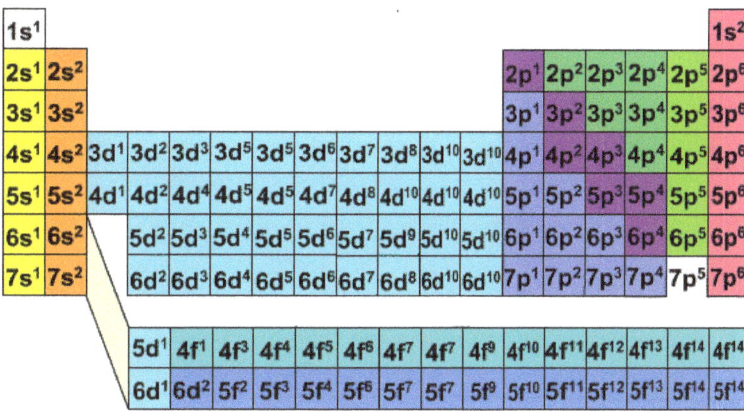

When we look at the eighteen (18) periodic table Groups (or Families) that run vertically, we can see that the elements are grouped by similar outer valence shells (4d, 5p, 6p, etc.) which means they have similar properties. The layout of the table also allows us to know how many valence electrons each element has simply by the column it is in. With the exception of groups 3–12 (the transition metals in light blue), the units digit of the group number identifies how many valence electrons are associated with a neutral atom of an element listed under that particular column as follows:

- Group 1 Alkali Metals (yellow): 1 Valence Electron

- Group 2 Alkaline Earth Metals (orange): 2 Valence Electrons

- Group 3-12 Transition Metals (light blue): 3 – 12 Valence Electrons respectively

- Group 13 Boron Group: 3 Valence Electrons

- Group 14 Carbon Group: 4 Valence Electrons

- Group 15 Nitrogen Group: 5 Valence Electrons

- Group 16 Oxygen Group: 6 Valence Electrons

- Group 17 Halogen Group (light green): 7 Valence Electrons

- Group 18 Noble Gases (light pink): 8 Valence Electrons

Barton E. Taylor

The Octet Rule

In chemistry, the rule of thumb is that main group elements (not transitional metals) tend to bond in such a way that each atom has eight (8) electrons in the valence shell. Chemical bonding occurs through the process of ionic bonding between oppositely charged ions, one being positive and the other negative. By using the valence electron number from each element, we can see how this works when combining elements together as follows.

<u>Example 1</u>

Sodium Chloride – NaCl

- Sodium (Na) is in column 1 on the periodic table which means it has 1 valence electron

- Chlorine (Cl) is in column 7 on the periodic table which means it has 7 valence electrons

- Na (1 VE) + Cl (7VE) = 8 Valence electrons when combined which produces NaCl

<u>Example 2</u>

Calcium Chloride – $CaCl_2$

- Calcium (Ca) is in column 2 on the periodic table which means it has 2 valence electrons

- Chlorine (Cl) is in column 7 on the periodic table which means it has 7 valence electrons

- Ca (2 VE) + Cl (7VE) + Cl (7VE) = 16 Valence electrons when combined which produces $CaCl_2$

<u>Example 3</u>

Water – H_2O

- Hydrogen (H) is in column 1 on the periodic table which means it has 1 valence electron

- Oxygen (O) is in column 6 on the periodic table which means it has 6 valence electrons

- H (1 VE) + H (1VE) + O (6VE) = 8 Valence electrons when combined which produces H_2O

Ionic Bonding

The mechanism by which compounds either gain or lose electrons is called ionization. In either case, the transfer of electrons produces a net electrical effect on the molecule which is then in turn called an ion. The exchange of electrons creates either a positive (+) molecule called a cation, or negative (-) molecule called an anion. There needs to be at least one electron donor and at least one electron acceptor to complete the transfer of the valence electron(s).

Ionic bonding is based on the attraction between these two oppositely charged ions since compounds need to be electrically balanced and neutral. In chemistry gaining electrons is referred to as reduction while losing electrons is referred to as oxidation.

In ionic bonding, the electron is donated or given up by an element which is usually a metal. When this metal loses an electron, there is now a surplus of positively charged protons now within the nucleus which makes this a positive ion (cation). The element that accepts the electron is usually a non-metal. When this non-metal accepts the electron, there is now a surplus of negatively charged electrons which makes this a negative ion (anion). In general, the strong electrostatic interaction between the ions result in both higher melting points and electrical conductivity properties than found in covalent bonds.

Example 1

Sodium Chloride – NaCl

- Sodium (Na) is a metal in column 1 on the periodic table which means it has 1 valence electron to donate (metal), so it will have a positive charge when it gives up it's valence electron and then be identified as a positive charge as Na^+

- Chlorine (Cl) is a non-metal in column 7 on the periodic table which means it has 7 valence electrons and needs to accept an electron (non-metal) so it will have a negative charge when it gains another electron and then be identified as Cl^-

- Since compounds need to be electrically neutral: $Na^+ + Cl^- = NaCl$

<u>Example 2</u>

Calcium Chloride – $CaCl_2$

- Calcium (Ca) is a metal in column 2 on the periodic table which means it has 2 valence electrons to donate (metal), so it will have a positive charge when it gives up it's valence electron and then be identified as a positive charge as Ca^{2+}

- Chlorine (Cl) is a non-metal in column 7 on the periodic table which means it has 7 valence electrons and can only accept one electron (non-metal) so it will have a negative charge when it gains another electron and then be identified as Cl^-

- Since compounds need to be electrically neutral and we have two positive charges from calcium and only one negative charge in chlorine, we need two chlorine ions to accept the 2 electrons donated by calcium as follows: $Ca^{2+} + Cl^- + Cl^- = CaCl_2$

We see this when we look at an element such as sodium metal when the process of donating the electron is violent and often explosive in nature. As sodium donates the electron and becomes positively charged, each neighbouring sodium particle rapidly repels the other in a manner similar to a magnet repelling the similar pole. However, this repulsion occurs at extremely high speed with a large release of energy in a reaction called a Coulomb Explosion, and we see the metal "explode".

Covalent Bonding

Unlike ionic bonding, covalent bonding occurs between atoms of the same electronegativity (i.e. have the same affinity for electrons) and share electrons cooperatively. Covalent bonding happens between the same element or elements close to each other in the periodic table and is generally between non-metallic elements. Instead of a "give-take" relationship found in ionic bonding, both atoms do not tend to donate electrons, so they share these electrons to achieve the octet configuration and become stable.

We see this in hazardous materials frequently where the vast majority of hazardous materials comprise the most reactive non-metal group that consists of carbon, hydrogen and oxygen, followed by the lesser reactive non-metal group that consists of the halogens, sulphur and phosphorous. Covalent bonds tend to have less electrostatic attraction than ionic bonds which generally result in both lower melting points and less electrical conductivity than found in ionic bonds. Ionic bonds tend to be shorter and much stronger than covalent bonds. Since covalent bonds are sharing electrons and don't have the strong ionic attraction, covalent bonds tend to be weaker in strength but allow for the formation of very large molecules that are not common with ionic bonds since they are easier to bond with. This is seen in the formation of large organic compounds that are formed from the combination of carbon and hydrogen.

The simplest example of a covalent bond is found between carbon (C) and hydrogen (H) in the simplest form of methane, CH_4. Carbon is in the 6th column of the periodic table which if you remember means it has six (6) valence electrons. As discussed earlier, this means two (2) electrons sit in the first "s" orbital with the remaining four (4) electrons sitting in the second "p" orbital. These four electrons need to have 4 more electrons brought in to become stable for the Octet Rule as seen in the following table.

Orbitals and Electron Capacity of the First Four Principle Energy Levels				
Principle energy level (n)	Type of sublevel	Number of orbitals per type	Number of orbitals per level(n^2)	Maximum number of electrons ($2n^2$)
1	s	1	1	2
2	s	1	4	8
	p	3		
3	s	1	9	18
	p	3		
	d	5		
4	s	1	16	32
	p	3		
	d	5		
	f	7		

Hydrogen is in the first column of the periodic table which means it has one (1) valence electron. It is very important to note that **even though hydrogen sits in column 1, it is not considered a metal** and therefore is the exception to the rule. Again, covalent bonding occurs between non-metals, and both hydrogen and carbon are non-metals.

Carbon needs four (4) more electrons in the outer orbit therefore, and hydrogen needs one (1) more electron to fill the "s" orbital. However, both elements are similar in electronegativity (in this case both cations or positive), with carbon being C^{4+} and hydrogen being H^+, so they form a covalent bond with each element sharing the other electrons. Carbon needs 4 more electrons and shares it with four (4) individual molecules if hydrogen:

- $C^{4+} + (H^+ \times 4) = CH_4$

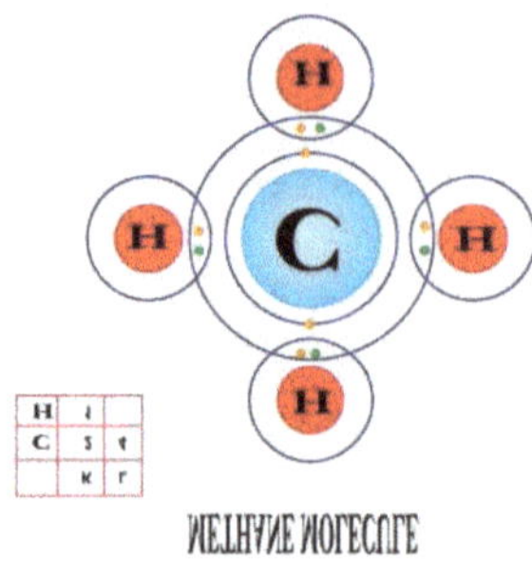

The example above shows the carbon and hydrogen each sharing an electron to make one pair of electrons. This is referred to as a Single Covalent Bond.

If the elements share two (2) pairs of electrons, it is referred to as a Double Covalent Bond as we would see in oxygen which has 6 valence electrons in the outer shell so that two oxygen atoms combine to form an oxygen molecule and share two (2) pairs of electrons:

- $O^{2-} + O^{2-} = O_2$

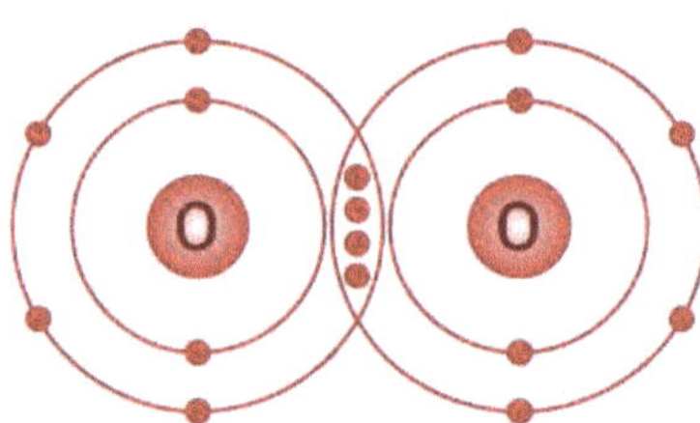

If the elements share three (3) pairs of electrons, it is referred to as a Triple Covalent Bond as we would see in nitrogen which has 3 valence electrons in the outer shell so that two nitrogen combine to form a nitrogen molecule and share three (3) pairs of electrons:

- $N^{3-} + N^{3-} = N_2$

Covalent bonds share electrons equally or disproportionally which is referred to as:

- Nonpolar Covalent Bond – electrons are shared equally between atoms who exert the same amount of pull on each electron

- Polar Covalent Bond – electrons are unequally shared due to one of the atoms having a stronger pull on the electrons than the other atom

Elements

Chemical elements are made up of atoms that are exactly the same with the same number of protons in the atomic nucleus. When these identical atoms combine, they form what is known as a chemical element. An element is a substance that cannot be decomposed into a simpler substance by a chemical process. There currently are 118 elements identified (2019) with first 94 on the periodic table occurring naturally on Earth and the remaining 24 being man-made and synthetic.

80 of the elements have at least one stable isotope - a variant of an element that has the same number of protons in the nucleus but a different number of neutrons in the nucleus. 38 of the elements are radionuclide – an unstable atom that decays over time to create a different element. Of all the elements, iron is the most abundant on Earth (by mass) and oxygen is the most common overall.

Each element is identified on the periodic table with a unique identifying symbol that consists of either one (1) of two (2) letters. If the symbol uses one letter, that letter is capitalized. If the symbol uses two letters, the first is capitalized and the second letter is lower case. The symbols for the elements are based within the Latin and Greek alphabet and can be seen in examples such as Lead, Pb, which in Latin is Plumbum.

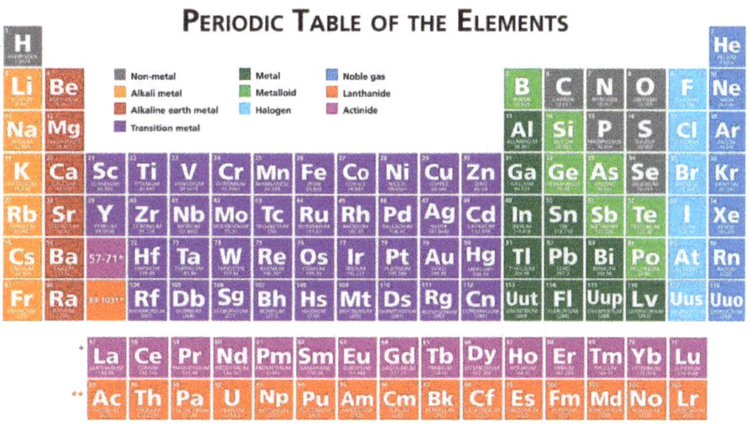

Personnel that work with hazardous materials clearly can be exposed to any of these elements depending on environment but should be well versed in a particular group of elements that in many circles are referred to as the "HazMat Elements". These thirty-nine (39) elements have been identified by various agencies and groups as being the predominant elements that have historically been encountered by first responders. These are:

H-Hydrogen	Cu-Copper	O-Oxygen
Li-Lithium	Ag-Silver	S-Sulphur
Na-Sodium	Au-Gold	F-Fluorine
K-Potassium	Zn-Zinc	Cl-Chlorine
Be-Beryllium	Hg-Mercury	Br-Bromine
Mg-Magnesium	B-Boron	I-Iodine
Ca-Calcium	Al-Aluminum	U-Uranium
Ba-Barium	C-Carbon	He-Helium
Ti-Titanium	Si-Silicon	Ne-Neon
Cr-Chromium	N-Nitrogen	Ar-Argon
Mn-Manganese	P-Phosphorous	Kr-Krypton
Fe-Iron	As-Arsenic	Xe-Xenon
Co-Cobalt	Pu-Plutonium	Pb-Lead

Gas
Metal
Non-metal
Halogen
Noble Gas

Atomic Number

Neutral atoms of an element contain an equal number of protons and electrons. The number of protons (positive charge) determines an element's atomic number (Z) and distinguishes one element from another. For example, carbon's atomic number (Z) is 6 because it has 6 protons. The number of neutrons (neutral charge) can vary to produce isotopes, which are atoms of the same element that have different numbers of neutrons. The number of electrons (negative charge) can also be different in atoms of the same element, thus producing ions (charged atoms). For instance, iron, Fe, can exist in its neutral state, or in the +2 and +3 ionic states.

Atomic Mass

An element's weight, or mass number (A), is the sum of the number of protons and the number of neutrons. The small contribution of mass from electrons is disregarded in calculating the mass number. This approximation of mass can be used to easily calculate how many neutrons an element has by simply subtracting the number of protons from the mass number. Protons and neutrons both weigh about one atomic mass unit, or "amu". Isotopes of the same element will have the same atomic number but different mass numbers.

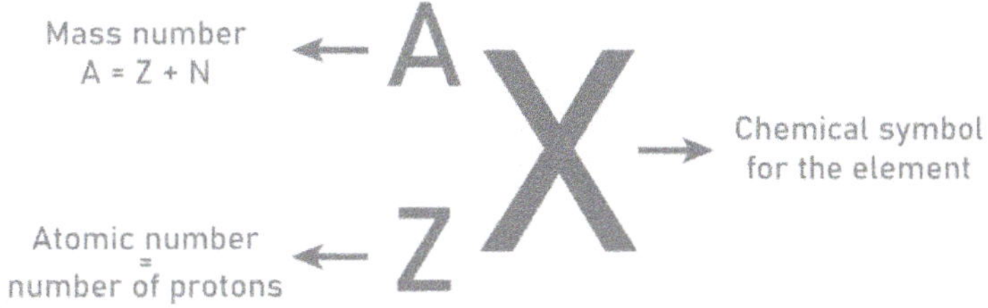

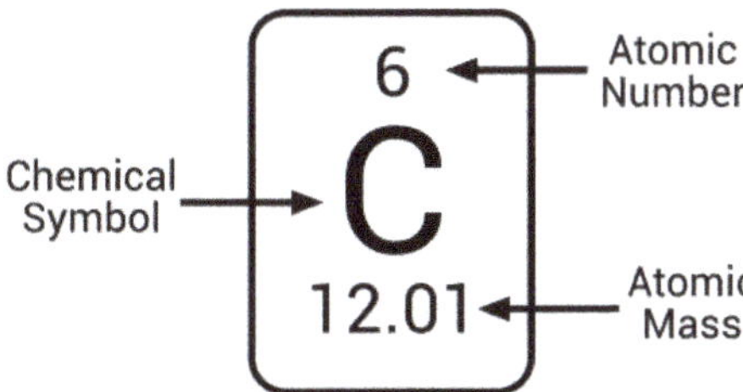

Inorganic Compounds

Inorganic compounds include substances that do not contain:

- a carbon–carbon bond or

- a carbon–hydrogen bond.

Inorganic chemistry is riddled with exceptions however which contradict the above statement with several exceptions to the rule. In the very broadest sense, inorganic compounds are substances that are of mineral origin and do not contain carbon in their molecular structure. However, again compounds such as carbon monoxide (CO), carbon dioxide (CO_2), and carbonate (CO_3) are considered inorganic and are exceptions to that rule.

Inorganic compounds primarily involve acids, bases, and salts and the resulting products that deal with:

- Oxides – a chemical compound that contains at least one oxygen atom and one other element in its chemical formula

- Sulphates – polyatomic compounds that include SO^{2-}_4

- Carbonates – salts that come from carbonic acid and include $CO2^-_3$.

- Halides - halide anions: fluoride (F^-), chloride (Cl^-), bromide (Br^-), iodide (I^-), astatide (At^-)

Several inorganic compounds are essential for life and include water, oxygen, carbon dioxide, nitrogen and various minerals. Generally inorganic compounds are smaller than organic compounds and are formed from ionic bonds.

Acid

The word acid comes from the Latin word *acidus* which means sour. In the simplest terms according to the Arrhenius Theory, acids are compounds that contain hydrogen and can release hydrogen ions, **H^+**, into water, and are thus referred to as aqueous acids. The higher the availability of the hydrogen ions when an acid dissociates or breaks apart as in the case of hydrochloric acid, HCl, the higher the acidity of the acid.

The definition of acids was expanded in 1923 to include non-aqueous solvents and are referred to as Brønsted–Lowry acids. Aqueous acid has a pH less than 7. The lower the pH, the higher the acidity or presence of the hydrogen ion. Each pH unit represents a factor of 10 difference in the concentration of the hydrogen ion.

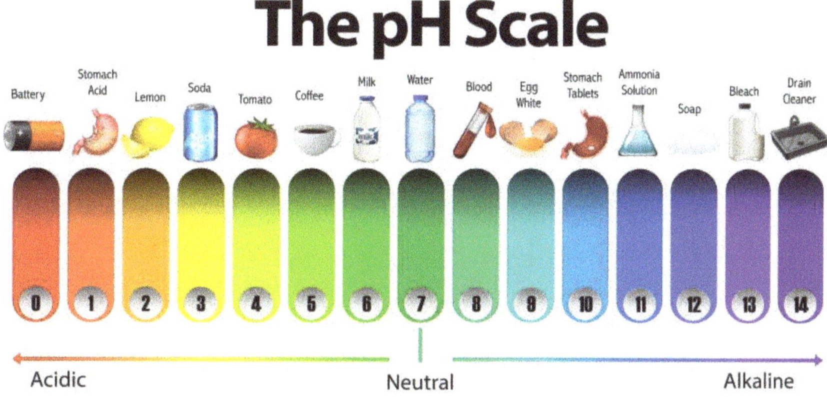

Alkaline

The work alkali comes from the Arabic word *al-qaly* which means the ashes of the saltwort plant. In the simplest terms according to the Arrhenius Theory, alkaline compounds can be considered the opposite of acids and are commonly referred to as bases. Bases are substances that when mixed in water:

- create an increase in the aqueous hydroxide ion concentration, **OH⁻**

- decrease the aqueous hydrogen ion concentration, **H⁺**

Bases react with acids to form salts and are often used as catalysts to encourage certain chemical reactions. Aqueous bases have a pH greater than 7. The higher the pH, the higher the basicity, or in simpler terms, the lower the presence of the hydroxide ion.

It is important to also understand that technically there is a difference between basicity and alkalinity even though they are very often interchanged in conversation. To clarify:

- Bases are substances that react with acids to *neutralize* them and usually consists of one or two metal atoms bonded with an oxygen to create an Oxide. Basicity is measured using pH which measures how much of the hydrogen ion is present.

- An alkaline is similar to a base but consists of a hydrogen atom bonded with an oxygen to create a Hydroxide (OH⁻). Alkalinity is the measurement of how much carbonate is in the water, not the pH. Therefore, alkalinity is the *capacity* of water to resist change to pH that would make the water more acidic.

Salts

Salts are solid compounds that are formed when a metal reacts with a non-metal and forms an ionic bond between the positive cations and negative anions. When a salt dissolves in water and produces the hydroxide ion (OH⁻), it is referred to as an alkali salt. When a salt dissolves in water and produces the hydrogen ion, H^+ it is referred to as an acid salt. Due to the strength of the ionic bond, most salts have high melting points and are also generally soluble in water.

Solid salts tend to be transparent, with the opacity of the salt being related to the size of the molecule with large crystal compounds being relatively transparent and large polycrystalline molecules appearing as powders. As well, the colour of the salt will vary depending on the positive cations or negative anions that form the molecule. These same ions when bound in solid form tend to make salts behave as insulators that do not conduct electricity. When liquified however, the salt behaves as what is referred to as an electrolyte and becomes an active conductor of electricity.

Binary Salts

Binary salts are made up of two (2) elements, one metal and one non-metal as in sodium chloride, NaCl. They are easily identified by the ending of their name being "ide" as noted in the previous example. Based on the varying hazards that come with binary salts, the group itself does not have one basic hazard identified with it and requires additional product review to determine the specific hazard.

However, there are four (4) specific binary salts that present specific concerns when introduced to water:

- Nitride Salts – release ammonia when in contact with water

- Carbide salts – produce acetylene when in contact with water

- Phosphide salts – produce phosphine gas when in contact with water

- Hydride salts – produce hydrogen gas when in contact with water

Each of these salts also create a corrosive base when reacted with water due to the creation of the hydroxide ion that will then attach to the metal ion of the salt during decomposition.

<u>Example 1</u>

Calcium carbide (CaC_2) + Water (H_2O) = Acetylene (C_2H_2) + Calcium Hydroxide ($CaOH_2$)

Example 2

Calcium phosphide (Ca_3P_2) + Water (H_2O) = Phosphine (PH_3) + Calcium Hydroxide ($CaOH_2$)

Binary Oxide Salts

Binary oxides salts are made up of two (2) elements, one metal and oxygen (non-metal) as in potassium oxide, K_2O. They are easily identified by the ending of their name being "oxide" as noted previously.

Binary Oxide salts are also violently water reactive and as with Binary salts, create a corrosive base when reacted with water due to the creation of the hydroxide ion that will then attach to the metal ion of the salt during decomposition. Additionally, the water reaction creates a large amount of heat that is released during decomposition.

Peroxide Salts

Peroxide salts are made up of a metal element and a non-metal peroxide group, O_2^{-2} and are easily identified by the prefix of their name being "per".

Peroxide salts are also violently water reactive and create a corrosive base when reacted with water due to the creation of the hydroxide ion that will then attach to the metal ion of the salt during decomposition. More importantly, the water reaction creates a large amount of heat that is released during decomposition as well as releasing oxygen. Unlike binary oxide salts, peroxide salts have an excess of oxygen and is why they release oxygen whereas binary oxides do not. Therefore when water reacts with peroxide salts, the salt acts as an oxidizer which creates a dangerous environment for both fire and explosion.

Hydroxide Salts

Hydroxide salts are made up of a metal element and a non-metal hydroxide ion, OH^-, and are easily identified by the ending of their name being "hydroxide" such as calcium hydroxide. When in contact with water, hydroxide salts release heat and creates a corrosive base.

Oxysalts

Oxysalts are made up of a metal element and the oxy-ion, O_3. Oxysalts are not water reactive but do however behave as an oxidizer and release oxygen as they decompose and accelerate combustion. These include the following base state radicals:

- Fluorate - $FO_3{}^{-1}$

- Chlorate - $CLO_3{}^{-1}$

- Bromate - $BrO_3{}^{-1}$

- Iodate - $IO_3{}^{-1}$

- Nitrate - $NO_3{}^{-1}$

- Manganate - $MnO_3{}^{-1}$

- Carbonate - $CO_3{}^{-2}$

- Chromate - $CrO_4{}^{-2}$

- Sulphate - $SO_4{}^{-2}$

- Phosphate - $PO_4{}^{-3}$

- Borate - $BO_3{}^{-3}$

- Arsenate - $AsO_4{}^{-3}$

Key things to understand identifying oxysalt suffixes and prefixes:

- Base state radicals end in "ate" : Sulphate, $SO_4{}^{-2}$
- Remove an oxygen from the sulphate, the radical name ends in "ite": Sulphite, $SO_3{}^{-1}$
- Remove two (2) oxygen from the sulphate, the prefix "hypo" is added: Hyposulphite, $SO_2{}^{-2}$
- Add one (1) oxygen to the sulphate, the prefix "per" is added: Persulphate, $SO_5{}^{-2}$

Cyanide Salts

Cyanide salts are made up of a metal element and a cyanide ion, CN, and are easily identified by the ending of their name being "cyanide" such as potassium cyanide. When dissolved in water, cyanide salts create a corrosive base when reacted with water due to the creation of the hydroxide ion that will then attach to the metal ion of the salt during decomposition. When dissolved in an acid, decomposition creates hydrogen cyanide which is extremely toxic.

Ammonium Salts

Ammonium salts are made up of a non-metal ammonium ion, NH_4^{-1} attached to an anion such as ammonium chloride. Ammonium salts are identified by the prefix "ammonium". Ammonium salts can be relatively non-hazardous as in the case of ammonium sulphite and ammonium chloride or can have oxidizing properties as in the case of ammonium nitrate. In all case, the ammonium salt properties will be governed by the attached negative anion.

Organic compounds

Organic compounds deal with chemical compounds that contain carbon in one of two (2) forms:

- a carbon–carbon bond

- a carbon–hydrogen bond.

Carbon is an element that has a very strong ability to join with other carbon atoms in a long chain or ring shape through the process known as catenation. Carbon forms covalent bonds with other carbon atoms to form both short and long organic compounds, all of which are the basis of all known life. The simplest organic compound is methane which consists of a carbon atom covalently bonded to four (4) hydrogen atoms as follows:

$$\begin{array}{c} H \\ | \\ H-C-H \\ | \\ H \end{array}$$

Organic compounds come in several orientations with varying physical and chemical properties and are referred to in various ways depending on their structure and composition. Compounds that are entirely comprised of carbon and hydrogen are referred to as Hydrocarbons.

Each compound is identified by both:

- the number of carbons that are bonded together within the structure

- the type of bond between the carbons

Organic structures all use the same prefix to indicate the number of carbons bonded together within the structure. The bonding of carbons is endless in theory and abides to the following format:

Name	Molecular Formula	Condensed Formula	Structural Formula
Methane	CH_4	CH_4	
Ethane	C_2H_6	H_3CCH_3	
Propane	C_3H_8	$H_3CCH_2CH_3$	
Butane	C_4H_{10}	$H_3C(CH_2)_2CH_3$	
Pentane	C_5H_{12}	$H_3C(CH_2)_3CH_3$	
Hexane	C_6H_{14}	$H_3C(CH_2)_4CH_3$	
Heptane	C_7H_{16}	$H_3C(CH_2)_5CH_3$	
Octane	C_8H_{18}	$H_3C(CH_2)_6CH_3$	
Nonane	C_9H_{20}	$H_3C(CH_2)_7CH_3$	
Decane	$C_{10}H_{22}$	$H_3C(CH_2)_8CH_3$	

It is important to note that organic compounds that have fewer than four (4) carbons are usually in gas form and can be reviewed in more detail in Module 4.2, Compressed Gases.

Structurally, organic compounds are in one (1) of two forms:

- tree-shaped structure referred to as Aliphatic

- or in a ring-shaped structure that is referred to as Cyclic.

Aliphatic compounds come from the Greek word *aleiphar*, which means a fat oil. Aliphatic compounds are often also referred to non-aromatic compounds. Cyclic compounds have carbons that are connected together in a circular manner. Very stable cyclic compounds are termed Aromatic compounds and often referred to informally as "benzene rings" since benzene is the most stable aromatic structure. These are discussed further in the module.

Alkanes

Alkanes are also known as paraffins and are aliphatic with the exception of the Cyclic Alkanes. All carbon bonds in alkanes are strong single bonds that are not easily broken and resist adding other elements into the existing compound. Since the bonds are "full", they are referred to as *Saturated Bonds*. Alkanes end in the suffix "ane", such as methane. They occur naturally and consist of the primary hazard of flammability and likelihood of asphyxiation due to oxygen displacement.

The number of carbon and hydrogens within an alkane is determined by the formula C_nH_{2n+2}.

Cyclic Alkanes are a unique alkane and exist only with five (5), six (6), seven (7) or eight (8) carbon lengths. All cyclic alkanes are flammable and generally have anesthetic properties. Since the carbons are bonded to each other in a circle, each carbon loses attachment to two (2) hydrogen, so the formula for cyclic alkanes is C_nH_{2n}. As well, cyclic alkanes have the prefix "cyclo" as with cyclohexane vs hexane.

Alkenes

Alkenes can be either aliphatic or cyclic and contain at least one carbon-carbon double bond. Since this double bond can easily be broken and is not as strong as an alkane single bond, they are referred to as *Unsaturated Bonds*. Alkenes end in the suffix "ene" such as ethylene. The primary hazard of alkenes is in the release of heat when the double bond is broken. Additionally, the addition of hydrogen converts many alkenes into catalysts which tend to react violently.

The number of carbon and hydrogens within an alkane is determined by the formula C_nH_{2n}.

Alkynes

Alkynes are also known as acetylenes and can be either aliphatic or cyclic and contain at least one carbon-carbon triple bond. Since this triple bond can easily be broken as well, alkynes are referred to as *Unsaturated Bonds*. Due to the low ratio of hydrogen atoms to carbon atoms, alkynes tend to be highly combustible. As well, as bonds are broken, they generate a large amount of heat as well as rapidly expand which creates a violent and reactive environment.

The number of carbon and hydrogens within an alkane is determined by the formula C_nH_2.

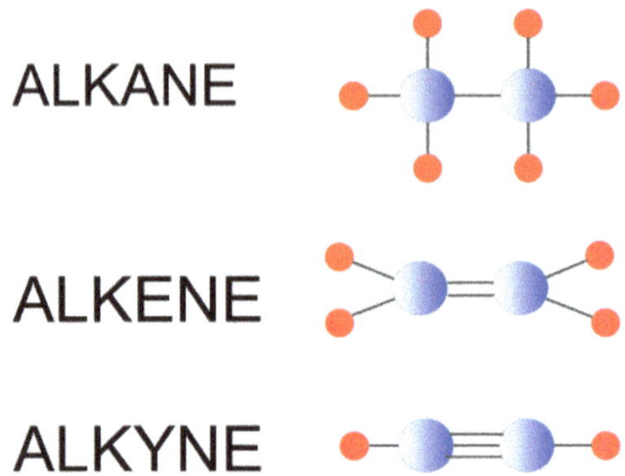

Aromatics

Aromatics are very stable cyclic compounds that by design have an additional electron to share that creates a series of single and double bonds between the carbons which is referred to as a resonant bond. Aromatics are often referred to informally as benzene rings. When the benzene ring attaches to another group, the ring is known as a *phenyl group*.

Aromatic rings visually appear to look like a honeycomb structure with benzene being the simplest of aromatic compounds. With the structure, the resonant bond, or extra electron that freely floats between the carbons to create a double bond, is shown as a line to indicate double bonds as noted below.

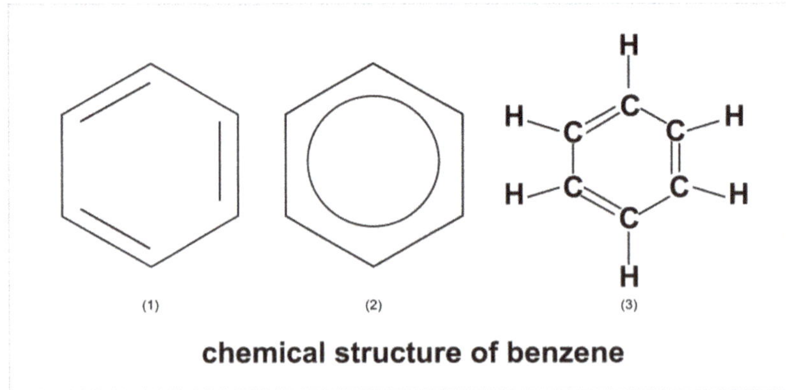

chemical structure of benzene

Due to the high ratio of carbon-hydrogen bonds in aromatic compounds, often 1:1, the rings are extremely stable and difficult to break apart which makes aromatic rings very hard to destroy.

Alkyl Halides

Alkyl halides are a subgroup within the Halocarbons and are more commonly referred to as Haloalkanes due to these compounds being derived from alkanes and also containing one of more halogens. Haloalkanes are very diverse and widespread within the industry and have several various properties, characteristics and names with some being flammable and toxic, while others are used for fire extinguishing media and anesthetic.

In general haloalkanes have high flash points and ignition temperatures and even though flammable, are less flammable than alkanes in general since they have fewer carbon-hydrogen bonding. However with the addition of the halogen group, haloalkanes tend to also be more reactive than their alkane parent group and are not miscible with water.

Haloalkanes present an additional environmental hazard due to the ability to release the halogens into the atmosphere as they do when present in chlorofluorocarbons (CFC), hydrofluorocarbons (HFC) and hydrochlorofluorocarbons (HCFC). Additionally, it is estimated that one fifth of all pharmaceuticals contain the halogen fluorine since the carbon-fluorine bond is the one halogen that is not reactive and pose a health hazard if releases into the water table.

Other halogens such as chlorine are common in metal degreasers, solvents and paint removers as seen with ethylene dichloride as seen below, dichloromethane. Chloroform (trichloromethane) is a well known haloalkane used for anaesthetic purposes.

$$\mathrm{Cl}-\underset{\underset{\displaystyle H}{|}}{\overset{\overset{\displaystyle H}{|}}{C}}-\underset{\underset{\displaystyle H}{|}}{\overset{\overset{\displaystyle H}{|}}{C}}-\mathrm{Cl}$$

Amines

Amines are derived from ammonia and therefore contain a nitrogen atom within the compound. Amines attach to other compounds (denoted as R) and have the structure as noted below. Amines are the core building block of amino acids and play very important roles with biology and life.

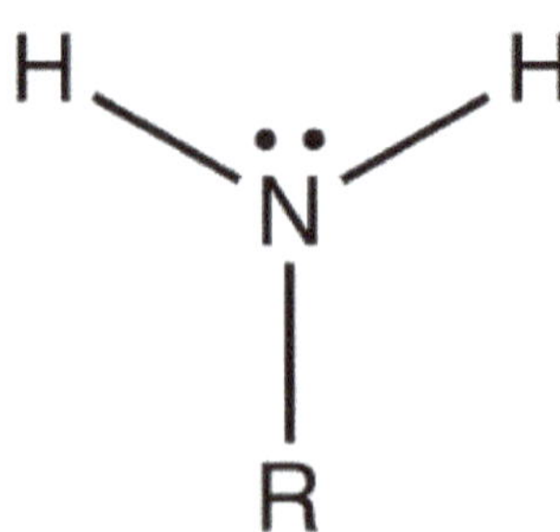

Generally amines are flammable but have a narrow flammability range and higher ignition temperatures. They are characterized by a pungent odour that is compared to the smell of rotting fish, fecal decay and ammonia, and generally pose both a toxicity and irritant hazard. As the amine increases in size, generally solubility decreases. Many amines are found in pharmaceuticals and insecticides.

Ethers

Ethers have the primary hazard of flammability due to their inability to form hydrogen bonds. They have a broad flammability range (2%-48%) and have low boiling points which make them highly volatile. Additionally they have low flash points and low ignition temperatures. They are also compounded by their anaesthetic properties.

Ethers pose a substantial hazard when exposed to oxygen over a period of time and generally need to be stored for less than 6 months at a time due to the small amount of additional oxygen that is required to form an unstable compound. When oxygen is introduced to an ether, it bounds with the oxygen already within the ether and creates a very unstable and volatile peroxide formation as outlined in Section 3.6. To compound this problem, ethers are light sensitive and decompose violently over time.

Alcohols

Alcohols have the primary hazard of flammability They have a broad flammability range (1%-36%)

but have high boiling points, moderate flash points and high ignition temperatures. Alcohols are based on the hydroxyl group, OH⁻, and as such are miscible with water.

$$R-O-H$$

Alcohols can be identified by the ending "ol" as in ethanol and methanol. Alcohol can be categorized into three (3) primary groups:

- Isopropyl alcohol: Commonly referred to as rubbing alcohol, isopropyl alcohol is toxic by ingestion. It has a high rate of evaporation which creates a cooling effect hence the nickname rubbing alcohol.

- Methyl Alcohol: Commonly known as wood alcohol and methanol. Methyl alcohol toxic by ingestion and causes blindness in small quantities. It is used primarily in solvents and is often also used in fuels due to its very low freezing point.

- Ethyl Alcohol: Commonly known as ethanol. Ethyl alcohol is used for beverages and is relatively non-toxic in small doses. It is also used as a solvent and is often also used in fuels due to its very low freezing point.

Ketones

Ketones have the primary hazard of flammability with a narrow flammability range and have moderate boiling points, moderate flash points and high ignition temperatures. They are also compounded by their anaesthetic and narcotic properties.

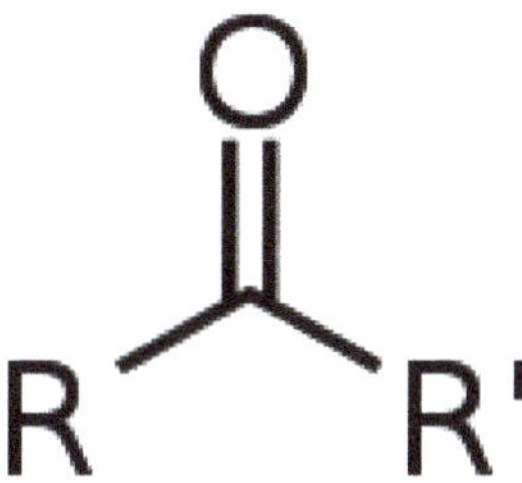

Ketones are generally liquid and due to their high vapour pressure are capable of forming explosive mixtures with air. They ae highly reactive with acids and bases, and react violently with nitric acid, hydrogen peroxide and perchloric acid. Ketones can be identified by the ending "one" as in the most common industrial ketone encountered, acetone.

Aldehydes

Aldehydes have the primary hazard of toxicity. They have a broad flammability range (3%-55%) and have moderate boiling points, moderate flash points and high ignition temperatures. Aldehydes have very diverse properties that depend entirely on what functional group (R) that it attaches to.

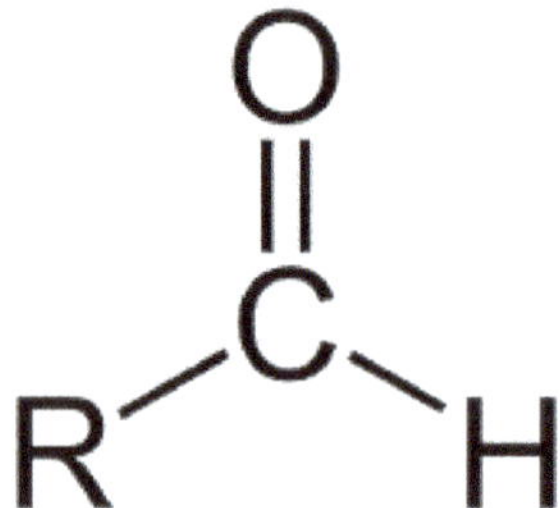

Many aldehydes have a sweet and fruity odour. Examples of this are found in vanilla extract which is a phenolic aldehyde called Vanillin. Others include the almond smell in almond extract which is the aldehyde called Benzaldehyde. However less pleasant pungent odours are also found in some aldehydes including Formaldehyde which is naturally occurring and often found in indoor air quality tests. When formaldehyde is mixed less than 37% with water, it is a product we commonly find in the hazardous waste industry and is known as Formalin.

Esters

Esters have the primary hazard of polymerization. They have a narrow flammability range and have moderate boiling points, moderate flash points and high ignition temperatures. Esters come from blending alcohols with organic acids and make up the biological group referred to as Lipids.

Esters make up the majority of animal fats and vegetable oils in our daily life. An oil is an ester that has a melting point below room temperature and is liquid, such as common cooking vegetable oil. A fat is an ester that is solid at room temperature, such as butter. From this it is easy to see that small chain esters may be soluble in water, while larger chain esters will not be soluble in water at all.

Esters are the primary constituent of common fragrances including essential oils which are commonly referred to as ethereal oils. As well, common human, animal and insect pheromones are within the ester group. Esters are not easily identifiable by name since the word "ester" will never appear in the name of a compound which is often confusing Common esters include glycerides which are esters of glycerol and acetates such as vinyl acetate.

Metallic Compounds

Metals

Metals contain one of more of the metal elements listed on the periodic table bonded to another element or compound. The metal acts as a positive ion or cation as explained earlier in Section 3.2 that is bonded to a non-metallic anion or ionic group. When metals bond to other metals, they form what is referred to as an Alloy which are mixtures that show metallic properties but are not considered to be a metallic compound. Alloys can be:

- Substitutional Alloys: alloys where the primary metal atom is replaced by a metal atom of similar size. An example is brass where the copper atom is replaced with a zinc atom.

- Interstitial Alloys: alloys where smaller atoms occupy the holes in the lattice of the host metal. An example is steel where carbon atoms fill in the lattice of the iron atoms.

Examples of metallic compounds include:

- Potassium Chloride: KCl

- Sodium Chloride: NaCl

- Silver Nitrate: $AgNO_3$

Metals have the following properties:

- They are malleable and can be altered into various shapes and are ductile in holding their integrity

- They are conductors both of electricity and heat

- They are shiny and lustrous in appearance

NOTE: Metallic elements fall within Group 1 of the periodic table. Hydrogen falls within Group 1 but is not considered a metal even though it *behaves* as a metal. Hydrogen is considered non-metal as we see in the most common hydrogen compound we know, water – H_2O.

Metalloids

As the name suggests, metalloids are chemical elements that exhibit properties both of a metal and as a non-metal and are often viewed as hybrids There is ongoing debate and disagreement on this subject to date but nonetheless remains a term that is used within the chemical community.

There are six (6) recognized metalloids:

- Boron

- Silicon

- Germanium

- Arsenic

- Antimony

- Tellurium

There are an additional five (5) elements that are often put into this class. These are:

- Carbon

- Aluminum

- Selenium

- Polonium

- Astatine

Metalloids have the following properties:

- They are a metallic appearance but tend to be more brittle

- They are only moderately conductive of electricity

- They are duller in appearance

Heavy Metals

Heavy metals pose a very unique concern in our industry due to the nature of what they are. Heavy metals are dense elements that pose a high toxicity hazard at low concentrations. These metals include:

- Lead

- Mercury

- Cadmium

- Chromium

- Thallium

- Arsenic

Many of these compounds are referred to as bio-accumulators – materials that do not break down within the body, and over time, tend to build up and stay within the organisms system. If this organism is eaten by another, the compound passes to the next member of the food chain, and it goes on until it reaches humans. An example of this is mercury build up in fish.

Non-Metals

As the name suggests, non-metals lack any characteristics of metals. Non-metals act as negative ions or anions as explained earlier in Section 3.2 that is bonded to a positive cation or ionic group.

Non-metals are divided into two (2) groups on the periodic table:

- Reactive non-metals: tend to form covalent bonds with metals

- Noble Gases: inherently reluctant to form compounds with other elements in general

Two of the non-metals, hydrogen and helium make up over 99% of what is called the observable universe with another non-metal, oxygen, following up in a close third place. Non-metals have a very diverse set of properties simply based on the variety of covalent and ionic bonds they form with other compounds.

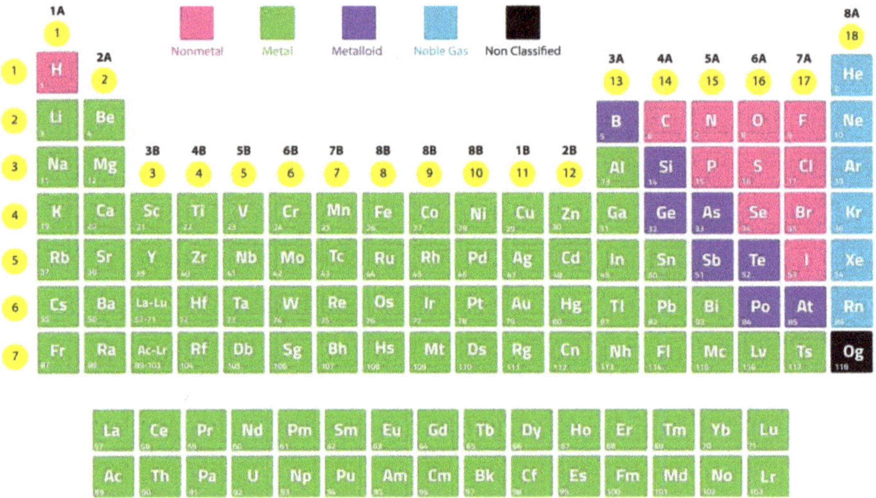

Halogens

The name halogen comes from the Greek word halogens are listed in column 7 of the periodic table and include six (6) elements:

- Fluorine

- Chlorine

- Bromine

- Iodine

- Astatine

- Tennessine

Each halogen is both toxic and a strong oxidizer with fluorine actually being a stronger oxidizer than oxygen itself. Halogens don't burn but due to their oxidizer properties, they substantially enhance combustion and are also considered highly reactive in their interactions with other compounds.

Halogens all react with hydrogen to create hydrogen halides, all of which are very reactive. Reactivity decreases as the halogen increases in mass however. Hydrogen fluoride, HF, is explosively reactive in a cold and dark environment whereas hydrogen chloride, HCL, is explosive in the presence of light and heat. Both examples exist in gas form and have aqueous counterparts known as hydrofluoric acid and hydrochloric acid respectively. Bromine exists in a liquid state, and iodine and astatine exist in solid state.

Units of Measure

Units of measure all have two (2) parts:

- a numerical value that is used for comparison and

- a unit which is used to evaluate scale

Chemistry deals with atoms that can be extremely large or small and use scientific notation that is based on the power of 10, 10^n. If n is a positive (+) number, the decimal point will move to the right of the non-zero integer as seen below (think of the positive number as the number of zeros behind the 1):

- $10^2 = 10 \times 10 = 100$

- $10^3 = 10 \times 10 \times 10 = 1,000$

- $10^4 = 10 \times 10 \times 10 \times 10 = 10,000$

If n is a negative (-) number, the decimal point will move to the left of the non-zero integer as seen below (think of the negative as number of zeros in front of the 1)

- $10^{-2} = 0.1 \times 0.1 = 0.001$

- $10^{-3} = 0.1 \times 0.1 \times 0.1 = 0.0001$

- $10^{-4} = 0.1 \times 0.1 \times 0.1 \times 0.1 = 0.00001$

Scientific notation is always in metric as follows:

- Mass: Measured in kilogram, kg

- Length: Measured in metre, m

- Volume: Measured in cubic metre. m^3

- Temperature: Measured in Celsius, C^o, Fahrenheit, F^o, Kelvin, K^o

Common prefixes are as follows:

- mega: M or 10^6

- kilo: k or 10^3

- deci: d or 10^{-1}

- centi: c or 10^{-2}

- milli: m or 10^{-6}

- micro: μ or 10^{-9}

We deal in absolutes when it comes to numbers and analytical. Understanding various criteria and conversions is essential.

- 1 % = 10,000 parts per million (100% is 1,000,000 parts per millions)

Parts per Million (ppm) has several different conversions that we normally see:

- milligram per kilogram: mg/kg

- microgram per gram: μg/g

- milliliter per litre: ml/L

- microlitre per millilitre: μg/ml

Parts per Million (ppb) has several different conversions as well:

- microgram per kilogram: μg/kg

- microlitre per litre: μl/L

Total Petroleum Hydrocarbons

Total Petroleum Hydrocarbons, TPH, is a term generally used for several hundred hydrocarbon compounds that are found within crude oil. To measure each separately is not practical, so generally the total amount of TPH is measured. TPH is the measurement of the sum of what are referred to as volatile petroleum hydrocarbons, VPH, and extractable petroleum hydrocarbons, EPH. TPH is evaluated in several ways:

- TPH for the gasoline range organics, GRO, that have 6-10 carbon atoms (C6 – C10)

- TPH for diesel range organics, DRO, that have 10-28 carbon atoms (C10-C28)

- TPH for oil or residual range organics, ORO/RRO, that have 28-36 carbon atoms (C28-C36)

Volatile petroleum hydrocarbons, VPH, have 5 to 12 carbon atoms (C5-C12), as well as what is referred to as BTEX, MTBE, naphthalene, and aromatic rings that have 9-10 carbon atoms (C9-C10).

Extractable petroleum hydrocarbons, EPH, have 9-36 carbon atoms (C9-C36), and aromatic rings that have 11-22 carbon atoms (C11-C22).

BTEX

- Benzene/toluene/ethylbenzene/xylene. Major components found in petroleum hydrocarbon waste. These are all aromatic hydrocarbons based on the benzene ring that are stable.

  - **Benzene:** Benzene is a natural constituent of crude oil and may be synthesized from other compounds present in petroleum. Benzene is a 6-carbon aromatic chain (C6)

  - **Toluene:** also known as methylbenzene, phenylmethane, and *Toluol*, is a clear water -insoluble liquid with the typical smell of paint thinner. Toluene is a 7-carbon aromatic chain (C7)

  - **Ethylbenzene:** important in the petrochemical industry as an intermediate in the production of styrene, which in turn is used for making polystyrene, a commonly used plastic material. Although often present in small amounts in crude oil, ethylbenzene is produced in bulk quantities by combining benzene and ethylene. Ethylbenzene is an 8-carbon aromatic chain (C8)

- o **Xylene:** clear, colorless, sweet-smelling liquid that is very flammable. It is usually refined from crude oil. Xylene is an 8-carbon aromatic chain (C8)

Naphthalene

- A fusion of a pair of benzene rings referred to as a polycyclic aromatic hydrocarbon often used in household mothballs. Naphthalene is a 10-carbon aromatic chain (C10)

MTBE

- Methyl tert-butyl ether is a flammable and volatile compound primarily used as a fuel additive. MTBE is a 5-carbon aromatic chain (C5)

PAH

- Polyaromatic hydrocarbon. These are a series of aromatic hydrocarbons that are combined. The bigger the group, the harder it is to "farm" and treat it out.

Leachable

- Is determined by the Toxicity Characteristic Leaching Procedure, or TCLP

- TCLP procedure is designed to determine the mobility of both organic and inorganic analytes present in liquid, solid, and multiphasic wastes.

- The TCLP analysis simulates landfill conditions. Over time, water and other liquids percolate through landfills. The percolating liquid often reacts with the solid waste in the landfill and may pose public and environmental health risks because of the contaminants it absorbs. The TCLP analysis determines which contaminants are present in the leachate and their concentrations

- Express analytically as weight per volume, or usually, milligrams per litre, mg/L

Totals

Is a total weight measurement: weight of COC in a defined weight of the matrix – mg/kg

Chapter 3:

Hazardous Materials Classification

Class 1 Explosives

Overview

Definition

Class 1 Explosive materials are defined by various agencies as substances, articles or devices that are designed to either function by explosion, or when subjected to heat, impact, or friction undergo rapid chemical transformation forming other products whose combined volume is much greater than the original substance. The National Fire Protection Association further defines explosion as a rapid release of high-pressure gas into the environment that creates an overpressure within the surrounding area.

Components

Explosives are either physical or chemical in nature and fall into two primary classifications:

- High Explosives – the conversion of a solid to gas extremely rapidly by creating a wave that passes through the explosive material instantly and creates a high heat and pressure shock wave that moves at a speed greater than the speed of sound (343 m/s or 1,125 f/s @200C). This is referred to as detonation.

- Low Explosives – the conversion of a solid to gas over a sustained period of time that moves at a speed less than the speed of sound. This is referred to as deflagration.

Additionally, explosives fall into the following sub-categories:

- Overpressure Explosion - the physical over-pressurization of a container that results in container rupture. This may result from overfilling, faulty pressure-relief valves or damaged containers creating vulnerable weak points.

- Mechanical Explosion - the physical/mechanical increase of temperature within a container due to a heat source which creates additional vapour content and subsequent vapour pressure within the container.

- Chemical Explosion - the rapid combustion of a chemical mixture that creates a high-pressure reaction. This group also includes combustible dusts which are compounds with an increased surface area that when suspended in air and exposed to an ignition source become explosive.

- Nuclear Explosion – the result of a tactical deployment, weapon malfunction, or act of terrorism. Nuclear explosions are either air-burst explosions designed to disrupt electronics or ground-burst explosions which are designed for mass destruction.

Explosions pose three primary effects as follows:

- Blast Pressure – the high-pressure gas wave discharge from the explosion (referred to as the Positive Phase) as well as the secondary vacuum that pulls materials toward the area of origin (referred to as the Negative Phase)
- Fragmentation – smaller parts of objects that are in the path of the explosion.
- Thermal Wave – the generation of heat by the explosion though initial flash and fireball.

Families Of Explosives

Explosives can be comprised of pure compounds or mixtures and are divided further into four (4) families based on their molecular structure.

- Inorganic Explosive Compounds – these compounds include three (3) primary materials which are:
  - Fulminates – based on the structure of carbon, nitrogen and oxygen (CNO). When attached to metals such as mercury become very unstable and sensitive to friction, heat, pressure and electricity. In many cases such as silver fulminate, the compound tends to self-detonate under its own weight.
  - Silver acetylide – highly sensitive material that also is light sensitive
  - Ammonium nitrate – hard to initiate under normal conditions but acts as an oxidizer and is very powerful if mixed with fuels as with the common material ANFO.
- Metal Azides - based on the structure of nitrogen (N3). When attached to metals such as sodium become very explosive when heated or shaken. Sodium azide is used in air-bag deployment and is a chemical asphyxiant that behaves similarly to cyanide within the body.
- Aliphatic Nitro Compounds – a hydrocarbon derivative that is based on the nitro group

structure of nitrogen and oxygen (NO2) where the oxygen bond is highly unstable and reacts explosively. Examples include nitroglycerine and nitroglycerine-based explosives commonly called Dynamite.

- Aromatic Explosive Nitro Compounds – as with aliphatic nitro compounds, these are based on the nitro group structure of nitrogen and oxygen (NO2) being added to an aromatic hydrocarbon of benzene or toluene. Aromatic nitro compounds are more stable than aliphatic nitro compounds and detonate only if vigorously shocked or heated above 2320C (4500F). Examples include trinitrotoluene (TNT) and trinitrophenol (picric acid).

Transportation of Dangerous Goods Classification

Transport Canada defines Explosives as follows under SOR/2017-253, Part 2:

- capable, by chemical reaction, of producing gas at a temperature, pressure and speed that would damage the surroundings; or
- designed to produce an explosive or pyrotechnic effect by heat, light, sound, gas or smoke or a combination of those means as a result of non-detonative, self-sustaining exothermic chemical reactions

Department of Transportation Classification

Department of Transport defines Explosive as follows under 49 CFR 173.50:

- For the purposes of this subchapter, an explosive means any substance or article, including a device, which is designed to function by explosion (i.e., an extremely rapid release of gas and heat) or which, by chemical reaction within itself, is able to function in a similar manner even if not designed to function by explosion, unless the substance or article is otherwise classed under the provisions of this subchapter. The term includes a pyrotechnic substance or article, unless the substance or article is otherwise classed under the provisions of this subchapter.

Division 1.1 Mass Explosion Hazard

Division 1.1 is the highest level of explosives and comprises explosives that have a Mass Explosion Hazard. A mass explosion hazard is defined as an explosion that affects the entire load instantaneously. Division 1.1 explosives are very sensitive to heat and shock. Examples: hand grenades, general purpose bombs.

Division 1.2 Projection Hazard

Division 1.2 comprises explosives that have a Projection Hazard but not a mass explosion hazard. A projection hazard is defined as an airborne hazard generated from disintegration during explosion such as shrapnel and flying debris. Examples: Mortars, tank rounds.

Division 1.3 Fire Hazard

Division 1.3 comprises explosives that have a Fire Hazard but not a mass explosion hazard. Division 1.3 materials also include a minor blast and/or projection hazard. Examples: Flares, display fireworks.

Division 1.4 Minor Explosion Hazard

Division 1.4 comprises explosives that have a Minor Explosion Hazard. The explosive effects are not significant and primarily contained to the individual package with no projection hazard expected. Examples: Ammunition – 7.62 mm, 5.56 mm, 9 mm, 45 caliber rounds, consumer fireworks.

Division 1.5 Insensitive Explosion Hazard

Division 1.5 comprises explosives that are Very Insensitive but also present a mass explosion hazard. The compounds are considered very insensitive with very little probability of initiation or transition from burning to detonation under normal conditions. An external fire must not cause instantaneous explosion of the majority of the package contents. Examples: Blasting agents

Division 1.6 Extremely Insensitive Explosion Hazard

Division 1.6 comprises explosives that are Extremely Insensitive but do not present a mass explosion hazard. The compounds are considered extremely insensitive with negligible probability of initiation or propagation.

Compatibility Groups

Class 1 Explosives are broken further from the 6 Divisions into thirteen (13) Compatibility Groups which is used to determine which explosives can be transported together.

- Group A: Primary explosive substance.
    - Division 1.1.
- Group B: Primary explosive substance with less than two effective protective features. Detonators for blasting, detonator assemblies for blasting, and cap-type primers, are also included here.
    - Division 1.1, 1.2, 1.4.
- Group C: Propellant explosive or other deflagrating explosive.
    - Division 1.1, 1.2, 1.3, 1.4.
- Group D: Secondary detonating explosive or black powder without the means of initiation or propelling charge or containing a primary explosive substance and two or more effective protective features.
    - Division 1.1, 1.2, 1.4, 1.5.
- Group E: A secondary detonating explosive, without means of initiation, with a propelling

charge (other than one containing a flammable liquid or gel or hypergolic liquids).

- o Division 1.1, 1.2, 1.4.
- Group F: A secondary detonating explosive, with its own means of initiation, with a propelling charge (other than one containing a flammable liquid or gel, or hypergolic liquids) or without a propelling charge.
    - o Division 1.1, 1.2, 1.3, 1.4.
- Group G: Pyrotechnic substance, or article containing both an explosive substance and an illuminating, incendiary, tear or smoke producing substance (other than a water activated article or one containing white phosphorus, phosphides, a pyrophoric substance, a flammable liquid or gel, or hypergolic liquids).
    - o Division 1.1, 1.2, 1.3, 1.4/
- Group H: Article containing an explosive substance and white phosphorous.
    - o Division 1.2, 1.3.
- Group J: Article containing an explosive substance and a flammable liquid or gel.
    - o Division 1.1, 1.2, 1.3.
- Group K: Article containing an explosive substance and a toxic substance.
    - o Division 1.2, 1.3.
- Group L: Special explosive risk (e.g. due to water-activation or presence of hypergolic liquids, phosphides or a pyrophoric substance) needing isolation of each type.
    - o Division 1.1, 1.2, 1.3.
- Group N: Extremely insensitive detonating substances.
    - o Division 1.6.
- Group S: Packed or designed to minimize any hazardous effects from possible accidental activation are confined within the package unless the container has been degraded by fire, in which case all blast or projection effects are limited to the extent that they do not significantly hinder or prohibit firefighting or other emergency response efforts in the immediate vicinity of the means of containment.
    - o Division 1.4.

Explosives may only be transported together if they ae compatible based on the 13 Groups.

Column 1	Column 2
A	A
B	B, S
C	C, D, E, N, S
D	C, D, E, N, S
E	C, D, E, N, S
F	F, S
G	G, S
H	H, S
J	J. S
K	K, S
L	L
N	C, D, E, N, S
S	B, C, D, E, F, G, H, J, K, N, S

Class 2 Compressed Gases

Overview

Definition

Class 2 materials are composed of gases that exist under pressure either in completely gaseous states or in liquified gaseous states. A compressed gas is defined as a gas which when packaged under pressure is entirely gaseous at -500C (-580F), including all gases with a critical temperature less than -500C (-580F). In all cases, the primary hazard associated with compressed gases is pressure which can cause a violent reaction if the cylinder is compromised.

Compressed gases are broken into four (4) categories:

- Non-Liquified Gases – a gas that when packaged under pressure is entirely gaseous at -500C (-580F), including all gases with a critical temperature less than -500C (-580F). Also known as compressed, pressurized or permanent gases. These gases do not become liquid when they are compressed at normal temperatures even at very high pressure. Examples include oxygen, nitrogen, helium, argon.

- Liquified Gases – a gas that when packaged under pressure is partially liquid at temperatures greater than -500C (-580F). Includes liquified petroleum gas (LPG). Examples include anhydrous ammonia, chlorine, propane, carbon dioxide. These gases also can be further quantified as:
    - High Pressure Liquified Gas – a gas with critical temperature between -500C (-580F) and +650C (1490F)
    - Low Pressure Liquified Gas - a gas with critical temperature above +650C (1490F)
- Cryogenic Liquified Gases – a cryogenic liquid means a liquified gas that has a boiling point colder than -900C (-1300F). Includes liquified natural gas (LNG) which is composed predominantly with methane. Examples include anhydrous ammonia, chlorine, propane, carbon dioxide.
- Dissolved Gas – a gas that when packaged under pressure is dissolved in a liquid phase solvent. Example is acetylene.

CRITICAL POINT

Critical point is also referred to as critical state. It is at which two phases of a substance, such as gas and liquid, become indistinguishable from each other and the density of the liquid and vapour are equal. At this point the compound is referred to as a supercritical fluid. Gases have a very low density and viscosity and easily expand and contract in response to both temperature and pressure changes. Critical point is therefore a function of both critical temperature and critical pressure.

CRITICAL TEMPERATURE

Gases have more difficulty converting to a liquid as the temperature increases due to the push towards a gaseous state as the temperature increase. The temperature at which this vapour can no longer be converted into a liquid regardless of how much pressure is applied is called the critical temperature.

CRITICAL PRESSURE

Critical pressure is a function of critical temperature and is defined as the pressure needed to convert a gas into a liquid at that gases critical temperature.

Transportation of Dangerous Goods Classification 🇨🇦

Transport Canada defines a gas as follows under SOR/2017-253, Part 2:

- a gas included in one of the three divisions set out in section 2.14;
- a mixture of gases;
- a mixture of one or more gases with one or more vapours of substances included in other classes;
- an article charged with a gas;
- tellurium hexafluoride; or
- an aerosol.

Department of Transportation Classification

- Department of Transport defines a gas as follows under 49 CFR 173.115:
- Division 2.1 (Flammable gas). For the purpose of this subchapter, a flammable gas (Division 2.1) means any material which is a gas at 20 °C (68 °F) or less and 101.3 kPa (14.7 psia) of pressure (a material which has a boiling point of 20 °C (68 °F) or less at 101.3 kPa (14.7 psia)
- Division 2.2 (non-flammable, non-poisonous compressed gas) - including compressed gas, liquefied gas, pressurized cryogenic gas, compressed gas in solution, asphyxiant gas and oxidizing gas). For the purpose of this subchapter, a non-flammable, non-poisonous compressed gas (Division 2.2) means any material (or mixture)
- Division 2.3 (Gas poisonous by inhalation). For the purpose of this subchapter, a gas poisonous by inhalation (Division 2.3) means a material which is a gas at 20 °C (68 °F) or less and a pressure of 101.3 kPa (14.7 psia) (a material which has a boiling point of 20 °C (68 °F) or less at 101.3 kPa (14.7 psia)

Division 2.1 Flammable Gases

Division 2.1 are gases that are flammable and can be in the form of liquified gas, cryogenic liquids and compressed gas. Flammable gases are often referred to as hydrocarbon gases due to the presence of both hydrogen (H) and carbon (C). Hydrogen is the lightest element in the periodic table as well as the most abundant substance in the universe and when in molecular form (H_2) is extremely flammable. Examples: methane, propane, butane.

Division 2.2 Non-Flammable Non-Toxic Gases

Division 2.2 are gases that are both non-flammable and non-toxic and are also referred to as non-reactive. However, Division 2.2 gases pose an asphyxiation hazard since they dilute or replace the oxygen in the atmosphere. These gases can be in the form of liquified gas, cryogenic liquids, compressed gas and gases in solution. Examples: carbon dioxide, helium, neon, argon, nitrogen, xenon.

OXIDIZING GASES 2.2/5.1

Division 2.2/5.1 gases are non-flammable gases that have a subclass of 5.1 due to their nature of being an oxidizer. Oxidizers can initiate or greatly accelerate the combustion of other materials even if not flammable themselves. Example: oxygen.

Division 2.3 Toxic Gases

Division 2.3 are gases that have a Toxic by Inhalation Hazard (TIH). These gases in some cases can also be absorbed through the skin and are either known to be toxic to humans or presumed to be toxic based on animal testing. Examples: anhydrous ammonia, chlorine, hydrogen sulphide, boron trifluoride, phosgene.

Aerosols

Aerosol means any non-refillable receptacle containing a gas compressed, liquefied or dissolved under pressure, and fitted with a release device allowing the contents to be ejected as particles in suspension in a gas, or as a foam, paste, powder, liquid or gas.

In all cases, aerosols cannot be used for Division 2.3 Toxic Gases and are shipped under UN1950 as:

- Class 2.1 if the gas contains 85% or more by mass of a flammable component. Flammable components do not include pyrophoric, self-heating or water-reactive chemicals.
- Class 2.2. if the gas contains less than 1% by mass of a flammable component.

Additionally, if the product (other than the propellant) presents additional hazard, it must carry a subsidiary Class 6.1 Toxic Substance Packing Group III (Canada allows Packing Group II as well), or Class 8 Corrosive Substance Packing Group II or III. Packing Group I is forbidden for aerosols.

Class 3 Flammable Liquids

Class 3 materials are defined as chemicals that exist at ambient temperature in a liquid form with sufficient vapour pressure to ignite in the presence of an ignition source. Flammable liquids are defined by several agencies including National Fire Protection Agency (NFPA), Occupational Safety and Health Association (OSHA), and most recently the Global Harmonized System (GHS).

Historical Classification

Prior to the effective date of December 1, 2018 for GHS, OSHA 29 CFR 1910.106 had the following historical definitions before it aligned with the GHS categorizations:

- Flammable Liquid – Any liquid having a flashpoint below 100 0F, or 37.8 0C
  - Class IA liquids had flash points below 73°F (22.8°C) and boiling points below 100°F (37.8°C).
  - Class IB liquids had flash points below 73°F (22.8°C) and boiling points above 100°F (37.8°C).
  - Class IC liquids had flash points at or above 73°F (22.8°C) and below 100°F (37.8°C)
- Combustible Liquid – Any liquid with a flashpoint at or above 100 0F (37.8 0C) but below 200 0F (93.3 0C)
  - Class II liquids had flash points at or above 100°F (37.8°C) and below 140°F (60°C).
  - Class IIIA liquids had flash points at or above 140°F (60°C) and below 200°F (93.3°C)
  - Class IIIB liquids had flash points at or above 200°F (93.3°C). When these chemicals were heated within 30°F (16.7°C) of their flash points, they were treated as Class IIA liquids.

Current Classification

Effective December 1, 2018, GHS (and subsequently OSHA) defines Flammable Liquids as:

- Flammable Liquid – Any liquid having a flashpoint 199.4°F (93°C)
  - Category 1 liquids have flash points below 73.4°F (23°C) and boiling points at or

below 95°F (35°C).

- o Category 2 liquids have flashpoints below 73.4°F (23°C) and boiling points above 95°F (35°C).
- o Category 3 liquids have flashpoints at or above 73.4°F (23°C) and at or below 140°F (60°C). When Category 3 liquids with flash points at or above 100°F (37.8°C) are heated for use to within 30°F (16.7°C) of their flash point, they must be handled in accordance with the requirements for a Category 3 liquid with a flashpoint below 100°F (37.8°C).
- o Category 4 liquids have flash points above 140°F (60°C) and at or below 199.4°F (93°C). When Category 4 flammable liquids are heated for use to within 30°F (16.7°C) of their flash points, they must be handled in accordance with the requirements for a Category 3 liquid with a flashpoint at or above 100°F (37.8°C).
- o In addition, the new rules specify that when a liquid with a flash point greater than 199.4°F (93°C) is heated for use to within 30°F (16.7°C) of its flash point, it must be handled in accordance with the requirements for a Category 4 flammable liquid.

	<73.4°F (23°C)	<100°F (37.8°C)	<140°F (60°C)	<199.4°F (93°C)	>199.4°F (93°C)
Old 1910.106	Flammable		Combustible		
Classes	IA, IB	IC	II	IIIA	IIIB
New GHS	Flammable				
Categories	1,2	3		4	

Transportation Of Dangerous Goods Classification

Transport Canada defines a Flammable Liquid as follows under SOR/2017-253, Part 2:

- Flammable Liquid - Substances that are liquids or liquids containing solids in solution that have a flash point less than or equal to 60°C
  - o Packing Group I, if they have an initial boiling point of 35°C or less at an absolute pressure of 101.3 kPa and any flash point;
  - o Packing Group II, if they have an initial boiling point greater than 35°C at an

absolute pressure of 101.3 kPa and a flash point less than 23°C; or

- o Packing Group III, if the criteria for inclusion in Packing Group I or II are not met.

Department Of Transportation Classification

Department of Transport defines a Flammable Liquid and Combustible Liquid as follows under 49 CFR 173.120 Part (a) and (b):

- Flammable Liquid - a liquid with a flash point ≤60°C (≤140°F), or any liquid in bulk packaging with a flashpoint ≥37.8°C (≥100°F) that is intentionally heated and transported above its flashpoint

- Combustible Liquid - any liquid that does not meet the definition of any other hazard class and has a flash point of >60°C (>140°F) and <93°C (<200°F). To be classified as a Combustible Liquid under exemption 49 CFR 173.150 (f) the liquid must meet the following conditions:
  - o Doesn't meet the definition of any other hazard class.
  - o To be transported by rail or highway within the U.S. only.
  - o Has a flashpoint of ≥100°F and ≤140°F.
  - o Is not a flammable liquid that is also an elevated temperature material that has been intentionally heated and is transported above its flashpoint.

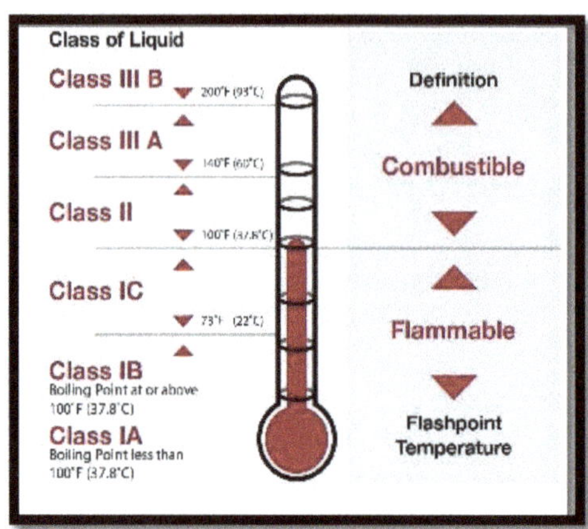

Technical

Temperature

It becomes critical to understand the different temperature scales that are listed throughout various reference literature in order to correctly evaluate the chemical nature of a flammable liquid.

- Centigrade (°C) - the centigrade scale is used predominantly throughout the world as well as within the scientific and technical community in the United States.
- Fahrenheit (°F) - the Fahrenheit scale is familiar to most emergency responders because it is the temperature used most commonly in the United States
- Kelvin and Rankine (K or R) – the Kelvin scale is used primarily in chemical calculations and is also known as Absolute Temperature. Temperatures are expressed either by (1) Kelvin when dealing with centigrade temperatures and (2) Rankine when dealing with Fahrenheit temperatures.

Conversion is as follows:

- From (°F) to (°C): $°C = 5(°F - 32) \div 9$
- From (°C) to (°F): $°F = [9 \times °C \div 5] + 32$

- From (°F) to (R): °F = °F – 460
- From (°C) to (K): °C = °C + 273

Boiling Point

Classification of Flammable Liquids incorporates the boiling point which is directly affected by both the temperature of the liquid and the atmospheric pressure. Boiling point is therefore defined as the temperature at which the vapour pressure of a liquid equals the atmospheric pressure of the air.

Clearly the temperature of the liquid will also dictate how much vapour is present whether it is in a closed vessel or open to the atmosphere during a spill. Once the temperature reaches the boiling point, the liquid is driven into a vapour state which will

- increase the pressure within a closed vessel or
- produce a vapour cloud from an open spill that will travel away from the area.

Each compound has a different boiling point which requires review of the three primary factors that come into play when looking at the boiling point of a flammable liquid.

a) Molecular Weight

Molecular weight is the sum of the atomic weight of each atom within the molecule relative to the most common isotope of Carbon which has a mass of 12. Molecules are comprised of a combination of elements that we see on the periodic table that when joined provide a collective weight for that molecule. As more elements are added into a molecule and the size increases, the more energy it will take to boil that liquid so that it exceeds the atmospheric pressure that is holding it in liquid form. The greater the molecular weight, the greater the boiling point.

b) Polarity

Polarity deals with the positive (+) and negative (-) electric charge that is found between atomic bonds. Like a magnet, molecules work on the basis of attraction between positive and negative charges, and the strength of that attraction is referred to as polarity. As a liquid is heated, the molecules increase in motion and eventually reach a point that the molecular attraction of the positive and negative charge is not sufficient enough to keep them together, and they break apart causing the liquid to become a gas. The stronger the attraction, referred to as the polarity of a molecule, the more energy it will take to break this apart which means a higher boiling point.

c) Polymer Branching

Polymers are large molecules that generally consist of repeating small molecules called monomers. Polymer branching refers to the chemical structures that extend off of the main trunk of the molecule similar to a branch on a tree. The larger the core size or trunk of the molecule, the larger the surface area and ability for molecules to attract each other which in turn increases the boiling point due to the strength of these attractions. Branching however reduces the core size of the molecule by splitting some of the polymer chemical structures out of the core which subsequently reduces the surface area and therefore decreases the boiling point. In many cases, these hydrocarbon molecules have the same molecular structure but have the carbon and hydrogen branches connected in a different structural formation. These molecules are referred to as isomers.

Vapour Pressure

a) Atmospheric Pressure

Atmospheric pressure, also known as the barometric pressure, is the pressure exerted by the weight of the surrounding atmosphere on the surface of a liquid. Vapour pressure in turn is the pressure exerted by the liquid back onto the surrounding atmospheric pressure.

It is important to understand that liquids naturally want to become a gas and the pressure exerted down on them by the surrounding air is what determines if they stay as a liquid or become a vapour (mixture phase of both a gas and liquid). Atmospheric pressure is defined as the pressure at sea level, and expressed in two primary ways:

- 1 ATM = 760 millimetres of mercury (760 mm Hg)
- 1 ATM = 14.7 pounds per square inch (14.7 lb/in2)

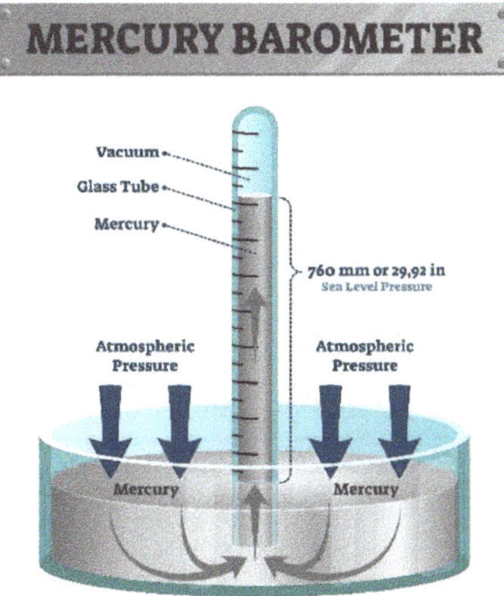

Subsequently, the higher the elevation where the atmosphere is referred to as "thinner", the less weight the air has pressing down on the liquid. The boiling point for any given material therefore will be less at higher elevations since it requires less effort to drive the liquid into a gas state.

b) Density

Vapour density is the "weight" of the vapour in comparison to the weight of dry air. Air is primarily a mixture of nitrogen (78%) and oxygen (21%) with trace volumes of water vapour, argon and carbon dioxide. Dry air has no water vapour and has a defined molecular weight of 28.97 grams per mole. When determining the vapour density of a compound, the molecular weight of the material is divided by 28.97 and then compared to air which is given a weight value of 1.0.

Vapour Density = Molecular Mass of Gas/28.97

For example, methane has a molecular mass of 16.04 grams/mole. Therefore methane has a vapour density as follows:

- Vapour Density = 16.04/28.97 = 0.55

If the vapour density of a compound is greater than 1.0, the vapour will be heavier than air and settle close to the ground. If the vapour density of the compound is less than 1.0, the vapour will be lighter than air and will move to elevated places.

Specific Gravity

Specific gravity is also referred to as Relative Density and is defined as the ratio of the density of a material when compared to the density of a reference substance. For liquids, the reference substance is usually water. For gases, the reference substance is air as outlined previously in vapour density. Generally, specific gravity is used when comparing the density of a liquid to water.

A compound's density is a measure of how heavy something is in a given volume. For specific gravity, density is measured as grams per millilitre or kilograms per litre. To find the density of a material the mass or weight is divided by the volume as follows:

Density = Weight/Volume

For example, 10 litres of gasoline weighs 7.7 kilograms. Therefore, gasoline has a density as follows:

- Density = 7.7 kg/10 litres = 0.77 kg/litre

Water, which is used as the reference substance, has a density of 1 gram per millilitre, or 1 kilogram per litre.

Specific Gravity = Density of the Substance/Density of Water

Therefore the Specific Gravity of Gasoline is:

- Specific Gravity Gasoline = (0.77 kg/litre) / (1 kg/litre) = 0.77

If the specific gravity of a liquid is greater than 1.0, the liquid will be heavier than water and sink below the surface. If the specific gravity of a liquid is less than 1.0, the liquid will be lighter than water and will float on the surface.

Class 4 Flammable Solids

Overview

Definition

Flammable solids are comprised of solid phase materials that under normal conditions undergo combustion in the presence of an ignition source. The primary hazards of flammable solids are that they ignite readily, burn fiercely and are difficult if not impossible to extinguish. They constitute two (2) primary types of materials that include:

- Desensitized Explosives – explosives that when dry are Class 1 Explosives excluding those explosives that are under "wet" conditions to suppress explosive properties.
- Self Reactive – thermally unstable compounds that undergo a strong and often violent exothermic reaction due to decomposition of the compound.
- Flammable solids are separated into five (5) primary categories based on the individual hazards associated with the solid:
- Water Reactive – Compounds that react violently in the presence of water.
    - These compounds often produce flammable hydrogen gas that can ignite when mixed with air. These include alkali metals, organometallic compounds, and various hydrides.
    - Generate large amounts of heat when contacted by water resulting in a violent reaction.
- Highly Unstable and Reactive – Compounds that are inherently unstable and self-reactive under normal conditions.
    - These compounds generally react alone due to self-decomposition and liberate large amounts of heat and toxic by-product gas. Include azides, ethers, many nitrates and organometallics.
    - Reaction rates always substantially increase as the temperature increases which requires heat dissipation mechanisms to stabilize the compound.
- Incompatible Reactive – Compounds that react violently in the presence of incompatible materials.
    - Often generate large amounts of heat when mixed resulting in a violent exothermic reaction and often toxic gases.

- Pyrophoric Reactive – Compounds that ignite spontaneously when expose to oxygen and the moisture in the air at or below 54.4°C or 130°F.
  - Include organometallics, metal hydrides and finely divided metals such as lithium, magnesium and aluminum.
- Shock Reactive – Compounds that react violently in the presence of light, friction or mechanical shock (when struck, vibrated or agitated).
  - Generally thought of as shock or impact sensitive and include nitroglycerine, nitrogen triiodide and various peroxides.

Sublimation And Flash Point Solids

A small group of flammable solids go through a process referred to as sublimation. Sublimation refers to a chemical change of state and is the transition of a solid directly to a gas/vapour phase without going through the intermediate liquid phase. Since these compounds still have a flash point and are reactive, they are referred to as Flash Point Solids. When ignited, these materials ignite in a similar manner as a flammable liquid and will in fact melt and flow like a flammable liquid when ignited. Examples of these materials include naphthalene (moth balls), paraformaldehyde, and camphor.

Subclass 4.1 Flammable Solids

Effective December 1, 2018, GHS (and subsequently OSHA) defines a flammable solid as a readily combustible solid or a solid that is liable to cause or contribute to fire through friction. A readily combustible solid means a powdered, granular or pasty mixture or substance that can be easily ignited by brief contact with an ignition source and, when ignited, has a flame that spreads rapidly.

Flammable Solids are categorized as:

- Flammable Solids Category 1 – A solid that is:
  - Other than a metal powder, in respect of which
    - The burning time is less than 45 seconds, or the burning rate is greater than 2.2 millimetres per second and
    - The wetted zone does not stop the fire or stops the fire for less than 4 minutes, or

- A metal powder, in respect if which the burning time is less than or equal to 5 minutes

- Flammable Solids Category 2 – A solid that is:
  - Other than a metal powder, in respect of which
    - The burning time is less than 45 seconds, or the burning rate is greater than 2.2 millimetres per second and
    - The wetted zone stops the fire for at least 4 minutes, or
    - A metal powder, in respect if which the burning time is greater than 5 minutes and less than or equal to 10 minutes

Transportation Of Dangerous Goods Classification

Transport Canada defines a 4.1 Flammable Solid as follows under SOR/2017-137, Part 2:

- readily combustible, as determined in accordance with section 2.4.2.2 of Chapter 2.4 of the UN Recommendations,
- under normal conditions of transport, liable to cause fire through friction,
- solid desensitized explosives, which are solid explosives desensitized through wetting with water or alcohols or diluted with other substances to form a homogeneous solid mixture to suppress their explosive properties so that they are not included in Class 1, Explosives,

Substances that have one of the following UN numbers meet the criterion in subparagraph (iii): UN1310, UN1320, UN1321, UN1322, UN1336, UN1337, UN1344, UN1347, UN1348, UN1349, UN1354, UN1355, UN1356, UN1357, UN1517, UN1571, UN2555, UN2556, UN2557, UN2852, UN2907, UN3270, UN3319, UN3344.

- self-reactive substances that are liable to undergo a strongly exothermic decomposition even without the participation of oxygen (air), as determined in accordance with section 2.4.2.3 of Chapter 2.4 of the UN Recommendations, but Class 4.1 does not include substances that have
  - a primary class of Class 1, Explosives, Class 5.1, Oxidizing Substances, or Class 5.2, Organic Peroxides,
  - a heat of decomposition less than 300 J/g, or
  - a self-accelerating decomposition temperature (SADT) that is greater than 75°C for

a 50 kg means of containment, as determined in accordance with section 2.4.2.3.4 of Chapter 2.4 of the UN Recommendations,

- polymerizing substances that, without stabilization, are liable to undergo a strongly exothermic reaction resulting in the formation of larger molecules or resulting in the formation of polymers under conditions normally encountered in transport, SOR/2017-137

- identified by one of the following UN numbers: UN2956, UN3241, UN3242 or UN3251, or

- are in the list of currently assigned self-reactive substances in section 2.4.2.3.2.3 of Chapter 2.4 of the UN Recommendations;

Department Of Transportation Classification

Department of Transport defines a 4.1 Flammable Solid as follows under 49 CFR 173.124 Part (a) and (b):

- Desensitized explosives that:
  - When dry are Explosives of Class 1 other than those of compatibility group A, which are wetted with sufficient water, alcohol, or plasticizer to suppress explosive properties; and
  - Are specifically authorized by name either in the Hazardous Materials Table in § 172.101 of this subchapter or have been assigned a shipping name and hazard class by the Associate Administrator under the provisions of –
    - (A) A special permit issued under subchapter A of this chapter; or
    - (B) An approval issued under § 173.56(i).
- Self-reactive materials that are thermally unstable and can undergo an exothermic decomposition even without participation of oxygen (air). A material is excluded from this

definition if any of the following applies:

- The material meets the definition of an explosive as prescribed in subpart C of this part, in which case it must be classed as an explosive;
- The material is forbidden from being offered for transportation according to § 172.101 of this subchapter or § 173.21;
- The material meets the definition of an oxidizer or organic peroxide as prescribed in this subpart, in which case it must be so classed;
- The material meets one of the following conditions:
  - Its heat of decomposition is less than 300 J/g; or
  - Its self-accelerating decomposition temperature (SADT) is greater than 75 °C (167 °F) for a 50 kg package; or
  - It is an oxidizing substance in Division 5.1 containing less than 5.0% combustible organic substances; or
  - The Associate Administrator has determined that the material does not present a hazard which is associated with a Division 4.1 material.

- Readily combustible solids are materials that:
  - Are solids which may cause a fire through friction, such as matches;
  - Show a burning rate faster than 2.2 mm (0.087 inches) per second when tested in accordance with the UN Manual of Tests and Criteria (IBR, see § 171.7 of this subchapter); or
  - Any metal powders that can be ignited and react over the whole length of a sample in 10 minutes or less, when tested in accordance with the UN Manual of Tests and Criteria.

- Polymerizing materials are materials which, without stabilization, are liable to undergo an exothermic reaction resulting in the formation of larger molecules or resulting in the formation of polymers under conditions normally encountered in transport. Such materials are considered to be polymerizing substances of Division 4.1 when:
  - Their self-accelerating polymerization temperature (SAPT) is 75 °C (167 °F) or less under the conditions (with or without chemical stabilization) as offered for transport in the packaging, IBC or portable tank in which the material or mixture is to be transported. An appropriate IBC or portable tank for a polymerizing material

must be determined using the heating under confinement testing protocol from boxes 7, 8, 9, and 13 of Figure 20.1 (a) and (b) (Flow Chart Scheme for Self-Reactive Substances and Organic Peroxides) from the UN Manual of Tests and Criteria (IBR, see § 171.7 of this subchapter) by successfully passing the UN Test Series E at the "None" or "Low" level, or by an equivalent test method with the approval of the Associate Administrator;

o   They exhibit a heat of reaction of more than 300 J/g; and

o   Do not meet the definition of hazard classes 1-8 (including combustible liquids).

o   The provisions concerning polymerizing substances in paragraph (a)(4) will be effective until January 2, 2019.

Subclass 4.2 Spontaneously Combustible Materials

Spontaneously combustible materials have three (3) primary categories within it:

- Self-reactive substances and mixtures
- Pyrophoric Liquids and Pyrophoric Solids
- Self heating substances and mixtures

Self Reactive Substances And Mixtures

Effective December 1, 2018, GHS (and subsequently OSHA) defines Class 4.2 as self-reactive substances and mixtures as:

- Type A – A liquid or solid that, as packaged, is liable to detonate, or deflagrate rapidly
- Type B - A liquid or solid that possesses explosive properties and, as packaged, neither detonates, nor deflagrates rapidly, but is liable to undergo a thermal explosion in that package
- Type C - A liquid or solid that possesses explosive properties and, as packaged, neither

detonates, nor deflagrates rapidly, nor undergoes a thermal explosion in that package

- Type D - a liquid or solid that:
    - detonates partially, does not deflagrate rapidly and shows no violent effect when heated under confinement
    - does not detonate, deflagrates slowly and shows no violent effect when heated under confinement, or
    - neither detonates nor deflagrates, and shows a medium effect when heated under confinement
- Type E - In laboratory testing, a liquid or solid that neither detonates nor deflagrates, and shows low or no effect when heated under confinement
- Type F - a liquid or solid that neither detonates in the cavitated state nor deflagrates and
- shows low or no effect when heated under confinement, as well as low or no explosive power
- shows no effect when heated under confinement nor any explosive power, and either
    - has a SADT < 60°C when evaluated in a 50 kg package, or
    - in the case of a liquid mixture, has a diluent that is used for desensitization with a boiling point < 150°C
- Type G - a liquid or solid that neither detonates in the cavitated state nor deflagrates, shows no effect when heated under confinement nor any explosive power, and either
    - has a SADT of 60°C to 75°C when evaluated in a 50 kg package, or
    - in the case of a liquid mixture, has a diluent that is used for desensitization with a boiling point ≥ 150°C

Pyrophoric Liquids And Solids

Effective December 1, 2018, GHS (and subsequently OSHA) defines a pyrophoric liquid as a liquid which, even in small quantities, is liable to ignite within 5 minutes after coming into contact with air. GHS identifies pyrophoric liquids as:

- Pyrophoric Liquids Category 1 – A liquid that, within 5 minutes either:
    - ignites when added to an inert carrier and after coming into contact with air, or
    - ignites or chars a filter paper, after coming into contact with air

Effective December 1, 2018, GHS (and subsequently OSHA) defines a pyrophoric solid as a solid that is liable to ignite within 5 minutes after coming into contact with air. GHS identifies a pyrophoric solid as:

- <u>Pyrophoric Solids Category 1</u> – A solid that ignites within 5 minutes after coming into contact with air

Self Heating Substances And Mixtures

Effective December 1, 2018, GHS (and subsequently OSHA) defines self-heating substances as:

- <u>Self Heating Category 1</u> - A solid or liquid in respect of which a positive result is obtained in a test using a 25 mm sample cube at 140°C and the spontaneous ignition temperature of a 450 l volume of the solid or liquid is ≤ 50 °C
- <u>Self Heating Category 2</u> - A solid or liquid in respect of which:
  - a positive result is obtained in a test using a 100 mm sample cube at 140°C, a negative result is obtained in a test using a 25 mm sample cube at 140°C and
    - the solid or liquid is packed in packages with a volume > 3 m3,
    - a positive result is obtained in a test using a 100 mm sample cube at 120°C and the solid or liquid is packed in packages with a volume > 450 l, or
    - a positive result is obtained in a test using a 100 mm sample cube at 100°C; or
  - a positive result is obtained in a test using a 25 mm sample cube at 140°C and the spontaneous ignition temperature of a 450 l volume of the solid or liquid is >50°C

Transportation Of Dangerous Goods Classification

Transport Canada defines Class 4.2, Substances Liable to Spontaneous Combustion as follows under SOR/2017-137, Part 2:

- pyrophoric substances that spontaneously ignite within 5 minutes after coming into contact with air, as determined in accordance with section 2.4.3.2 of Chapter 2.4 of the UN recommendations,
- self-heating substances that, when in large amounts (kilograms), spontaneously ignite on contact with air after long periods (hours or days), as determined in accordance with section 2.4.3.2 of Chapter 2.4 of the UN Recommendations

Department Of Transportation Classification

Department of Transport defines a Spontaneously Combustible Material Class 4.2 as follows under 49 CFR 173.124 Part (a) and (b):

- A pyrophoric material is a liquid or solid that, even in small quantities and without an external ignition source, can ignite within five (5) minutes after coming in contact with air when tested according to UN Manual of Tests and Criteria.

- Self-heating material. A self-heating material is a material that through a process where the gradual reaction of that substance with oxygen (in air) generates heat. If the rate of heat production exceeds the rate of heat loss, then the temperature of the substance will rise which, after an induction time, may lead to self-ignition and combustion. A material of this type which exhibits spontaneous ignition or if the temperature of the sample exceeds 200 °C (392 °F) during the 24-hour test period when tested in accordance with UN Manual of Tests and Criteria (IBR; see§ 171.7 of this subchapter), is classed as a Division 4.2 material.

Subclass 4.3 Water Reactive Substance And Mixtures

Effective December 1, 2018, GHS (and subsequently OSHA) defines a water reactive substance and mixture as substances and mixtures which, in contact with water, emit flammable gases are liquids and solids that, by interaction with water, are liable to become spontaneously flammable or give off flammable gases in dangerous quantities, that is, in quantities that are equal to or greater than one litre of gas per kilogram of the mixture or substance per hour.

Water reactive substances are categorized as:

- Substances and mixtures which in contact with water emit flammable gases - Category 1 – a liquid or solid that:
    - reacts with water at ambient temperature and produces a gas that is liable to ignite spontaneously;
    - reacts with water at ambient temperature such that the rate of evolution of flammable gas is ≥ 10 l/kg of liquid or solid over any one minute; or
    - reacts with water at ambient temperature to ignite spontaneously in any step of the test procedure
- Substances and mixtures which in contact with water emit flammable gases - Category 2 – a liquid or solid that:
    - reacts with water at ambient temperature such that the maximum rate of evolution of flammable gas is ≥ 20 l/kg of liquid or solid per hour
- Substances and mixtures which in contact with water emit flammable gases - Category 3 – a liquid or solid that:
    - reacts with water at ambient temperature such that the maximum rate of evolution of flammable gas is ≥ 1 l/kg of liquid or solid per hour

Transportation Of Dangerous Goods Classification

Transport Canada defines Class 4.3, Water Reactive as follows under SOR/2017-137, Part 2:

- Water-reactive Substances, which consists of substances that, in tests performed in accordance with section 2.4.4.2 of Chapter 2.4 of the UN Recommendations, emit a flammable gas at a rate greater than 1 L/kg of substance per hour or spontaneously ignite at any step in the test procedure.
- For the purposes of subparagraph (1)(a) (iv.1), a substance is considered to be a polymerizing substance of Class 4.1 if it:
    - has a self-accelerating polymerization temperature (SAPT) that is less than or equal to 75°C under the conditions in which the substance or mixture is to be transported, with or without chemical stabilization as offered for transport, and in the means of containment in which the substance or mixture is to be transported;
    - exhibits a heat of reaction of more than 300 J/g; and

o   does not meet any other criteria for inclusion in Classes 1 to 8.

SOR/2017-137

Department Of Transportation Classification

Department of Transport defines Class 4.3, Water Reactive 2 as follows under 49 CFR 173.124 Part (a) and (b):

- Division 4.3 (Dangerous when wet material). For the purposes of this chapter, dangerous when wet material (Division 4.3) means a material that, by contact with water, is liable to become spontaneously flammable or to give off flammable or toxic gas at a rate greater than 1 L per kilogram of the material, per hour, when tested in accordance with UN Manual of Tests and Criteria.

Class 5 Oxidizers

Overview

Definition

Oxidizing compounds are materials that either provide oxygen to other materials or force other materials to yield or release their oxygen. Oxidizers themselves do not burn but substantially enhance combustion and are regulated under two (2) primary types of materials that include:

- General Oxidizers Class 5.1
- Organic Peroxides Class 5.2

NFPA expands on these categories and identifies four (4) classes of oxidizers as follows from least to greatest hazard:

- Class 1 Oxidizer – Solids or liquids that readily yield oxygen or an oxidizing gas, or readily reacts to oxidizer combustible materials.
    - slightly increase the burning rate of combustible materials.
    - do not cause spontaneous ignition when they come in contact with them.
- Class 2 Oxidizer – Oxidizing material that can cause spontaneous ignition when in contact with combustible materials.
    - increase the burning rate of combustible materials moderately with which they come in contact.
    - may cause spontaneous ignition when in contact with a combustible material.
- Class 3 Oxidizer – Oxidizing material that can undergo vigorous self-sustained decomposition when catalyzed or exposed to heat.
    - severely increase the burning rate of combustible materials with which they come in contact.
    - will cause sustained and vigorous decomposition if contaminated with a combustible material or if exposed to sufficient heat.
- Class 4 Oxidizer – Oxidizing material that can undergo an explosive reaction when catalyzed or exposed to heat, shock or friction.
    - can explode when in contact with certain contaminants.
    - can explode if exposed to slight heat, shock, or friction.

- o will increase the burning rate of combustibles.
- o can cause combustibles to ignite spontaneously.

Subclass 5.1 Oxidizing Substance

Effective December 1, 2018, GHS (and subsequently OSHA) defines an oxidizing liquid whether or not combustible, that is liable to cause or contribute to the combustion of other material. Oxidizers are both liquids and solids.

Oxidizing liquids are categorized as:

- Oxidizing Liquids Category 1:
  - o A liquid that, when tested in a 1:1 mixture, by mass, with cellulose, spontaneously ignites, or exhibits a mean pressure rise time < the mean pressure rise time of a 1:1 mixture, by mass, of 50.0% perchloric acid and cellulose
- Oxidizing Liquids Category 2:
  - o A liquid that, when tested in a 1:1 mixture, by mass, with cellulose, exhibits a mean pressure rise time ≤ the mean pressure rise time of a 1:1 mixture, by mass, of 40.0% aqueous sodium chlorate solution and cellulose
- Oxidizing Liquids Category 3:
  - o liquid that, when tested in a 1:1 mixture, by mass, with cellulose, exhibits a mean pressure rise time ≤ the mean pressure rise time of a 1:1 mixture, by mass, of 65.0% aqueous nitric acid and cellulose

Effective December 1, 2018, GHS (and subsequently OSHA) defines an oxidizing solid whether or not combustible, that is liable to cause or contribute to the combustion of other material.

Oxidizing solids are categorized as:

- Oxidizing Solids Category 1:
  - o A solid that, when tested in a 4:1 or 1:1 mixture, by mass, with cellulose, exhibits a mean burning time < the mean burning time of a 3:2 mixture, by mass, of potassium bromate and cellulose
- Oxidizing Solids Category 2:
  - o A solid that, when tested in a 4:1 or 1:1 mixture, by mass, with cellulose, exhibits a mean burning time ≤ the mean burning time of a 2:3 mixture, by mass, of

potassium bromate and cellulose

- Oxidizing Liquids Category 3:
    - A solid that, when tested in a 4:1 or 1:1 mixture, by mass, with cellulose, exhibits a mean burning time $\leq$ the mean burning time of a 3:7 mixture, by mass, of potassium bromate and cellulose

Halogens

Halogens in pure elemental form constitute strong oxidizers even though they are often identified as toxic materials due to the hazard priority for exposure. Common halogens and properties encountered in the hazardous materials industry are:

- Fluorine – the strongest oxidizer known and is known to be able to cause concrete to burn. Fluorine is in a gaseous state and like many halogens is known to be toxic by inhalation.
- Chlorine – one of the most common halogen gases used in industry, chlorine is not combustible itself but strongly supports combustion. Chlorine can be a gas or a liquified gas and is known to be toxic by inhalation.
- Bromine – bromine is in liquid form and reacts often explosively with metals. As with chlorine, bromine is extensively used in the pharmaceutical and plastics industry and creates corrosive fumes.
- Iodine – the least reactive of all halogens, iodine is a granular solid that is extremely toxic by inhalation and ingestion and a strong eye and tissue irritant.

Oxysalts

As outlined in Section 3 Hazardous Materials Chemistry, oxysalts are made up of a metal element and the oxy-ion, O3. Oxysalts are not water reactive but do however behave as an oxidizer and release oxygen as they decompose and accelerate combustion. Oxysalts can be easily identified by the suffix "ate" or "ite" and the prefix "per" or "hypo".

Most oxysalts are soluble in water but can form explosive mixtures with acid. Additionally, they often can release halogens such as fluorine and chlorine which enhances oxidation.

Peroxide Salts

Peroxide salts are made up of a metal element and a non-metal peroxide group, O2-2 and are easily identified by the prefix of their name being "per". Peroxide salts are also violently water reactive and create a corrosive base when reacted with water due to the creation of the hydroxide ion that will then attach to the metal ion of the salt during decomposition.

Peroxide salts are inorganic and are not to be confused with organic peroxides which will be discussed later in this module. Peroxide salts are often referred to as metal peroxides due to the metal cation being ionically bonded to oxygen which makes them both reactive and volatile in nature. Metal peroxides are often explosively reactive with organic compounds and water and can create self-igniting mixtures with powdered metals.

Inorganic Acid Oxidizers

Certain inorganic acids such as nitric acid, chromic acid and perchloric acid are very strong oxidizers and will cause combustion when in contact with organic material such as paper. In some cases such as chromic acid, the reaction can be explosive in nature.

As with all oxidizers, each chemical can be corrosive and toxic as well as explosive. Generally inorganic acid oxidizers are highly volatile in the presence of organic material and often are also water reactive.

Transportation Of Dangerous Goods Classification

Transport Canada defines Class 5.1 Oxidizing Substance as follows under SOR/2017-137, Part 2:

- Class 5.1, Oxidizing Substances, which consists of substances that yield oxygen thereby causing or contributing to the combustion of other material, as determined in accordance with section 2.5.2 of Chapter 2.5 of the UN Recommendations

Department Of Transportation Classification 

Department of Transport defines Class 5.1 Oxidizing Substance as follows under 49 CFR 173.127 Part (a):

- For the purpose of this subchapter, oxidizer (Division 5.1) means a material that may, generally by yielding oxygen, cause or enhance the combustion of other materials.
- A solid material is classed as a Division 5.1 material if, when tested in accordance with the UN Manual of Tests and Criteria (IBR, see § 171.7 of this subchapter):
    - If test O.1 is used (UN Manual of Tests and Criteria, sub-section 34.4.1), the mean burning time is less than or equal to the burning time of a 3:7 potassium bromate/cellulose mixture; or
    - If test O.3 is used (UN Manual of Tests and Criteria, sub-section 34.4.3), the mean burning rate is greater than or equal to the burning rate of a 1:2 calcium peroxide/cellulose mixture.
- A liquid material is classed as a Division 5.1 material if, when tested in accordance with the UN Manual of Tests and Criteria, it spontaneously ignites or its mean time for a pressure rise from 690 kPa to 2070 kPa gauge is less than the time of a 1:1 nitric acid (65 percent)/cellulose mixture.

Subclass 5.2 Organic Peroxides

Effective December 1, 2018, GHS (and subsequently OSHA) defines organic peroxides as solid or liquid organic chemicals (i.e., chemicals containing carbon) that are characterized by a weak oxygen-oxygen (-O-O-) bond (also called a peroxy group or peroxide group). This bond can break or decompose easily, releasing heat (i.e., exothermic reaction). The rate of decomposition increases with increasing temperature. Decomposition can also be initiated by heat, mechanical shock, friction, or contaminants such as amines, metal ions (by themselves or as a result of contact with metal surfaces), strong acids and bases, and strong reducing and oxidizing agents.

In addition to being thermally unstable, organic peroxides may have one or more of the following properties:

- be liable to explosive decomposition
- burn rapidly
- be sensitive to impact or friction
- react dangerously with other substances.

GHS also states that "An organic peroxide is regarded as possessing explosive properties when in laboratory testing the formulation is liable to detonate, to deflagrate rapidly or to show a violent effect when heated under confinement." (GHS, 5th revised edition, 2013, paragraph 2.15.1.2). Organic peroxides have what is referred to as a self-accelerating decomposition temperature, SADT, which is the temperature at which the compound will begin to decompose. SADT will be explored in more detail in Section 6.10.1.2.2.

Organic peroxides are categorized in one (1) of seven (7) types based on the degree of danger they present defined by their ability to detonate, deflagrate, and react to heat under confinement as follows from greatest to least hazard:

• Organic Peroxide Type A:

    o A liquid or solid that, as packaged, is liable to detonate, or deflagrate rapidly

• Organic Peroxide Type B:

    o A liquid or solid that possesses explosive properties and, as packaged, neither detonates, nor deflagrates rapidly, but is liable to undergo a thermal explosion in that package

• Organic Peroxide Type C

    o A liquid or solid that possesses explosive properties and, as packaged, neither detonates, nor deflagrates rapidly, nor undergoes a thermal explosion in that package

• Organic Peroxide Type D

    o A liquid or solid that

        □ detonates partially, but does not deflagrate rapidly and shows no violent effect when heated under confinement

☐ does not detonate, but deflagrates slowly and shows no violent effect when heated under confinement, or

☐ neither detonates nor deflagrates, but shows a medium effect when heated under confinement

• Organic Peroxide Type E

o A liquid or solid that neither detonates nor deflagrates, and shows low or no effect when heated under confinement

• Organic Peroxide Type F

o A liquid or solid that neither detonates in the cavitated state nor deflagrates and

☐ shows low or no effect when heated under confinement, as well as low or no explosive power; or

☐ shows no effect when heated under confinement nor any explosive power, and either

• has a SADT < 60°C when evaluated in a 50 kg package, or

• in the case of a liquid mixture, has a diluent that is used for desensitization with a boiling point < 150°C

• Organic Peroxide Type G

o a liquid or solid that neither detonates in the cavitated state nor deflagrates, shows no effect when heated under confinement nor any explosive power, and either

☐ has a SADT of 60°C to 75°C when evaluated in a 50 kg package, or

☐ in the case of a liquid mixture, has a diluent that is used for desensitization with a boiling point ≥ 150°C

Transportation Of Dangerous Goods Classification 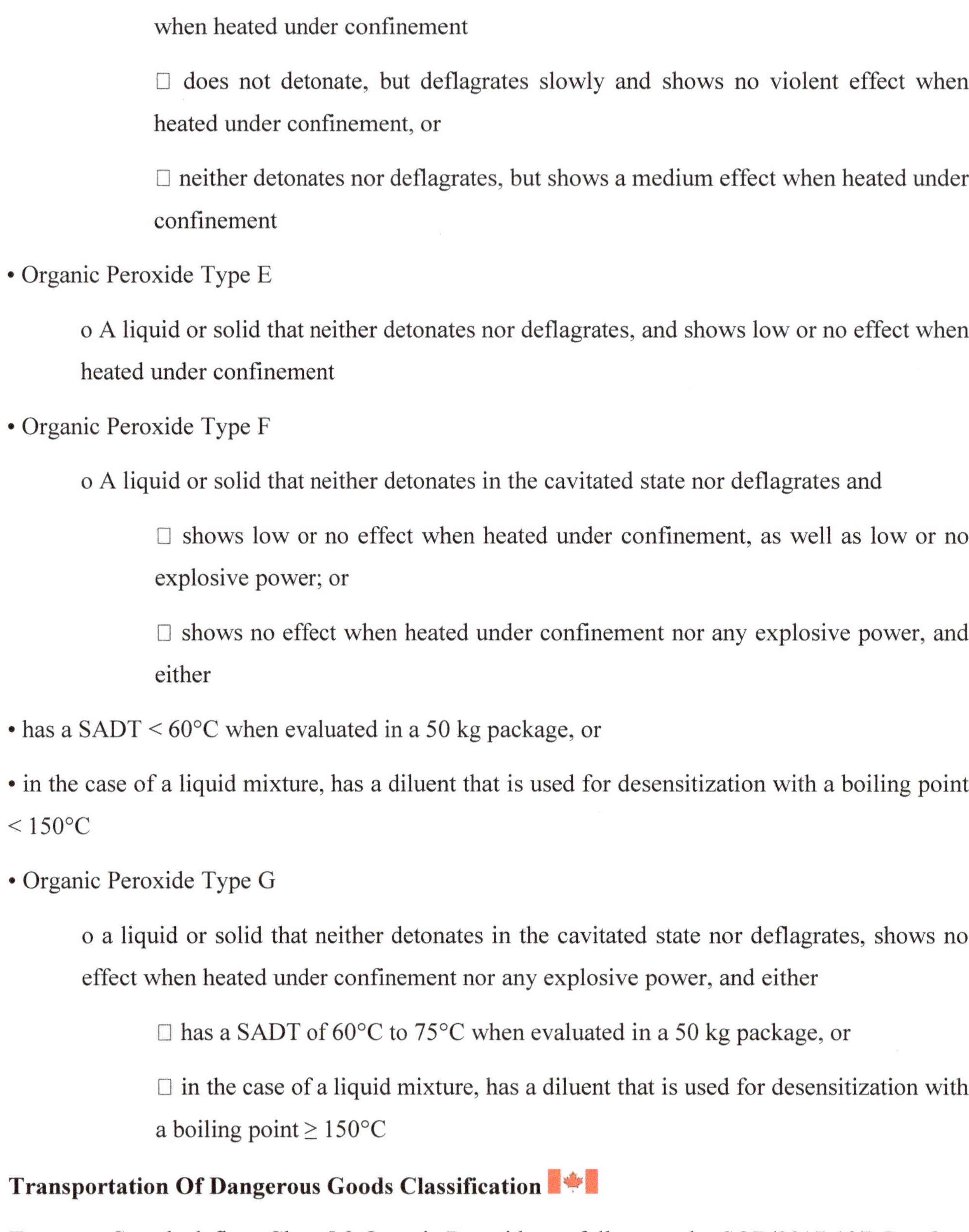

Transport Canada defines Class 5.2 Organic Peroxides as follows under SOR/2017-137, Part 2:

• Class 5.2, Organic Peroxides, which consists of substances that o are thermally unstable organic compounds that contain oxygen in the bivalent "-O-O-" structure, as determined in accordance with section 2.5.3 of Chapter 2.5 of the UN Recommendations,

o are liable to undergo exothermic self-accelerating decomposition,

o (iii) have one or more of the following characteristics:

☐ they are liable to explosive decomposition,

☐ they burn rapidly,

☐ they are sensitive to impact or friction,

☐ they react dangerously with other substances, or

☐ they cause damage to the eyes, or

• are in the list of currently assigned organic peroxides in section 2.5.3.2.4 of Chapter 2.5 of the UN Recommendations. SOR/2017-137

Department of transportation classification

Department of Transport defines Class 5.2 Organic Peroxides as follows under 49 CFR 173.128 Part (a):

• For the purposes of this subchapter, organic peroxide (Division 5.2) means any organic compound containing oxygen (O) in the bivalent -O-O- structure and which may be considered a derivative of hydrogen peroxide, where one or more of the hydrogen atoms have been replaced by organic radicals, unless any of the following paragraphs applies:

o The material meets the definition of an explosive as prescribed in subpart C of this part, in which case it must be classed as an explosive;

o The material is forbidden from being offered for transportation according to § 172.101 of this subchapter or § 173.21;

o The Associate Administrator has determined that the material does not present a hazard which is associated with a Division 5.2 material; or

o The material meets one of the following conditions:

☐ For materials containing no more than 1.0 percent hydrogen peroxide, the available oxygen, as calculated using the equation in paragraph (a)(4)(ii) of this section, is not more than 1.0 percent, or

☐ For materials containing more than 1.0 percent but not more than 7.0 percent hydrogen peroxide, the available oxygen, content (Oa) is not more than 0.5 percent

Class 6 Toxics

Overview

Poisonous materials are substances that can harm an organism when exposed to a sufficient amount of the compound. The study of poisonous materials is referred to as toxicology and even though very interchangeable overall, there are some subtle differences between the term poisonous and the term toxic. In the simplest terms, a poison refers to a substance that will harmfully affect a biological organism. How strongly that poison affects that organism is referred to as how toxic that compound is.

Often, we hear the phrases "Time and Distance" or "How Much - How Often" associated with toxicology. These phrases summarize the premise that the longer and closer an organism is exposed to a poison, or the more a poison is taken in quickly, the likelihood that the toxicity of the exposure will exponentially increase. It stands to reason then that the shorter period that an organism is exposed and the further away they are from the source of the poison, the less toxic that compound will be. The critical point to remember with poisonous materials is that most compounds in excess pose a detrimental effect on an organism and need to be adequately gauged in context.

As with people, each organism will react uniquely to exposures with differing results and require diligent protocols to ensure that even the smallest amount of exposures are operationally controlled at all times. Small exposures over a long period of time as we see with the history of asbestos and the resulting mesothelioma often are equally as destructive as high one-time exposures. Toxicity encompasses the study of these adverse effects and provides comprehensive guidelines to help each of us ensure that we maintain a diligent work environment, but it is the responsibility of each person to understand the information available.

There are four (4) general types of toxic entities:

• Chemical – includes organic and inorganic compounds

• Biological – includes disease causing microorganisms and pathogens

• Radioactive – includes uranium, radium and ionizing radiation

• Physical – includes substances that physically interfere with biological process such as asbestos and silicon dioxide

Factors

Toxicity is dependent on several factors that need to be considered when evaluating the impact that a substance will have on a person. As previously noted, some individuals will have unpredictable reactions to a substance that are qualitatively different than what is observed in most individuals. These situations are referred to as idiosyncratic responses due to their unpredictability and the fact that they are uncommon overall.

The primary factors taken into account when evaluating toxicity are as follows:

• Form of substance – the physical state of a substance has a profound impact on the toxicology. Vapour, gas, liquid and solid states all impact the route of exposure as does the number of substances that a person is exposed to.

• Chemical Activity – the rate at which the substance impacts the organism at a cellular level. Some chemicals immediately damage cells while others alter cell structure over time.

• Dosage – dosage is by far the most important factor to be considered and determine if a substance is an acute toxicant or a chronic toxicant.

• Route of exposure – the route that a substance is presented to a person is very important. Different organs are targeted by different routes which in turn determine if the body has time to detoxify the substance before it is distributed throughout the body.

• Absorption – absorption is associated with the route of exposure and the rate at which that absorption occurs is critical.

• Organism Species – each organism with metabolize substances differently as we find with items like insecticides that will not harm livestock.

• Age – an individual's age often plays a formidable part in the persons response to exposure.

• Gender – as with age, gender often is important to evaluate due to the way each gender metabolizes substances.

• Health – again, an individual's physical health can play a large role in the effect a substance has on a person.

• Metabolism – metabolism is the process of which an organism converts one chemical into another and is very individual for each person. Metabolism plays two (2) key roles when dealing with toxicity:

o Detoxification – the process of converting a toxin into a less toxic form

     o Bioactivation – the process of converting a substance into a more reactive or toxic form

• Distribution – where a toxicant is distributed throughout the body will ultimately determine where toxicity occurs within an organism.

• Excretion – how quickly and effectively substances are excreted from the body and by which method (i.e.) kidney, gastrointestinal, lungs, sweat, tears, milk.

Effects

Acute

Acute toxicity refers to adverse effects occurring following oral or dermal administration of a single dose of a substance or mixture, or multiple doses given within 24 hours, or an inhalation exposure to a substance or mixture of four hours or of a duration that is converted to four hours. For an exposure to be considered acute, the adverse affects need to occur within 14 days of exposure. As part of acute toxicity, another exposure that involves multiple exposures with a period of time between each is referred to as Subacute.

Acute toxicity is measured in several ways including:

• Generally Recognized as Safe, GRAS – the substance is generally recognized, among qualified experts, as having been adequately shown to be safe under the conditions of its intended use.

• No Observed Adverse Effect Level, NOAEL - the highest experimental point that is without adverse effect.

• Short-Term Exposure Limit, STEL - The concentration which no person should be exposed to for more than 15 minutes during an 8-hour workday.

• Threshold Limit Value Short Term Exposure Limit, TLV-STEL- The maximum concentration to which a worker can be exposed every workday (8 hours) and experience no adverse health effects.

• Threshold Limit Value Ceiling, TLV-C – The concentration to which no person should be exposed to.

• LD50 – Median Lethal Dose. The value of LD50 for a substance is the dose required to kill half the members of a tested population after a specified test duration. A lower LD50 is indicative of increased toxicity. LD50 is expressed as a mass per unit.

• LC50 – Median Lethal Concentration. Similar to LD50 but expressed as a concentration value.

• Permissible Exposure Limit, PEL – the OSHA legal limit for exposure based on an 8-hour workday, 40 hours per week

• Recommended Exposure Limit, REL – the NIOSH recommended limit for exposure based on a 10-hour workday, 40 hours per week

• Immediately Dangerous to Life and Health, IDLH - an atmosphere that poses an immediate threat to life, would cause irreversible adverse health effects, or would impair an individual's ability to escape from a dangerous atmosphere.

As part of the Global Harmonized System, acute toxicity is defined under routes of exposure:

Column 1		Column 2
Item	Category	Ranges for LD_{50} or for Acute Toxicity Point Estimates (mg/kg body weight (bw))
1	Acute Toxicity (Oral) — Category 1	≤ 5
2	Acute Toxicity (Oral) — Category 2	> 5 and ≤ 50
3	Acute Toxicity (Oral) — Category 3	> 50 and ≤ 300
4	Acute Toxicity (Oral) — Category 4	> 300 and ≤ 2000

Column 1		Column 2
Item	Category	Ranges for LD_{50} or for Acute Toxicity Point Estimates (mg/kg bw)
1	Acute Toxicity (Dermal) — Category 1	≤ 50
2	Acute Toxicity (Dermal) — Category 2	> 50 and ≤ 200
3	Acute Toxicity (Dermal) — Category 3	> 200 and ≤ 1000
4	Acute Toxicity (Dermal) — Category 4	> 1000 and ≤ 2000

Column 1		Column 2	Column 3	Column 4
Item	Category	Ranges for LC_{50} or for Acute Toxicity Point Estimates		
		Gases (ppmV)	Vapours (mg/l)	Dusts and Mists (mg/l)
1	Acute Toxicity (Inhalation) — Category 1	≤ 100	≤ 0.5	≤ 0.05
2	Acute Toxicity (Inhalation) — Category 2	> 100 and ≤ 500	> 0.5 and ≤ 2	> 0.05 and ≤ 0.5
3	Acute Toxicity (Inhalation) — Category 3	> 500 and ≤ 2500	> 2 and ≤ 10	> 0.5 and ≤ 1
4	Acute Toxicity (Inhalation) — Category 4	> 2500 and ≤ 20 000	> 10 and ≤ 20	> 1 and ≤ 5

Chronic

Similar in ways to subacute exposure, chronic exposures are multiple exposures over a long period of time, often years. Unlike subacute exposures where there are no cumulative effects however, chronic exposures continue to build upon each exposure and increase the level of toxicity within the body. Over time, this increased toxicity can cause illness, permanent damage, and death.

Chronic toxicity is caused by repeated exposure to a harmful substance for part of the lifespan of an animal, for a major portion of its lifespan, or for all of its lifespan. Repeat dose toxicity studies are usually conducted in animals with the main aim of defining a No Observed Adverse Effect Level, NOAEL. Chronic toxicity is principally due to the progressive accumulation of damage in one or more critical target organs.

Effective December 1, 2018, GHS (and subsequently OSHA) includes the following exposure criteria:

• Skin corrosion - a substance must penetrate through the epidermis into the dermis within four hours of application and must not reverse the damage within 14 days.

• Skin irritation - shows damage less severe than corrosion if: the damage occurs within 72 hours of application; or for three consecutive days after application within a 14-day period; or causes inflammation which lasts for 14 days in two test subjects.

• Mild skin irritation - is minor damage (less severe than irritation) within 72 hours of application or for three consecutive days after application.

• Serious eye damage - involves tissue damage or degradation of vision which does not fully reverse in 21 days. Eye irritation involves changes to the eye which do fully reverse within 21 days.

• Respiratory sensitizer - cause breathing hypersensitivity when the substance is inhaled.

• Skin sensitizer - causes an allergic response from a dermal application.

• Reproductive toxicity - cause adverse effects in either sexual function or fertility to either a parent or the offspring.

• Specific target organ toxicity - damage only specific organs.

• Aspiration hazard - solids or liquids which can cause damage through inhalation.

• Germ cell mutagenicity – the ability of some substances and mixtures to modify the genetic material of cells or organisms in ways that allow changes to be transmitted during cell division.

• Carcinogenicity – a mixture or substance liable to lead to cancer or increase the incident of cancer.

• Biohazardous infectious materials – any microorganism, nucleic acid or protein that causes or is a probable cause of infection, with or without toxicity, in humans or animals.

Routes Of Exposure

Inhalation

For most chemicals in the form of vapors, gases, mists, or particulates, inhalation is the major route of entry. Once inhaled, chemicals are either exhaled or deposited in the respiratory tract. If deposited, damage can occur through direct contact with tissue, or the chemical may diffuse into the blood through the lung-blood interface.

Upon contact with tissue in the upper respiratory tract or lungs, chemicals may cause health effects ranging from simple irritation to severe tissue destruction. Substances absorbed into the blood are circulated and distributed to organs that have an affinity for that particular chemical. Health effects can then occur in the organs, which are sensitive to the toxicant.

Absorption

Skin (dermal) contact can cause effects that are relatively innocuous such as redness or mild dermatitis; more severe effects include destruction of skin tissue or other debilitating conditions. Many chemicals can also cross the skin barrier and be absorbed into the blood system. Once absorbed, they may produce systemic damage to internal organs.

The eyes are particularly sensitive to chemicals. Even a short exposure can cause severe effects to the eyes, or the substance can be absorbed through the eyes and be transported to other parts of the body causing harmful effects.

Ingestion

Chemicals that inadvertently get into the mouth and are swallowed do not generally harm the gastrointestinal tract itself unless they are irritating or corrosive. Chemicals that are insoluble in the fluids of the gastrointestinal tract (stomach, small, and large intestines) are generally excreted. Others that are soluble are absorbed through the lining of the gastrointestinal tract. They are then transported by the blood to internal organs where they can cause damage.

Injection

Substances may enter the body if the skin is penetrated or punctured by contaminated objects. Effects can then occur as the substance is circulated in the blood and deposited in the target organs.

Cancer Slope Factors

Cancer Slope Factors (CSF) are mathematical models used to estimate and predict the potential risk of cancer development that will arise in response to a lifetime exposure to an agent. The CSF is estimated at the upper bound of 95% confidence level and is often referred to as the "potency factor". CSF fall into the following categories:

• Group A: Human carcinogens

• Group B1: Probable human carcinogens based on limited human data

• Group B2: Sufficient evidence in animals, limited or no human evidence

• Group C: Possible human carcinogens

• Group D: Not classified as to human carcinogenicity

• Group E. Evidence of non-carcinogenicity in humans

When calculating exposure to a known compound, we calculate the Time-Weighted average and then compare it to the Permissible Exposure Limit, PEL.

Example

Amyl Acetate, PEL @ 100 ppm.

An employee is exposed to amyl acetate at 80 ppm for 6 hours and 110 ppm for 2 hours. What is the time weighted exposure for this person?

$$\text{TWA} = \frac{(\text{Exposure A X Time A}) + (\text{Exposure B X Time B})}{(\text{Time A} + \text{Time B})}$$

$$= \frac{(80 \text{ ppm X 6 Hours}) + (110 \text{ ppm X 2 Hours})}{(6 \text{ Hours} + 2 \text{ Hours})}$$

$$= \frac{(480 + 220) \text{ ppm Hours}}{(8 \text{ Hours})}$$

$$= \mathbf{87.5 \text{ ppm}}$$

COMMON CHEMICALS	COMMON SCENES	OSHA PEL (PPM)	IDLH (PPM)
Lithium Hydride	Drug labs	0.025	0.5
Iodine	Drug Labs, Hospitals, University	0.1	2
Phosgene Gas	Drug Labs, Hospitals, University	0.1	2
Mercury	Industry, Residence, Drug Lab, University	0.01	2
Chlorine Dioxide	Pulp & Paper, Drug Lab, Water Treatment Plants, Swimming Pools	0.1	5
Yellow Phosphorous	Drug Labs, Hospitals, University	0.1	5
Chlorine Gas	Rail, Truck, Farm, Drug Lab, Swimming Pools	1 (NIOSH 0.5 REL)	10
Hydrogen Peroxide	Pulp & Paper, Drug Lab, Water Treatment Plants, Swimming Pools	1	75
Hydrogen Sulphide	Oil Field, Swamps, Sewers, Manholes	20 (NIOSH 10 REL)	100
Anhydrous Ammonia	Rail, Truck, Farm, Drug Lab	50	300
Toluene	Industry, Drug Lab, Nail Polish, White-Out	200	500
Methanol	Everywhere	200	6000
Benzene	Industry, Oilfield	1	500 (Ca)

Subclass 6.1 Toxic Substance

Transportation Of Dangerous Goods Classification

Transport Canada defines Class 6.1 Toxic Substance as follows under SOR/2017-137, Part 2:

• Class 6.1, Toxic Substances, which consists of substances that are liable to cause death or serious injury or to harm human health if swallowed or inhaled or if they come into contact with human skin;

• Substances included in Class 6.1, Toxic Substances, are grouped by oral toxicity, dermal toxicity and inhalation toxicity by dust, mist or vapour. Toxicity by inhalation of a gas is covered in Class 2.3, Toxic Gases. A substance is included in Class 6.1

o due to oral toxicity if its LD50 (oral) is less than or equal to 300 mg/kg;

SOR/2008-34

o due to dermal toxicity if its LD50 (dermal) is less than or equal to 1 000 mg/kg; or

o due to inhalation toxicity

☐ (i) by dust or mist if dust or mist is likely to be produced in a transport accident and its LC50 (inhalation) is less than or equal to 4 mg/L, or

SOR/2008-34

☐ (ii) by vapour if its LC50 (inhalation) is less than or equal to 5 000 mL/m3.

2.29 Packing Groups

• When a substance is known to be included in Class 6.1 and that knowledge is based on documentary evidence published in technical journals or government publications and testing is not done to determine the packing group, the substance must be included in Packing Group I.

• Substances that are included in Class 6.1 due to

o oral toxicity is included in one of the following packing groups:

☐ Packing Group I, if the LD50 (oral) is less than or equal to 5 mg/kg,

☐ Packing Group II, if the LD50 (oral) is greater than 5 mg/kg but less than or equal to 50 mg/kg, or

☐ Packing Group III, if the LD50 (oral) is greater than 50 mg/kg but less than or equal to 300 mg/kg;

SOR/2008-34

o dermal toxicity is included in one of the following packing groups:

☐ Packing Group I if the LD50 (dermal) is less than or equal to 50 mg/kg,

☐ Packing Group II if the LD50 (dermal) is greater than 50 mg/kg but less than or equal to 200 mg/kg, or

☐ Packing Group III if the LD50 (dermal) is greater than 200 mg/kg but less than or equal to 1 000 mg/kg;

SOR/2008-34

o inhalation toxicity by dust or mist are included in one of the following packing groups:

☐ Packing Group I if the LC50 (inhalation) is less than or equal to 0.2 mg/L,

SOR/2012-245

☐ Packing Group II if the LC50 (inhalation) is greater than 0.2 mg/L but less than or equal to 2 mg/L, or

☐ Packing Group III if the LC50 (inhalation) is greater than 2 mg/L but less than or equal to 4 mg/L; or

SOR/2008-24

o inhalation toxicity by vapour are included in one of the following packing groups, where "V" is the saturated vapour concentration in millilitres per cubic metre of air at 20°C and at 101.3 kPa:

☐ Packing Group I, if

☐ (A) V is greater than or equal to 10 multiplied by the LC50, and

☐ (B) the LC50 is less than or equal to 1 000 mL/m3,

☐ Packing Group II, if

☐ (A) V is greater than or equal to the LC50,

☐ (B) the LC50 is less than or equal to 3 000 mL/m3, and

☐ (C) the criteria for Packing Group I are not met, or

☐ Packing Group III, if

☐ (A) V is greater than or equal to 0.2 multiplied by the LC50,

☐ (B) the LC50 is less than or equal to 5 000 mL/m3, and

☐ (C) the criteria for inclusion in Packing Group I or II are not met.

Department Of Transportation Classification

Department of Transport defines Class 6.1 Poisonous Substance as follows under 49 CFR 173.132 Part (a) through (c):

o For the purpose of this subchapter, poisonous material (Division 6.1) means a material, other than a gas, which is known to be so toxic to humans as to afford a hazard to health during transportation, or which, in the absence of adequate data on human toxicity:

o Is presumed to be toxic to humans because it falls within any one of the following categories when tested on laboratory animals (whenever possible, animal test data that has been reported in the chemical literature should be used):

o Oral Toxicity. A liquid or solid with an LD50 for acute oral toxicity of not more than 300 mg/kg.

o Dermal Toxicity. A material with an LD50 for acute dermal toxicity of not more than 1000 mg/kg.

o Inhalation Toxicity.

o A dust or mist with an LC50 for acute toxicity on inhalation of not more than 4 mg/L; or o A material with a saturated vapor concentration in air at 20 °C (68 °F) greater than or equal to one-fifth of the LC50 for acute toxicity on inhalation of vapors and with an LC50 for acute toxicity on inhalation of vapors of not more than 5000 mL/m 3; or

o Is an irritating material, with properties similar to tear gas, which causes extreme irritation, especially in confined spaces.

o For the purposes of this subchapter

o LD50 (median lethal dose) for acute oral toxicity is the statistically derived single dose of a substance that can be expected to cause death within 14 days in 50% of young adult albino rats when administered by the oral route. The LD50 value is expressed in terms of mass of test substance per mass of test animal (mg/kg).

o LD50 for acute dermal toxicity means that dose of the material which, administered by continuous contact for 24 hours with the shaved intact skin (avoiding abrading) of an albino rabbit, causes death within 14 days in half of the animals tested. The number of animals tested must be sufficient to give statistically valid results and be in conformity with good pharmacological practices. The result is expressed in mg/kg body mass.

o LC50 for acute toxicity on inhalation means that concentration of vapor, mist, or dust which, administered by continuous inhalation for one hour to both male and female young adult albino rats, causes death within 14 days in half of the animals tested. If the material is administered to the animals as a dust or mist, more than 90 percent of the particles available for inhalation in the test must have a diameter of 10 microns or less if it is reasonably foreseeable that such concentrations could be encountered by a human during transport. The result is expressed in mg/L of air for dusts and mists or in mL/m 3 of air (parts per million) for vapors. See § 173.133(b) for LC50 determination for mixtures and for limit tests.

o When provisions of this subchapter require the use of the LC50 for acute toxicity on inhalation of dusts and mists based on a one-hour exposure and such data is not available, the LC50 for acute toxicity on inhalation based on a four-hour exposure may be multiplied by four and the product substituted for the one-hour LC50 for acute toxicity on inhalation.

o When the provisions of this subchapter require the use of the LC50 for acute toxicity on inhalation of vapors based on a one-hour exposure and such data is not available, the LC50 for acute toxicity on inhalation based on a four-hour exposure may be multiplied by two and the product substituted for the one-hour LC50 for acute toxicity on inhalation.

o A solid substance should be tested if at least 10 percent of its total mass is likely to be dust in a respirable range, e.g. the aerodynamic diameter of that particle-fraction is 10 microns or less. A liquid substance should be tested if a mist is likely to be generated in a leakage of the transport containment. In carrying out the test both for solid and liquid substances, more than 90% (by mass) of a specimen prepared for inhalation toxicity testing must be in the respirable range as defined in this paragraph.

• For purposes of classifying and assigning packing groups to mixtures possessing oral or dermal toxicity hazards according to the criteria in § 173.133(a)(1), it is necessary to determine the acute LD50 of the mixture.

Subclass 6.2 Infectious Substance

Category A Infectious Affecting Humans

An infectious substance is defined a substance, such as viruses, bacteria, parasites, fungi or other agents that is known or reasonably believed to contain a pathogen and cause disease in humans or animals. Infectious substances might also be blood, tissue, organs, body fluids, or cultures that contain pathogenic microorganisms. Exposure in Class 6.2 occurs when a substance is released outside of the protective packaging and results in physical contact with humans or animals.

Category A Infectious Substances pose the highest risk of infection and are capable of causing permanent disability, life-threatening or fatal disease in otherwise healthy humans or animals. Examples of Category A include Hantaviruses, Hepatitis B, Dengue virus and Human immunodeficiency virus (HIV).

The proper shipping name of a Category A infectious substance is, as appropriate:

• UN2814 – INFECTIOUS SUBSTANCE, AFFECTING HUMANS

• UN2900 – INFECTIOUS SUBSTANCE, AFFECTING ANIMALS only

Category B Infectious Affecting Animals

Category B infectious substances may be responsible for causing disease in human or animals, but the conditions in transport are such that the likelihood of contracting the disease upon exposure is extremely remote. Examples of Category A include specimens with body fluids such as blood, urine or feces, and clinical biopsy samples.

The proper shipping name of a Category B infectious substance is:

• UN3373 – BIOLOGICAL SUBSTANCE, CATEGORY B

Transportation Of Dangerous Goods Classification

Transport Canada defines Class 6.2 Infectious Substances as follows under SOR/2017-137, Part 2:

An infectious substance is defined in Part 1, Coming into Force, Repeal, Interpretation, General Provisions and Special Cases, as "a substance known or reasonably believed to contain viable micro-organisms such as bacteria, viruses, rickettsia, parasites, fungi and other agents such as prions that are known or reasonably believed to cause disease in humans or animals and that are listed in Appendix 3 to Part 2, Classification, or that exhibit characteristics similar to a substance listed in Appendix 3". (1) Substances are included in Class 6.2, Category A or Category B if they are infectious substances and are listed in Appendix 3 to this Part or exhibit characteristics similar to a substance listed in that appendix. SOR/2008-34

• (2) Infectious substances that are included in Category A and that are in a form other than a culture may be handled, offered for transport or transported as Category B in accordance with the conditions set out in paragraphs 1.39(a) to (c) of Part 1, Coming into Force, Repeal, Interpretation, General Provisions and Special Cases. SOR/2008-34

• (3) Despite subsection (2), the following infectious substances included in Category A, and any substance that exhibits characteristics similar to these substances, must always be handled, offered for transport or transported as Category A

2.36.1 Medical or Clinical Waste

SOR/2014-306

Dangerous goods that are medical or clinical waste must be classified

- (a) under UN2814 or, as applicable, under UN2900, if they contain Category A infectious substances;

- (b) under UN3291, if they contain Category B infectious substances; or

- (c) under UN3291, if the shipper has reasonable grounds to believe that they have a low probability of containing infectious substances.

   SOR/2016-95

For the classification of medical or clinical wastes, international, national or provincial reference catalogues may be taken into account.

Note: The shipping name for UN3291 is "CLINICAL WASTE, UNSPECIFIED, N.O.S." or "(BIO)MEDICAL WASTE, N.O.S." or "REGULATED MEDICAL WASTE, N.O.S." SOR/2014-306

Department Of Transportation Classification

Department of Transport defines Class 6.2 Infectious Substance as follows under 49 CFR 173.128 Part (a):

- For the purposes of this subchapter, the following definitions and classification criteria apply to Division 6.2 materials.

   o Division 6.2 (Infectious substance) means a material known or reasonably expected to contain a pathogen. A pathogen is a microorganism (including bacteria, viruses, rickettsiae, parasites, fungi) or other agent, such as a proteinaceous infectious particle (prion), that can cause disease in humans or animals. An infectious substance must be assigned the identification number UN 2814, UN 2900, UN 3373, or UN 3291 as appropriate, and must be assigned to one of the following categories:

o Category A: An infectious substance in a form capable of causing permanent disability or life-threatening or fatal disease in otherwise healthy humans or animals when exposure to it occurs. An exposure occurs when an infectious substance is released outside of its protective packaging, resulting in physical contact with humans or animals. A Category A infectious substance must be assigned to identification number UN 2814 or UN 2900, as appropriate. Assignment to UN 2814 or UN 2900 must be based on the known medical history or symptoms of the source patient or animal, endemic local conditions, or professional judgment concerning the individual circumstances of the source human or animal.

o Category B: An infectious substance that is not in a form generally capable of causing permanent disability or life-threatening or fatal disease in otherwise healthy humans or animals when exposure to it occurs. This includes Category B infectious substances transported for diagnostic or investigational purposes. A Category B infectious substance must be described as "Biological substance, Category B" and assigned identification number UN 3373. This does not include regulated medical waste, which must be assigned identification number UN 3291.

• Biological product means a virus, therapeutic serum, toxin, antitoxin, vaccine, blood, blood component or derivative, allergenic product, or analogous product, or arsphenamine or derivative of arsphenamine (or any other trivalent arsenic compound) applicable to the prevention, treatment, or cure of a disease or condition of human beings or animals. A biological product includes a material subject to regulation under 42 U.S.C. 262 or 21 U.S.C. 151-159. Unless otherwise excepted, a biological product known or reasonably expected to contain a pathogen that meets the definition of a Category A or B infectious substance must be assigned the identification number UN 2814, UN 2900, or UN 3373, as appropriate.

• Culture means an infectious substance containing a pathogen that is intentionally propagated. Culture does not include a human or animal patient specimen as defined in paragraph (a)(4) of this section.

• Patient specimen means human or animal material collected directly from humans or animals and transported for research, diagnosis, investigational activities, or disease treatment or prevention. Patient specimen includes excreta, secreta, blood and its components, tissue and tissue swabs, body parts, and specimens in transport media (e.g., transwabs, culture media, and blood culture bottles).

• Regulated medical waste or clinical waste or (bio) medical waste means a waste or reusable material derived from the medical treatment of an animal or human, which includes diagnosis and immunization, or from biomedical research, which includes the production and testing of biological products. Regulated medical waste or clinical waste or (bio) medical waste containing a Category A infectious substance must be classed as an infectious substance, and assigned to UN2814 or UN2900, as appropriate.

• Sharps means any object contaminated with a pathogen or that may become contaminated with a pathogen through handling or during transportation and also capable of cutting or penetrating skin or a packaging material. Sharps includes needles, syringes, scalpels, broken glass, culture slides, culture dishes, broken capillary tubes, broken rigid plastic, and exposed ends of dental wires.

• Toxin means a Division 6.1 material from a plant, animal, or bacterial source. A toxin containing an infectious substance or a toxin contained in an infectious substance must be classed as Division 6.2, described as an infectious substance, and assigned to UN 2814 or UN 2900, as appropriate.

• Used health care product means a medical, diagnostic, or research device or piece of equipment, or a personal care product used by consumers, medical professionals, or pharmaceutical providers that does not meet the definition of a patient specimen, biological product, or regulated medical waste, is contaminated with potentially infectious body fluids or materials, and is not decontaminated or disinfected to remove or mitigate the infectious hazard prior to transportation.

Other Hazards Of Concern

Biohazard Level 1-4

The United States Centers for Disease Control and Prevention (CDC) categorizes various diseases in levels of biohazard, Level 1 being minimum risk and Level 4 being extreme risk. Laboratories and other facilities are categorized as BSL (Biosafety Level) 1–4 or as P1 through P4 for short (Pathogen or Protection Level).

• Biohazard Level 1:

> o Bacteria and viruses including Bacillus subtilis, canine hepatitis, Escherichia coli, and varicella (chicken pox), as well as some cell cultures and non-infectious bacteria.

> o At this level precautions against the biohazardous materials in question are minimal, most likely involving gloves and some sort of facial protection.

• Biohazard Level 2:

> o Bacteria and viruses that cause only mild disease to humans, or are difficult to contract via aerosol in a lab setting, such as hepatitis A, B, and C, some influenza A strains, Lyme disease, salmonella, mumps, measles, scrapie, dengue fever, and HIV.

> o Routine diagnostic work with clinical specimens can be done safely at Biosafety Level 2, using Biosafety Level 2 practices and procedures.

> o Research work (including co-cultivation, virus replication studies, or manipulations involving concentrated virus) can be done in a BSL-2 (P2) facility, using BSL-3 practices and procedures.

• Biohazard Level 3:

> o Bacteria and viruses that can cause severe to fatal disease in humans, but for which vaccines or other treatments exist, such as anthrax, West Nile virus, Venezuelan equine encephalitis, SARS virus, MERS coronavirus, hantaviruses, tuberculosis, typhus, Rift Valley fever, Rocky Mountain spotted fever, yellow fever, and malaria.

• Biohazard Level 4:

> o Viruses that cause severe to fatal disease in humans, and for which vaccines or other treatments are not available, such as Bolivian hemorrhagic fever, Marburg virus, Ebola virus, Lassa fever virus, Crimean–Congo hemorrhagic fever, and other hemorrhagic diseases. Variola virus (smallpox) is an agent that is worked with at BSL-4 despite the existence of a vaccine, as it has been eradicated.

> o When dealing with biological hazards at this level, the use of a positive pressure

personnel suit with a segregated air supply is mandatory. The entrance and exit of a Level Four biolab will contain multiple showers, a vacuum room, an ultraviolet light room, autonomous detection system, and other safety precautions designed to destroy all traces of the biohazard. Multiple airlocks are employed and are electronically secured to prevent both doors opening at the same time. All air and water service going to and coming from a Biosafety Level 4 (P4) lab will undergo similar decontamination procedures to eliminate the possibility of an accidental release.

o Currently there are no bacteria classified at this level.

Human Body Fluids

Blood or body fluids should always be treated as potentially infectious since the infections that can be spread from one person to another through infected blood or other body fluids are hepatitis B, hepatitis C and HIV (human immunodeficiency virus). Body fluids capable of spreading any of these infections include blood, semen, vaginal fluid, cerebral spinal fluid, body tissues and organs.

Saliva does not contain HIV or hepatitis C but may contain small amounts of hepatitis B. Breast milk can contain HIV. Urine, feces, vomit, and tears do not carry these infections. However, any of the body fluids listed here can carry hepatitis B, hepatitis C or HIV if blood is present. The risk of becoming infected from an exposure to blood or body fluids is greater:

• when the amount of blood is of a large volume

• when the cut or entry point into your body is large or deep

Risk will also depend on what infections the other person has, and whether or not you have previously been vaccinated against Hepatitis B. Contact between infected blood and healthy skin will not spread infections, as healthy skin acts as a very good barrier to viruses.

Exposure routes are as follows:

• Percutaneous exposure through puncture of skin by needlestick or another sharp object

• Permucosal exposure through contact with mucous membranes

• Non-intact skin exposure through eczema, scratches, and damaged skin.

Animal Waste

Humans can be exposed to pathogens from poorly managed animal feces, particularly in communities where animals live in close proximity to humans. Exposure to animal feces has been associated with diarrhea, soil-transmitted helminth infection, trachoma, environmental enteric dysfunction, and growth faltering. Children may experience long-term growth shortfalls after exposure to these pathogens, and pregnant women and the immunocompromised may also experience severe and/or long-term adverse health effects after infection with pathogens carried in animal feces.

There are at least 39 important diseases people catch directly from animals and at least 48 important diseases people get from the bite of bugs that have previously bitten an infected animal. Additionally, there are at least 42 important diseases that people get by ingesting or handling food or water contaminated with animal feces. Some are familiar such as rabies, bubonic plague, food poisoning. Others have only recently emerged - monkeypox, West Nile encephalitis, and Legionnaires' disease. Some such as highly lethal bird flu, we fear even though they haven't spread in humans, yet.

Nearly two-thirds of human pathogens and three-quarters of emerging pathogens are zoonotic in origin. While research has focused on zoonotic transmission of respiratory and vector-borne pathogens, such as Ebola and West Nile Virus, less attention has been given to pathogens found in animal feces that are transmitted via water, sanitation, and/or hygiene related pathways.

Sharps

Sharps and needlestick injuries are wounds caused by needles and other sharp medical instruments (e.g. scalpel, blades and scissors) that accidentally puncture or cut the skin. Sharps and needles may only cause small wounds in the skin, but the effects can be worse. Such instruments come in contact with blood and other body fluids and may carry the risk of infections. More than 20 dangerous bloodborne pathogens including HIV and hepatitis may be transmitted through accidental injuries with contaminated needles and sharps.

According to the Centre for Disease Control and Prevention, CDC, Occupational exposure to bloodborne pathogens from needlesticks and other sharps injuries is a serious problem, resulting in approximately 385,000 needlesticks and other sharps-related injuries to hospital-based healthcare personnel each year.

Sharps injuries are primarily associated with occupational transmission of hepatitis B virus (HBV), hepatitis C virus (HCV), and human immunodeficiency virus (HIV), but they have been implicated in the transmission of more than 20 other pathogens.

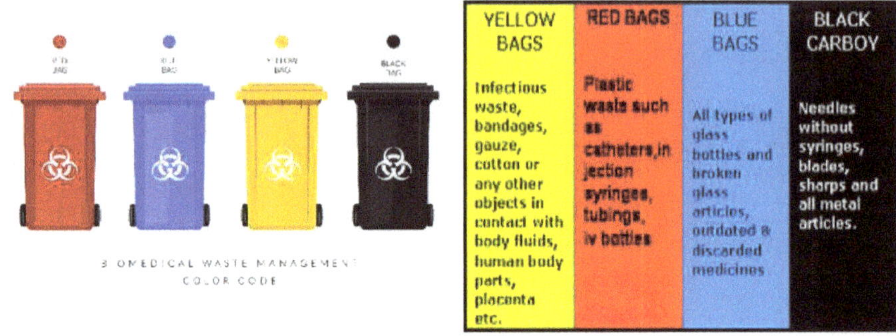

Class 7 Radioactives

Overview

Radioactivity is a term that is used for both naturally occurring and man-made radioactive compounds that release energy as they strive to achieve a more stable state. Radioactive elements are the elements that are on the periodic table with the atomic number of 83 or higher.

Radioactivity is a very robust topic and includes energy behaving in patterns that are similar to those of individual particles as well as patterns that are more wave-like in nature. There are several units of measurement and methods of measuring that come into play with radioactive materials which requires extensive understanding of the behaviour of materials and the nature of their hazard.

Frequently used terms associated with radioactivity that needs to be understood are as follows:

• Isotope - the different states of stability that the element goes through as it decays. Isotopes have the same number of positively charged protons in the nucleus but differ in the number of neutrons that the nucleus has.

• Decay - as the element releases energy to become more stable, the energy that is released is referred to the element's radioactivity and the process of achieving a more stable state is called decay.

• Half-Life - the length of time it takes for a radioactive element to decay.

For example, Carbon 14 is an isotope of Carbon 12 that is created on an ongoing basis as carbon reacts with the atmosphere. Carbon 14 decays over a period of 5,730 years and as an organic object gets older, there is less and less Carbon 14 present. By measuring the amount of Carbon 14 in an old artifact, scientists can accurately date how old an object is. This process is one we all have heard of and is called Carbon Dating.

Types Of Radiation

There are two (2) types of categories used for radiation:

• Non-ionizing radiation – this type of radiation does not carry enough energy to ionize molecules and remove electrons as energy which makes it relatively benign in nature. Non-ionizing radiation is slow with long wavelengths and generally does not require extra protective measures for individual safety

• Ionizing radiation – Ionizing radiation carries enough energy to detach electrons from a molecule which is tune creates an ion, hence the term ionizing radiation. Ionizing are very high frequency and fast moving with short wavelengths which can cause extensive damage to tissue and organs. Ionizing radiation is generally the concern within the hazardous materials industry.

Ionizing radiation comes in three (3) primary forms:

• Alpha radiation – Alpha particles are positively charged particles that are proportionally very large in size which makes them both heavy and slow. Alpha particles can only travel short distances, usually between 7-10 centimetres (3-4 inches) and will not penetrate the skin. The danger from alpha particles however come from them entering the body either through broken skin or more often through inhalation or ingestion. Once alpha particles are inside the body, they slowly emit radiation which in turns causes low-level irradiation to surrounding tissue and organs.

• Beta radiation – Beta particles are negatively charged particles that are faster, lighter and smaller than alpha particles. Beta particles are about 1/1800th the size of an alpha particle, can travel between 1 and 30 metres (3-100 feet), and can easily penetrate the skin. Beta radiation behaves like individual particles, so the concern they pose comes from the ability they have to cause extensive contamination of clothing and equipment.

• Gamma radiation – Gamma radiation is the strongest form of radiation that unlike alpha and beta particles, behaves as a wave. Gamma radiation is extremely high in energy and travels at the speed of light and can easily penetrate skin and other personal protective equipment. Protection from gamma radiation comes only from the shielding with several layers of lead, dense concrete or several metres of dirt. Since gamma radiation acts like a wave and not as a particulate such as alpha and beta, gamma radiation does not create as source of contamination and is strictly an exposure hazard as we see with X-rays.

Measuring Radioactivity

Ionizing radiation can be measured using units of electron volts, ergs, and joules. The electron-volt (abbreviated eV) is a unit of energy associated with moving electrons around. An electron is "tightly bound" in a hydrogen atom (one proton and one electron). It takes energy to move this electron away from the proton. It takes 13.6 electron-volts of energy to move this electron completely away from the proton. We say then that the atom is "ionized." In the jargon, the "ionization energy" of the tightly bound electron in hydrogen is 13.6 electron volts.

Electrons are very light objects, so we don't expect an electron-volt to represent very much energy. One electron-volt is only 1.6 x 10-19 joules of energy, in other words, 0.16 billion-billionth of a joule. One joule (abbreviated J) is equivalent to the amount of energy used by a one-watt light bulb lit for one second. The energy associated with the radioactive decay ranges from thousands to millions of electron-volts per nucleus, which is why the decay of a single nucleus typically leads to a large number of ionizations.

The radioactivity of a substance is measured in the number of nuclei that decay per unit time. The standard international unit or radioactivity is called a becquerel (abbreviated Bq), which is equal to one disintegration per second (dps). Radioactivity is also measured in curies, a historical unit based on the number of disintegrations per second in one gram of radium-226 (37 billion). Hence 1 curie = 37 billion Bq. One picocurie (a trillionth of a curie) = 0.037 Bq, and 1 Bq = 27 picocuries. Radioactivity is also measured in disintegration per minute (dpm). One dpm = 1/60 Bq.

Specific activity measures the radioactivity of a unit weight of substance. The units are curies per gram or becquerels per gram. This allows us to compare whether a substance is more or less radioactive than another. The specific activity of a radionuclide is inversely proportional to its atomic weight and its half-life.

Environmental and biological measurements of radioactivity are generally expressed as concentrations of radioactivity in soil, water, air, or tissue. Examples of units include picocuries per liter, becquerels per cubic meter, picocuries per gram, and disintegrations per minute per 100 square centimeters. One picocurie (abbreviated pCi) is 10-12 (or 0.000000000001) curie. Sometimes, the weight of a radioactive material per unit of soil or tissue might be given and expressed in parts per million, or ppm, can be expressed in terms of mass. This can be converted into radioactivity units, since we know the specific activities of various radionuclides. Disintegrations per minute per 100 square centimeters (dpm/100 cm2) is a unit commonly used to measure the surface contamination of an object, such as concrete or metal.

Measuring Dose

Placing your body near a radioactive source results in exposure. To evaluate the hazard from this exposure one must compute the absorbed dose. This is defined as the energy imparted to a defined mass of tissue. Dose is generally not uniform over the body. A radioactive substance can be selectively taken up by different organs or tissue.

Physically speaking, the most elementary way to measure the effect of radiation is to measure the amount of energy deposited in a given weight of material. However, the deposition of energy is only one aspect of the potential of radiation to cause biological damage. The damage caused per unit of deposited energy is greater when it is deposited over a shorter distance. Hence an alpha particle, which would deposit its entire energy over a very short distance, causes far more damage per unit of energy than a gamma ray, which deposits its energy over a longer track. The weight of biological matter in which the energy is deposited is also important. The sensitivities of different organs also vary. The concept of relative biological effectiveness (RBE) has been created to try to capture the relative efficiency of various kinds of radiation in producing biological damage.

Radiation doses are often calculated in the units of rad (short for Radiation Absorbed Dose). One rad is 100 ergs/gram, in other words, 100 ergs of energy absorbed by one gram of a given body tissue. An erg is one-ten-millionth of a joule. One hundred rad equals one Joule/kilogram (J/kg), which also equals one Gray (Gy), the standard international unit for measuring radiation dose.

When time is factored in, it is referred to as dose rate (or dose per unit time). An example of the units for dose rate is millirad/hour. In everyday terms, a joule (and even more so, an erg) is a rather small amount of energy. But in terms of ionization potential of molecules or elements, a joule is a huge amount of energy. One joule of ionizing radiation can cause tens of thousands of trillions of ionizations.

To summarize:

- Rem

    O roentgen equivalent man

    O A unit of equivalent absorbed dose of radiation which takes into account the relative biological effectiveness of different forms of ionizing radiation, or the varying ways in which they transfer their energy to human tissue. The dose in rem equals the dose in rad multiplied by the quality factor (Q). For beta and gamma radiation, the quality factor is taken as one, that is, rem equals rad. For alpha radiation, the quality factor is taken as 20, that is, rems equal 20 times rads. Rem is essentially a measure of biological damage.

    O REM = rad X Q

- Sievert (Sv)

    o A unit of equivalent absorbed dose equal to 100 rem.

    o 1 Sv = 100 REM

- Rad

    o Radiation absorbed dose

    o A unit of absorbed dose of radiation. Rad is a measure of the amount of energy deposited in tissue.

- Gray (Gy)

    o A unit of absorbed radiation dose equal to 100 rad. Gray is a measure of deposition of energy in tissue.

- Curie (Ci)

    o The traditional unit of radioactivity, equal to the radioactivity of one gram of pure radium-226.

    o 1 Ci = 37 billion Bq

- Becquerels (Bq)

    o The standard international unit of radioactivity equal to one disintegration per second.

    o 1 dps = 1 Bq

- Disintegrations per second (dps)

    o The number of subatomic particles (e.g. alpha particles) or photons (gamma rays) released from the nucleus of a given atom over one second. One dps = 60 dpm (disintegrations per minute).

    o 1dps = 1Bq

Packaging

Radioactive materials fall into three (3) primary categories:

- Category I Low Risk:

    - Extremely low radiation levels 0.5 mrem/hr (0.005 mSv/hr) maximum on surface

- Category I Medium Risk:

    o Low radiation levels >0.5 – 50 mrem/hr (0.5 mSv/hr) maximum on surface

    o 1.0mrem.hr (0.01 mSv/hr) maximum at 1 metre

- Category I High Risk:

    o Higher radiation levels >50 - 200 mrem/hr (2 mSv/hr) maximum on surface

    o 10 mrem.hr (0.1 mSv/hr) maximum at 1 metre

Excepted

Excepted packages are for extremely low levels of radioactivity with very low hazard.

• Excepted packaging are authorized for limited quantities of radioactive material that would pose a very low hazard if released in an accident.

• Examples of material typically shipped in excepted packaging include consumer goods such as smoke detectors.

• Excepted packaging are excepted (excluded) from specific packaging, labeling, and shipping paper requirements; they are however, required to have the letters "UN" and the appropriate four-digit UN identification number marked on the outside of the package, UN2910.

• Label reads "Radioactive Material Excepted Package. This package contains radioactive material, excepted package and is in all respects in compliance with the applicable international and national governmental regulations."

Industrial

Industrial packages: low levels of radioactivity with very low hazard; used in certain shipments of low activity material and contaminated objects, which are usually categorized as radioactive waste.

• Most low-level radioactive waste is shipped in these packages.

• Department of Transportation (DOT) regulations require that these packages allow no identifiable release of the material to the environment during normal transportation and handling.

• There are three categories of industrial packages: IP-1, IP- 2, and IP-3. The category of package will be marked on the exterior of the package.

Type A

Type A packages: used to transport small quantities of radioactive material with higher concentrations of radioactivity than those shipped in industrial packaging

• They are typically constructed of steel, wood, or fiberboard, and have an inner containment vessel made of glass, plastic, or metal surrounded with packing material made of polyethylene, rubber, or vermiculite.

• Examples of material typically shipped in Type A Packages include nuclear medicines (radiopharmaceuticals), radioactive waste, and radioactive sources used in industrial applications.

• Type A packaging and its radioactive contents must meet standard testing requirements designed to ensure that the package retains its containment integrity and shielding under normal transport conditions.

Type B

Type B packages: designed to transport material with the highest levels of radioactivity

• Designed to survive severe accidents conditions (e.g., impact, fire, water immersion)

• Designed to transport material with the highest levels of radioactivity

• Type B packaging range from small hand-held radiography cameras to heavily shielded steel casks that weigh up to 125 tons. (See photos below.)

• Life-endangering amounts of radioactive material are required to be transported in Type B Packages.

• Examples of material transported in Type B packaging include spent nuclear fuel, high-level radioactive waste, and high concentrations of other radioactive material such as cesium and cobalt.

• These package designs must withstand all Type A tests, AND a series of tests that simulate severe or "worst-case" accident conditions.

Type B package can have designations "(U)" or "(M)" (e.g., Type B (U) or Type B (M))

• U = Unilateral: the package design is approved by the country of origin.

• M = Multilateral: the package design is approved by each country through or into which the package is to be transported.

Naturally Occurring Radioactive Materials, NORM

NORM is the acronym for Naturally Occurring Radioactive Material, which potentially includes all radioactive elements found in the environment. However, the term is used more specifically for all naturally occurring radioactive materials where human activities have increased the potential for exposure compared with the unaltered situation.

All minerals and raw materials contain radionuclides of natural origin. The most important for the purposes of radiation protection are the radionuclides in the U-238 and Th-232 decay series. For most human activities involving minerals and raw materials, the levels of exposure to these radionuclides are not significantly greater than normal background levels and are not of concern for radiation protection. However, certain work activities can give rise to significantly enhanced exposures that may need to be controlled by regulation. Material giving rise to these enhanced exposures has become known as naturally occurring radioactive material (NORM).

Long-lived radioactive elements such as uranium, thorium and potassium and any of their decay products, such as radium and radon are examples of NORM. These elements have always been present in the Earth's crust and atmosphere, and are concentrated in some places, such as uranium orebodies which may be mined. The term NORM exists also to distinguish 'natural radioactive material' from anthropogenic sources of radioactive material, such as those produced by nuclear power and used in nuclear medicine, where incidentally the radioactive properties of a material maybe what make it useful. However from the perspective of radiation doses to people, such a distinction is completely arbitrary.

The acronym TENORM, or technologically enhanced NORM, is often used to refer to those materials where the amount of radioactivity has actually been increased or concentrated as a result of industrial processes. This paper addresses some of these industrial sources, and for simplicity the term NORM will be used throughout.

Excluding uranium mining and all associated fuel cycle activities, industries known to have NORM issues include:

• The coal industry (mining and combustion)

• The oil and gas industry (production)

• Metal mining and smelting

• Mineral sands (rare earth minerals, titanium and zirconium).

• Fertiliser (phosphate) industry

• Building industry

• Recycling

Classification

Transportation Of Dangerous Goods Classification

Transport Canada defines Class 7 Radioactive Substance as follows under SOR/2017-137, Part 2:

• Substances defined as Class 7, Radioactive Materials in the Packaging and Transport of Nuclear Substances Regulations are included in Class 7, Radioactive Materials.

• In these Regulations, the words "Class 7, Radioactive Materials" are used rather than the words that are used in the schedule to the Act, "Class 7, Nuclear Substances, within the meaning of the 'Nuclear Safety and Control Act', that are radioactive so that the Regulations are more easily read in conjunction with international documents incorporated by reference in them.

Department Of Transportation Classification

Department of Transport defines Class 7 Radioactive Substance as follows under 49 CFR 173.40:

• A1 means the maximum activity of special form Class 7 (radioactive) material permitted in a Type A package. This value is either listed in § 173.435 or may be derived in accordance with the procedures prescribed in § 173.433.

• A2 means the maximum activity of Class 7 (radioactive) material, other than special form material, LSA material, and SCO, permitted in a Type A package. This value is either listed in § 173.435 or may be derived in accordance with the procedures prescribed in § 173.433.

• Class 7 (radioactive) material See the definition of Radioactive material in this section.

• Closed transport vehicle means a transport vehicle or conveyance equipped with a securely attached exterior enclosure that during normal transportation restricts the access of unauthorized persons to the cargo space containing the Class 7 (radioactive) materials. The enclosure may be either temporary or permanent, and in the case of packaged materials may be of the "see-through" type, and must limit access from top, sides, and bottom.

• Consignment means a package or group of packages or load of radioactive material offered by a person for transport in the same shipment.

• Containment system means the assembly of components of the packaging intended to retain the Class 7 (radioactive) material during transport.

Class 8 Corrosives

Overview

Corrosives are materials that can attack and chemically destroy the structure of an object such as exposed body tissues and metal. They begin to cause damage as soon as they touch the skin, eyes, respiratory tract, digestive tract, or the metal. They might be hazardous in other ways too, depending on the particular corrosive material.

Corrosion of non-living surfaces such as metals is a distinct process. For example, a water-air electrochemical cell corrodes iron to rust, corrodes copper to patina, and corrodes copper, silver, and other metals to tarnish.

Corrosive materials can be solids, liquids or gases and consist of two (2) primary types of materials:

• Acids – referred to as corrosive

• Bases – referred to as caustic and is used particularly when dealing with alkali compounds

Additionally, corrosives can also fall within the oxidizer classification in some cases such as nitric acid which is both an oxidizer Class 5.1, and corrosive Class 8.

Effective December 1, 2018, GHS (and subsequently OSHA) defines corrosive to metals as substances or mixtures that are liable to undergo an irreversible chemical reaction with metals and leads to significant damage or, in some cases, even full destruction of metals.

Corrosive to metal are categorized as:

• <u>Corrosive to Metals Category 1:</u>

    o A mixture or substance that has a corrosion rate on either steel or aluminium surfaces that is > 6.25 mm per year at a test temperature of 55°C

• Skin corrosion and irritation under GHS are as follows:

• <u>Skin corrosion</u> - the production of irreversible damage to the skin, namely, visible necrosis through the epidermis and into the dermis, and includes ulcers, bleeding, bloody scabs and, within a 14-day observation period, discoloration due to blanching of the skin, complete areas of alopecia, and scars.

• <u>Skin-corrosive</u> - in relation to a mixture or substance, liable to cause skin corrosion.

• <u>Skin-irritant</u> - in relation to a mixture or substance, liable to cause skin irritation.

• <u>Skin irritation</u> - the production of reversible damage to the skin.

Skin corrosion is categorized as:

• <u>Skin Corrosion Category 1A</u>:

> o A substance that, according to animal data acquired from a scientifically validated method, produces irreversible damage to the skin after an exposure of three minutes or less, and within one hour of observation, in at least one of three animals.

• <u>Skin Corrosion Category 1B</u>:

> o A substance that, according to animal data acquired from a scientifically validated method, produces irreversible damage to the skin after an exposure of more than three minutes and up to and including one hour, and within 14 days of observation, in at least one of three animals.

• <u>Skin Corrosion Category 1C</u>:

> o A substance that, according to animal data acquired from a scientifically validated method, produces irreversible damage to the skin after an exposure of more than one hour and up to and including four hours, and within 14 days of observation, in at least one of three animals.

Skin irritation is categorized as:

• <u>Skin Irritation Category 2</u>:

> o A substance that, according to human data, is skin-irritant; or
>
> o in respect of which animal data reveal
>
> > □ in the case of data acquired from a test performed in accordance with the OECD Guideline for the Testing of Chemicals, No. 404, entitled Acute Dermal Irritation/Corrosion, as amended from time to time, a mean score of ≥ 2.3 and ≤ 4.0 for erythema and eschar or for edema in at least two of three animals from gradings at 24, 48 and 72 hours after patch removal or, if reactions are delayed, from gradings

on three consecutive days after the onset of skin reactions,

☐ in the case of data acquired from a scientifically validated method, inflammation, namely, local alopecia, hyperkeratosis, hyperplasia and scaling, that persists to the end of the observation period specified by the method in at least two animals, or

☐ in the case of data acquired from a scientifically validated method, evidence of severe skin irritation in only one animal

Acids

Inorganic Acids

As discussed in Section 3.4 Hazardous Materials Chemistry, acids donate positive hydrogen ions (H+). Inorganic acids, also referred to as mineral acids, contain no carbon and are derived from one of more inorganic compounds. Inorganic acids are easily identified by the chemical formula beginning with hydrogen as in the common examples:

• hydrochloric acid: HCl

• sulphuric acid: H2SO4

• hydrofluoric acid: HF

• nitric acid: HNO3

There are two (2) core types of inorganic acids:

• binary – composed of only two elements and start with the prefix "hydro" and end with the suffix "ic" such as hydrochloric acid, HCl

• oxyacids – composed of hydrogen, oxygen and other non-metal elements such as nitric acid, HNO3.

The higher the availability of the hydrogen ions when an acid dissociates or breaks apart as in the case of hydrochloric acid, HCl, the higher the acidity of the acid. Acids have a pH less than 7 – the lower the pH, the higher the acidity or presence of the hydrogen ion.

Organic Acids

Organic acids are derived from hydrocarbon compounds and as such are flammable as well as corrosive. They also are characterized by their ability to polymerize in the presence of heat and often shock and friction. Organic acids are easily identified by the chemical formula beginning with the hydrocarbon name as the prefix and ending with the suffix "ic" as in the common examples:

• formic acid: HCOOH

• acetic acid: CH3COOH

• butyric acid C2H7COOH

The most common organic acids are the carboxylic acids as noted in the previous examples but also include other acids such as citric acid and lactic acid. Organic acids are considered weak acids and do not dissociate completely in water like mineral (inorganic) acids do.

Bases

Alkaline compounds can be considered the opposite of acids and are commonly referred to as bases. Bases are substances that when mixed in water:

• create an increase in the aqueous hydroxide ion concentration, OH-

• decrease the aqueous hydrogen ion concentration, H+

There are three (3) core classification of bases:

• Monoacidic Base – when one (1) molecule of the base produces one (1) hydroxide ion. Example: sodium hydroxide, ammonium hydroxide

• Diacidic Base – when one (1) molecule of the base produces two (2) hydroxide ions. Example: barium hydroxide, magnesium hydroxide

• Triacidic Base – when one (1) molecule of the base produces three (3) hydroxide ions. Example: aluminum hydroxide, ferrous hydroxide

Dilution And Neutralization

Dilution is the process of mixing an acid or base (called the solute) with a compound (called the solvent) into a homogenous mixture (called the solution) to decrease the concentration of the solute overall.

It is very important when diluting acids to remember to add acid to water and not vice versa (remember the abbreviation "A-A", which stands for "Add-Acid") since the addition of acid and water releases a great deal of heat. If water is added into acid, the concentration of the acid causes the water to essentially boil instantaneously and vigorously and results in a violent splashing of the acid.

The same holds true for strong bases which are also exothermic and can result in splattering of the strong base if mixed incorrectly.

 Neutralization is a chemical reaction that occurs between an acid and a base that balance or cancel each other out.

Neutralization is dealing with the equalization of the hydrogen ions H+ and the hydroxide ions OH- which inherently causes the release of large amounts of heat. This heat can produce biproducts such as vapours and gases, as well as be physically violent with splattering behaviour of the mixture.

In both cases of dilution and neutralization, large volumes of a solvent such as water or neutralizing agent will be required to bring the pH of the product into a range of 7.

Classification

Transportation Of Dangerous Goods Classification

Transport Canada defines Class 8 Corrosive Substance as follows under SOR/2017-137, Part 2:

• are known to cause full thickness destruction of human skin, that is, skin lesions that are permanent and destroy all layers of the outer skin through to the internal tissues;

• cause full thickness skin destruction, as determined in accordance with OECD Guidelines 430 or OECD Guidelines 431; or SOR/2014-306

• do not cause full thickness destruction of skin but exhibit a corrosion rate that exceeds 6.25 mm per year at a test temperature of 55°C, as determined in accordance with section 37 of Part III of the Manual of Tests and Criteria.

SOR/2017-137

Department Of Transportation Classification 

Department of Transport defines Class 8 Corrosive Substance as follows under 49 CFR 173.136 Part (a):

• For the purpose of this subchapter, "corrosive material" (Class 8) means a liquid or solid that causes full thickness destruction of human skin at the site of contact within a specified period of time. A liquid, or a solid which may become liquid during transportation, that has a severe corrosion rate on steel or aluminum based on the criteria in § 173.137(c)(2) is also a corrosive material. Whenever practical, in vitro test methods authorized in § 173.137 of this part or historical data authorized in paragraph (c) of this section should be used to determine whether a material is corrosive.

Class 9 Miscellaneous Hazardous Substances

Overview

Class 9 hazardous materials are defined as those materials in solid, liquid or gas form which present a hazard during transport but do not meet the classification of any of the other hazard classes. These can be both health and physical hazards, and include items that included:

• hazardous waste

• noxious and anesthetic materials that would discomfort a flight crew and interfere with their ability to perform their duty

• materials with elevated temperatures

• marine pollutants which prove to be environmentally detrimental when released.

Effective December 1, 2018, GHS (and subsequently OSHA) defines two (2) categories that are used in many cases with Class 9 materials since they do not fit into any of the other hazard classifications. These categories are:

• Physical Hazards Not Otherwise Classified, PNOC

• Health Hazards Not Otherwise Classified, HNOC

Physical Hazards Not Otherwise Classified means a physical hazard presented by a product, mixture, material or substance that is different from any other physical hazard addressed by any other Subpart in this Part, and that has the characteristic of occurring by chemical reaction and resulting in the serious injury or death of a person at the time the reaction occurs. PNOC under GHS is as follows:

• <u>Physical Hazards Not Otherwise Classified Category 1:</u>

    o A product, mixture, material or substance that presents a physical hazard not otherwise classified.

Health Hazards Not Otherwise Classified means a health hazard presented by a mixture or substance that is different from any other health hazard addressed by any other Subpart in this Part and that has the characteristic of occurring via acute or repeated exposure and having an adverse effect on the health of a person exposed to it, including an injury, or resulting in the death of that person. PNOC under GHS is as follows:

• <u>Health Hazard Not Otherwise Classified Category 1:</u>

    o A substance that presents a health hazard not otherwise classified

Asbestos

Asbestos is the common name given to a group of naturally occurring mineral silicates that can be separated into flexible fibres. The name asbestos comes from the Greek word meaning "unquenchable or indestructible." The main properties that make asbestos useful are its incombustibility, strength and flexibility when separated into fibres. It is also effective as a reinforcing or binding agent when combined with cement or plastic. Asbestos fibres are virtually indestructible - extremely heat and chemical resistant, they do not evaporate of dissolve in water, and they do not decompose over time. This is why they have been used for centuries as a heat insulator.

Asbestos, Asbestos Containing Materials referred to as ACM, and Presumed Asbestos Containing Materials referred to as PACM, fall into two (2) primary areas:

• Friable – this term means easily crumpled and is used for materials with asbestos that can be easily reduced to a powder when dry becoming an airborne contaminant.

• Non-friable – this refers to asbestos material that is firmly bound within the matrix of a material and cannot easily become separated or airborne.

Commercial asbestos fibres belong in two broad mineralogical groups There are two main mineralogical classifications of asbestos based on the rock types which form the asbestos:

• Serpentine Asbestos – UN2590

o formally known as Chrysotile and often referred to as "white" asbestos

o represents approximately 93% of all asbestos used in the world

o is hydrated magnesium silicate which is in a long wavy-shaped fibre that is white

• Amphibole Asbestos – UN2212

o amosite or "brown" asbestos which has much shorter and straighter fibres

o crocidolite or "blue" asbestos which is shaped similarly to amosite

o tremolite, actinolite, anthophyllite, or "grey" asbestos

• Tremolite: variety of colours, not often used commercially or industrially, could be found in certain talcum powders, some paints and sealants

• Actinolite: harsh and not very flexible, not often used, airborne fibres can be easily inhaled and cause severe lung damage

• Anthophyllite: grey-brown colour, not often used commercially or industrially, found in some composite flooring

• Chrysotile: white asbestos with serpentine fibres, less friable, used in construction and vehicles, considered safest form of asbestos

• Amosite: brown asbestos, used in cement, ceiling tiles, and insulators

• Crocidolite: blue asbestos, best heat resistance, most dangerous asbestos

Dry Ice

Solid carbon dioxide is known as dry ice and has a much cooler temperature than traditional water ice. It is a preferred method of cooling since dry ice leaves no residue when it warms. Unlike water ice, when dry ice warms it produces carbon dioxide gas and no liquid. Carbon dioxide even though non- toxic is considered to be a simple asphyxiant since it will displace oxygen.

Due to the extreme cold of dry ice, handling procedures are paramount to avoid any form of frostbite. The UN identification for solid carbon dioxide is UN1845.

Molten Sulphur

Sulphur is a bright yellow powder that historically was referred to as Brimstone. When sulphur is transported above the melting point of 118OC or 245OC, it is referred to as molten sulphur and shipped under UN2448. Molten sulphur is an amber coloured liquid that is very common within the rail industry especially in western Canada due to the use in petroleum refining.

Molten sulphur not only poses a thermal hazard to personnel but also poses an inhalation hazard. Molten sulphur produces flammable and toxic hydrogen sulphide gas. Additionally, molten sulphur can also be ignited which in turn will produce sulphur dioxide gas as a biproduct. Mixing molten sulphur with water also poses the risk of forming sulphuric acid as a biproduct.

Formaldehyde Solutions

Formaldehyde is the simplest of aldehydes and occurs naturally as a gas in nature. In the hazardous waste industry formaldehyde is commonly encountered in a liquid form which is actually a mixture of both 37% formaldehyde gas and water. Since this solution will polymerize, addition of 10-15% of methyl alcohol is used to keep the mixture stable in solution. When methyl alcohol is added, the final product is referred to as Formalin.

Formalin is an extremely strong disinfectant as well as a tissue hardener. It is used for sterilizing surgical equipment as well as preserving biological samples and specimens. Since the toxicity of formalin falls outside of the requirements for Class 6, it falls into Class 9. It is important to remember however that in many cases formalin contains biological materials and poses other potential health hazards and requires the proper personal protective equipment when handling. The UN identification for formalin is UN2209.

Lithium Batteries

Lithium batteries are composed of several elements including lithium, sulphur, selenium, tellurium and even chlorine. They are shipped depending on the composition and use of the battery under the UN identification as follows:

• UN3090, Lithium Metal Batteries

• UN3091, Lithium Metal Batteries Contained in Equipment or Lithium Metal Batteries Packed With Equipment

• UN3480, Lithium Ion Batteries

• UN3481, Lithium Ion Batteries Contained in Equipment of Lithium Ion Batteries Packed with Equipment

Lithium batteries have a well-known history of self-heating and catching on fire. This process is referred to as Thermal Runaway which creates both pressure and heat that cannot be dissipated as quickly as the heat is generated which creates a fire. The problem however is that when these batteries ignite, they cannot be dealt with as a regular fire since the metal such as lithium within the battery generally is a flammable solid.

Polychlorinated Biphenyls

Polychlorinated biphenyls are commonly referred to as PCBs and are composed of two (2) highly stable benzene rings that are attached together with at least two (2) chlorine atoms attached to the compound. Benzene is very stable and difficult to destroy which is why PCBs have been used extensively in heat-sensitive situations such as transformers. It is also the reason why the destruction of PCBs must occur in a high temperature chemical incinerator.

PCBs are highly toxic and heavy and settle into the human body within the liver and fat cells for long periods of time due to the fact that they do not biodegrade. The UN identification for formalin is UN2315.

Other Regulated Materials, Consumer Commodities

Many other products are packaged in small containers that present a very limited hazard during transportation due the form, packaging and quantity of the product. Other Regulated Materials for Consumer Commodities are referred to as ORM-D.

Generally, these types of products are destined to be used in the home, institutions and industry. These include low concentration acids, lighter fluids, aerosol paints, and household cleaners.

Over The Counter Pharmaceuticals And Controlled Substances

Over the Counter medicines are commonly referred to as OTC and are commonly found in medical and dental institutions, household waste collection events, and even jobsites. However, many of these medicines require a prescription and are not intended to be handled without authorization and as such cannot be simply discarded into the trash due to the legal implications associated with the drug. Anti-depressants, anti-inflammatories, and in particular pain medications that are received from a medical institution will require several additional steps to both handle, receive and dispose of in many cases. Both the Government of Canada and the U.S. Food and Drug Administration have programs and guidelines for the disposal of unused medicines.

Controlled substances pose another concern for the hazardous materials industry, and both Health Canada and the U.S. Drug Enforcement Agency have programs and strict guidelines for controlled substances.

Controlled substances are those compounds whose manufacture, possession or use is regulated by the government. These include illicit drugs and prescription medications. Both Canada and the U.S. have established lists of drugs in a compendium of Schedules that fall within identified controlled substances.

Classification

Transportation Of Dangerous Goods Classification

Transport Canada defines Class 9 Miscellaneous Products, Substances or Organisms as follows under SOR/2017-137, Part 2:

• is included in Class 9 in column 3 of Schedule 1; or

• is not included in Class 9 in column 3 of Schedule 1 and does not meet the criteria for inclusion in any of Classes 1 to 8 and SOR/2008-34

    o Repealed SOR/2014-306

    o is a marine pollutant under section 2.7 of Part 2 (Classification), or

    SOR/2014-306

For a liquid, the UN number and shipping name are UN3082, ENVIRONMENTALLY HAZARDOUS SUBSTANCE, LIQUID, N.O.S., and for a solid, the UN number and shipping name are UN3077, ENVIRONMENTALLY HAZARDOUS SUBSTANCE, SOLID, N.O.S.

    o except for asphalt or tar, is offered for transport or transported at a temperature greater than or equal to 100°C if it is in a liquid state or at a temperature greater than or equal to 240°C if it is in a solid state,

For a liquid, the UN number and shipping name are UN3257, ELEVATED TEMPERATURE LIQUID, N.O.S., and for a solid, the UN number and shipping name are UN3258, ELEVATED TEMPERATURE SOLID, N.O.S.

o Repealed SOR/2008-34

o Repealed SOR/2008-34

Lithium Cells and Batteries SOR/2014-306

• A person must not handle, offer for transport or transport lithium cells and batteries under any of the following shipping names unless the cells and batteries meet the conditions set out in subsection (2):

o UN3090, LITHIUM METAL BATTERIES;

o UN3091, LITHIUM METAL BATTERIES CONTAINED IN EQUIPMENT or LITHIUM METAL BATTERIES PACKED WITH EQUIPMENT;

o UN3480, LITHIUM ION BATTERIES; or

o UN3481, LITHIUM ION BATTERIES CONTAINED IN EQUIPMENT or LITHIUM ION BATTERIES PACKED WITH EQUIPMENT.

Lithium cells and batteries are classified under

o UN3090, LITHIUM METAL BATTERIES, if they contain lithium metal or lithium alloy;

o UN3091, LITHIUM METAL BATTERIES CONTAINED IN EQUIPMENT or LITHIUM METAL BATTERIES PACKED WITH EQUIPMENT, if they contain lithium metal or lithium alloy and are contained in or packed with equipment;

o UN3480, LITHIUM ION BATTERIES, if they contain any type of lithium ion; and

o UN3481, LITHIUM ION BATTERIES CONTAINED IN EQUIPMENT or LITHIUM ION BATTERIES PACKED WITH EQUIPMENT, if they contain any type of lithium ion and are contained in or packed with equipment.

• The conditions are as follows:

o the cell or battery type passes each test set out in subsection 38.3 of Part III of the Manual of Tests and Criteria;

o each cell or battery has a safety venting device or is designed to prevent a violent rupture under normal conditions of transport;

o each cell or battery is equipped to prevent external short circuits; and

o each battery containing cells or a series of cells connected in parallel is equipped with diodes, fuses or other devices that prevent dangerous reverse current flow.

SOR/2017-137

Department Of Transportation Classification 

Department of Transport defines Class 8 Corrosive Substance as follows under 49 CFR 173.155 Part (a) though (c):

• General Exceptions for hazardous materials shipments in the following paragraphs are permitted only if this section is referenced for the specific hazardous material in the § 172.101 table of this subchapter.

• Limited quantities of Class 9 materials. Limited quantities of miscellaneous hazardous materials in Packing Groups II and III are excepted from labeling requirements, unless the material is offered for transportation or transported by aircraft, and are excepted from the specification packaging requirements of this subchapter when packaged in combination packaging according to this paragraph. Unless otherwise specified in paragraph (c) of this section, packages of limited quantities intended for transportation by aircraft must conform to the applicable requirements (e.g., authorized materials, inner packaging quantity limits and closure securement) of § 173.27 of this part. A limited quantity package that conforms to the provisions of this section is not subject to the shipping paper requirements of subpart C of part 172 of this subchapter, unless the material meets the definition of a hazardous substance, hazardous waste, marine pollutant, or is offered for transportation and transported by aircraft or vessel, and is eligible for the exceptions provided in § 173.156 of this part. In addition, packages of limited quantities are not subject to subpart F

(Placarding) of part 172 of this subchapter. Each package must conform to the packaging requirements of subpart B of this part and may not exceed 30 kg (66 pounds) gross weight. Except for transportation by aircraft, the following combination packaging are authorized:

• For miscellaneous materials in Packing Group II, inner packaging not over 1.0 L (0.3 gallon) net capacity each for liquids or not over 1.0 kg (2.2 pounds) net capacity each for solids, packed in a strong outer packaging.

• For miscellaneous materials in Packing Group III, inner packaging not over 5.0 L (1.3 gallons) net capacity each for liquids or not over 5.0 kg (11 lbs) net capacity each for solids, packed in a strong outer packaging.

• Consumer commodities. Until December 31, 2020, a limited quantity package containing a "consumer commodity" as defined in § 171.8 of this subchapter, may be renamed "Consumer commodity" and reclassed as ORM-D or, until December 31, 2012, as ORM-D-AIR material and offered for transportation and transported in accordance with the applicable provisions of this subchapter in effect on October 1, 2010.

CBRNE Fundamentals

Overview

CBRNe is an acronym for Chemical, Biological, Radiological, Nuclear and Explosive materials that when used with intent are referred to as Weapons of Mass Destruction, WMD. The hazardous materials industry is predicated on the ability to respond to uncontrolled events and situations as a measure of control in an effort to mitigate the impact of an event or incident on people, property and the environment. Personnel such as you that undertake these roles need to have substantially more than a fundamental understanding of the hazards associated with various agents that may affect you to ensure that there is a clear understanding of the actions and procedures required. By having a basic understanding of what is involved at a CBRNe incident, personnel will have the ability to recognize, survive and respond to an incident in a limited but knowledgeable capacity.

Comprehensive CBRNe training is both intense and challenging in nature and often taken by both military personnel and first response personnel to provide the tools to be able to think quickly while ensuring that a measured response is provided. Training usually consists of three (3) primary areas:

• Simulation Training

• Simulation Agent Training

• Live Agent Training

In this module the specific types of CBRNe incidents will be covered in detail to address the core pillars that CBRNe response needs to address. These pillars are:

• Scale and type of the incident and the resources needed to provide a measured response

• Protection of responders and appropriate levels of equipment needed

• Population affected

• Animals in the area

• Environment, particularly food and water resources for people

• Preservation of forensic evidence from the scene of the incident

CBRN Canada

The term CBRN is in common use in disaster and emergency services organizations across the country. Since July 2005, the Canadian Armed Forces also started using the term CBRN Defence, instead of NBC Defence, due to the increased threat of dirty bomb use which is radiological in nature.

CBRNE is a new term that is being used in both civilian and military organisations. The Canadian Joint Incident Response Unit is a Canadian Forces unit, under the direction of the Canadian Special Operations Forces Command, charged with supporting "the Government of Canada in order to prevent, control and mitigate CBRN threats to Canada, Canadians and Canadian interests."

All members of the Canadian Armed Forces are trained in CBRN defense, and maintain minimum standards, tested at least every three years.

At the provincial level, cities are provided opportunities for their emergency services with CBRN training. In Ontario for example, emergency services in Windsor, Peterborough, Toronto, and Ottawa have obtained CBRN standing at NFPA Standard 472 Awareness Level 3.

CBRN United States

The United States Army uses CBRN as an abbreviation for their Chemical, Biological, Radiological, and Nuclear Operations Specialists (MOS). The United States Army trains all US Army soldiers pursuing a career in CBRN at the United States Army CBRN School (USACBRNS) at Fort Leonard Wood. US Marines training exercise for temporary critical support to enable community recovery after a CBRNE incident.

The USAF uses Air Force Specialty Code (AFSC 3E9X1) U.S. Air Force Emergency Management, who are also CBRN Specialists. The USAF trains all US Airmen pursuing a career in counter-CBRN operations at the USAF CBRN School at Fort Leonard Wood.

The USMC uses CBRN as an abbreviation for two military occupational specialties. The Marine Corps runs a CBRN School to train Marine CBRN Defense Officers and Marine CBRN Defense Specialists at Fort Leonard Wood, Missouri. The USN requires all personnel to take a web-based CBRNE training annually to get a basic understanding of facts and procedures related to responding to a CBRNE incident.

Chemical Agents

Chemical warfare agents are defined by the World Health Organization, WHO, as a substance that is intended for use in military or non-military operations to kill, seriously injure or otherwise incapacitate people, or do harm or destroy their habitat or economy.

There are several important factors to take into consideration when evaluating chemical agents including:

• Concentration

• Duration of contact

• Chemical agent and mode of attack

• What is the intent of the agent – kill a mass group or a small group, injure and weaken resources

WHO has listed seventeen (17) chemicals that are listed as warfare agents and have broken them into five (5) categories based on properties and chemical characteristics. These are:

• Nerve Agents – known as Organophosphates, nerve agents are substances that disrupt the chemical communications through the nervous system. Poisoning by these nerve agents leads to an accumulation of acetylcholine producing a perpetual excited state in the nerve (e.g. constant muscle contraction). The eventual exhaustion of muscles leads to respiratory failure and death

> o G Series - high volatility nerve agents that are typically used for a nonpersistent to semipersistent effect (Sarin)

> o GV Series - have a volatility between the V and G agents and are typically used for a semi-persistent to persistent effect

> o V Series - low volatility and are typically used for a persistent effect or liquid contact hazard

> o T Series - related to the puffer fish toxin

• Blood Agents – Blood agents are chemicals that interfere with the blood's ability to uptake oxygen. Ultimately, without oxygen getting into the blood, death occurs from chemical asphyxiation. A well-known example of a blood agent is Cyanide.

• Blistering Agents – a chemical compound that irritates and causes injury to the skin, creates blisters and impedes breathing. These substances also attack the eyes, or any other tissue they contact. A well-known example of a blistering agent was Mustard Gas that was used in WWI.

o Vesicants

  ☐ produce large fluid-filled blisters on the skin

  ☐ Nitrogen Mustards, Sulphur Mustards

o Urticants

  ☐ produce a painful wound on the skin.

  ☐ sometimes termed skin necrotizers

  ☐ known as the most painful substances produced

• Choking Agents – known as pulmonary agents, choking agents are chemicals that cause pulmonary edema or excess fluid in the lungs which in turn causes death by asphyxiation. A well-known example of a choking agent is Chlorine.

• Riot Control and Incapacitating Agents – these are non-lethal localized chemicals that temporarily impair a person functions and ability to perform routine tasks. A well-known example of a riot control agent is Pepper Spray.

o Harassing Agents are not intended to kill or injure. They are often referred to as Riot Control Agents (RCAs) and may be used by civilian police forces against criminals and rioters, or in the military for training purposes. In general, harassing agents are sensory irritants that have fleeting concentration dependent effects that resolve within minutes after removal. Casualty effects are not anticipated to exceed 24-hours nor require medical attention

  ☐ Tearing Agents

• These sensory irritants produce immediate pain to the eyes and irritate mucous membranes

• Lachrymator

  ☐ Vomiting Agents

• These sensory irritants are also termed sternators or nose irritants.

• Irritate the mucous membranes to produce congestion, coughing, sneezing, and eventually nausea.

□ Malodorant Agents

• These are compounds with a very strong and unpleasant smell

• produce powerfully aversive effects without the toxic effects of tear agents or vomiting agents.

o Incapacitating Agents produce debilitating effects with limited probability of permanent injury or loss of life. The casualty effects typically last over 24 hours, and though medical evacuation and isolation is recommended, it is not required for complete recovery. These, together with harassing agents, are sometimes called nonlethal agents. There may be as high as 5% fatalities with the use of these agents

o Psychological Agents are substances that produce casualty effects through mental disturbances such as delirium or hallucination

The universal chemical agent weapon symbol is as follows:

Biological Agents

Biological agents are used in bioterrorism and are defined as agents used in the deliberate release of viruses, bacteria or other germs (agents) used to cause illness of death in people, animals or plants. Typically, these agents are found in nature but are altered to enhance their ability to cause disease, be more resistant to current medication and have the ability to readily spread into the environment through the air, water or food.

There are several important factors to take into consideration when evaluating biological agents including:

• The Agent

o is the agent a virus, bacteria or other pathogen

• Transmissibility

o is the agent is spread person-to-person

o is the agent spread from animals to humans referred to as zoonotic

o is the agent spread from animals to human via mosquitoes, ticks, fleas, referred to as vector

o is the agent spread through the air, water of food supply

• Incubation

o does the agent takes hours, days or weeks to incubate

• Severity of the disease

o how deadly or severe is the agent

• Countermeasure availability

o vaccines, antibiotics and antivirals

• Intent

o is the intent to kill mass population or simply insight panic.

Biological agents are broken into three (3) distinct categories:

• Viral Agents - Viruses are intracellular organisms that lack a system for their own metabolism, and are, therefore, dependent on host cells. Every virus requires its own special type of host. The host cells can be from humans, animals, plants, or bacteria. Viruses are much smaller than bacteria. A well-known example of a viral agent is Smallpox.

• Bacterial Agents - Bacteria generally cause disease in humans and animals by one of two mechanisms: invading host tissues, and/or producing toxins. The diseases they produce often respond to specific therapy with antibiotics. A well-known example of a viral agent is Anthrax.

• Toxins - Toxins are deadly substances produced by living organisms (animals, plants, microbes). Exposed persons are not infectious. A well-known example of a viral agent is Ricin.

The universal biological agent weapon symbol is as follows:

Radiological And Nuclear Agents

All matter is made up of atoms and when those atoms are unstable, they try to become form stable by emitting or releasing energy. This energy is released as radiation.

Radiation is separated into two (2) categories:

• Non-Ionizing Radiation – radiation such as Ultraviolet (UV) rays, microwaves, lasers, and electromagnetic fields (EMFs) from electric power lines. Although there are some health hazards associated with certain types and levels of nonionizing radiation, the hazards are generally small.

• Ionizing Radiation - is radiation that may cause damage to the human body by interacting with cells. It is this type of radiation that is dealt with in this course and unless otherwise specified, references to "radiation" should be taken to mean ionizing radiation.

Ionizing radiation is separated further into four (4) types:

• Alpha Particles

> o large atomic particles. They have little external penetrating power but can be harmful if alpha particle emitting radioactive material enters the respiratory tract, is swallowed or enters through an open wound.

> o a typical alpha particle will travel no more than a few centimetres in air and can be stopped by the outer layer of skin or a sheet of paper.

• Beta Particles

> o small atomic particles (electrons) that are fast moving and have limited penetrating ability.

> o they can be harmful if beta particles emitting radioactive material enters the respiratory tract, is swallowed or enters through an open wound.

> o a typical beta particle can travel up to several metres in the air and is stopped by skin, thin layers of wood or plastic.

• Gamma Radiation and X-Rays

> o electromagnetic waves.

> o Gamma radiation and X-Rays are capable of penetrating all parts of the body and can

actually pass right through the body.

o waves can travel several metres in air and may be shielded by using concrete, steel, lead, or other dense materials.

• Neutrons

o particles that have been emitted from an atom's nucleus and are capable of penetrating all parts of the body.

o normally associated with the operation of nuclear power plants and nuclear weapons.

o neutrons can travel long distances and may be shielded by using materials such as wax, water, or concrete.

The three (3) primary concerns with radiological agents are:

• dirty bombs – a device that causes the intentional dissemination of radioactive material without a nuclear detonation

• exposure device – a device that is hidden intentional to expose people to large doses of radiation without their knowledge

• improvised nuclear device – an illicit nuclear weapon

The universal radiological and nuclear agent weapon symbols are as follows:

Explosive Agents

Improvised explosive devices, referred to as IEDs are a significant concern when dealing with terrorist situations. The main reason that IEDs are such a concern is due to their relative ease of construction, the availability of components to build an IED, the destructive power and capacity, and the ability to remotely detonate these devices. These reasons are why explosive devices remain the most commonly used weapon of terrorists.

Explosives create not only a physically hazardous environment, but also creates an environment of fear that is often associated with the use of multiple devices during these events as we saw at the Boston Marathon on April 15, 2013. Physically, the hazards of explosive devices are:

• penetration trauma caused by flying debris

• blunt trauma caused by falling debris

• primary blast trauma where the explosive wave contacts body tissue

• crush injuries from blunt trauma, microvascular compression or hypoxia

• thermal trauma that is caused by thermal exposure to the explosion

• toxic inhalation caused by biproducts of combustion

• contamination of wounds

• hearing impairment

The universal explosive agent weapon symbol is as follows:

Chapter 4:
Hazard Assessment

Reference Literature

The following manuals and reference materials are intended to be used on an ongoing basis to assist the employee with research and the understanding of fundamental concepts. The list is not extensive however and consists of critical manuals that are universally accepted within the hazardous waste and emergency response community.

Most reference manuals are not intended to be read cover-to-cover and are provided to act as a research and consultation resource as needed. It is important to note that in some cases the need to understand the entire overview of the manual is necessary, as is in the case with the Emergency Response Guidebook and requires a more detailed understanding that with other resource materials.

Hazardous Materials Management Desk Reference second edition, ACHMM

The Academy of Certified Hazardous Materials Managers, ACHMM, established in 1985, is a non-profit membership organization dedicated to fostering professional development through continuing education, peer group interaction, and the exchange of ideas and information relating to hazardous materials management. Then purpose of ACHMM is to educate and instruct members in hazardous materials management and environmental health and safety.

http://www.achmm.org

Managing Hazardous Materials, A Definitive Text

The Institute of Hazardous Materials Management, IHMM, is a non-profit corporation dedicated to raising the professional level of persons managing hazardous materials.

IHMM has a primary role of overseeing the Certified Hazardous Materials Manager (CHMM) program. Additionally, IHNN works to improve the professional standing of CHMM candidates and to encourage entry of persons into the field through academic competencies and programs.

https://www.ihmm.org/

Hazcat Chemical Identification System, HAZTECH Systems Inc.

The HazCat® Chemical Identification System is a unique time saving tool designed especially for on-site use by emergency response personnel, environmental health specialists, hazardous materials specialists, and anyone who has competency in the storage, transportation or handling of hazardous materials.

The easy to use kit contains all test supplies, instructions and flow charts for non-chemist personnel to perform field testing on unknown substances to allow the assignment of twenty-five (25) unknown properties in a decision tree format.

The HazCat® Chemical Identification System also provides specialized kits for

- Weapons of Mass Destruction, WMD

- Methamphetamine

- Asbestos

- Lead

- https://hazcat.com/

2024 Emergency Response Guidebook

The 2024 Emergency Response Guidebook, ERG, is primarily a guide to aid first responders in quickly identifying the specific or generic hazards of the material(s) involved in the incident and protecting themselves and the general public during the initial response phase of the incident. This guidebook will assist responders in making initial decisions upon arriving at the scene of a dangerous goods incident. The ERG is updated every three to four years to accommodate new products and technology.

2024 Emergency Response Guidebook – Transport Canada

- **PDF Version**

    o http://www.tc.gc.ca/eng/canutec/guide-ergo-221.htm

- **Mobile Download**

o   http://www.tc.gc.ca/eng/canutec/guide-ergo-otherversion-443.htm

2024 Emergency Response Guidebook – Department of Transport

- **PDF Version**

    o   https://www.phmsa.dot.gov/sites/phmsa.dot.gov/files/2020-08/ERG2020-WEB.pdf

- **Mobile Download**

    o   https://www.phmsa.dot.gov/hazmat/erg/erg2020-mobileapp

NIOSH Pocket Guide To Chemical Hazards

The Pocket Guide presents key information and data in abbreviated tabular form for 633 chemicals or substance groupings that are found in the work environment.

Key data provided for each chemical/substance includes name (including synonyms/trade names), structure/formula, CAS/RTECS Numbers, DOT ID, conversion factors, exposure limits, IDLH, chemical and physical properties, measurement methods, personal protection, respirator recommendations, symptoms, and first aid.

The Pocket Guide has been designed to provide chemical-specific data to supplement general industrial hygiene knowledge. To maximize the amount of data provided in this limited space, abbreviations and codes have been used extensively. These abbreviations and codes, which have been designed to permit rapid comprehension by the regular user, should help users recognize and control occupational chemical hazards.

https://www.cdc.gov/niosh/docs/2005-149/default.html

- **PDF Version**

    o   https://www.cdc.gov/niosh/docs/2005-149/default.html

- **Mobile Download**

    o   https://www.cdc.gov/niosh/npg/mobilepocketguide.html

ASKRAIL®

Launched in 2014, the app provides immediate access to accurate and timely data about what type of hazardous materials a railcar is carrying so that responders can make an accurate descision during an incident. AskRail is intended to be a backup resource if information from the train crew or train consist is unavailable for incidents that occur on any North American Class 1 railroad and Amtrak. The app is available in the United Staes, Canada, and Mexico.

https://askrail.us/

Technical Information Centres

CANUTEC – 1-888-226-8832

CANUTEC is the Canadian Transport Emergency Centre operated by the Transportation of Dangerous Goods (TDG) Directorate of Transport Canada. The Directorate's overall mandate is to promote public safety in the transportation of dangerous goods by all modes. CANUTEC was established in 1979 and is one of the major safety programs Transport Canada delivers to promote the safe movement of people and goods throughout Canada.

IN THE EVENT OF AN EMERGENCY

In the event of an emergency involving dangerous goods:

- call CANUTEC at 1-888-CAN-UTEC (226-8832), 613-996-6666 or *666 on a cellular phone.

INFORMATION

- Phone

    o (613) 992-4624 (call collect)

- Fax

    o (613) 954-5101

- E-mail:

    o canutec@tc.gc.ca

- Mail:

- o 330 Sparks Street Office 1415 Place de Ville, Tower C Ottawa, Ontario, Canada K1A 0N5

CHEMTREC – 1-800-262-8200 (US), 1-703-741-5500 (worldwide)   

Established in 1971 as a public service of the American Chemistry Council (ACC), CHEMTREC is an around-the-clock service available to fire fighters, law enforcement officials and other emergency responders who need immediate critical response information for emergency incidents involving chemicals, hazardous materials and dangerous goods. CHEMTREC's highly trained personnel receive hundreds of calls every day and provide assistance during incidents that range from minor to critical.

CHEMTREC also provides services that allow shippers of hazardous materials to comply with government hazardous materials regulations. CHEMTREC continues to build new relationships with international manufacturers, shippers and emergency response organizations, as well as offering expanded services for customers who ship globally.

IN THE EVENT OF AN EMERGENCY

In the event of an emergency involving dangerous goods:

- call CHEMTREC at 1-800-262-8200 (US)

- 1-703-741-5500 (worldwide)

INFORMATION

- E-mail:

  - o chemtrec@chemtrec.com

Databases

CCOHS Safety Data Sheet Search

Canadian Centre for Occupational Health and Safety, CCOHS, is Canada's national resource for the advancement of workplace health and safety. CCOHS was established in 1978 by the Canadian Centre for Occupational Health and Safety Act, which was passed by unanimous vote in the Canadian Parliament. CCOHS promotes the total well-being – physical, psychosocial and mental health – of working Canadians by providing information, training, education, management systems and solutions that support health, safety and wellness programs. A federal department corporation, CCOHS is governed by a tripartite Council - representing government, employers and labour - to ensure a balanced, approach to workplace health and safety issues. CCOHS offers a range of workplace health and safety services to help your organization raise awareness, assess risks, implement prevention programs, and improve health, safety and well-being.

CCOHS fulfills its mandate to promote workplace health and safety and encourage attitudes and methods that will lead to improved worker physical and mental health, through a wide range of products and services. These products and services are offered in both English and French, and are designed in cooperation with national and international occupational health and safety organizations with an emphasis on preventing illnesses, injuries and fatalities. CCOHS provides a variety of both public service initiatives at no charge to the user, such as OSH Answers, the person-to-person Inquiry Service, newsletters, and podcasts. Services for specialty resources provided on a cost recovery basis and include databases, publications and training and education.

(M)SDS Search

http://ccinfoweb.ccohs.ca/msds/search.html

Monitoring

Medical Monitoring

Pre-employment

Pre-employment medical testing can determine whether an employee meets the physical demands of a particular job, and whether or not they can safely perform the role. Through this testing an employer is able to identify any health problems that could put the employee's health and safety at risk. The examination also establishes baseline metrics, which are essential in assessing potential insurance claims, and can reduce medical costs associated with injury and illness.

Pre-employment screening has two major functions:

- determination of an individual's fitness for duty, including the ability to work while wearing protective equipment,

- provision of baseline data for comparison with future medical data.

Workers at hazardous waste sites are often required to perform strenuous tasks and wear personal protective equipment, such as respirators and protective clothing, which may cause heat stress and other problems. To ensure that prospective employees are able to meet work requirements, the pre-employment screening should focus on the following areas:

- Occupational and Medical History

- Physical Examination

- Ability to Work While Wearing PPE

- Baseline Data for Future Exposures

Periodic

Periodic medical examinations should be developed and used in conjunction with pre-employment screening examinations. Comparison of sequential medical reports with baseline data is essential to determine biologic trends that may mark early signs of adverse health effects, and thereby facilitate appropriate protective measures.

The frequency and content of examinations will vary, depending on the nature of the work and exposures. Generally, medical examinations have been recommended at least yearly. More frequent examinations may be necessary, depending on the extent of potential or actual exposure, the type of chemicals involved, the duration of the work assignment, and the individual worker's profile.

Periodic screening exams can include:

- Interval medical history, focusing on changes in health status, illnesses, and possible work related symptoms. The examining physician should have information about the worker's interval exposure history, including exposure monitoring at the job site, supplemented by worker-reported exposure history and general information on possible exposures at previously worked sites

- Physical examination

- Additional medical testing, depending on available exposure information, medical history, and examination results. Testing should be specific for the possible medical effects of the worker's exposure

Termination

At the end of employment at a hazardous waste site, all personnel should have a medical examination as described in the previous sections. This examination may be limited to obtaining an interval medical history of the period since the last full examination (consisting of medical history, physical examination, and laboratory tests) if all three following conditions are met:

- The last full medical examination was within the last 6 months

- No exposure occurred since the last examination

- No symptoms associated with exposure occurred since the last examination.

If any of these criteria are not met, a full examination is medically necessary at the termination of employment.

Air Monitoring Quantitative Testing

Electrochemical

Electrochemical gas detectors work by allowing gases to diffuse through a porous membrane to an electrode where it is either chemically oxidized or reduced. The amount of current produced is determined by how much of the gas is oxidized at the electrode, indicating the concentration of the gas.

Manufactures can customize electrochemical gas detectors by changing the porous barrier to allow for the detection of a certain gas concentration range. Also, since the diffusion barrier is a physical - mechanical barrier, the detector tends to be more stable and reliable over the sensor's duration and thus required less maintenance than other early detector technologies. However, the sensors are subject to corrosive elements or chemical contamination and may last only 1–2 years before a replacement is required.

Electrochemical sensors can be sensitive to interferences from changes in temperature, relative humidity, and pressure, especially when operating at the lower limit of their sensing capabilities.

Catalytic Bead

Catalytic bead sensors, also referred to as Pellistors (combination of pellet and resistor) are commonly used to measure combustible gases that present an explosion hazard when concentrations are between the lower explosion limit (LEL) and upper explosion limit (UEL).

Active and reference beads containing platinum wire coils are situated on opposite arms of a Wheatstone bridge circuit and electrically heated, up to a few hundred degrees C. The active bead contains a catalyst that allows combustible compounds to oxidize, thereby heating the bead even further and changing its electrical resistance. The resulting voltage difference between the active and passive beads is proportional to the concentration of all combustible gases and vapors present.

The sampled gas enters the sensor through a sintered metal frit, which provides a barrier to prevent an explosion when the instrument is carried into an atmosphere containing combustible gases. Pellistors measure essentially all combustible gases, but they are more sensitive to smaller molecules that diffuse through the sinter more quickly. The measurable concentration ranges are typically from a few hundred ppm to a few volume percent.

Such sensors are inexpensive and robust but require a minimum of a few percent oxygen in the atmosphere to be tested and they can be poisoned or inhibited by compounds such as silicones, mineral acids, chlorinated organic compounds, and sulfur compounds.

Photoionization

Photoionization detectors (PIDs) use a high-photon-energy UV lamp to ionize chemicals in the sampled gas. If the compound has an ionization energy below that of the lamp photons, an electron will be ejected, and the resulting current is proportional to the concentration of the compound. Common lamp photon energies include 10.0 eV, 10.6 eV and 11.7 eV; the standard 10.6 eV lamp lasts for years, while the 11.7 eV lamp typically last only a few months and is used only when no other option is available.

A broad range of compounds can be detected at levels ranging from a few ppb to several thousand ppm. Detectable compound classes in order of decreasing sensitivity include:

- aromatics and alkyl iodides

- olefins, sulfur compounds, amines, ketones, ethers, alkyl bromides and silicate esters

- organic esters, alcohols, aldehydes and alkanes

- H_2S, NH_3, PH_3 and organic acids.

Major advantages of PIDs are their excellent sensitivity and simplicity of use. The main limitation is that measurements are not compound-specific. Recently PIDs with pre-filter tubes have been introduced that enhance the specificity for such compounds as benzene or butadiene. Fixed, hand-held and miniature clothing-clipped PIDs are widely used for industrial hygiene, hazmat, and environmental monitoring.

Instrumentation

Combustible Gas Indicator, CGI

Combustible Gas Indicators monitor for combustible gases and vapours and measure the concentration of either. CGI monitors have a filament, usually made of platinum, which is heated by burning the combustible gas/vapour. This increase in heat is what is measured.

Generally easy to use, CGI monitors have the following limitations that require understanding of use:

- Temperature differences between calibration and sampling environments can create a substantial difference in measurement

- CGI monitors work on sensitivity between the calibration gas and the gas being sampled. Therefore calibration gases must be similar in both physical and chemical properties the to the gas to be sampled for

- The platinum filament can be easily damaged by environments that are oxygen enriched or contain halides, silicones or tetraethyl lead.

- CGI monitors will NOT provide accurate measurement under oxygen enriched environments.

CGI monitors need to be calibrated immediately before use and are subject to regular calibration.

Flame Ionization Detector, FID

Flame Ionization Detectors monitor for several organic gases and vapours. FID monitors function by ionizing gases and vapours in a flame which then produces a current based on the proportion of the number of carbon atoms that are generated and present.

FID monitors require experience to properly interpret data that is displayed, especially when set to "Gas Chromatography Mode". In GC mode, the FID identifies specific compounds by separating all volatile species into individual components. Additionally, FID monitors require calibration with the specific analyte being sought.

FID monitors have the following limitations that require understanding of use:

- FID does not detect inorganic gas or vapours. This includes many synthetics compounds.

- They do not operate accurately at temperatures less than 4^0C (40^0F)

- FID monitors are not absolute in identifying compounds

- High concentrations of contaminants or oxygen enriched environments require the system to be modified in advance

- In GC mode readings are directly correlated to the calibration analyte used.

FID monitors need to be calibrated routinely.

Oxygen Meter

Oxygen meters monitor for oxygen as O_2. Oxygen monitors function by using an electrochemical sensor to measure the partial pressure of oxygen in air and converts that pressure reading to concentration. Oxygen monitors are generally relatively easy in use and require experience to properly operate the equipment.

Oxygen meters have the following limitations that require understanding of use:

- Must be calibrated prior to use to compensate for altitude and barometric pressure

- Certain gases such as ozone can affect the readings

- Carbon dioxide destroys the detector cell. If the ambient air is more than 0.5% carbon dioxide, the oxygen detector must be replaced frequently.

Photoionization Detector, PID

Photoionization detectors measure many organic and some inorganic gases and vapours. PID monitors detect concentrations of gases by utilizing ultra-violet radiation (UV) which when exposed the gas or vapour, produces a current that is proportional to the number of ions emitted.

PID monitors are generally relatively easy in use and require experience to properly operate the equipment as well as understand the limitations of what is being interpreted for data.

PID meters have the following limitations that require understanding of use:

- Does not detect methane

- Does not detect a compound that has an ionization potential (IP) greater than what the PID can create

- Data response is subjective to mixtures of gases and is therefore very dependant on calibration gas used

- High humidity can affect PID response.

Portable Infrared Spectrophotometer, IR

Portable infrared spectrophotometers measure many organic and inorganic gases and vapours. IR monitors pass UV radiation through the gas and vapour and then measure the frequencies that are absorbed by the material. Each compound absorbs very specific light making the IR monitors very accurate. Generally they work best in quantifying one or two gas mixtures.

IR monitors require extensive experience and are generally not easy to interpret without through knowledge. IR meters have the following limitations that require understanding of use:

- Requires repeated passes to achieve reliable results
- Requires 115Volt AC power source
- Not approved in flammable or explosive environments
- Water vapour, high moisture and carbon dioxide substantially interfere with IR measurements.

Qualitative Testing

Colourimetric Indicator Tubes

Direct-Read Colourimetric Tubes measure for specific gases and vapours by reacting the suspect gas or vapour with the indicator chemical within the tube. The resulting stain or colour change is directly proportional to the gas or vapours concentration.

Generally tubes are easy to use and require thorough understanding of the sampling technique prior to use. Primarily, different manufactures use various media which may result in varying concentration results.

Colourimetric tubes require operator experience and are easily misinterpreted. Tubes have the following limitations that require understanding of use:

- Humidity affects reliability of results and staining

- Operator may judge stain end-point differently which affects accuracy.

Multiphase pH Strips

A simple definition of pH is that it is a measure of the relative concentration of Hydrogen ions. The more Hydrogen ions there are, the more acidic the solution is; the fewer, the more alkaline. pH test strips only work on aqueous or water based solutions.

Chemical Test Strips

Mercury

Mercury test strips are simple in application and allow for the onsite indication and concentration of mercury. A change in color indicates the associated concentration of mercury present.

The strips require little training or experience and are simply dipped into the compound and then colourimetrically evaluated.

Multi Test Strips – Smart Strip

Chemical Detection Reagent strip instantly identifies nerve, cyanide, hydrogen sulfide, arsenic, acids/caustics, fluoride, oxidizers and chlorine. These strips are ideal for emergency responders in hazardous environments. The disposable HazMat Smart-Strip changes colors when exposed to nerve agents, cyanide and other chemicals

The baseball card-sized Smart Strip can detect chlorine, pH, fluoride, nerve agents, oxidizers, arsenic, sulfides and cyanide in liquid or aerosol form at minute levels. A change in color in any of the eight categories alerts users to get additional gear, decontaminate or evacuate.

The HazMat Smart Strip requires little training and attaches with either a peel-and-stick adhesive strip or a clip like those used for identification badges. Once the protective film is peeled off, the cards are operational for 12 hours, or until they are exposed to one of the eight chemical substances.

Radioactive Quantitative Monitoring

Personal Dosimeters

A radiation dosimeter is a device that measures dose uptake of external ionizing radiation. It is worn by the person being monitored when used as a personal dosimeter and is a record of the radiation dose received.

Modern electronic personal dosimeters can give a continuous readout of cumulative dose and current dose rate, and can warn the wearer with an audible alarm when a specified dose rate or a cumulative dose is exceeded. Other dosimeters, such as thermoluminescent or film types, require processing after use to reveal the cumulative dose received, and cannot give a current indication of dose when being worn.

- The electronic personal dosimeter (EPD) is an electronic device that has a number of sophisticated functions, such as continual monitoring which allows alarm warnings at preset levels and live readout of dose accumulated. These are especially useful in high dose areas where residence time of the wearer is limited due to dose constraints. The dosimeter can be reset, usually after taking a reading for record purposes, and thereby re-used multiple times.

- A thermoluminescent dosimeter measures ionizing radiation exposure by measuring the intensity of visible light emitted from a crystal in the detector when heated. The intensity of light emitted is dependent upon the radiation exposure. These were once sold surplus and one format resembled a dark green wristwatch containing the active components and a highly sensitive IR diode mounted to the LiF glass chip. The main advantage is that the chip records dosage passively until exposed to light or heat so even a used sample can provide valuable scientific data.

- Film badge dosimeters are for one-time use only. The level of radiation absorption is indicated by a change to the film emulsion, which is shown when the film is developed. They are now mostly superseded by electronic personal dosimeters and TLDs.

- Quartz fibre dosimeter (QFD) use the property of a quartz fiber to measure the static electricity held on the fiber. Before use by the wearer a dosimeter is charged to a high voltage, causing the fiber to deflect due to electrostatic repulsion. As the gas in the dosimeter chamber becomes ionized by radiation the charge leaks away, causing the fiber to straighten and thereby indicate the amount of dose received against a graduated scale, which is viewed by a small in-built microscope.[3] They are only used for short durations, such as a day or a shift, as they can suffer from charge leakage, which gives a false high reading. They are now largely superseded by electronic personal dosimeters for short term monitoring.

- Geiger tube dosimeters (GM) use a conventional Geiger-Muller tube typically a ZP1301 or similar energy compensated tube requiring between 600 and 700V and a low power counter IC with display driver. The display on most was a bubble type with 4 digits though some newer units used an LCD module, and a button to enable the display for long battery life. The voltage was derived from a small step-up that often used a unijunction transistor (UJT) which though expensive was reliable over time and especially in high radiation environments common with tunnel diodes. These have the disadvantage that the stored Bq or uSv count is volatile and vanishes if the power supply gets disconnected though there can be a capacitor to prevent this. The fix was to use a long life battery, knurled high quality contacts and security screws to hold the typically glass front panel in place.

Geiger Counter

Geiger counter is an instrument used for detecting and measuring ionizing radiation. Also known as a Geiger–Mueller counter (or Geiger–Müller counter), it is widely used in applications such as radiation dosimetry, radiological protection, experimental physics, and the nuclear industry.

It detects ionizing radiation such as alpha particles, beta particles, and gamma rays using the ionization effect produced in a Geiger–Müller tube, which gives its name to the instrument. In wide and prominent use as a hand-held radiation survey instrument, it is perhaps one of the world's best-known radiation detection instruments.

Bubble Detector

Bubble chamber detection is a radiation detector that uses as the detecting medium a superheated liquid that boils into tiny bubbles of vapour around the ions produced along the tracks of subatomic particles. Bubble detectors serve as inexpensive, simple-to-use dosimeters. Neutrons produce tiny vapor trails in a special gel. The vapor forms bubbles, and the bubbles accumulate. The number of bubbles relates to the number of neutrons, which helps determine exposure to neutron radiation.

Helium 3 Detector

An isotope of Helium, ^{3}He provides for an effective neutron detector material because ^{3}He reacts by absorbing thermal neutrons, producing a ^{1}H and ^{3}H ion. Its sensitivity to gamma rays is negligible, providing a very useful neutron detector. Unfortunately the supply of ^{3}He is limited to production as a biproduct from the decay of tritium (which has a 12.3 year half-life); tritium is produced either as part of weapons programs as a booster for nuclear weapons or as a biproduct of reactor operation.

A helium 3 detector can monitor levels of neutron radiation much as a Geiger counter does for ionizing radiation. The high cost of helium 3 detectors limits their use to specialized laboratory and industrial applications.

Sampling

Sampling of compounds from spill response, site remediation, or to perform analysis of unknown compounds is one of the key measures in assessing the level of risk involved with the work while allowing all personnel to adequately don the appropriate Level of PPE. Unless each sample is approached in a systematic and prescribed method, the whole reasoning for sampling can be compromised resulting in false analytical that can create both substantial health and economic impacts on a job.

The term "sample" is extremely diverse and means different things to different people and industries and needs to be acknowledged and understood at the very onset of any sampling program. In each case the core question to ask is what is the purpose of the sample and what information will it provide.

- As an Emergency Responder, we use sampling to help us identify the characteristics of the material in an effort to evaluate the toxicity or danger of the material, subsequently determining our Risk Assessment for our personnel based on Risk = Toxicity + Exposure. The higher the toxicity, the less exposure time our personnel will want to have with this compound which helps us in deciding what Level (A,B,C,D) of protection we need for that situation

- As a hazardous materials worker, we use the analytical as a finger-print of the site, determining where the contamination is, what it exactly is, and how long it has been there. We also look at the environmental fate of the contaminant - what this does to the habitat(s) that it is impacting, where it will disperse itself to, where it will flow to and how quickly, and finally how long it will take to degrade.

- As a client, we look at how much will this cost, and what are our alternatives, and if in fact that client is responsible for that impact, or if indeed it was there before they were.

Sampling and site investigations usually fall into one of four (4) categories:

- Transaction Screening: the review and off-site inquiries used to determine whether there were site activities or systems used that may have caused contamination of this site. This includes the use of interviews, site visits, and some documentation review.

- Phase I Environmental Site Assessment (ESA): the Transaction Screening will determine if there is a need for a Phase I, which is a non-intrusive investigation performed by a recognized environmental professional (not the owner as is possible with the Transaction Screening). This includes an in-depth review of the 4 main criteria which are

    o a complete records review

    o site visit

    o interviews

    o report reviews

- Phase II ESA: this is a combination of non-intrusive and intrusive sampling of a site to collect accurate and additional information pertaining to Contaminants of Concern (COC) for that site. Non-intrusive examples include colourimetric sampling, head space, and electromagnetic surveys, while intrusive includes collection of sub-surface samples, building materials, and oils.

- Phase III ESA: ensures that the cleanup of contaminated sites has been successful to the level of criteria governed by that Province/Country. These samples are the confirmation samples that a site is clean after remediation

Canada 

The Canadian Association for Laboratory Accreditation Ince, CALA, is an internationally recognized leader in providing the highest-quality accreditation of laboratories. They are committed to objectivity and data integrity gives CALA-accredited laboratories lower risk and competitive advantage by ensuring that their customers receive data that can be trusted. CALA works with ANSI, ISO and the Canadian Council of Ministers of the Environment to provide sampling procedures that are internationally recognized.

https://cala.ca/

United States

The American Association for Laboratory Accreditation, A2LA, was established in 1978 as a non-profit, public service membership society dedicated to the formal recognition of competent testing and calibration laboratories, inspection bodies, proficiency testing providers, and reference material producers. A2LA works with ANSI, ISO and the Environmental Protection Agency to provide sampling procedures that are internationally recognized.

https://www.a2la.org/

General Sampling Protocols

Grab Samples

A grab sample refers to a small representative subset of a larger quantity, concentration or measurement that is taken at a specific time. Grab samples of air and water environments are often tested to determine the degree of corrosion that may be experienced by metals in the vicinity. Grab samples can only provide a "snapshot" of information. By their nature they are not representative, but they do have an important role in data collection during an investigation.

A sample collected at a particular time and place can represent only the composition of the source at that time and place. This involves manual sampling and minimal equipment but may be unduly costly and time-consuming for routine or large-scale sampling programs. As the name implies, Grab samples are simple scoops of the compound being sampled and are appropriate where conditions are constant or well mixed and slow to change.

Care should always be taken that a grab sample is representative of the whole and should be taken from well-mixed areas on all occasions.

It has become common practice to use organic vapour detectors (OVDs) to sample for soil contamination, referred to as "Head Space Testing". Although this technique is a useful method for identifying the presence of contamination, it is not good for quantitative measurements. The results are often quite different from those obtained from laboratory analysis. OVDs may be used as site-screening tools to determine the general location and degree of contamination, but sample collection for laboratory analysis is absolutely necessary.

All sampling equipment should be either stainless steel or polytetrafluoroethylene (e.g. Teflon ®). The equipment used for sample collection should not be the same as that used to advance the hole. Clean gloves should be worn and should be changed before each new sample is collected. When possible, a different set of equipment should be used for each sample collection. When this is not possible, the equipment should be cleaned between each sampling event.

For test pits, boreholes, and surface sampling, the location and number of samples required are site specific, and will depend on the type of contaminant, its mobility in the environment, and the physical features of the site. The preliminary site assessment and site-screening procedures should be used to determine the appropriate number and location of samples to be taken.

An adequate number of sampling locations should be established in order to determine the horizontal and vertical extent of soil contamination. The sampling density should be increased in areas of anomalies. If no information is available for predicting the location of hot spots, a grid pattern can be used to identify sampling locations.

The first step that should be undertaken in a sampling program is the development of a sampling protocol, a written description of the detailed procedures that should be followed. It should contain the following elements, which are described later in detail:

- Sample collection method(s) to be used

- Sample Locations (use a map)

- Equipment (calibration and maintenance)

- The number of field samples required

- Quality control samples (number and type)

- The laboratory to be used, as well as their QA/QC procedures

- Order of sampling

- Type, number, and size of containers (Laboratories should be able to provide containers)

- Preservation instructions (The laboratory will provide the necessary preservatives, if needed)

- Chain of custody procedures

- Transportation plans

- Field preparations

- Field measurements

Quality control samples are used to determine background levels of chemicals for comparison with the contaminated material. Two (2) control site samples (duplicate sample blanks) should be obtained and analyzed for each site that is being assessed.

The control site should have common characteristics with the contaminated site, but obviously should not be contaminated. It should be located near the contaminated site, and upgradient from the contamination. If there is no suitable sample blank location nearby, a site in the general region should be chosen. The control site sample should be taken just prior to the field samples.

Three types of quality control blanks are used during sampling:

- Trip Blanks: Used to verify if sample contamination occurred in the sample containers and/or as a result of sample cross contamination during sample transport and storage.

- Field Blanks: Used to verify if sample contamination occurred as a result of reagent and/or environmental contamination, such as from contaminated air at the sampling location.

- Equipment Blanks: These are designed to check for contamination from sampling equipment (e.g. pumps and bailers) Equipment blanks are useful for evaluating the effectiveness of equipment decontamination procedures.

Procedures:

- Clean gloves should be worn and should be changed before each new sample is collected

- Completely fill each sample vial so that no headspace exists. Minimize aeration and air contact

- Clean threads of jar thoroughly with a disposable wipe

- Cap the vial and affix a chain of custody sticker

- Label the vial

- Wrap vial in aluminum foil

- Place on ice in a covered cooler

- Complete the necessary documentation

Sample Handling and Transport

Keep samples cool (4 degrees C) and in the dark. Use ice cubes or crushed ice to chill samples as soon as they are collected, and ice packs to maintain internal temperatures in shipping containers.

Deliver samples to the laboratory as soon as possible after collection, noting the recommended maximum holding times as outlined by CCME.

Composite Samples

Composite samples are either amalgamated or made up of smaller time-related grab samples which are made up of sub samples of equal volume taken at specific time intervals (hourly usually) to make a single daily sample.

A composite sample representing a 24hr period is considered standard for most determinations. Under other circumstances, however, a composite representing a longer time period, or a shorter time period may be preferable. Often flow proportional sampling is used, which requires a purpose-designed sampler that take samples of materials proportional to the flow. This latter form of sampling is extremely accurate and preferable.

Monitoring Well Samples

The primary objective of a monitoring well is to provide an access point for measuring ground-water levels and to permit the procurement of ground-water samples that accurately represent in-situ ground-water conditions at the specific point of sampling.

The basic water-level measuring device is a steel tape typically coated with ordinary carpenter's chalk. This is the simplest water-level measuring device and is considered by many to be the most accurate device at moderate depths. In addition to a standard steel tape, the five main types of water level measuring devices are:

- Float type
- Pressure transducers
- Acoustic probes
- Electric sensors
- Air lines

Bailers are the simplest of the sampling devices commonly used for ground-water sampling. They can be constructed from a variety of materials including polytetrafluorethylene (PTFE), polyvinyl chloride (PVC) and stainless steel. Diameters of 0.5 inches or larger are common. Because bailers are lowered by hand or winch, the maximum sampling depth is limited by the strength of the winch and the time required for bailing.

Drum Samples

Drums are the most frequent type of containers sampled by field investigators for chemical analyses and/or physical testing. Caution should be exercised by the field investigators when sampling drums because of the potential presence of explosive/flammable gases and/or toxic vapors.

COLIWASAs (Composite Liquid Waste Samplers) or drum thieves are used to collect liquid samples from drums. The COLIWASA or drum thief is slowly lowered to the bottom of the container and then the COLIWASA is closed with the inner rod to create a vacuum with the sampler's gloved thumb on the end. The device is then slowly removed from the drum and the contents are released from the device into one sample container. The procedure is repeated until a sufficient sample volume is obtained.

Shoreline Cleanup And Assessment Techniques, Scat

The National Oceanic and Atmospheric Administration, NOAA, developed the Shoreline Cleanup and Assessment Technique (SCAT) which is a systematic method for surveying an affected shoreline after an oil spill. The SCAT method originated during the response to the 1989 *Exxon Valdez* oil spill, when responders needed a systematic way to document the spill's impacts on many miles of affected shoreline.

The SCAT approach uses standardized terminology to document shoreline oiling conditions and is designed to support decision-making for shoreline cleanup. It is flexible in its scale of surveys and a regular part of the oil spill response. SCAT surveys begin early in the response to assess initial shoreline conditions, and ideally continue to work in advance of operational cleanup.

Surveys continue during the response to verify shoreline oiling, cleanup effectiveness, and eventually, to conduct final evaluations of shorelines to ensure they meet cleanup endpoints. The SCAT process includes eight basic steps:

- Conduct reconnaissance survey(s).

- Segment the shoreline.

- Assign teams and conduct SCAT surveys.

- Develop cleanup guidelines and endpoints.

- Submit survey reports and shoreline oiling sketches to the ICS Planning Section.

- Monitor effectiveness of cleanup.

- Conduct post-cleanup inspections.

- Conduct final evaluation of cleanup activities.

https://response.restoration.noaa.gov/oil-and-chemical-spills/oil-spills/resources/shoreline-cleanup-and-assessment-technique-scat.html

Cleaning Sampling Equipment

Improperly handled cleaning solutions may easily become contaminated. Storage and application containers must be constructed of the proper materials to ensure their integrity.

Following are acceptable materials used for containing the specified cleaning solutions based on the EPA Field Equipment and Decontamination Procedure:

- Detergent must be kept in clean plastic, metal, or glass containers until used. It should be poured directly from the container during use.

- Tap water may be kept in tanks, hand pressure sprayers, squeeze bottles, or applied directly from a hose.

- Deionized water must be stored in clean, glass or plastic containers that can be closed prior to use. It can be applied from plastic squeeze bottles.

- Organic-free water must be stored in clean glass or Teflon® containers prior to use. It may be applied using Teflon® squeeze bottles, or with the portable system.

Equipment used to collect samples of environmental media from investigation sites should be field cleaned before returning from the study. Based on the condition of the sampling equipment, one or more of the following options must be used for field cleaning:

- Wipe the equipment clean

- Water-rinse the equipment

- Wash the equipment in detergent and water followed by a tap water rinse.

When equipment must be decontaminated in the field, the following procedures are to be utilized.

Decontamination pads constructed for field cleaning of sampling and drilling equipment should meet the following minimum specifications:

- The pad should be constructed in an area known or believed to be free of surface contamination

- The pad should not leak

- If possible, the pad should be constructed on a level, paved surface and should facilitate the removal of wastewater. This may be accomplished by either constructing the pad with one corner lower than the rest, or by creating a sump or pit in one corner or along one side. Any sump or pit should also be lined

- Sawhorses or racks constructed to hold equipment while being cleaned should be high enough above ground to prevent equipment from being splashed

- Water should be removed from the decontamination pad frequently

- A temporary pad should be lined with a water impermeable material with no seams within the pad. This material should be either easily replaced (disposable) or repairable.

Chain Of Custody

A critical activity within any data collection phase involving physical samples is the handling of sample media prior to sampling, handling/transporting sample media to the field, handling samples from the field at the time of collection, storage of samples (at field or other locations), transport of samples from the field site, and the analysis of the samples. Documentation ensuring that proper handling has occurred throughout these activities is part of the custody record, which provides a mechanism for tracking samples through sample collection, processing and analysis.

Custody records document the "chain of custody"; the date and person responsible for the various sample handling steps associated with each sample. Custody records also provide a reviewable trail for quality assurance purposes and as evidence in legal proceedings.

In order to use the results of a sampling program as evidence, a written record must be available listing the location of the samples at all times. This is also an important component of good laboratory practices. The COC record is necessary to make a prima facie showing of the integrity of the samples. Without it, one cannot be sure that the samples and sampling data analyzed were the same as the samples and data reported to have been taken at a particular time. Procedures may vary, but an actual COC record sheet with the names and signatures of the relinquishers/receivers works well for tracking physical samples. The samples should be handled only by persons associated in some way with the monitoring program. A good general rule to follow is "the fewer hands the better," even though a properly sealed sample may pass through a number of hands without affecting its integrity.

Each person handling the samples must be able to state from whom and when the item was received and to whom and when it was delivered. A COC form should be used to track the handling of the samples through various stages of storage, processing, and analysis at the laboratory. It is recommended practice to have each person who relinquishes or receives samples sign the COC form for the samples.

When using professional services to transport physical samples, only reliable services that provide a tracking number should be used. Information describing the enclosed samples should be placed on the bill of lading. A copy of the shipping receipt and tracking number should be kept as a record. The package should be addressed to the specific person authorized to receive the package, although it is recognized that staff not typically part of the COC may receive the samples and deliver them to the authorized addressee. A procedure must be in place to ensure that samples are delivered to the appropriate person without being opened or damaged. In this circumstance, the sample is considered still in transport until received by the authorized addressee. It may be necessary to ship and/or receive samples outside of normal business hours. A procedure should be developed in advance that considers staff availability, secure storage locations, and appropriate storage conditions (e.g., temperature-controlled).

Barton E. Taylor

Hazards

Unknown Hazardous Materials And Categorization, HAZCAT Liquids

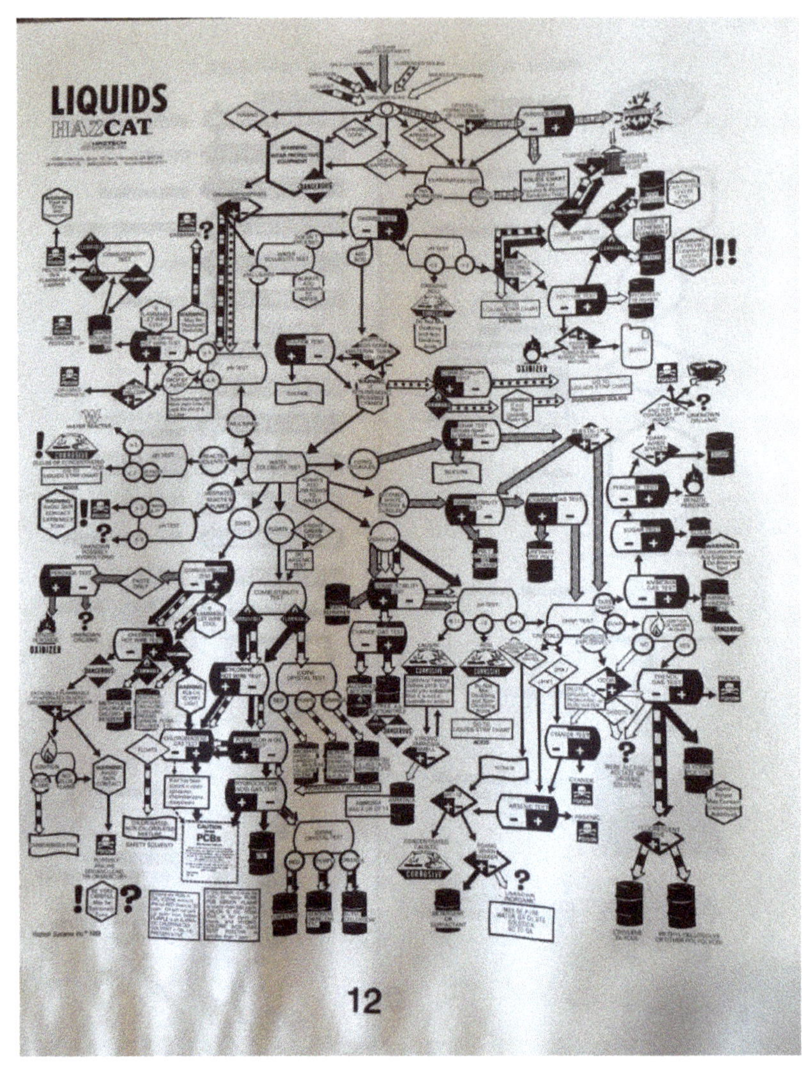

Courtesy of HAZTECH SYSTEMS INC. HAZCAT® CHEMICAL IDENTIFICATION SYSTEM, HAZCAT® 1496226, JULY 19, 1988

Solids

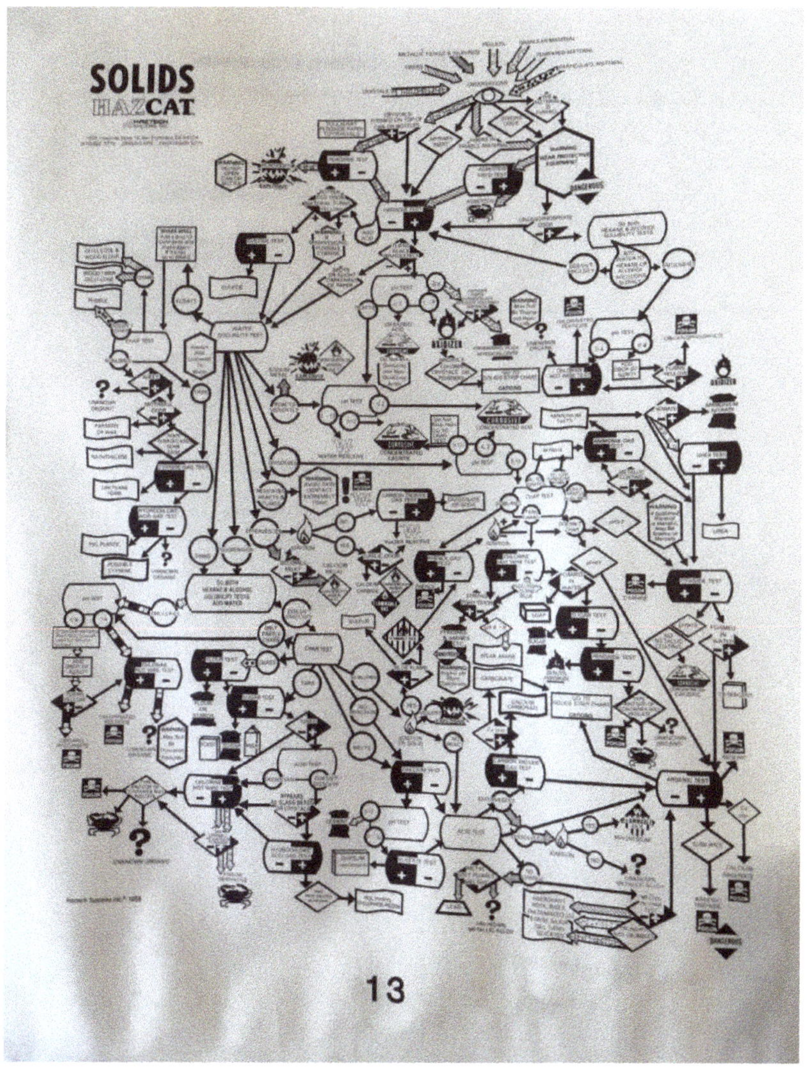

COURTESY OF HAZTECH SYSTEMS INC. HAZCAT® CHEMICAL IDENTIFICATION
SYSTEM, HAZCAT® 1496226, JULY 19, 1988

Quick Test

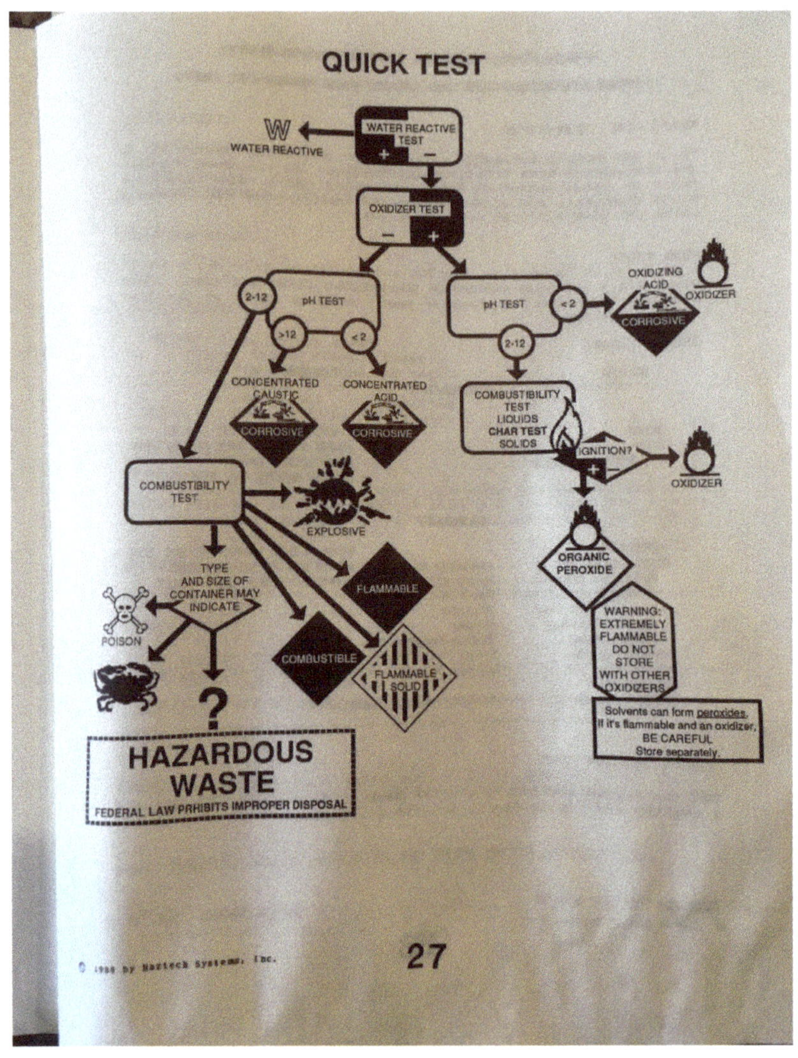

COURTESY OF HAZTECH SYSTEMS INC. HAZCAT® CHEMICAL IDENTIFICATION SYSTEM, HAZCAT® 1496226, JULY 19, 1988

Mixtures

Liquid

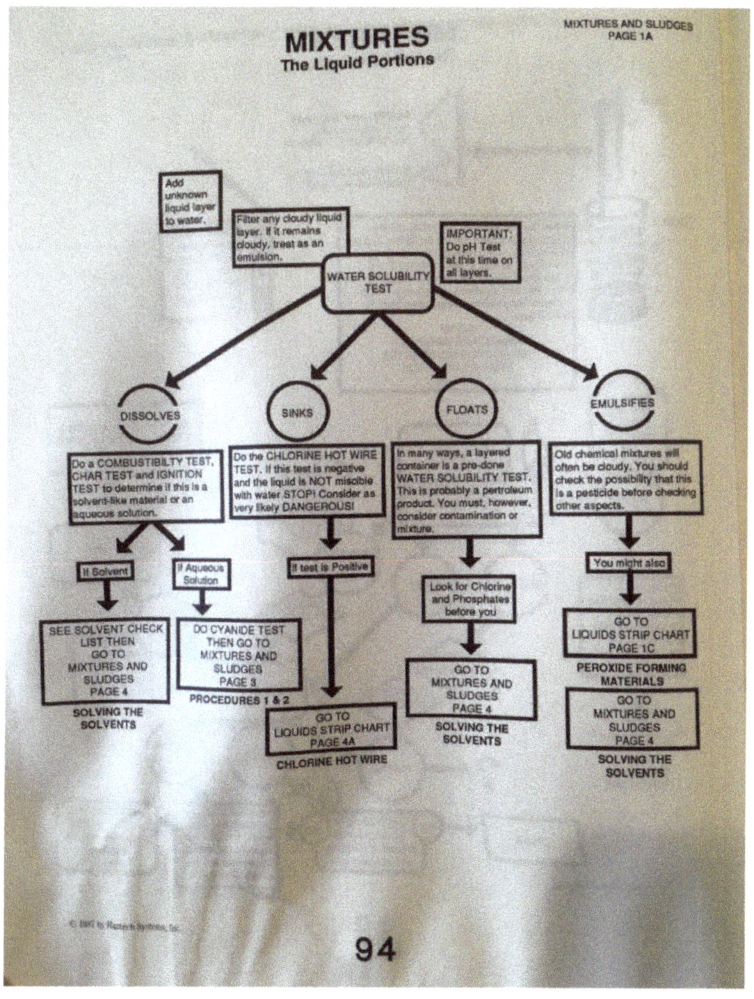

Courtesy of HAZTECH SYSTEMS INC. HAZCAT® CHEMICAL IDENTIFICATION SYSTEM, HAZCAT® 1496226, JULY 19, 1988

Solid

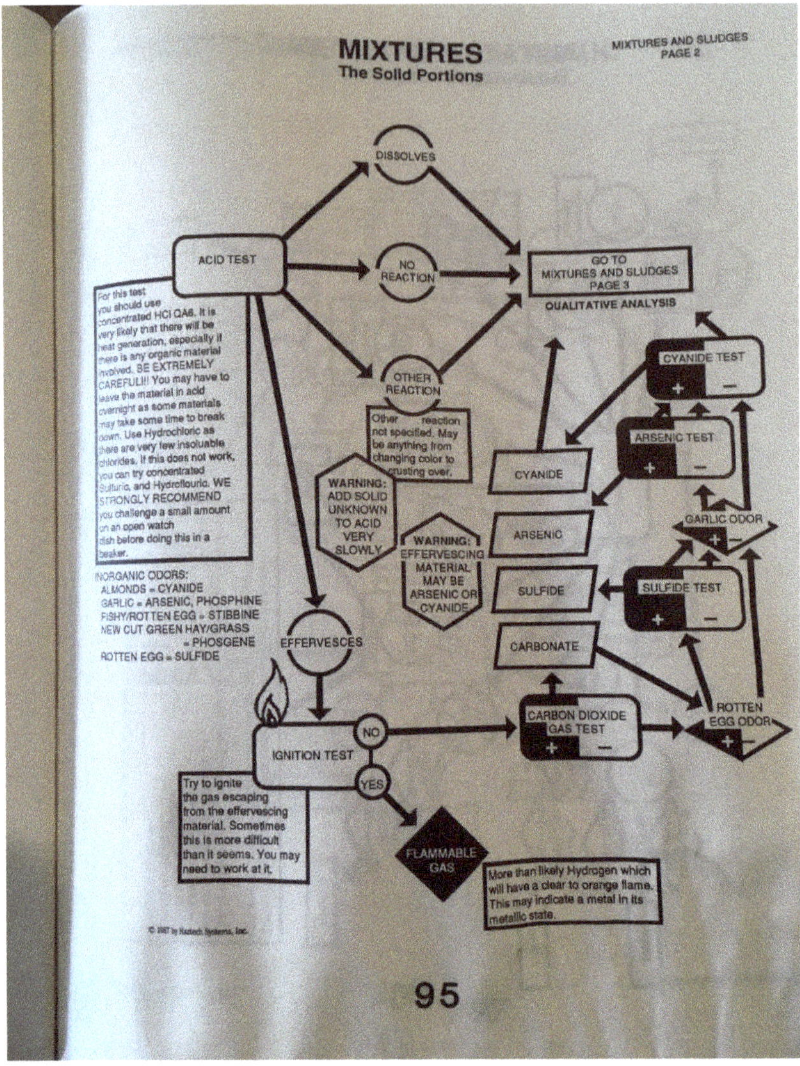

COURTESY OF HAZTECH SYSTEMS INC. HAZCAT® CHEMICAL IDENTIFICATION SYSTEM, HAZCAT® 1496226, JULY 19, 1988

Quick Field Test

One for simplest roadside tests to perform that allow for a high level of accuracy in determining the personality of an unknown is what the author crudely refers to as his "*Eph-Off* Test". It is critical to understand that this is a simple test that mirrors the Quick Test chart previously noted, and that it provides a superficial understanding of the nature of the unknown material being handled. Caution must always be taken to understand the concerns associated with doing this test, and each situation will need to be reviewed prior to attempting any of these tests.

The test is as follows:

- **<u>Eye: Visual Appearance</u>**

  - Is this a liquid or solid?

  - Are there layers or emulsions within the liquid indicating a mixture?

  - What colour(s) are evident?

  - If solid, is it granular, a fine dust, or course?

  - Is there crystallization around the cap?

  - Is there particulate floating in the mixture?

  - Has the solid formed a clump?

- **<u>pH</u>:**

  - pH less than 2, greater than 12.5

  - Neutral (pH = 7)

- **<u>Oxidizer Test</u>**

  - Test the compound with potassium iodide paper to see if it turns black. Turning black, and the speed at which the paper turns black, provides an indication of if the compound is an oxidizer

- **<u>Flammability/Organic Test</u>**

  - Put the compound into a ceramic dish and ignite with a match to establish if it is flammable, non-flammable, or combustible

  - Not the colour and content of the smoke: No smoke often indicates a non-organic compound, or a compound that has a low carbon content. Black smoke and the presence of soot, generally indicates an organic compound of high carbon content

- **<u>Firework Test</u>**

  - Using a copper wire, dip the cold wire into the chemical and expose to a butane flame. The colour of the resulting flame indicates various constituents present in the compound

The compound can also be aspirated into the intake port of the flame to generate potential colour

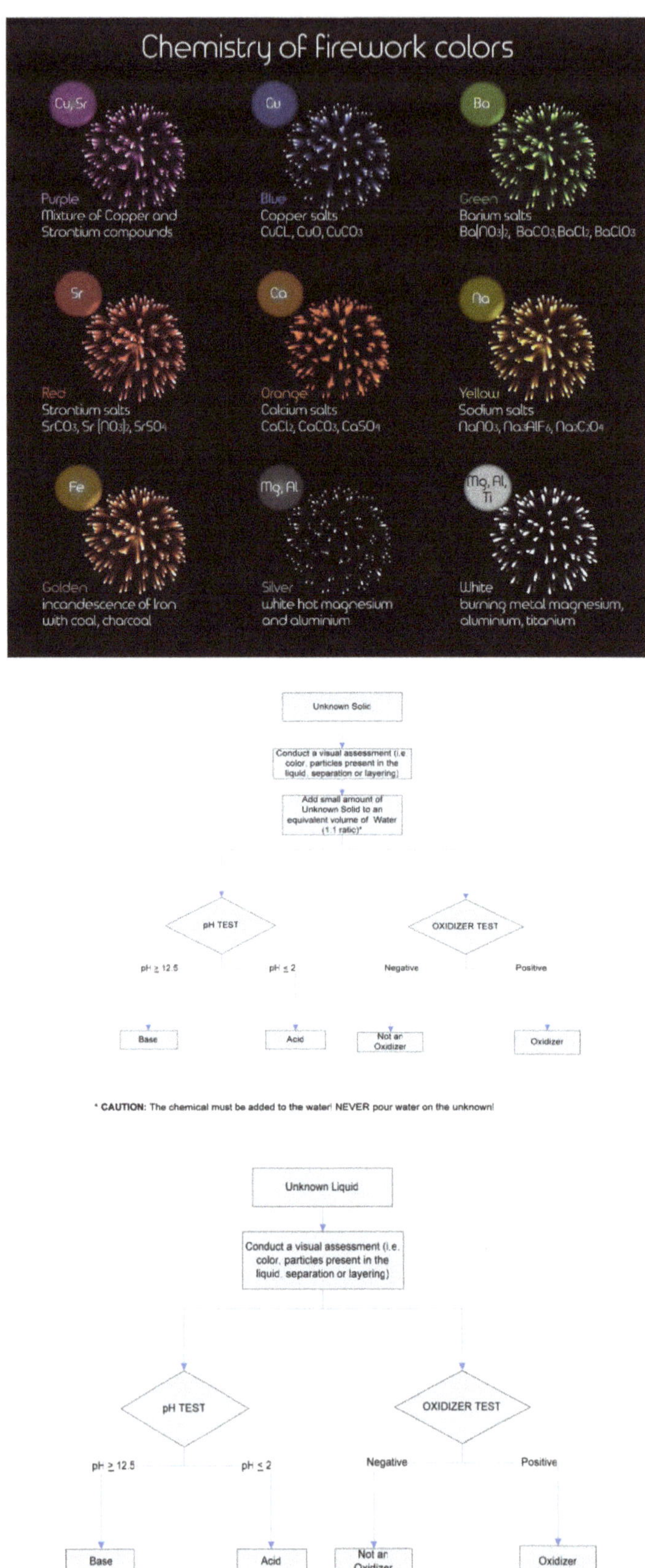

Corrosivity hazards

Corrosive - acid

Organic

Numerous organic acids are used in the laboratories (for example formic acid, acetic acid, benzoic acid, citric acid, picric acid); acetic acid and trichloroacetic acid are widely employed for the preparation of microscopic pieces and for protein electrophoresis. Such substances expose the personnel to the following occupational risks:

- Fire, outbursts and explosions.

- Irritations and caustic injuries (chemical burns).

- Acute intoxications

- Chronic intoxications.

- Allergies.

- Carcinogenesis and mutagenesis.

Inorganic

The specific hazards of the industrially important inorganic acids will be found below; however, it should be noted that all these acids have certain dangerous properties in common. Solutions of inorganic acids are not flammable in themselves; however, when they come into contact with certain other chemical substances or combustible materials, a fire or explosion may result.

- React with certain metals with the liberation of hydrogen, which is a highly flammable and explosive substance when mixed with air or oxygen.

- They may also act as oxidizing agents and, when in contact with organic or other oxidizable materials, may react destructively and violently.

- Corrosive, especially in high concentrations; they will destroy body tissue and cause chemical burns when in contact with the skin and mucous membranes. In particular, the danger of eye accidents is pronounced.

- Inorganic acid vapours or mists are respiratory tract and mucous membrane irritants

- Repeated skin contact may lead to dermatitis. Accidental ingestion of concentrated inorganic acids will result in severe irritation of the throat and stomach, and destruction of the tissue of internal organs, perhaps with fatal outcome, when immediate remedial action is not taken.

- Certain inorganic acids may also act as systemic poisons.

Caustic – base

Caustic compounds are materials that can attack and chemically destroy exposed body tissues. Caustic can also damage or even destroy metal. Common bases are ammonium hydroxide, potassium hydroxide (caustic potash) and sodium hydroxide (caustic soda).

- burn and destroy body tissues on contact. The stronger, or more concentrated, the corrosive material is and the longer it touches the body, the worse the injuries will be

- some corrosives are toxic and can cause other health problems

- can severely irritate, or in come cases, burn the eyes. Touching the skin can severely irritate or even badly burn and blister the skin

- vapours or particles irritates and burns the inner lining of the nose, throat, windpipe and lungs. In serious cases, this results in pulmonary edema, a buildup of fluid in the lungs that can be fatal.

- swallowing corrosives burns the sensitive lining of the mouth, throat, esophagus and stomach

- can also attack some metals like aluminum, zinc, galvanized metal, and tin to produce hydrogen gas

- some corrosives are also flammable or combustible and can easily catch fire and burn or explode.

- some corrosives are incompatible with other chemicals. They may undergo dangerous chemical reactions and give off toxic or explosive products if they contact each other.

Flammability Hazards

Fire Chemistry

Fire is the rapid oxidation of a material in the exothermic chemical process of combustion, releasing heat, light, and various reaction products. In the hazardous materials industry, the threat of fire or combustion must always be considered.

Fires start when a flammable or a combustible material, in combination with a sufficient quantity of an oxidizer such as oxygen gas or another oxygen-rich compound (though non-oxygen oxidizers exist), is exposed to a source of heat or ambient temperature above the flash point for the fuel/oxidizer mix, and is able to sustain a rate of rapid oxidation that produces a chain reaction. This is commonly called the fire tetrahedron. Fire cannot exist without all of these elements in place and in the right proportions.

Once ignited, a chain reaction must take place whereby fires can sustain their own heat by the further release of heat energy in the process of combustion and may propagate, provided there is a continuous supply of an oxidizer and fuel.

Classes of Fire

Combustibles

Class A fires are defined as ordinary combustibles. These types are fires use commonly flammable material as their fuel source. Wood, fabric, paper, trash, and plastics are common sources of Class A fires. This is essentially the common accidental fire encountered across several different industries. Trash fires are one such example. Class A fires are commonly put out with water or monoammonium phosphate.

Flammable Liquids

The Class B fire is defined as one that uses a flammable liquid or gas as its fuel base. Common liquid based fuel sources include petroleum based oils and paints, kerosene, and gasoline. Flammable gases such as butane or propane are also common fuel sources in Class B fires. Class B fires are a common hazard in industries dealing with fuels, lubricants, and certain types of paint. Smothering these types of fires to remove oxygen is a common solution as are chemical reactions that produce similar effects.

Electrical

The Class C fire is defined as a fire that uses electrical components and/or energized equipment as its fuel source. Electrical fires are often fueled by motors, appliances, and electronic transformers. Electrical fires are common in industries that deal with energy or make use of heavy electrically-powered equipment. However, electrical fires can occur on smaller scales in all businesses (i.e. an overloaded surge protector or bad wiring) and should be taken seriously. To extinguish such fires you cut the power off and use non-conductive chemicals to extinguish the fire.

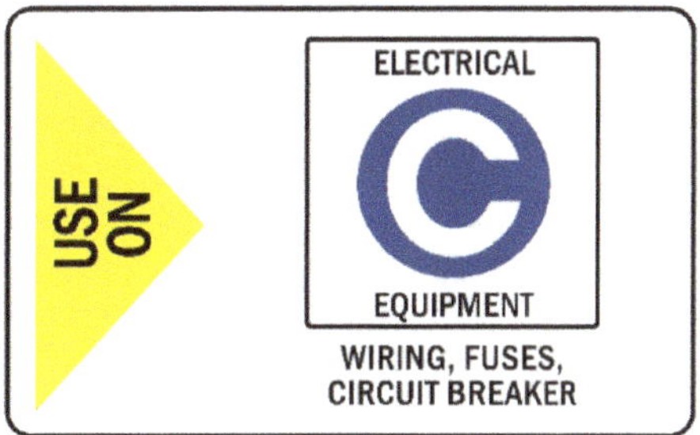

Combustible Metals

The Class D fire is defined as one that uses a combustible metal as its fuel source. Examples of such combustible metals include titanium, magnesium, aluminum, and potassium. Note that there are also other metals with combustive properties you may encounter. Class D fires are a danger in laboratory environments. However, be aware that combustible metals are used as part of production and other industry processes, and you need to be certain of what materials you are using for day-to-day operations. When confronted with such a fire, common extinguishing agents such as water are ineffective and can be hazardous. To extinguish a Class D fire, use a dry powder agent. This absorbs the heat the fire requires to burn and smothers it as well.

Cooking Oils and Animal Fats

A Class K fire is defined as a cooking fire involving combustion from liquids used in food preparation. Technically a type of liquid fire, Class K fires are distinct enough to warrant their own classification. Cooking fires are fueled by a wide range of liquid cooking materials. Greases, cooking oils, vegetable fat, and animal fat are all fuel sources found in Class K fires. Class K fires are naturally of concern in the food service and restaurant industry. Such fires can be very dangerous and far more destructive than you may think. Wet chemical fire extinguishers have become popular in putting out these types of fires.

Barton E. Taylor

Radioactivity Hazards

Activity

Measurement

Radioactivity refers to the amount of ionizing radiation released by a material. Whether it emits alpha or beta particles, gamma rays, x-rays, or neutrons, a quantity of radioactive material is expressed in terms of its radioactivity (or simply its activity), which represents how many atoms in the material decay in a given time period. Radioactive elements are the elements that are on the periodic table with the atomic number of 83 or higher. Frequently used terms associated with radioactivity that needs to be understood are:

- Isotope - the different states of stability that the element goes through as it decays. Isotopes have the same number of positively charged protons in the nucleus but differ in the number of neutrons that the nucleus has.

- Decay - as the element releases energy to become more stable, the energy that is released is referred to the element's radioactivity and the process of achieving a more stable state is called decay.

For measuring radioactivity, three types of devices are available:

- Gas-filled tube counters e.g. the Geiger Muller Counter

- Scintillation Counters

- Semi-conductor Detectors

There are various measurement units for radioactivity:

- **Rem**

- Roentgen equivalent man

- Equals the dose in rad multiplied by the quality factor (Q). REM = rad X Q

- **Sievert (Sv)**

- A unit of equivalent absorbed dose equal to 100 rem. 1 Sv = 100 REM

- **Rad**

- Radiation absorbed dose. A measure of the amount of energy deposited in tissue.

- **Gray (Gy)**

- Unit of absorbed rad dose equal to 100 rad. Measure of deposition of energy in tissue.

- **Curie (Ci)**

- The traditional unit of radioactivity, equal to the radioactivity of one gram of pure radium-226. 1 Ci = 37 billion Bq

- **Becquerels (Bq)**

- The standard international unit of radioactivity. 1 disintegration per second = 1 Bq

- **Disintegrations per second (dps)**

- The number of subatomic particles (e.g. alpha particles) or photons (gamma rays) released from the nucleus of a given atom over one second. One dps = 60 dpm (disintegrations per minute).

- 1dps = 1Bq

Half Life

Half-life is the interval of time required for one-half of the atomic nuclei of a radioactive sample to decay (change spontaneously into other nuclear species by emitting particles and energy), or, equivalently, the time interval required for the number of disintegrations per second of a radioactive material to decrease by one-half.

Half-lives are characteristic properties of the various unstable atomic nuclei and the particular way in which they decay. Alpha and beta decay are generally slower processes than gamma decay. Half-lives for beta decay range upward from one-hundredth of a second and, for alpha decay, upward from about one one-millionth of a second. Half-lives for gamma decay may be too short to measure (around 10^{-14} second), though a wide range of half-lives for gamma emission has been reported.

Exposure

Absorbed Dose

Exposure describes the amount of radiation traveling through the air. Many radiation monitors measure exposure. The units for exposure are the roentgen (R) and coulomb/kilogram (C/kg).

Absorbed dose describes the amount of radiation absorbed by an object or person (that is, the amount of energy that radioactive sources deposit in materials through which they pass). The units for absorbed dose are the radiation absorbed dose (rad) and gray (Gy). When time is factored in, it is referred to as dose rate (or dose per unit time).

- **ALARA:** keeping your radiation dose **As Low As Reasonably Achievable**.
  - TIME
    - Less Time = Less Exposure
  - DISTANCE
    - Greater Distance = Less Exposure
  - SHIELDING
    - More Shielding = Less Exposure

Quality Factor

The quality factor of a radiation type is defined as the ratio of the biological damage produced by the absorption of 1 Gy of that radiation to the biological damage produced by 1 Gy of X-rays or gamma rays.

Effective Dose Equivalent

Dose equivalent (or effective dose) combines the amount of radiation absorbed and the medical effects of that type of radiation. For beta and gamma radiation, the dose equivalent is the same as the absorbed dose. By contrast, the dose equivalent is larger than the absorbed dose for alpha and neutron radiation, because these types of radiation are more damaging to the human body.

Units for dose equivalent are the roentgen equivalent man (rem) and sievert (Sv), and biological dose equivalents are commonly measured in 1/1000th of a rem (known as a millirem or mrem).

Naturally Occurring Radioactive material, norm

NORM potentially includes all radioactive elements found in the environment. However, the term is used more specifically for all naturally occurring radioactive materials where human activities have increased the potential for exposure compared with the unaltered situation. Long-lived radioactive elements such as uranium, thorium and potassium and any of their decay products, such as radium and radon are examples of NORM. The most important for the purposes of radiation protection are the radionuclides in the U-238 and Th-232 decay series

These elements have always been present in the Earth's crust and atmosphere, and are concentrated in some places, such as uranium orebodies which may be mined.

Technologically Enhanced Naturally Occurring Radioactive Material, TENORM

The acronym TENORM is used to refer to those materials where the amount of radioactivity has actually been increased or concentrated as a result of industrial processes. Industries known to have NORM issues include:

- The coal industry and the oil and gas industry

- Metal mining and smelting

- Mineral sands (rare earth minerals)

- Fertilizer (phosphate) industry

- Building industry

- Recycling

Reactivity Hazards

Incompatible Chemicals

Mixing of chemicals may cause a number of reactions ranging from mild to violent. Incompatible chemicals generally involve reactions created from accidental contact of incompatible materials that liberate excessive heat, toxic vapours, or fire/explosion.

The most common example is Acids and Bases. Acids and bases can be used as neutralizing agents under controlled circumstances but tend to react violently when mixed. Even through both are categorized as Class 8 materials, segregation at storage is highly important.

Oxidizing Potential

Oxidizers with Organic Material

When oxidizers interact with organics, the organic compound becomes a fuel and the reaction may produce enough heat for combustion to occur. Examples of this are nitric acid mixing with paper towel. Reactions may vary from simple dissolving to extreme contact explosions as we see with oxygen mixing with asphalt.

Self Accelerated Decomposition Temperature

The self-accelerating decomposition temperature, SADT, is the lowest temperature at which an organic peroxide in a typical vessel or shipping package will undergo a self-accelerating decomposition within one week. The SADT is the point at which the heat evolution from the decomposition reaction and the heat removal rate from the package of interest become unbalanced. When the heat removal is too low, the temperature in the package increases and the rate of decomposition increases uncontrollably.

A self-accelerating decomposition occurs when the rate of peroxide decomposition is sufficient to generate heat at a faster rate than it can be dissipated to the environment. Temperature is the main factor in determining the decomposition rate, although the size of the package is also important since its dimensions will determine the ability to dissipate heat to the environment.

Maximum Storage Temperature

The maximum safe storage temperature is the highest temperature to store a chemical (like an organic peroxide) above which slow decomposition and explosion may occur. Although a number of organic peroxides can safely be stored at room temperature, most require some form of temperature control.

Minimum Storage Temperature

Many chemicals require to be stored within certain temperature parameters, with a minimum temperature that they can be stored at. If the temperature goes outside the assigned minimum parameters, the chemical will be adversely affected and may be no longer usable or worse still, may become volatile and dangerous.

Shelf Life

The shelf life of aqueous trace metals standards is dependent upon numbers 1 and 2 above. Shelf Life is the amount of time that a properly packaged and stored standard will last without undergoing chemical or physical changes, remaining within the specified uncertainty. A change greater than that uncertainty ($\pm 0.5\%$ relative for our standards) means the standard has gone over (passed) its shelf life.

In general:

- Never allow chemicals to freeze or be close to freezing

- Store chemicals in a place that stays below 37°C (100°F)

- Store away from direct sunlight

- Ensure all lids are closed and secured

Aging Chemicals

In many cases, incompatibility comes from chemicals that are stored too long and subsequently become unstable. Oxygen from the air can react with chemicals to form highly unstable organic peroxides that are highly explosive when exposed to heat, friction or even shock. This reaction is further enhanced by regular exposure to sunlight which substantially increases the peroxidation reaction.

Chemicals that are old are considered highly reactive and include chemicals that:

- are inherently unstable and susceptible to rapid decomposition

- under specific conditions, can react alone, or with other substances in a violent uncontrolled manner, liberating heat, toxic gases, or leading to an explosion

- increase in reaction as the temperature increases.

As discussed earlier, organic peroxides pose SADT concerns which in turn can create a high viscosity in the liquid and eventually crystalline formations around the opening of the container that is highly unstable. The slightest addition of shock or friction to these crystals will result in an explosive reaction.

Some of the more common examples of chemicals that are of concern when old are:

- Hydrogen Peroxide – decomposes to create oxygen and water with release of substantial amounts of heat

- Diethyl Ether – very common in schools, industry and vehicles

- Picric Acid – also known as trinitrophenol, picric acid is stable when kept moist under 20% water but is similar in structure and behaviour as trinitrotoluene, TNT

- Acetylenic compounds, Aluminum, Azides

- Carbon disulfide, Chromium trioxide

- Diazomethane, Dimethyl sulfoxide, Dry benzoyl peroxide

- Ethers, Ethylene oxide

- Halogenated compounds

- Lithium aluminum hydride

- Nitrates, nitro and nitroso

- Organometallics

- Palladium, Platinum, Perchlorates, Permanganates, Phosphorus trichloride

- Sodium, Sodium amide

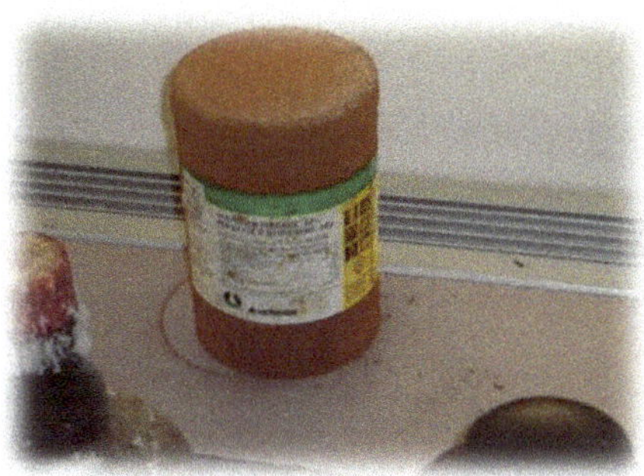

Water Reactive Chemicals

Water reactive compounds react violently with water. Many produce flammable hydrogen gas that can then ignite when mixed with air and include alkali metals, organometallic compounds and some hydrides. Others give off large amounts of heat when mixed with water resulting in a violent reaction if the heat produced is not sufficiency dissipated.

Virtually all water reactive chemicals produce a bi-product off-gas that is considered Toxic by Inhalation, TIH, and found in the Green section, Table 2 of the 2016 Emergency Response Guidebook. It is critical to understand that the gases produced are not the same as the chemical that was exposed to water. It is also important to understand that some of the water reactive chemicals are TIH compounds themselves such as bromine trifluoride.

Barton E. Taylor

TABLE 2 - WATER-REACTIVE MATERIALS WHICH PRODUCE TOXIC GASES

Materials Which Produce Large Amounts of Toxic-by-Inhalation (TIH) Gas(es) When Spilled In Water

ID No.	Guide No.	Name of Material	TIH Gas(es) Produced
1715	156	Acetyl bromide	HBr
1717	155	Acetyl chloride	HCl
1724	155	Allyltrichlorosilane, stabilized	HCl
1725	137	Aluminum bromide, anhydrous	HBr
1726	137	Aluminum chloride, anhydrous	HCl
1728	155	Amyltrichlorosilane	HCl
1732	157	Antimony pentafluoride	HF
1741	125	Boron trichloride	HCl
1745	144	Bromine pentafluoride	HF Br_2
1746	144	Bromine trifluoride	HF Br_2
1747	155	Butyltrichlorosilane	HCl
1752	156	Chloroacetyl chloride	HCl
1753	156	Chlorophenyltrichlorosilane	HCl
1754	137	Chlorosulfonic acid	HCl
1754	137	Chlorosulfonic acid and Sulfur trioxide mixture	HCl
1754	137	Chlorosulphonic acid	HCl
1754	137	Chlorosulphonic acid and Sulphur trioxide mixture	HCl
1754	137	Sulfur trioxide and Chlorosulfonic acid	HCl
1754	137	Sulphur trioxide and Chlorosulphonic acid	HCl
1758	137	Chromium oxychloride	HCl
1762	156	Cyclohexenyltrichlorosilane	HCl
1763	156	Cyclohexyltrichlorosilane	HCl
1765	156	Dichloroacetyl chloride	HCl

Chemical Symbols for TIH Gases:

Br_2	Bromine	HF	Hydrogen fluoride	NO_2	Nitrogen dioxide
Cl_2	Chlorine	HI	Hydrogen iodide	PH_3	Phosphine
HBr	Hydrogen bromide	H_2S	Hydrogen sulfide	SO_2	Sulfur dioxide
HCl	Hydrogen chloride	H_2S	Hydrogen sulphide	SO_2	Sulphur dioxide
HCN	Hydrogen cyanide	NH_3	Ammonia		

Page 346 — Use this list only when material is spilled in water.

TABLE 2 - WATER-REACTIVE MATERIALS WHICH PRODUCE TOXIC GASES

Materials Which Produce Large Amounts of Toxic-by-Inhalation (TIH) Gas(es) When Spilled In Water

ID No.	Guide No.	Name of Material	TIH Gas(es) Produced
1766	156	Dichlorophenyltrichlorosilane	HCl
1767	155	Diethyldichlorosilane	HCl
1769	156	Diphenyldichlorosilane	HCl
1771	156	Dodecyltrichlorosilane	HCl
1777	137	Fluorosulfonic acid	HF
1777	137	Fluorosulphonic acid	HF
1781	156	Hexadecyltrichlorosilane	HCl
1784	156	Hexyltrichlorosilane	HCl
1799	156	Nonyltrichlorosilane	HCl
1800	156	Octadecyltrichlorosilane	HCl
1801	156	Octyltrichlorosilane	HCl
1804	156	Phenyltrichlorosilane	HCl
1806	137	Phosphorus pentachloride	HCl
1808	137	Phosphorus tribromide	HBr
1809	137	Phosphorus trichloride	HCl
1810	137	Phosphorus oxychloride	HCl
1815	132	Propionyl chloride	HCl
1816	155	Propyltrichlorosilane	HCl
1818	157	Silicon tetrachloride	HCl
1828	137	Sulfur chlorides	HCl SO_2 H_2S
1828	137	Sulphur chlorides	HCl SO_2 H_2S
1834	137	Sulfuryl chloride	HCl
1834	137	Sulphuryl chloride	HCl

Chemical Symbols for TIH Gases:

Br_2	Bromine	HF	Hydrogen fluoride	NO_2	Nitrogen dioxide
Cl_2	Chlorine	HI	Hydrogen iodide	PH_3	Phosphine
HBr	Hydrogen bromide	H_2S	Hydrogen sulfide	SO_2	Sulfur dioxide
HCl	Hydrogen chloride	H_2S	Hydrogen sulphide	SO_2	Sulphur dioxide
HCN	Hydrogen cyanide	NH_3	Ammonia		

Use this list only when material is spilled in water. — Page 347

Air Reactive Chemicals

Often the terms Water Reactive and Pyrophoric are interchanged which is incorrect and needs to be clearly understood.

Pyrophoric materials are referred to as Air Reactive compounds, and are solid, liquid and gas materials that ignite spontaneously when exposed to air at or below 54°C (130°F). Pyrophoric materials react with the oxygen in the air, not the moisture. In comparison, water reactive compounds become spontaneously flammable or emit flammable gases when in contact with moisture in the air.

The confusion and hence the incorrect association of the two terms comes in that many pyrophoric materials are ***also*** water reactive as well as pyrophoric. Some common examples of pyrophoric chemicals are:

- organo-metallic reagents (i.e. Grignard reagents)

- alkali earth elements (sodium, potassium, cesium)

- finely divided metals (Raney nickel, aluminum powder, zinc dust)

- metal hydrides (sodium hydride, germane, lithium aluminum hydride)

- alkyl metal hydrides (butyllithium, trimethylaluminum, triethylboron)

- metal carbonyls (nickel carbonyl, iron pentacarbonyl)

- gases (arsine, diborane, phosphine, silane)

- silicon halides (dichloromethylsilane)

Many of the unstable chemicals that are air, light, heat or mechanical agitation sensitive are referred to as Shock Reactive. These compounds react violently when struck, agitated or even vibrated. Many of these compounds behave as catalysts in industry and include the following common list:

Acetyl azide	Chloropicrin
Acetyl nitrate	Copper acetylide
Ammonium nitrate	Cyanuric triazide
Ammonium azide	Diazidoethane
Ammonium bromate	Diazomethane
Ammonium chlorate	Diazodinitrophenol
Ammonium dichromate	Dinitrophenol
Ammonium hexanitrocobaltate	Dinitrophenylhydrazlne
Ammonium nitrate	Diethylene glycol dinitrate
Ammonium nitrite	Dipentaerithritol hexanitrate
Ammonium periodate	Dipicryl amine
Ammonium permanganate	Disulfur dinitride
Ammonium picrate	Ethyl nitrite
Ammonium tetraperoxychromate	Fluorine azide
Azidocarbonyl guanidine	Glycol dinitrate
Barium azide	Glycol monolactate trinitrate
Barium chlorate	Guanyl nitrosaminoguanyl hydrazine
Benzene diazonium chloride	HMX
Benzotriazole	Hydrazoic acid
Benzoyl peroxide	Hydrazine azide
Bismith nitrate	Lead azide
Boron triazide	Lead dinitrorescorcinate (Styphnate)
Butenetroil trinitrate	Lead mononitrorescorcinate
t-butyl Hypochlorite	Mannitol hexanitrate
Cadmium azide	Lithium nitrate

Confined Space Hazards

A confined space is an enclosed or partially enclosed area that is big enough for a worker to enter. It is not designed for someone to work in regularly, but workers may need to enter the confined space for tasks such as inspection, cleaning, maintenance, and repair. A small opening or a layout with obstructions can make entry and exit difficult and can complicate rescue procedures.

Hazardous Atmospheres

The atmosphere in a confined space may pose several hazards, the primary ones being:

- too little oxygen

- too much oxygen

- toxic gas

- explosive gas

There are three (3) defined levels of a hazardous atmosphere in confined space:

- High Hazard Atmosphere

    o An atmosphere is one that may expose a person to death, immediate injury, acute illness or otherwise impair that person's ability to egress the space in an unaided manner if failure to ventilation or respiratory protection fails.

- Medium Hazard Atmosphere

    o An atmosphere that does not have clean, respirable air but is not likely to otherwise impair that person's ability to egress the space in an unaided manner if failure to ventilation or respiratory protection fails.

- Low Hazard

    o An atmosphere that is known by pre-testing to contain clean, respirable air and is not likely to change during the work activity.

The primary cause of death in confined spaces comes from the atmosphere lacking enough oxygen. Aside from monitoring protocols, low oxygen levels are virtually undetectable by a person which in turn provides no warning. Oxygen ranges need to be greater than 19.5% to be considered not oxygen deficient. Similarly, too much oxygen in an atmosphere creates an environment that is highly susceptible to both fire and explosion. Oxygen ranges exceeding 22.0% are deemed oxygen enriched.

Atmospheric oxygen which we refer to as "air" contains approximately 20.9% oxygen, 78% nitrogen and then various other gases including carbon dioxide and argon.

Toxic Atmospheres

Toxic atmospheres are ones that contain contamination from another source known as an asphyxiant that may result in injury or death to people within the space. Simple asphyxiants are gases which can become so concentrated that they displace oxygen in the air. Low oxygen levels can cause symptoms such as rapid breathing, rapid heart rate, clumsiness, emotional upset, and fatigue. Asphyxiants include argon, nitrogen, or carbon monoxide.

At extreme levels, the environment is deemed Immediately Dangerous to Life and Health, IDLH, which is a term used to describe an environment that will cause irreversible health effects or death even with the briefest of exposures.

Asphyxiants that have no other health effects are referred to as ***Simple Asphyxiants*** (or external asphyxiants) and include gases that dilute atmospheric oxygen causing suffocation. These include nitrogen, carbon dioxide, methane, helium and argon. In most cases simple asphyxiants are colourless and odourless and offer no warning properties.

Asphyxiants that interfere with the absorption and transportation of oxygen within the body are referred to as ***Chemical Asphyxiants*** (or internal asphyxiants). Gases such as hydrogen sulphide and carbon monoxide are examples of chemical asphyxiants, and need to be dealt with as a toxic gas.

In order to evaluate where a gas will sit in an enclosed space or in the open air, we need to be able to do the following things:

- Understand that the air around us has a weight of **28.96 (29) grams/mole** based on the composition of oxygen, nitrogen, and the other elements generally in air
  - 78.08% nitrogen
  - 20.95% oxygen

- o 0.93% argon

- o 0.04% trace gases

Use the atomic mass of each element to determine the molecular weight of the compound

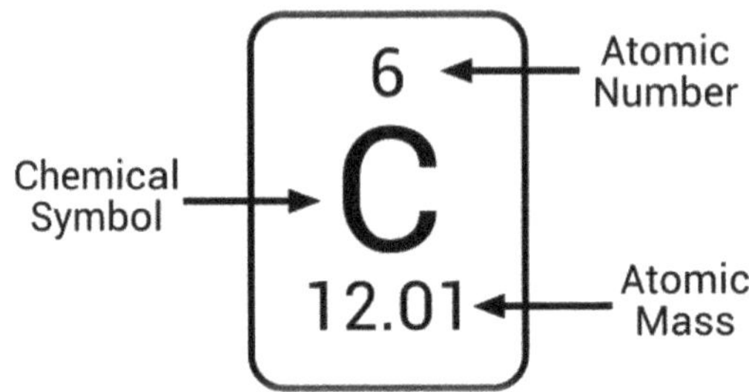

Example: Carbon Monoxide, CO:

- Carbon Atomic Mass is 12.01 g/mole, Oxygen Atomic Mass is 15.99 g/mol

- $12.01 + 15.99 = 28$ grams/molecule

- 28 is lighter than 28.96, so Carbon Monoxide will slightly float

- To figure CO specific gravity – 28 g/mol ÷ 28.96 g/mol air = 0.97

Example: Chlorine, Cl_2:

- Chlorine Atomic Mass is 35.45 g/mol

- $35.45 + 35.45 = 70.9$ g/mol

- 70.9 is heavier than 28.96, so Chlorine will sink

- To figure Cl_2 specific gravity – 70.9 g/mol ÷ 28.96 g/mol air = 2.45

GAS	MOLECULAR FORMULA	MOLECULAR WEIGHT (grams/Mole)	SPECIFIC GRAVITY	LOCATION IN AIR (29g/mole)
Anhydrous Ammonia	NH3	17.03	0.588052486	Float Above
Boron Trifluoride	BF3	67.81	2.341505525	Sink Below
Carbon Dioxide	CO2	44.01	1.51968232	Sink Below
Carbon Monoxide	CO	28.01	0.967196133	Float Above
Chlorine	Cl2	70.9	2.44820442	Sink Below
Ethylene Oxide	C2H4O	44.05	1.521063536	Sink Below
Helium	He	4	0.138121547	Float Above
Hydrogen	H	1	0.034530387	Float Above
Hydrogen Sulphide	H2S	34.1	1.177486188	Sink Below
Nitrogen	N	14.01	0.483770718	Float Above
Phosgene	COCl2	98.92	3.415745856	Sink Below

Explosive Atmospheres

In Section 6.8.1 fire chemistry was discussed using the Fire Tetrahedron model. When dealing with confined spaces, attention must be given to what is commonly referred to as the Explosion and Flammability Ranges.

There are four (4) main criteria that need to be evaluated and understood when it comes to these ranges as follows:

- Lower Explosive Limit

    o Known as "LEL"

    o The lowest concentration of a substance that will produce a fire or flash when an ignition source is present

- Upper Explosive Limit

    o Known as "UEL"

    o The highest concentration of as substance that will burn or explode when an ignition source is present

- Flammability Range

    o The range of concentrations between the LEL and UEL where the gas-air mixture will support combustion

- Flash Point

    - The minimum temperature at which a liquid will give off enough flammable vapour just above the surface to ignite in the presence of an ignition source

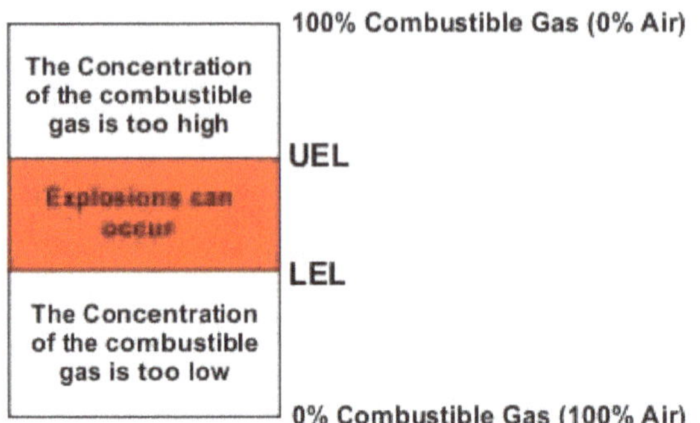

Field Considerations

In addition to the atmosphere concerns, physical hazards of confined space need to be clearly understood and identified at each scene. These include:

- Chemical exposures due to skin contact or ingestion as well as inhalation of 'bad' air.

- Process-related hazards such as residual chemicals, release of contents of a supply line.

- Physical hazards – noise, heat/cold, radiation, vibration, electrical, and inadequate lighting.

- Safety hazards such as moving parts of equipment, structural hazards, engulfment, entanglement, slips, falls.

- Vehicular and pedestrian traffic.

- Shifting or collapse of bulk material.

- Barrier failure resulting in a flood or release of free-flowing solid or liquid.

- Visibility (e.g., smoke particles in air).

- Biological hazards – viruses, bacteria from fecal matter and sludge, fungi, or moulds.

Electrical Hazards

Electricity

Electricity can result in:

- Electrocution

- Electric shock

- Burns (electrical or thermal contact)

- Fires

- Explosions

- Indirectly, injury from a fall, from cuts, or from broken bones.

Power Line Risks

Before working under or near overhead power lines, ensure that you maintain a safe distance to the lines and, for very high-voltage lines, ground any equipment such as cranes that can become energized. If working on power lines, ensure that the lines have been deenergized and grounded by the owner or operator of the lines. Other protective measures like guarding or insulating the lines help prevent accidental contact.

Employees unqualified to work with electricity, as well as mechanical equipment, should remain at least 10 feet (3.05 meters) away from overhead power lines. If the voltage is more than 50,000 volts, the clearance increases by 4 inches (10 centimeters) for each additional 10,000 volts.

When mechanical equipment is operated near overhead lines, employees standing on the ground should avoid contact with the equipment unless it is located outside the danger zone. When factoring the safe standoff distance, be sure to consider the equipment's maximum reach.

Electrocution

Electrocution is death or severe injury caused by electric shock, electric current passing through the body. The word is derived from "electro" and "execution", but it is also used for accidental death. The term "electrocution" was coined in 1889 in the US just before the first use of the electric chair and originally referred only to electrical execution and not to accidental or suicidal electrical deaths. However, since no English word was available for non-judicial deaths due to electric shock, the word "electrocution" eventually took over as a description of all circumstances of electrical death from the new commercial electricity.

Electric Shock

Electric shock occurs upon contact of a (human) body part with any source of electricity that causes a sufficient magnitude of current to pass through the victim's flesh, viscera or hair. Physical contact with energized wiring or devices is the most common cause of an electric shock.

In cases of exposure to high voltages, such as on a power transmission tower, physical contact with energized wiring or objects may not be necessary to cause electric shock, as the voltage may be sufficient to "jump" the air gap between the electrical device and the victim. The injury related to electric shock depends on the magnitude of the current.

Ground Fault Interrupter Circuits

Circuit protection devices limit or stop the flow of current automatically in the event of a ground fault, overload, or short circuit in the wiring system. Well-known examples of these devices are fuses, circuit breakers, ground-fault circuit interrupters, and arc-fault circuit interrupters.

- Fuses and circuit breakers open or break the circuit automatically when too much current flows through them. When that happens, fuses melt and circuit breakers trip the circuit open. Fuses and circuit breakers are designed to protect conductors and equipment. They prevent wires and other components from overheating and open the circuit when there is a risk of a ground fault.

- Ground-fault circuit interrupters, or GFCIs, are used in wet locations, construction sites, and other high-risk areas. These devices interrupt the flow of electricity within as little as 1/40 of a second to prevent electrocution. GFCIs compare the amount of current going into electric equipment with the amount of current returning from it along the circuit conductors. If the difference exceeds 5 milliamperes, the device automatically shuts off the electric power.

- Arc-fault devices provide protection from the effects of arc-faults by recognizing characteristics unique to arcing and by functioning to deenergize the circuit when an arc-fault is detected.

Ground Disturbance Hazards

The prevention of damage to buried facilities positively impacts worker safety, public safety, protection of the environment and preservation of the integrity of the underground infrastructure that provides goods and services essential to today's society.

Ground disturbance activities present a considerable risk to the large network of underground infrastructure throughout Canada and must be managed in a manner that will minimize the potential of damage that can impact workers, the general public, and the environment.

Unwanted contact with a buried facility has the potential for the following negative consequences:

- Injury or death to workers/the public

- Environmental consequences

- Interruption of critical services

- Buried facility and other equipment damage

- Production loss

- Corporate reputation loss

Typical hazards for ground disturbances include, but are not limited to:

- Excavation stability

- Shoring

- Entering and leaving an excavation

- Fall hazards

- Confined spaces

- Presence of hydrocarbon vapours or fumes, or other gases, e.g. H2S

- Presence of buried electrical facilities or overhead power lines

- Potential for unknown obstructions or buried facilities not located

- Interaction between workers and machinery

- Changing conditions such as job scope, personnel, weather, etc.

- Human behaviour

- Areas of historical, archaeological, or environmental significance Organizations shall consider the development of a Ground Disturbance Damage

Fundamentals

Approvals

Before ground disturbance is undertaken, an approval is required, in either of the following situations:

- The work takes place within the right-of-way (ROW) of a facility

- The work takes place within 5 m [five metres] of a pipeline / facility when no ROW exists.

An approval must be in writing. The acceptable approvals generally are:

- Crossing Agreement(s) between the owner of the underground facility and the company conducting the ground disturbance.

- Ground Disturbance Checklist/Permit for situations in which the company is both the Facility Owner of the underground facility and the company conducting the ground disturbance.

- Proximity Agreement when working within 30 m of another company's above or below-ground facilities.

Notifications

- Notify the Facility Owner of the work, search or controlled areas with the following information:

  - Nature/scope of the proposed ground disturbance, for example, location and purpose of the work and its extent.

  - Schedule of work, for example, the date work will commence and end.

- Notification must be received by the Facility Owner a minimum of two working days and not more than seven working days before commencing with the ground disturbance.

- If pipeline work is included, National Energy Board (NEB) notification must be received by the Facility Owner a minimum of three working days before the day on which a ground disturbance is planned to start before commencing with the ground disturbance.

- Notification is most commonly performed through provincial One-Call services; however, if the Facility Owner does not subscribe to One-Call services, notification must still be performed according to the requirements as previously stated.

Receiving Notification and Execution

- A Facility Owner of an underground facility who receives notification must provide any assistance that the party conducting the ground disturbance may reasonably require, to enable the latter to comply with the regulations.

- Upon being notified, the Facility Owner must:

  o Provide any information regarding an underground facility in existence within the ground disturbance work area and within 30 m of a search or controlled area.

  o Identify on the surface of the ground the alignment of the underground facility with clearly distinguishable warning signs and markers at adequate intervals. Markings must be at maximum intervals of 10 m along the pipeline or facility that are clearly visible and distinct from any other markings.

  o Provide locating and marking required by regulation to the person conducting the ground disturbance.

  o Inspect the pipeline to ensure that the locating and marking has been properly carried out if it is performed by another party other than the Facility Owner. This must be done before the ground disturbance may start.

  o Carry out inspections necessary to maintain safety of the underground facility.

Line Locating

- Locate all underground utilities within the thirty metre search area.

- Ensure that all lines in the area are accounted for, by identifying any potential sources of underground structures and positively verifying that none of the structures are within the thirty metres of the search area.

- Underground facilities within an existing lease or facility must be located by two different line locators conducting independent sweeps.

- All known pipelines and utilities, as noted on the plot plans/site drawings, maps, or facility searches that pass within the controlled area, must be located and staked, to indicate location alignment.

Exposure

Excavation and Trenching

The following criteria must be followed for mechanical excavation:

- Mechanical excavation may only be used up to the edge of the ROW or within 5 metres of the existing facility where there is no ROW, before using hand exposure or hydrovac to daylight the existing buried facility.

- Once the existing buried facility has been daylighted, mechanical excavation may be conducted closer than 5 m but not closer than 1 m to the buried facility

- Within 5 m of a buried facility, work must be done under the direct supervision of the Ground Disturbance Supervisor

- When mechanical excavation equipment is used and contacting an underground facility is possible, the Ground Disturbance Supervisor must direct the Equipment Operator or Spotter, both of whom must be fully visible to the Equipment Operator at all times

- Mechanical excavation equipment may be used closer than 1 m but not closer than 30 cm to an underground facility

Before a worker begins working in a trench that is more than 1.5 m in depth and is narrower than its depth, the Ground Disturbance Supervisor must ensure that workers are protected from cave-ins by proceeding as follows:

- Cutting back the walls to reduce the remaining vertical height to less than 1.5 m

- All excavations must be properly shored and back-sloped per provincial regulations

- The open side of an access route used by powered mobile equipment into an excavation has a barrier of sufficient height to prevent mobile equipment from sliding or rolling into the excavation

- If a worker is required to enter a trench that is more than 1.5 m, a safe point of entry and exit (for example, ladders and ramps) must be located within 8 m of the worker

- The excavation must be inspected by a competent person prior to entry

- Perform atmospheric monitoring in excavations that are greater than 1.5 m and when a hazardous atmosphere possibly exists.

Shoring

- When shoring or sloping is not practical, the Ground Disturbance Supervisor must ensure that temporary protective structures are installed, maintained and dismantled in accordance with the specifications of a professional engineer and that the structures are kept in place as long as workers are required to enter the trench or excavation

- Freezing, grouting and/or stabilizing must be designed and approved by a professional engineer

- Adjacent foundations must be supported, as required

- Natural freezing of the soil is not acceptable as an alternative or partial alternative to the installation of temporary protective structures

- Occupational Health and Safety (OH&S) regulations must be followed, to avoid danger of wall collapse

- Spoil piles must be at least 1 m from the side of the excavation and have a slope of not more than 45 degrees

- Power line poles must be protected from cave-ins

- When ground disturbance work is done near an overhead power line, the work must be performed in a manner that does not reduce the original support provided for the power line poles

- Equipment must not be closer to the edge of the trench than the vertical distance from the bottom of the trench to the same edge

- If equipment or heavy objects must be closer, a professional engineer must approve additional support in the trench.

Daylighting

- When a mechanical excavation is planned within 5 m of an underground facility, the underground facility must be exposed for visible inspection

- The Facility Owner must be contacted to arrange exposure or to confirm acceptable exposure methods

- The Ground Disturbance Supervisor must observe the exposure operations, to ensure the exposure is conducted with proper care for the safety of the workers and the integrity of the buried facility

- Before excavating, daylight all existing underground facilities (including anode beds) in the proposed ground disturbance work area, at one or more points by hand exposure or hydrovac, and identify for depth, size and direction

- Once exposed, the underground facilities must be protected at all times to prevent damage from slough-in material or objects falling or being placed in the daylight hole

- All daylight holes must be clearly marked to distinguish them from other excavations, for example, pile pilot holes

- The Ground Disturbance Supervisor must determine an appropriate method to protect and identify the daylight holes for underground facility

- When pile pilot holes have been drilled, all daylight holes must be fenced separately from other excavations

- The method used to identify or protect daylight holes must be documented on the permit/hazard assessment and ground disturbance documents and communicated to everyone involved in the ground disturbance.

Machinery and Equipment Hazards

Mechanical Hazards

Crushed hands and arms, severed fingers, blindness -- the list of possible machinery-related injuries is as long as it is horrifying. There seem to be as many hazards created by moving machine parts as there are types of machines. Safeguards are essential for protecting workers from needless and preventable injuries.

Dangerous moving parts in three basic areas require safeguarding:

- The point of operation: that point where work is performed on the material, such as cutting, shaping, boring, or forming of stock

- Power transmission apparatus: all components of the mechanical system which transmit energy to the part of the machine performing the work. These components include flywheels, pulleys, belts, connecting rods, couplings, cams, spindles, chains, cranks, and gears

- Other moving parts: all parts of the machine which move while the machine is working. These can include reciprocating, rotating, and transverse moving parts, as well as feed mechanisms and auxiliary parts of the machine.

A wide variety of mechanical motions and actions may present hazards to the worker. These can include the movement of rotating members, reciprocating arms, moving belts, meshing gears, cutting teeth, and any parts that impact or shear. These different types of hazardous mechanical motions and actions are basic in varying combinations to nearly all machines and recognizing them is the first step toward protecting workers from the danger they present.

Non-Mechanical Hazards

All power sources for machines are potential sources of danger.

- When using electrically powered or controlled machines, for instance, the equipment as well as the electrical system itself must be properly grounded

- Replacing frayed, exposed, or old wiring will also help to protect the operator and others from electrical shocks or electrocution. High pressure systems, too, need careful inspection and maintenance to prevent possible failure from pulsation, vibration, or leaks. Such a failure could cause, among other things, explosions or flying objects

- Machines often produce noise (unwanted sound) which can result in a number of hazards to workers. Noise can startle and disrupt concentration, and can interfere with communications, thus hindering the worker's safe job performance. Research has linked noise to a whole range of harmful health effects, from hearing loss and aural pain to nausea, fatigue, reduced muscle control, and emotional disturbance. Engineering controls such as the use of sound-dampening materials, and personal protective equipment, such as ear plugs and muffs, can help control the harmful effects of noise. Also, administrative controls that involve removing the worker from the noise source can be an effective measure when feasible

- Because some machines require the use of cutting fluids, coolants, and other potentially harmful substances, operators, maintenance workers, and others in the vicinity may need protection. These substances can cause ailments ranging from dermatitis to serious illnesses and disease. Specially constructed safeguards, ventilation, and protective equipment and clothing are possible temporary solutions to the problem of machinery-related chemical hazards until these hazards can be better controlled or eliminated from the workplace.

Access Hazards and Guarding

Moving machine parts have the potential to cause severe workplace injuries, such as crushed fingers or hands, amputations, burns, or blindness. Safeguards are essential for protecting workers from these preventable injuries. Any machine part, function, or process that may cause injury must be safeguarded. When the operation of a machine or accidental contact injure the operator or others in the vicinity, the hazards must be eliminated or controlled.

Machine safeguards must meet these minimum general requirements:

- Prevent contact

- Be secure

- Protect from falling objects

- Create no new hazards.

Lockout Tagout

In practice, lockout is the isolation of energy from the system (a machine, equipment, or process) which physically locks the system in a safe mode. The energy-isolating device can be a manually operated disconnect switch, a circuit breaker, a line valve, or a block (Note: push buttons, selection switches and other circuit control switches are not considered energy-isolating devices). In most cases, these devices will have loops or tabs which can be locked to a stationary item in a safe position (de-energized position). The locking device (or lockout device) can be any device that has the ability to secure the energy-isolating device in a safe position.

- Notify all affected employees that a lockout is required and the reason FOR THE LOCKOUT

- if the equipment is operating, shut it down by the normal stopping procedure (such as: depress stop button, open toggle switch)

- Operate the switch, valve, or other energy isolating devices so that the energy source(s) (electrical, mechanical, hydraulic, other) is disconnected or isolated from the equipment

- Lockout energy isolating devices with an assigned individual lock

- Stored energy, such as that in capacitors, springs, elevated machine members, rotating fly wheels, hydraulic systems, and air, gas, steam or water pressure, must also be dissipated or retained by methods such as grounding, repositioning, blocking, bleeding down

- After ensuring that no personnel are exposed and as a check on having disconnected the energy sources, operate the push button or other normal operating controls to make certain the equipment will not operate. CAUTION: Return operating controls to neutral position after the test

- The equipment is now locked out.

In the preceding steps, if more than one individual is required to lock out equipment, each shall place his/her own personal lock on the energy isolating device(s). One designated individual of a work crew or a supervisor, with the knowledge of the crew, may lock out equipment for the whole crew. In such cases, it may be the responsibility of the individual to conduct all steps of the lockout procedure and inform the crew when it is safe to work on the equipment. Additionally, the designated individual shall not remove a crew lock until it has been verified that all individuals are clear.

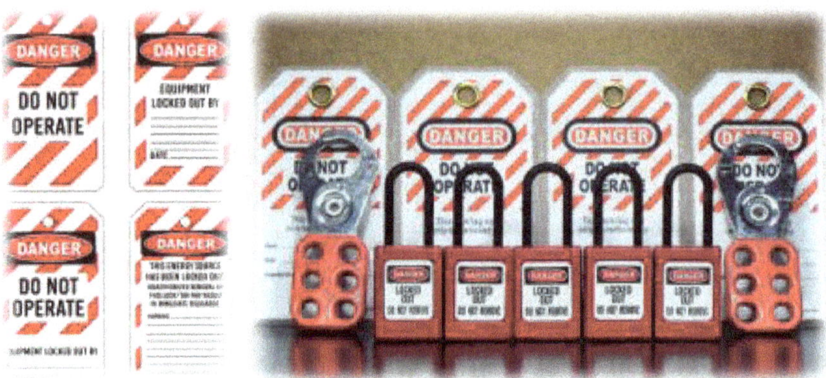

Energy Sources

De-energization is a process that is used to disconnect and isolate a system from a source of energy in order to prevent the release of that energy. By de-energizing the system, you are eliminating the chance that the system could inadvertently, accidentally or unintentionally cause harm to a person through movement, or the release of heat, light, or sound.

In general, examples include:

- Electrical energy - To find a specific method to discharge a capacitor for the system in question, contact the manufacturer for guidance. Many systems with electrical components, motors, or switch gears contain capacitors. Capacitors store electrical energy. In some cases, capacitors hold a charge and may release energy very rapidly (e.g., similar to the flash of a camera). In other cases, capacitors are used to remove spikes and surges in order to protect other electrical components. Capacitors must be discharged in the lockout process in order to protect workers from electrical shock.

- Hydraulic and Pneumatic potential energy - Setting the valves in the closed position and locking them into place only isolates the lines from more energy entering the system. In most cases, there will still be residual energy left in the lines as pressurized fluid. This residual energy can be removed by bleeding the lines through pressure relief valves. Verify depressurization or use flange-breaking techniques. Contact the manufacturer for more specific details, or if no pressure relief valves are available, what other methods are available.

- Mechanical potential energy - Carefully release energy from springs that may still be compressed. If this is not possible, use blocks to hold the parts that may move if the energy is released.

- Gravitational potential energy - If feasible, lower the part to a height where falling is impossible. If this is not possible, contact the manufacturer for guidance.

- Chemical energy - If available, bleed lines and/or cap ends to remove chemicals from the system.

Noise Hazards

Types of Hearing Protection

All employees should wear proper hearing protection (ear plugs, ear muffs, etc.) when noise exposures equal or exceed an 8-hour, time-weighted average sound level of 85 dBA.

There are three (3) types of hearing protection:

- **Ear Muffs**

e

- **Ear Plugs**

- **Ear Caps**

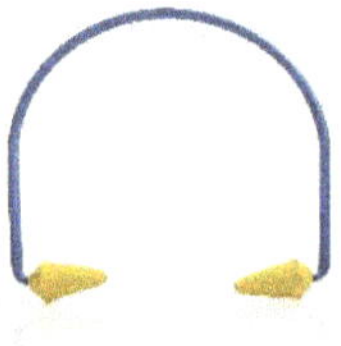

Noise Reduction Rating

The "Noise Reduction Rating" or "NRR" of hearing protection is measured in decibels. The NRR is how much noise (in decibels) the device will reduce for the wearer. In general, look for NRR of 25 or greater.

The NRR is found on the earmuff or earplug package. The higher the number, the greater the protection. Wearing both plugs and muffs at the same time will reduce the amount of noise exposure. However, the additional reduction from wearing both devices will be only 6 or 7 decibels, even if the NRR for both devices is above 25.

Noise Reduction Rating

All employees should wear proper hearing protection (ear plugs, ear muffs, etc.) when noise exposures equal or exceed an 8-hour, time-weighted average sound level of 85 dBA.

Table 1
Adjusted Noise Exposure Limits for Extended Work Shifts

Time (hours)	Noise limit (criterion level)	
T	85 dB	90 dB
8	85.00	90.00
9	84.49	89.49
10	84.03	89.03
11	83.62	88.62
12	83.24	88.24
13	82.89	87.89
14	82.57	87.57
15	82.27	87.27
16	81.99	86.99

(CCOHS Table 1: Adjusted Noise Exposure Limits for Extended Work Shifts, 2023-06-13)

Site Control Hazards

Situational Awareness

Situational awareness is being aware of what is happening around you in terms of where you are, where you are supposed to be, and whether anyone or anything around you is a threat to your health and safety. It involves perception of environmental elements with respect to time and space, the comprehension of their meaning, and the projection of their status after some variable has changed, such as time. Applied behavioral professionals associate situational awareness to terms such as intelligence, vigilance, attention, fatigue, stress, compatibility, and workload. In short, it involves being aware of what is happening around you to understand how information, events, and your own actions will impact your goals and objectives, both now and in the near future.

Behaviour becomes a function of the individual and the environment they are in. Everyone's situational awareness is individual and different than others so it becomes critical to be aware of this in order to make positive decisions and aid in the instruction of others. Furthermore, situational awareness is directly correlated and dependant of the familiarity a person has with the task. The more a person successfully completes a task, the perception of risk decreases and the individual feels more in control of their situation and subsequently willing to bear more risk.

(Endsley, 1995a 4, 1995b 5)

Perception, Comprehension and Projection

Perception of the Elements

The first step in achieving SA is to perceive the status, attributes, and dynamics of relevant elements in the environment which can lead to an awareness of multiple situational elements (objects, events, people, systems, environmental factors) and their current states (locations, conditions, modes, actions).

Unfortunately we cannot remain aware of everything which is going on around us. Due to the limitations of human memory and the complexity of any given situation, situational awareness will be suboptimal at any one time. If a person focusses on one or two things happening, situational decreases since there are usually more than two elements to any given situation. On the other hand, if a person focusses on all the elements, they will likely become overwhelmed and also lose situational awareness.

Comprehension of the Situation

The second step in achieving SA It requires integrating this information to understand how it will impact upon the individual's goals and objectives by identifying what is actually happening. As mentioned this is not easy in scope due to the problem that as a person gathers information, the mind tends to reject information that it deems unimportant even when it is not. SA is hindered when a person:

- Enters the situation with a preconceived idea

- Is excessively motivated or pressured to accomplish a task

- Is complacent or "running on automatic"

- Is overloaded or trying to multitask beyond their competency

- Is fatigued

- Experiences poor communication and has too much or too little information.

The core to comprehension in SA is to train your mind to retain the information you need to identify safe and unsafe atmospheres. By process of safety training programs, individuals are trained to program themselves to be able to identify safety hazards at the worksite. To comprehend this, each person must evaluate:

- The past – what were the circumstances in the past and what was the outcome

- The present – what are the variables currently in the workplace that could cause potential damage

- The future – what variables are changing and could any develop into a hazard in the future

Projection and Responding

The third and highest level of SA involves the ability to project the future actions of the elements in the environment. Projection and response is achieved through knowledge of the status and dynamics of the elements and comprehension of the situation, and then extrapolating this information forward in time to determine how it will affect future states of the operational environment.

How the individual responds to the information involves asking:

- How are you going to fix the different variables presented throughout the site?

- How you are going to maintain the safe atmosphere?

- How are you going to respond to added variables?

- How will you react to a given hazard?

Decision Making During High Stress Situations

It is a common saying that stress destroys your ability to make smart choices. The Centre for Disease Control, CDC identifies the following key issues with making sound decisions under stress:

- Stress is directly affected by and individual's perception and perceived demands

- Competence in judgement is always compromised under stress

- Stress itself is a function of information available

- Stress narrows the focus of attention

- The more dynamic the situation, the more the decision maker must achieve a trade-off between the cost of the action versus the risk of non-action.

The American Institute of Stress recommends the following ways to make decisions while experiencing high stress situations:

- Clarify what is really at stake and move away from the pitfalls that hinder that clarification

- Do not assume there is only one right way of doing things under a Win-Loss mentality

- Assign priorities to tasks at hand and review similar decision you've made in the past that have worked well

- Acknowledge when you are overloaded and bring in help

- Do not avoid making a decision with procrastination. Capture what needs attention and strategically attack.

Human Factors

Human factors are based on the relationship between people and the systems with which they are interacting with such as tools, equipment and workplace environment. How jobs are designed, aligning abilities with roles and individual perceptions of risk all need to be incorporated in any situation to evaluate how people perform under different situations and circumstances in order to improve efficiency, creativity, productivity and job satisfaction while minimizing errors, or in safety terms, injuries.

Human factors is about understanding human limitations due to:

- Cultural, economical & political differences

- Language, social & lifestyle differences

- Age & gender differences

- Technological & education differences

- Physical differences

The primary step is to understand "How" employees process information so we can identify "What" errors can arise. By obtaining this information, processes can be both simplified and standardized to help people avoid reliance on memory with the provision of clear procedures and communication methods.

Statistically, four (4) root causes exist in human factor evaluation that create 80% of all workplace errors and injuries. These are:

- Fatigue

- Stress

- Distractions

- Personal issues

Surface Hazards

Slips, Trips and Falls

Slips, trips and falls are a leading cause of injury in Canada according to Statistics Canada. In Canada over 42,000 workers get injured annually due to fall incidents. This number represents about 18% of the "time-loss injuries" that were accepted by workers' compensation boards or commissions across Canada (based on statistics from Association of Workers' Compensation Boards of Canada, 2016). Statistics show that the majority (67%) of falls happen on the same level resulting from slips and trips. The remaining 30% are falls from a height.

Slips

Slips happen where there is too little friction or traction between the footwear and the walking surface. Common causes of slips are:

- wet or oily surfaces

- occasional spills

- weather hazards

- loose, unanchored rugs or mats

- flooring or other walking surfaces that do not have same degree of traction in all areas

Trips

Trips happen when your foot collides (strikes, hits) an object causing you to lose the balance and, eventually fall. Common causes of tripping are:

- obstructed view

- poor lighting

- clutter in your way

- wrinkled carpeting

- uncovered cables

- bottom drawers not being closed

- uneven (steps, thresholds) walking surfaces

Falls

If you are at risk for falling three metres (10 feet) or more at your workplace, you should wear the appropriate fall protection equipment. If fall protection is required, establish a complete fall protection program if one is not in place. The program should include educating and training workers, selecting and fitting the equipment for the task and the worker, and knowing how to inspect the equipment.

The Fall Protection Hierarchy requires that the fall protection utilized shall be chosen in the following order, whereby if the first option is not feasible, the second option shall be considered and so on down the list:

- Guardrails

- Personal fall restraint

- Personal fall arrest

- Control zones (where allowed by local legislation)

Fall protection is required if a fall hazard is $\geq$ 3 m (10 ft.) OR there is an unusual possibility of injury for a fall <3 m (10 ft.). Workers using fall arrest or fall restraint must be tied off at all times when otherwise not protected from a fall $\geq$ 3 m (10 ft.).

An area easily accessible to workers must have guardrails installed if it is a raised floor, open-sided floor, ramp, or mezzanine, $\geq$ 1.2 m (4ft) above floor or ground level EXCEPT at a loading dock and during demolition (access must be restricted).

An area easily accessible to workers must have guardrails installed on both sides of a walkway constructed or installed over a hazardous condition or dangerous machinery.

Guardrails are used for fall protection wherever practicable as they are the best method for fall protection.

Loose and Unstable Material

According to the National Institute for Occupational Health and Safety, NIOSH, entrapment and suffocation are hazards associated with storage bins and hoppers where loose materials such as grain, sand, or gravel are stored, handled, or transferred. In some cases, material being drawn from the bottom of storage bins can cause the surface to act like quicksand.

When a storage bin is emptied from the bottom, the flow of material forms a funnel-shaped path over the outlet. The rate of material flow increases toward the center of the funnel. During a typical unloading operation, the flow rate can become so great that once a worker is drawn into the flow path, escape is virtually impossible.

A condition known as bridging can create hazardous situations. Bridging occurs when grain or other loose material clings to the sides of a silo or bin that is being emptied from below. A bridge of material may collapse without warning, entrapping workers who are standing below or on top of the bridge and who are unaware that the surface is unstable.

Bridging can occur in storage bins, silos, and hoppers that contain ground grains or meal such as soybean meal or other loose materials such as cement, limestone, coal, or sawdust. Unground grains such as barley, oats, and corn are less likely to form bridges, since the individual kernels do not adhere to the sides of the storage bin. Diameter of the storage vessel and moisture content of the stored materials are factors that contribute to bridging.

NIOSH makes the following recommendations:

- Workers should be trained to assume that all stored materials are bridged and that the potential for entrapment and suffocation associated with stored grain or other loose materials is constant. The training should include information on safe work practices and rescue.

- Workers should not be allowed to enter a storage area from the bottom when material is adhering to the sides or is bridged overhead.

- When workers must enter storage areas, they should stay above the material at all times and should never stand on top of stored material.

- Safety signs should be posted to warn workers of the hazards of working with stored grains and other loose materials. Safety signs alone are not sufficient to provide the information needed to prevent fatalities; such signs should be only one component of a comprehensive safety program.

- Bins, hoppers, silos, tanks, transport vehicles, and surge piles where loose materials are stored, handled, or transferred should be equipped with mechanical devices or other means of handling materials so that workers are not required to enter such storage areas. Bridging can usually be prevented by mechanical agitation or vibration of stored materials.

- Any time a worker enters a storage area (bin, tanks, etc.), the supply and discharge of materials must be stopped and the supply and discharge equipment must be locked out.

- Workers entering storage areas should wear safety belts or harnesses equipped with properly fastened life lines. A similarly equipped standby person should be stationed outside the area

Thermal Hazards

Heat Stress

Heat stress is a major hazard, especially for workers wearing protective clothing. The same protective materials that shield the body from chemical exposure also limit the dissipation of body heat and moisture. There are four (4) forms of heat stress.

Heat rash

- results from continuous exposure to heat or humid air. The sweat ducts become clogged and the sweat cannot get to the surface of the skin. Instead, it becomes trapped beneath the skin's surface causing a mild inflammation or rash. Heat rash is also called prickly heat.

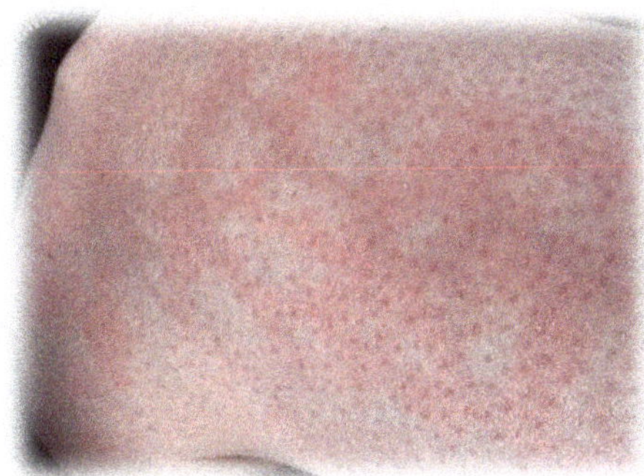

Heat cramps

- are caused by heavy sweating with inadequate electrolyte replacement which result in muscle spasms. Heat cramps are associated with cramping in the abdomen, arms and calves.

Heat exhaustion

- occurs from increased stress on various organs including inadequate blood circulation due to cardiovascular insufficiency or dehydration.

Heat stroke

- is the most serious form of heat stress that occurs when the body temperature regulation fails. Immediate action must be taken to cool the body before serious injury or death occur.

Cold Stress

When the body is unable to warm itself, serious cold related illnesses and injuries may occur, and permanent tissue damage and death may result. Hypothermia can even occur when land temperatures are ABOVE freezing or water temperatures are below 98.6°F / 37°C. Cold related illnesses can slowly overcome a person who has been chilled by low temperatures, brisk winds, or wet clothing.

Wind-chill or windchill

- (popularly wind chill factor) is the lowering of body temperature due to the passing-flow of lower-temperature air. Wind chill numbers are always lower than the air temperature for values where the formula is valid.

At any temperature, you feel colder as the wind speed increases. The combined effect of cold air and wind speed is expressed simply as the "wind chill" temperature in degrees Celsius or Fahrenheit. It is essentially the air temperature that would feel the same on exposed human flesh as the given combination of air temperature and wind speed. It can be used as a general guideline for deciding clothing requirements and the possible health effects of cold.

In Canada, the term "wind chill" or "wind chill index" is used. This factor is a measurement of a heat loss rate caused by exposure to wind and is expressed in temperature-like units

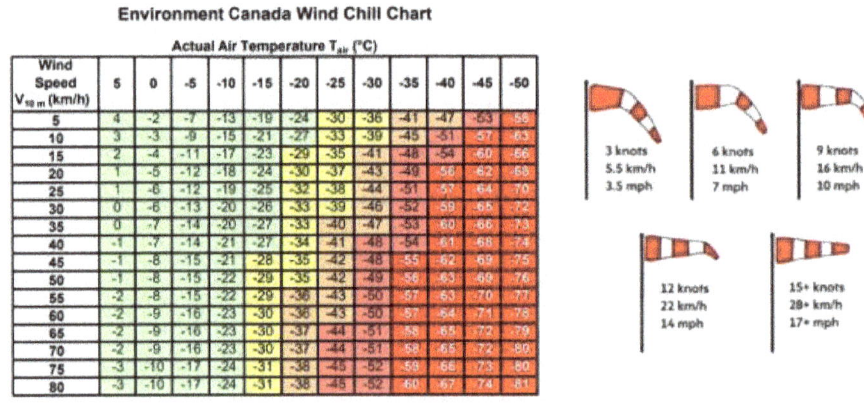

Environment Canada Wind Chill Chart

Wind Speed $V_{10\,m}$ (km/h)	Actual Air Temperature T_{air} (°C)											
	5	0	-5	-10	-15	-20	-25	-30	-35	-40	-45	-50
5	4	-2	-7	-13	-19	-24	-30	-36	-41	-47	-53	-58
10	3	-3	-9	-15	-21	-27	-33	-39	-45	-51	-57	-63
15	2	-4	-11	-17	-23	-29	-35	-41	-48	-54	-60	-66
20	1	-5	-12	-18	-24	-30	-37	-43	-49	-56	-62	-68
25	1	-6	-12	-19	-25	-32	-38	-44	-51	-57	-64	-70
30	0	-6	-13	-20	-26	-33	-39	-46	-52	-59	-65	-72
35	0	-7	-14	-20	-27	-33	-40	-47	-53	-60	-66	-73
40	-1	-7	-14	-21	-27	-34	-41	-48	-54	-61	-68	-74
45	-1	-8	-15	-21	-28	-35	-42	-48	-55	-62	-69	-75
50	-1	-8	-15	-22	-29	-35	-42	-49	-56	-63	-69	-76
55	-2	-8	-15	-22	-29	-36	-43	-50	-57	-63	-70	-77
60	-2	-9	-16	-23	-30	-36	-43	-50	-57	-64	-71	-78
65	-2	-9	-16	-23	-30	-37	-44	-51	-58	-65	-72	-79
70	-2	-9	-16	-23	-30	-37	-44	-51	-58	-65	-72	-80
75	-3	-10	-17	-24	-31	-38	-45	-52	-59	-66	-73	-80
80	-3	-10	-17	-24	-31	-38	-45	-52	-60	-67	-74	-81

(CANDAC/PEARL)

Frostnip

- is a milder form of cold injury that doesn't cause permanent skin damage. You can treat frostnip with first-aid measures, including rewarming the affected skin. All other frostbite requires medical attention because it can damage skin, tissues, muscle and bones. Possible complications of severe frostbite include infection and nerve damage.

Frostbite

- is an injury caused by freezing of the skin and underlying tissues. First your skin becomes very cold and red, then numb, hard and pale. Frostbite is most common on the fingers, toes, nose, ears, cheeks and chin. Exposed skin in cold, windy weather is most vulnerable to frostbite. But frostbite can occur on skin covered by gloves or other clothing.

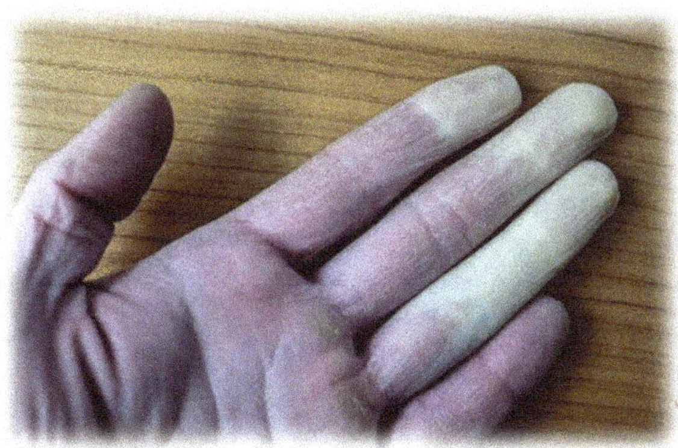

Hypothermia

- is a medical emergency that occurs when your body loses heat faster than it can produce heat, causing a dangerously low body temperature. Normal body temperature is around 98.6 F (37 C). Hypothermia occurs as your body temperature falls below 95 F (35 C).

When your body temperature drops, your heart, nervous system and other organs can't work normally. Left untreated, hypothermia can eventually lead to complete failure of your heart and respiratory system and eventually to death. Hypothermia is often caused by exposure to cold weather or immersion in cold water. Primary treatments for hypothermia are methods to warm the body back to a normal temperature.

Equipment Limitations

Low temperatures can adversely affect the tensile toughness of many commonly-used materials in the engineering world. Tensile toughness is a measure of a material's brittleness or ductility (the tendency to deform before fracturing); it is often estimated by calculating the area beneath the stress-strain curve.

- **Ductile materials** – These materials absorb significant amounts of impact energy before fracturing, resulting in tell-tale deformations.

- **Brittle materials** – Brittle materials, on the other hand, tend to shatter on impact.

In general, materials with high ductility and high strength have good tensile toughness. However, depending on the material, tensile toughness can be very sensitive to temperature changes.

Cold weather temperatures can negatively affect the safe working capacity of cranes and heavy-lifting equipment. The steel in these pieces of equipment can experience a shift from ductile to brittle if the temperature drops below a certain point. This shift is known as the "ductile-to-brittle-transition" temperature (DBTT), the "nil-ductility transition" temperature, or the "15 ft*lb transition" temperature, and the temperature at which this shift occurs varies from material to material.

Cold weather affects personal protective equipment as well on several levels ranging from regulator freeze-up to various materials being compromised for penetration rates and integrity. Tyvek, butyl, neoprene and rubber materials as well as others do not fair well in cold temperatures and need to be evaluated prior to use. Decontamination units and solutions may have limitations and regular use items such as hydraulic hoses become more rigid and the hydraulic fluid more viscous which create concerns with the seals.

HYPOTHERMIA

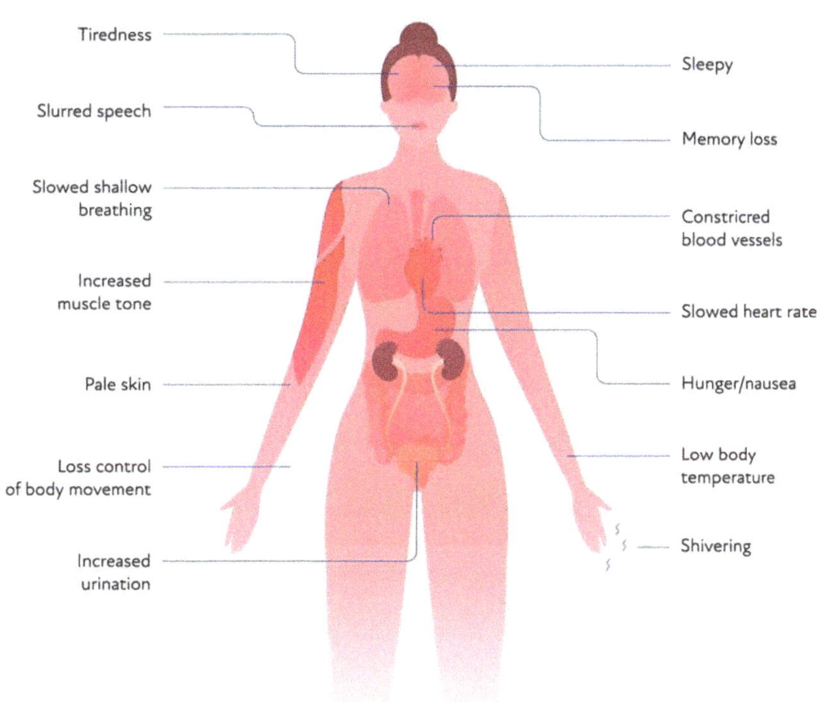

Traffic hazards

Highway, road, street, bridge, tunnel, utility, and other workers for the highway infrastructure are exposed to hazards from outside and inside the work zone. Falls, electrical, struck-by, and caught between are the common hazards found in this type of work.

According to OSHA, transportation incidents and workers struck by vehicles or mobile equipment account for the highest number of fatal work injuries, according to the Bureau of Labor Statistics. Workers such as emergency responders, clean-up, utility, demolition, construction, and others in areas where there are moving vehicles and traffic are exposed to being struck-by moving vehicles. Work zones are used to move traffic in an approved direction and are typically identified by signs, cones, barrels, and barriers.

- Standard highway signs for information, speed limits, and work zones will assist drivers in identifying, in designated traffic paths. Using standard highway signs for internal construction worksite traffic control will assist workers in recognizing the route they are to use at the construction site

- Standard traffic control devices, signals, and message boards will instruct drivers to follow a path away from where work is being done. The authority in charge will determine the approved traffic control devices such as cones, barrels, barricades, and delineator posts that will be used as part of the traffic control plan. These standard devices should also be used inside the work zone.

- Various styles of concrete, water, sand, collapsible barriers, crash cushions, and truck-mounted attenuators are available to limit motorist intrusions into the construction work zone.

- Flaggers and others providing temporary traffic control should wear high visibility clothing with a background of fluorescent orange-red or yellow-green and retroreflective material of orange, yellow, white, silver, or yellow-green. In areas of traffic movement, this personal protective equipment will make the worker visible for at least 1,000 feet, so that the worker can be seen from any direction, and make the worker stand out from the background. Check the label or packaging to ensure that the garments are performance class 2 or 3.

- Flagger stations should be illuminated. Lighting for workers on foot and equipment operators is to be at least 5 foot-candles or greater. Where available lighting is not sufficient, flares or chemical lighting should be used. Glare affecting workers and motorists should be controlled or eliminated.

Welding, Cutting and Brazing Hazards

Health hazards from welding, cutting, and brazing operations include exposures to metal fumes and to ultraviolet (UV) radiation. Safety hazards from these operations include burns, eye damage, electrical shock, cuts, and crushed toes and fingers. Many of these can be controlled with proper work practices and personal protective equipment (PPE).

Hexavalent Chromium

According to OSHA, Hexavalent chromium known as Chromium (VI) is known to cause cancer. In addition, it targets the respiratory system, kidneys, liver, skin and eyes.

Chromium metal is added to alloy steel to increase hardenability and corrosion resistance. A major source of worker exposure to Cr(VI) occurs during "hot work" such as welding on stainless steel and other alloy steels containing chromium metal. Cr(VI) compounds may be used as pigments in dyes, paints, inks, and plastics. It also may be used as an anticorrosive agent added to paints, primers, and other surface coatings. The Cr(VI) compound chromic acid is used to electroplate chromium onto metal parts to provide a decorative or protective coating.

Workplace exposures occur mainly in the following areas:

- Welding and other types of "hot work" on stainless steel and other metals that contain chromium

- Use of pigments, spray paints and coatings

- Operating chrome plating baths

Radiant Energy

Electromagnetic energy given off by an arc or flame can injure workers' eyes and is commonly referred to as radiant energy or light radiation. For protection from radiant energy, workers must use personal protective equipment, such as safety glasses, goggles, welding helmets, or welding face shields. This equipment must have filter lenses with a shade number that provides the appropriate level of protection.

A shade number indicates the intensity of light radiation that is allowed to pass through a filter lens to one's eyes. Therefore, the higher the shade number, the darker the filter and the less light radiation that will pass through the lens.

OSHA Recommendations			
Operation	Arc Current (Amperes)	OSHA Minimum Protective Shade Number	ANSI & AWS Shade Number Recommendations
Light Cutting	Under 300	8	9
Medium Cutting	300 to 400	9	12
Heavy Cutting	400 to 800	10	14

Controlling Fumes and Gases

Welding joins materials together by melting a metal work piece along with a filler metal to form a strong joint. The welding process produces visible smoke that contains harmful metal fume and gas bi-products.

The factors that affect worker exposure are:

- Type of welding process

- Base metal and filler metals used

- Welding rod composition

- Location (outside, enclosed space)

- Welder work practices

- Air movement

- Use of ventilation controls

The fumes and gases that are generated included:

Metals:

- Aluminum, Antimony, Arsenic

- Beryllium, Cadmium, Chromium, Cobalt

- Copper, Iron, Lead

- Manganese, Molybdenum

- Nickel, Silver, Tin, Titanium, Vanadium, Zinc.

Gases:

- Shielding Gases – argon, nitrogen, carbon dioxide

- Process gases – nitric oxide, phosgene, hydrogen fluoride

Working at Heights Hazards

Fundamentals

Falling from one level to another level is the most critical consequence of working at heights. Work positioning systems used to raise or lower workers to the desired height are a major cause of falling incidents. Examples of these systems are: ladders, scaffolds, elevating work platforms, vehicle mounted aerial devices, suspended access equipment (swing stage), boatswain's chairs and mast-climbing work platforms.

Regulations outline clothing, equipment and devices for workers who are at risk of the following:

- Falling more than 3 metres

- Falling more than 1.2 metres, if the work area is used as a path for a wheelbarrow or similar equipment

- Falling into operating machinery

- Falling into water or another liquid

- Falling into or onto a hazardous substance or object

- Falling through an opening on a work surface.

Workers exposed to these falling hazards must be adequately protected by a guardrail system that is designed by a professional engineer in accordance with good engineering practices. If it is not reasonably possible to install a guardrail system, a worker must be adequately protected by at least one of the following methods of protection:

- a travel restraint system

- a fall restricting system

- a fall arrest system (other than a restricting system designed for use in wood pole climbing) and a safety net.

Suspended platforms, and scaffolds must all be designed by a professional engineer. Several elevating devices listed in the Regulations must also meet CSA standards.

Systems and Components

There are three main systems of fall protection, fall arrest, travel restraint and safety net. Even though a travel restraint system is worn by the worker it is considered a control along the path because it prevents a worker from reaching the edge of the roof where they could fall.

Fall Arrest System

A Personal Fall Arrest System (PFAS) includes a full body harness, connector, lifeline, and certified anchorage components. An assembly of components joined together that when connected to a fixed support, is capable of arresting a worker's fall. It should stop a fall within 0.6 metres of the worker's original position.

A fall arrest system consists of the following Travel Restraint System:

- a full body harness (CSA-certified)

- lanyard (with locking snap hooks or D-rings)

- shock absorber

- rope grab

- lifeline and lifeline anchor.

Full body harnesses should be checked before use for flaws such as damage to webbing, bent or broken grommets, loose stitching and missing parts. Fall restricting systems, a type of fall arrest system, includes a harness and retractable device that restricts the distance a worker will fall.

Safety Net System

Protects workers from falling from a surface of more than three metres. It must be located and supported in such a way that it arrests the fall of workers who may fall into it without endangering them.

Anchorage

An anchor point should be independent of the supporting or suspension system of the worker.

Anchorage used for vertical fall arrest should be located directly above the work area.

Permanent Anchor Points

A permanent anchor system used as the fixed support in a fall arrest system, fall- restricting system or travel restraint system must adhere to the Building Code and it must be safe and practical to use as a fixed support.

Temporary Anchor Points

If the requirements for a permanent anchor system are not met, the minimum anchorage requirements for the temporary fixed support are outlined in the Regulations that include:

- travel restraint

- fall arrest

- fall restricting

Vertical Lifelines

- Vertical Lifelines (VLL) are for vertical access or ladder protection. Two typical examples are:

    - $\frac{5}{8}$" diameter (three-strand or kernmantle) synthetic fibre rope, with compatible rope grab.

- $\frac{3}{16}$" diameter Self-Retracting Lifeline (SRL) Independent Wire Rope Core (IWRC) wire rope, with fall-indicating snap hook.

- Vertical lifelines should be suspended separately from any work position or platform system, unless authorized by an engineer.

- Primary anchorage to a commercial lighting truss system is not recommended for any vertical lifeline system, unless authorized by an engineer.

- Overclimbing a self-retracting lifeline anchor point is not recommended by any manufacturer.

- An energy-absorbing lanyard should not be used in combination with a self-retracting lifeline, unless the lifeline manufacturer specifically includes one for use within the system.

- A self-retracting lifeline should be attached directly to the dorsal D-ring on a full-body harness. A sternal D-ring connection may be allowed in some applications for vertical ladder climbing only.

- Synthetic lifelines should not be used in direct proximity to pyrotechnics or high-heat luminaires.

- A self-retracting lifeline should not be stored in an extended position unless permitted by the manufacturer.

Horizontal Lifelines

- Horizontal Lifelines (HLL) installations include rigging grids and lighting systems. Two typical examples of manufactured systems are:

  - $\frac{5}{8}$"diameter (three-strand or kernmantle) synthetic fibre rope, with energy absorber, tensioning device and connecting O-rings.

  - $\frac{3}{8}$" diameter IWRC (independent wire rope core) wire rope, with energy absorber and tensioning device.

- Minimum anchorage requirements and vector force calculations vary by manufacturer. The interpretation of these calculations shall be made by a professional engineer.

- Snap hooks must be connected to the supplied O-ring on a synthetic horizontal lifeline.

- Commercially available horizontal lifelines should always be used as directed by the manufacturer.

- The number of workers using a horizontal lifeline system should not exceed the manufacturer's specifications.

- Synthetic lifelines should not be used in direct proximity to pyrotechnics or high-heat luminaries.

Chapter 5:

Containment Introduction

A vessel is a container in which materials are processed, treated or stored, and are extremely diverse in design and function. The core factors affecting which vessel is used are pressure requirements, type of product contained, temperature requirements, corrosion factors and volume needed.

Hazardous materials personnel and first responders will be exposed to a wide array of vessels throughout their career that will range from small waste collections drums to large industrial towers and tanks. In each case, personnel must be able to clearly identify the type of vessels being observed in order to ensure all safety measures are in place prior to engagement.

In this module, specific vessels will be discussed to provide a complete working knowledge of various vessels that may be encountered throughout various industrial sectors. It is important to note that various categories of vessels may also be broken further into smaller categories and requires thorough investigation prior to conducting any work.

Fundamental Terms

Articulated Drain – a hinged drain attached to the roof of an external floating roof tank that moves up and down as the roof and fluid levels rise and fall

Atmospheric Tank – an enclosed vessel that operates at atmospheric pressure, usually cylindrical in shape and equipped with either a fixed or floating roof that contains nontoxic vapour liquids

Bin/Hopper – a vessel that typically holds dry solids

Blanketing – the process of putting an inert gas such as nitrogen into the vapour space above the liquid in a tank to prevent air leakage into the tank

Boot – the section in the lowest are of the process vessel where water or other liquids are collected and removed

Containment Wall – an earthen berm or constructed wall used to protect against tank failures, runoff and spills

Cylinder – a vessel that can hold extremely volatile or high-pressure materials often referred to as high pressure tanks

Drum – a specialized type of storage tank or intermediary process vessel

Fixed Bed Reactor – a reactor vessel in which the catalyst bed is stationary, and the reactants are passed over it

Fixed Roof – a type of vessel cover used on storage tanks that is fixed to the tank and is used for liquids with high flash points and liquids with slightly higher than atmospheric pressure

Floating Roof – a type of vessel cover, either plastic or steel, used on storage tanks, that floats upon the surface of the stored liquid and is used to decrease vapour space and reduce the potential for evaporation

Foam Chamber – a reservoir and piping installed on liquid storage vessels and containing fire extinguishing media

Gauge Hatch – an opening on the roof of a tank used to check tank levels and obtain samples

Mist Eliminator – a device on the top of a tank that is composed of mesh, vanes or fibres, that collects droplets of mist from gas to prevent it from leaving the tank

Pressurized Tank – an enclosed vessel in which a greater-than-atmosphere pressure is maintained

Reactor – a vessel in which chemical reactions are initiated and sustained

Spherical Tank – a type of pressurized storage tank often referred to as a round tank that is used to store volatile or highly pressurized material

Stirred Tank Reactor – a reactor vessel that contains a mixer or agitator to improve mixing of reactants

Sump – an area of temporary storage located at the bottom of the tank from which an undesirable material is removed

Tank – a large container or vessel for holding liquids and/or gases

Vapour Recovery System – the process of recapturing vapours by methods such as chilling or scrubbing

Vessel – a container which materials are processed, treated, or stored

Vortex – a cone formed by swirling liquid or gas

Specifications

United Nations

Developed as a set of standards, by the United Nations, UN ratings are essential for shipping or storing hazardous materials. The UN Rating is a series of number and letter codes that show what a container is regulated to handle. They determine this through a series of tests that all containers must undergo if they are to be UN Rated.

Current UN Regulations are enforced by both Transport Canada through TDG and the Department of Transportation, D.O.T.

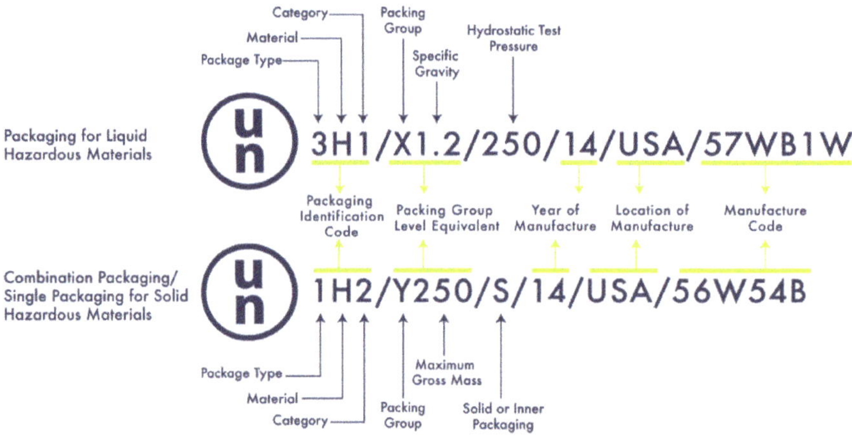

Package Type

1 – drums or pails

2 – wooden barrel

3 – jerrican

4 – box

5 – bag

6 – composite packaging

7 – pressure receptacle

Material

A – steel

B – aluminum

C – natural wood

D – plywood

F – reconstituted wood

G – fibreboard

H – plastic

L – textile

M -= paper, multi-wall

N – metal

P – glass, porcelain, stoneware

Category

1 – non-removable drum head

2 – removable drum head

Packing Group

X – packaging meets Group I, II and III tests

Y – packaging meets Group II and III tests

Z – packaging meets Group III tests

Density or Specific Gravity

Density – For solids that have inner packaging they need to be marked with the maximum gross mass (weight) in kilograms.

Specific Gravity – Stand alone packaging meant to hold liquids need to be marked with the specific gravity rounded down to the first decimal.

Solids/Inner Packaging

Solids – an "S" in upper case will follow the density

Liquids – must show the hydrostatic test pressure in kPa rounded to the nearest 10 kPa.

Underwriters Laboratories Of Canada 

Underwriters Laboratories of Canada (ULC) is an independent product safety testing, certification and inspection organization. ULC has tested products for public safety for 90 years and we are accredited by the Standards Council of Canada and International Accreditation Service, Inc.

ULC's safety certification services include testing, evaluation and factory surveillance of products to Canadian and international standards for safety. These certifications enhance the safety of products as well as the public's confidence in their compliance. Consumers, retailers, insurers, distributors and regulators recognize our familiar Marks as trusted symbols of safety.

The marks shown and explained below are owned and controlled by ULC and used to indicate a product has been certified using the Canadian Safety Scheme. A directory of certified products is available online via the Online Certifications Directory, however, only products bearing the mark are certified.

The traditional ULC Listing Mark consists of four required elements:

- ULC in a circle symbol

- The word LISTED

- Product name or company name/file number

- Issue/serial number or alphanumeric control number

Marking system

Labels

Marking and labeling are important steps when preparing a dangerous good package for transportation. Labels often communicate the hazards associated with the package, and markings ensure the shipment is handled so that spills, accidents and exposure are prevented. As such, they must be applied appropriately, reflect correct information, and comply with the regulations.

Marking means a descriptive name, identification number, instructions, cautions, weight, specification, or UN marks, or combinations thereof, required on outer packaging of hazardous materials or dangerous goods.

Labels identify the specific primary and subsidiary hazards posed by the materials in a dangerous goods package. These methods of communication rely on specific colors, codes, and pictograms to clearly and immediately identify the type of materials in the package.

Transportation of Dangerous Goods identify classification and marking under SOR/2014 Part 2.

Department of Transportation includes hazardous materials markings under 49 CFR 172, 173, and 178 as follows:

Placards

Placards provide information about hazards to transportation workers and emergency responders. Typically, placards are found on tank cars, cargo and portable tanks, bulk packages and vehicles. Please refer to Section 4 Hazmat Classification for a detailed explanation of each classification.

Transportation of Dangerous Goods

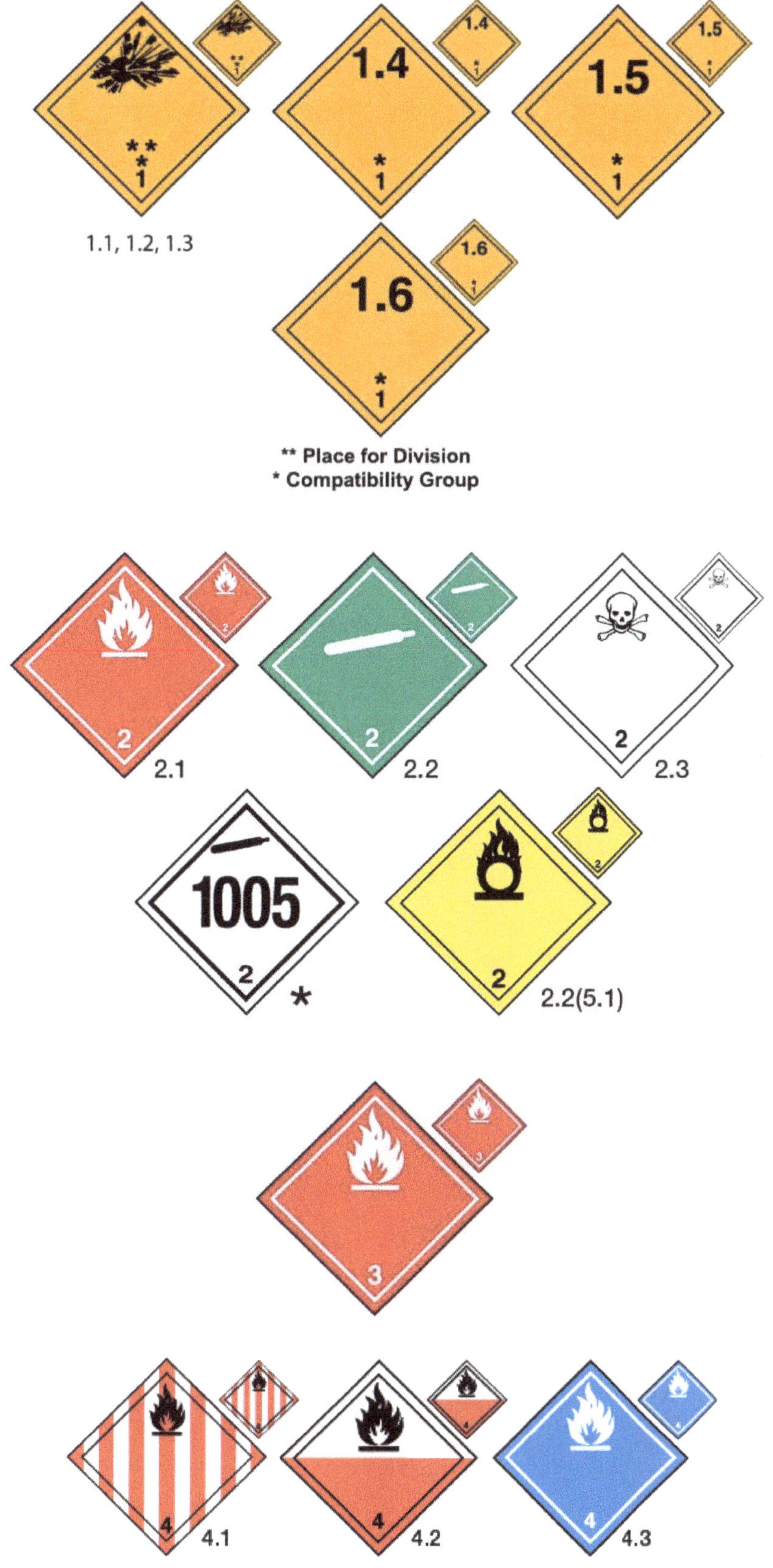

1.1, 1.2, 1.3
1.4
1.5
1.6
** Place for Division
* Compatibility Group
2.1
2.2
2.3
1005
2.2(5.1)
4.1
4.2
4.3

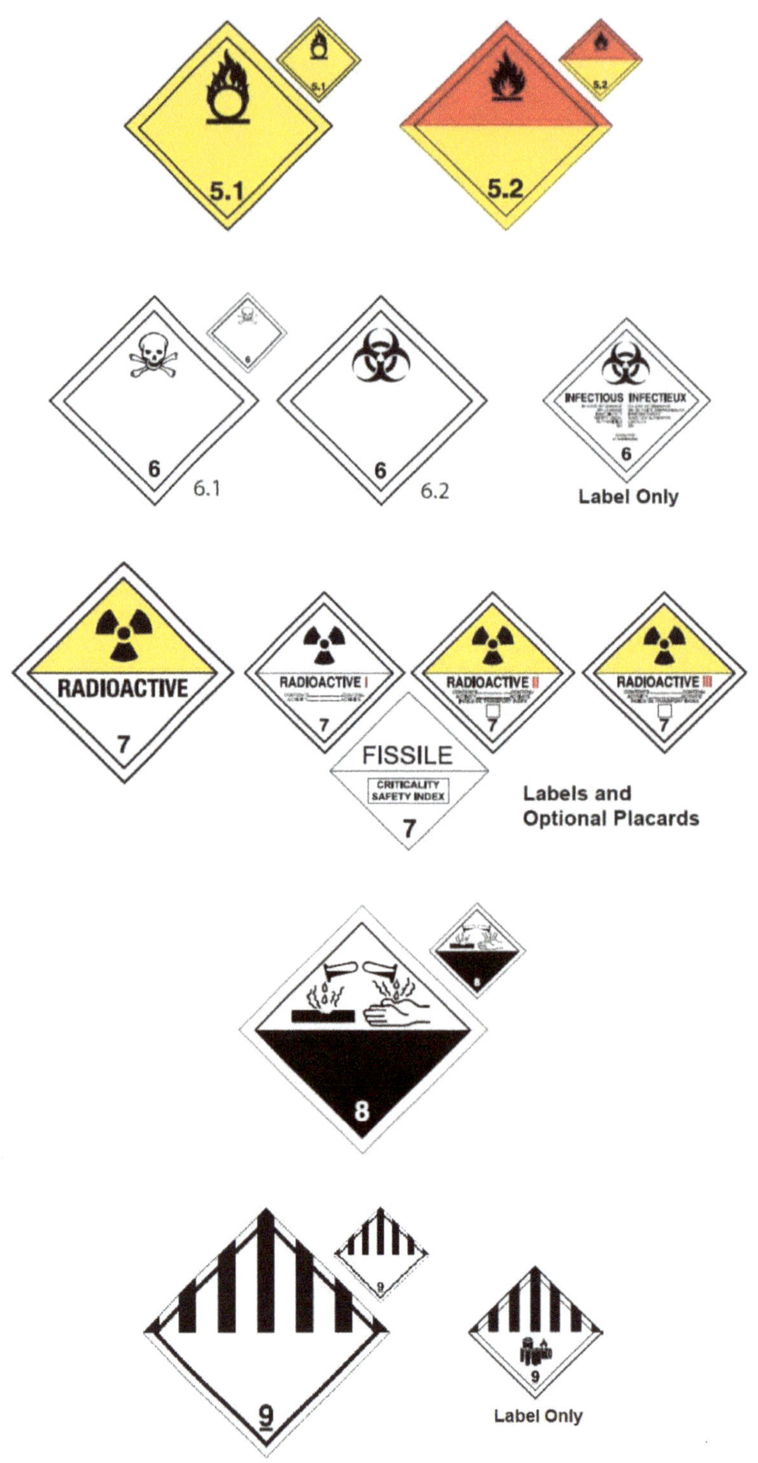

Department of Transportation 

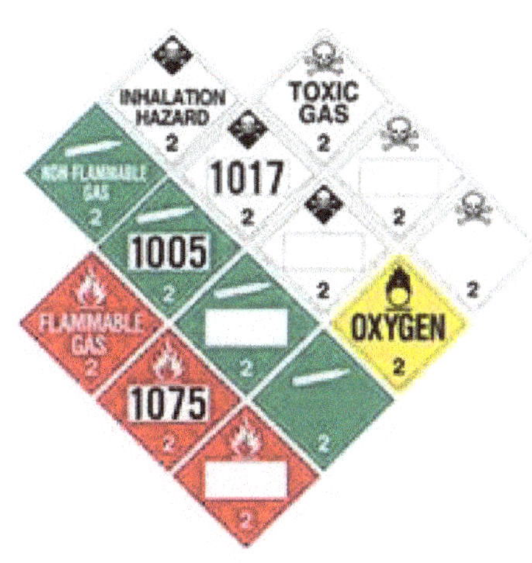

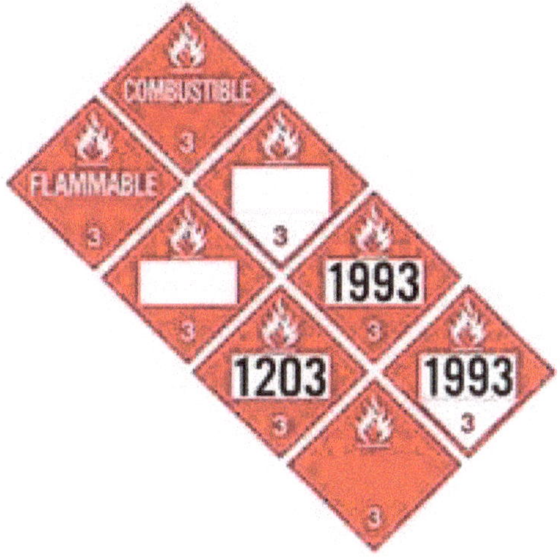

FLAMMABLE SOLID
DANGEROUS
1325
SPONTANEOUSLY COMBUSTIBLE
3170
3190

OXIDIZER
5.1
ORGANIC PEROXIDE
2014
5.2
5.1
5.2
5.1
5.1

POISON
6
TOXIC
6
INHALATION HAZARD
2811
6
6
6
PG III
6
6

NFPA 704 marking system 

The NFPA 704 Marking System provide information about hazards that occur during and emergency response. Typically placards are found outside buildings on doors, on tanks and are clearly visible for emergency responders.

NFPA 704 provides a simple, readily recognized, easily understood system for identifying the specific hazards of a material and the severity of the hazard that would occur during an emergency response. The system addresses the health, flammability, instability, and special hazards presented from short-term, acute exposures that could occur as a result of a fire, spill, or similar emergency.

NFPA Rating Explanation Guide

RATING NUMBER	HEALTH HAZARD	FLAMMABILITY HAZARD	INSTABILITY HAZARD	RATING SYMBOL	SPECIAL HAZARD
4	Can be lethal	Will vaporize and readily burn at normal temperatures	May explode at normal temperatures and pressures	ALK	Alkaline
3	Can cause serious or permanent injury	Can be ignited under almost all ambient temperatures	May explode at high temperature or shock	ACID	Acidic
				COR	Corrosive
2	Can cause temporary incapacitation or residual injury	Must be heated or high ambient temperature to burn	Violent chemical change at high temperatures or pressures	OX	Oxidizing
1	Can cause significant irritation	Must be preheated before ignition can occur	Normally stable. High temperatures make unstable	☢	Radioactive
				₩	Reacts violently or explosively with water
0	No hazard	Will not burn	Stable	₩ OX	Reacts violently or explosively with water and oxidizing

Military Marking System

The United States military tries to use markings such as the Department of Transportation (DOT) placards, labels, and NFPA 704 as much as possible both while materials are in transportation and once stored at a fixed facility. However, there are times when a special marking system developed by the military must be used since:

- the primary reason is that the military marking system is not language dependent

- the military uses the marking systems within facilities when working around ammunition such as rockets, missiles, and other devices.

Military hazardous materials markings provide information on

- explosives

- special chemical hazards.

Class 1, Division 1 - Materials that present a mass detonation hazard.

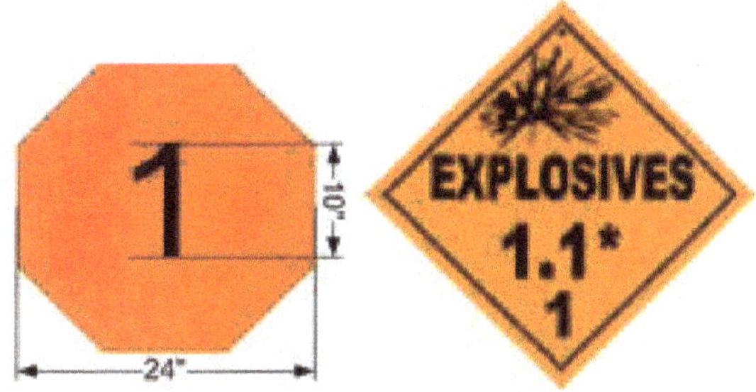

Examples – Hand grenades, general purpose bombs, 40 mm HEDP

Class 1, Division 2 – Projection Hazard.

Examples – HE Mortars, tank rounds

Class 1, Division 3 – Fire Hazard.

Examples – 155mm Illum, Flares, and signal illuminations.

Class 1, Division 4 – Minor Explosion Hazard.

Examples – 7.62mm, 5.56mm, 45 cal, 9mm ammunition

Set 1, Highly Toxic Chemical Agent

- Examples – Nerve and blistering agents

Set 2, Harassing Agent

- Examples – Choking gases, vomiting agents, screening smokes

Set 3, White Phosphorous Munitions

Apply No Water

Wear Breathing Apparatus

Documentation

Inventory

The following are the requirements that must be met to ensure proper labeling for the shipment and storage of containers.

- All Lab Packs require a Packing List. Additionally, all dangerous lab packs must be labeled in accordance with TDG Clear Language or Department of Transportation, D.O.T.

- Labels must include the Proper Shipping Name, Classification, and Packing Group Number.

The label is to be displayed on any side of the container, package or overpack, other than the side on which it is intended to rest.

Containers must have:

- An appropriate Class Label must be affixed to the container.

- A copy of the packing list must be attached to the container, preferably on the side for easy access, and protected from the elements (i.e. plastic cover for the packing list).

- Any cautionary notes if required

Bill of Lading

A bill of lading (sometimes abbreviated as B/L or BoL) is a document issued by a carrier (or their agent) to acknowledge receipt of cargo for shipment. Although the term historically related only to carriage by sea, a bill of lading may today be used for any type of carriage of goods.

This document is used for Non-Regulated Waste and must include a detailed description of the waste. Additionally, documentation is Province, Industry and Waste Specific and may be required.

Movement Document

Movement documents are required under the Export and Import of Hazardous Waste and Hazardous Recyclable Material Regulations (EIHWHRMR) and the Basel Convention to:

- Ease border crossings.

- Track shipments to their authorized destination for disposal or recycling.

- Report on actual transboundary movement of HW and HRM.

Part A - To be completed by the Generator (Consignor)

- **Provincial ID Number** - Enter Provincial Identification Number. It is a unique identifier used for provincial waste tracking purposes.

- **Generators Specific Information** - Enter Generators' name and mailing address. Enter physical address or LSD number of generating site. PO Box Numbers and R.R. Numbers are not allowed.

- **Intended Consignee Specific Information** - Complete name of Receiver and Receiver's Provincial Identification number. Enter Receiver's mailing address. Enter physical location (street address or LSD) of receiving site.

- **Physical State** - Enter physical state of waste (L = liquid, S = solid, X = gas). Write CL TDG shipping name, with Waste and description in parentheses after the CL TDG name.

- **Waste ID: Provincial Number** - The Provincial Number is not required in western Canada.

- **Product Identification Number (PIN)** - Enter PIN, as found in Schedule III, CL TDG Regulations.

- **Quantity Shipped** - Enter quantity of waste and units. Indicate units in KG (kilograms) for solids or L (liters) for liquids.

- **Classification** - Enter primary waste classification followed, in parenthesis, by subsidiary classifications.

- **Packing Group** - Enter Packing Group

- **Packing Instructions** - Packaging numbers and codes are entered to indicate how many packages are being shipped and the code for the type of packaging for shipping.

- o **Package Type**:

  - Drum   – 01
  - Tank   – 02
  - Bulk   – 03
  - Carton   – 04
  - Bag   – 05
  - Roll-off or Lugger Bin   – 06
  - Other   – 07

- **Special Handling Instructions** - List or attach special handling/emergency instructions to assist in the event of a spill or other emergency. Mark the appropriate box to indicate if the instructions are attached or are written in the area provided on the manifest.

- **Date Shipped** - Enter the shipping date (YY/MM/DD format); the time the shipment leaves the generating site; and the expected time of arrival at the receiving site.

- **Circulation Number** - Circulation Number is not required in western Canada.

- **Consignor Certification** - Consignor certification is to be completed by an authorized representative of the Generator. Provide printed name, signature, and telephone number.

Part B - To be Completed by the Carrier

- **Carrier Information** - The transporter company name and address must be shown.

- **Provincial ID Number** - The ABC # is required. Contact the individual trucking company to determine all the required information prior to moving the waste.

- **Name** - The driver's name, signature and telephone number is required to certify delivery.

Part C - To be Completed by the Consignee (Receiver)

- **Provincial ID Number** - The Receiver number

- **Receiver Information** - The receiver name, address and site location must be recorded in this section of the manifest. It is your responsibility to ensure that the Receiver is able to process the waste and that they have all the correct licenses in place.

- **Quantity Received** - This section will be completed by the receiver of the waste. It should be the same as the quantity shipped unless there was a problem weighing the waste or a discrepancy.

- **Handling Code** - This information will be completed by the receiver.

- **Authorized Person** – This should be signed by the Receiver of the waste.

Normal Distribution

- White Copy   Forward to applicable Provincial Authority, as instructed on back of manifest.

- Green Copy   Generator (Consignor) to Retain.

- Yellow Copy   Forward to appropriate provincial authority.

- Pink Copy   Retained by the carrier.

- Blue Copy   Receiving Facility to Retain.

- Brown Copy   Forwarded back to the Generator by the Receiver.

Inter-Provincial Manifest Distribution

White Copy (Copy 1) and Yellow Copy (Copy 3) are to be photocopied and are forwarded to the provincial authorities of the province of destination (receiver). The Original White Copy (Copy 1) and Yellow Copy (Copy 3) are sent to the provincial authority in the province from which the waste originated.

International shipments, Environment Canada receives copies.

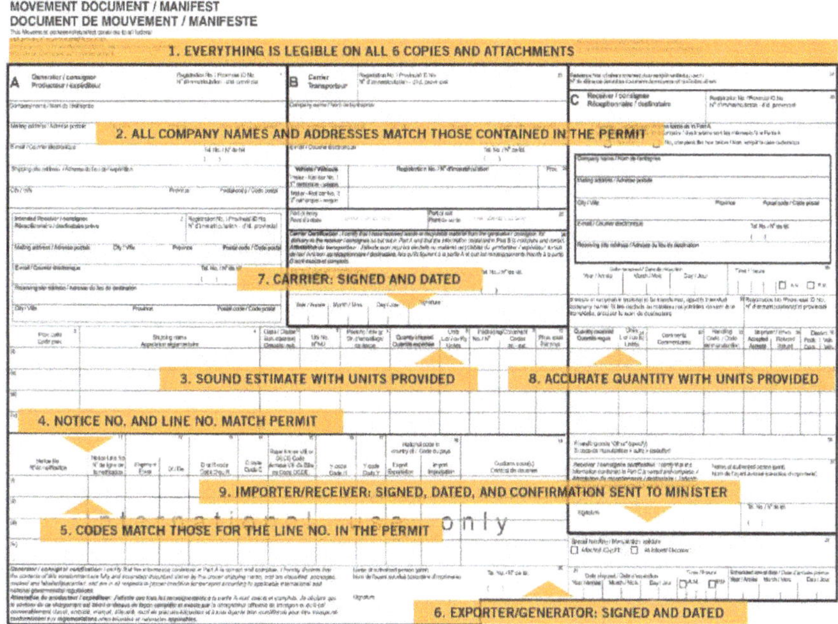

Oilfield Waste Form, Alberta

In addition to all of the various hazardous and non-hazardous waste streams, Alberta regulates oilfield waste under Directive 58, **Oilfield Waste Management Requirements for the Upstream Petroleum Industry.** This directive outlines comprehensive regulatory requirements for the handling, treatment, and disposal of upstream oilfield waste as well as a comprehensive overview of:

- oilfield waste characterization and classification

- waste manifesting and tracking

- oilfield waste management facilities and application requirements for oilfield waste management facilities

- waste management and disposal options.

In all cases, it is the responsibility of the waste generator to ensure that each waste has been properly identified, characterized and handled, treated, and disposed in a proper manner.

Wastes must be classified as either Dangerous Oilfield Waste (DOW) or non-DOW based on the criteria outlined in Table 4.1a, *Properties of Dangerous Oilfield Wastes* and Table 4.lb, *Dangerous Oilfield Wastes.* Sufficient historical data exists for some waste streams whereby common acceptable treatment and disposal practices have been established. These oilfield waste streams are included in Section 7.4 of Appendix 7.0, Waste Management Table

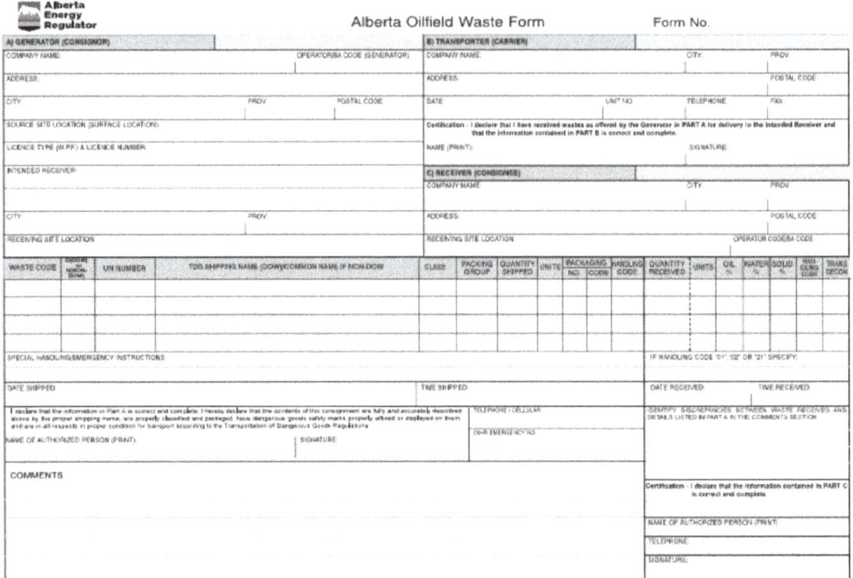

Containers

Small Containment

Bottles

A bottle is a container, typically made of glass or plastic and with a narrow neck, used for storing liquids. Bottles come in all shapes and sizes and are composed of various materials including glass, plastic and metal. Bottles may be clear or amber in colour and often depend on the material they hold.

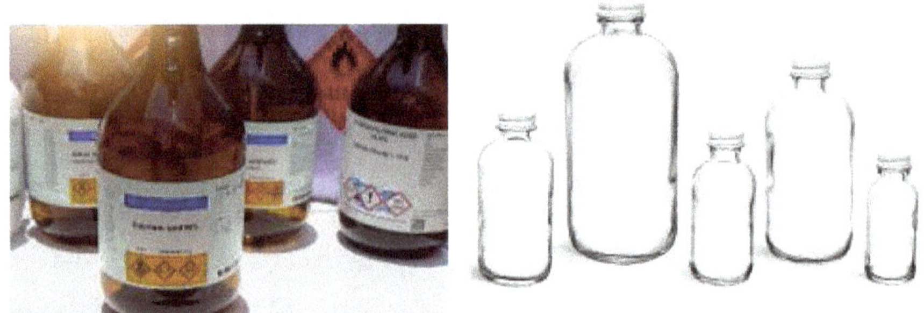

Pails and Jerricans

UN approved pails range in size from 4 litre to 30 litre containers and are generally round or square in shape. They are made of either high density polyethylene plastic or steel with epoxy phenolic lining, and include lids that screw on, snap on, or are closed-lid design.

Jerricans are also made of plastic or steel but unlike pails, are flat-sided

 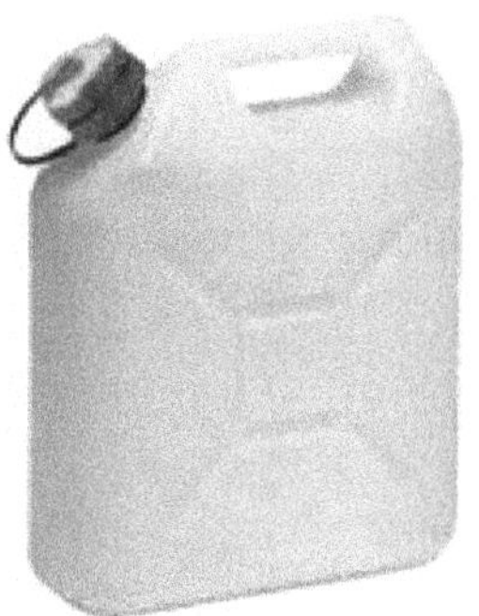

CARBOY

Carboys are also referred to as demijohns and refer to large glass vessels with a narrow neck. Carboys are generally used in transporting chemicals and are commonly used in home-brewing applications.

AEROSOL

An aerosol is defined as a suspension system of solid or liquid particles in a gas. An aerosol includes both the particles and the suspending gas, which is usually air.

Boxes

WOOD

UN approved wood boxes and crates are commonly used for items including machine parts and batteries. The crates themselves come in various sizes and shapes and need to be UN approved with the appropriate labelling on the container.

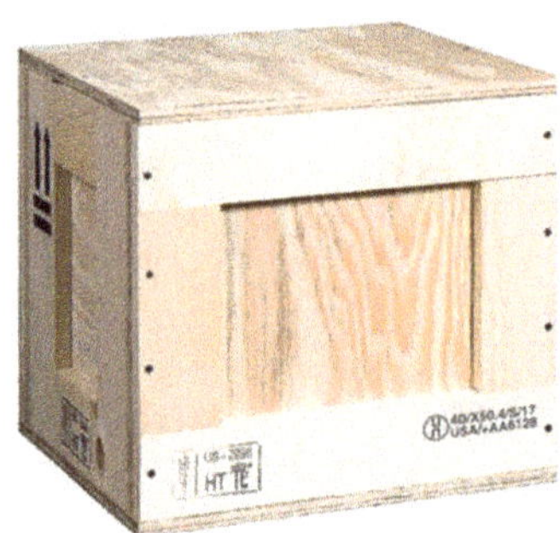

CORREGATED FIBREBOARD

Corrugated fibreboard is widely used in the manufacture of shipping containers and boxes. The material is a 'sandwich' of special purpose papers which can be made up in many different grades, ranging from single wall, comprising one corrugated layer glued between two flat layers, through to triple and occasionally quadruple wall board, of 7 or 9 papers respectively. Corrugated fibreboard is characterised by the weight of a given area of the material, which in Europe and many other parts of the world is expressed in grams per square metre (g/m2). This is often referred to as the board 'grammage'.

Drum

UN approved drums come in several configurations including lined/unlined steel UN drums, plastic and fibre drums, and are designed for a wide range of solids & liquid dangerous goods.

Open head drums (1A2 & 1H2) UN drums and closed head / tight head (1A1 & 1H1) UN drums comply with TDG, 49 CFR, IMDG Code, IATA, & ICAO. Closed-head (1A1) UN steel drums and open-head (1A2) UN steel drums are available in a variety of sizes from 1 gallon to 55 gallon (205 Litre). Phenolic lined & Epoxy-phenolic lined steel UN drums provide maximum protection from dangerous goods that are incompatible with carbon steel.

Totes

INTERMEDIATE BULK CONTAINER, IBC

An intermediate bulk container, IBC, is a pallet mounted, industrial grade reusable container that is used for storing and transporting bulk liquids and powders. Also known as a tote, the IBC is capable of stacking and can be moved by a pallet jack or forklift. The TWO broad types of IBCs in use today can be categorized under:

- Rigid - rigid intermediate bulk containers are stackable, reusable, versatile containers with an integrated pallet base mount that provides forklift and/or pallet jack maneuverability. These containers can be made from metal, plastic, or a composite construction of the two materials.

- Flexible - A standard flexible intermediate bulk container can hold 1,100 to 2,200 lb (499 to 998 kg) and manufacturers offer bags with a volume of 10–100 cu ft (283–2,832 L). In addition to the above materials, flexible IBCs can also be made of fiberboard, wood, aluminum, and folding plastic. Folding IBCs are also made of heavy plastic. Flexible intermediate bulk containers, made of woven polyethylene or polypropylene bags, are designed for storing or transporting dry, flowable products, such as sand, fertilizer, and plastic granules.

The term intermediate comes from the volume that intermediate bulk containers carry, which sits in between that of tanks and drums. The two most common volumes of the rigid IBC are the 1,000 litre (275 gallon) units.

COMPOSITE

Composite IBCs provide a cost-effective, reliable method of handling storing and shipping liquids. Composite totes are comprised of a high-density polyethylene (HPDE) bottle which is encased in a heavy-duty steel cage. This rigid, galvanized tubular steel grid is designed to offer superior protection and are approved for UN Packaging groups II & III. New tanks are often also rated as food-grade.

STAINLESS STEEL

Stainless steel IBCs are generally constructed from 10-gauge 304 stainless steel for strength and durability. They feature a one-piece sloped bottom, 22½" top opening, 2" top bung and a 2" bottom outlet with a ball valve and range in capacity. Generally the IBC features a standard base dimension of 42"x48" for ease when using s standard pallet. Stainless steel tanks are UN31A certified for the transport of flammable and combustible liquids and are used in a variety of industries including the petrochemical, pharmaceutical, flavor and fragrances, and food and beverage industries.

BAGS

A flexible intermediate bulk container (FIBC), bulk bag, or big bag, is an industrial container made of flexible fabric that is designed for storing and transporting dry, flowable products, such as sand, fertilizer, and granules of plastic.

FIBCs are most often made of thick woven polyethylene or polypropylene, either coated or uncoated, and normally measure around 45–48 inches (114–122 cm) in diameter and varies in height from 100 to 200 cm (39 to 79 inches). Its capacity is normally around 1,000 kg or 2,200 lb, but the larger units can store even more. A bulk bag designed to transport one metric ton (0.98 long tons; 1.1 short tons) of material will itself only weigh 5–7 lb (2.3–3.2 kg).

Cylinders

All compressed gases are hazardous because of the high pressures inside the cylinders. Gas can be released deliberately by opening the cylinder valve, or accidentally from a broken or leaking valve or from a safety device. Even at a relatively low pressure, gas can flow rapidly from an open or leaking cylinder.

There are three major groups of compressed gases stored in cylinders:

Liquified Gases:

- Gases which can become liquids at normal temperatures in cylinders under pressure.

- Exist inside the cylinder in a liquid-vapour balance or equilibrium.

- Anhydrous ammonia, chlorine, propane, nitrous oxide and carbon dioxide.

Non-Liquefied Gases:

- Non-liquefied gases are also known as compressed, pressurized or permanent gases.

- Do not liquefy when they are compressed at normal temperatures, even at very high pressures.

- Oxygen, nitrogen, helium and argon.

Dissolved Gases:

- Acetylene is the only common dissolved gas. Acetylene is chemically very unstable. Even at atmospheric pressure, acetylene gas can explode.

- Acetylene cylinders are fully packed with an inert, porous filler. When acetylene gas is added to the cylinder, the gas dissolves in the acetone.

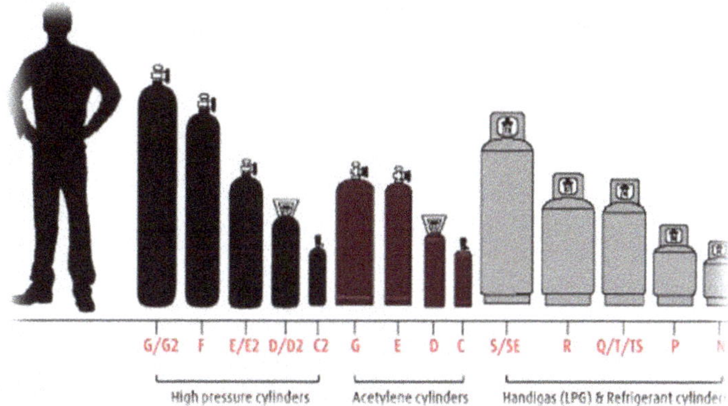

Cryogenic

Cryogenic liquid containers, also referred to as liquid cylinders, are double-walled vacuum vessels with multilayer insulation in the annular space. They are designed for the reliable and economic transportation and storage of liquefied gases at cryogenic temperatures, typically colder than −130°F (−90°C). There are two primary advantages of a liquid container:

- it contains a large volume of gas at a relatively low pressure compared to a compressed gas cylinder.

- it provides a source of cryogenic liquids which can be easily handled.

The cryogenic products normally found in liquid containers are:

- liquid nitrogen (LIN)

- liquid argon (LAR)

- liquid oxygen (LOX)

- liquid helium (LHE).

Carbon dioxide and nitrous oxide are also available as refrigerated liquids in similar containers.

NOTE: Cryogenic liquid containers *are often incorrectly referred to as Dewars* – Dewars are open, non-pressurized vessels for holding cryogenic liquids where liquid cylinders as noted above are pressurized.

Intermodal Containers

Intermodal Tank Markings

An intermodal container is a large standardized shipping container, designed and built for intermodal freight transport, meaning these containers can be used across different modes of transport, From ship to rail to truck, without unloading and reloading their cargo.

Intermodal containers are primarily used to store and transport materials and products efficiently and securely in the global containerized intermodal freight transport system, but smaller numbers are in regional use as well. These containers are known under a number of names, such as:

- container
- cargo or freight container

- ISO container

- shipping, sea or ocean container

- sea van or (Conex) box

- sea can or c can.

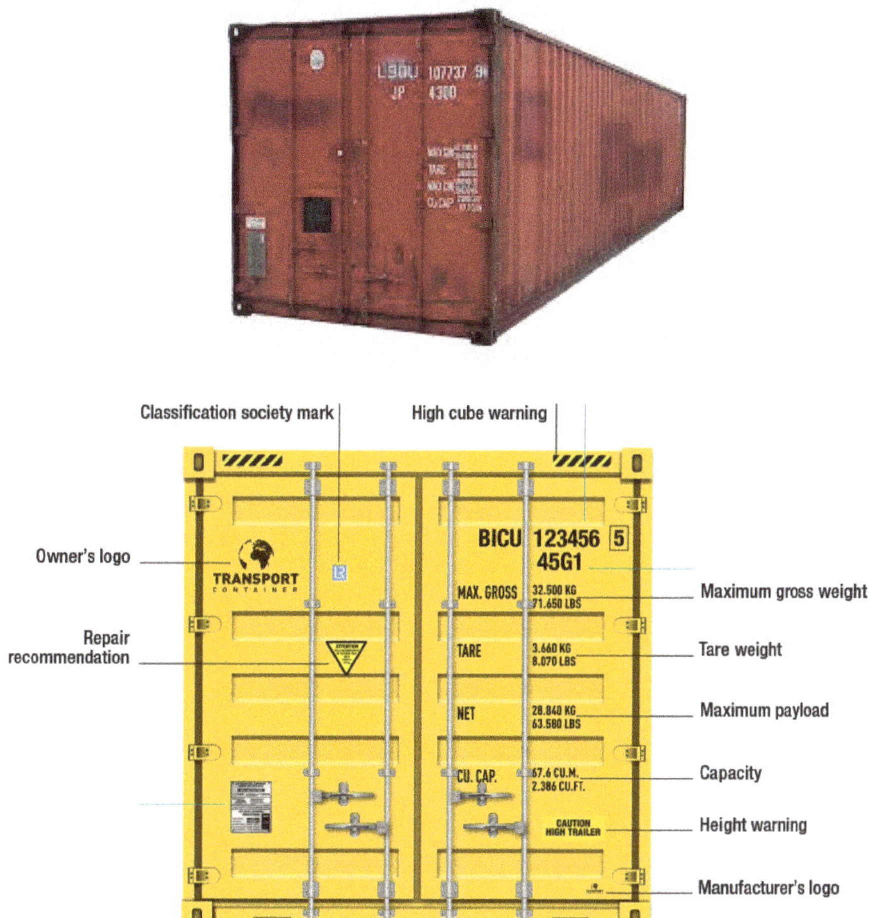

Hazard identification numbers, utilized under European and some South American regulations, may be found in the top half of an orange panel on some intermodal bulk containers. The United Nations 4-digit identification number is in the bottom half of the orange panel.

The hazard identification number in the top half of the orange panel consists of two or three digits. In general, the digits indicate the following hazards:

- 2 - Emission of gas due to pressure or chemical reaction

- 3 - Flammability of liquids (vapors) and gases or self-heating liquid

- 4 - Flammability of solids or self-heating solid

- 5 – Oxidizing (fire-intensifying) effect

- 6 - Toxicity or risk of infection

- 7 - Radioactivity

- 8 - Corrosivity

- 9 - Risk of spontaneous violent reaction

Note: The risk of spontaneous violent reaction within the meaning of digit 9 includes the possibility, due to the nature of a substance, of a risk of explosion, disintegration and polymerization reaction followed by the release of considerable heat or flammable and/or toxic gases.

- Doubling of a digit indicates an intensification of that particular hazard (i.e., 33, 66, 88)

- Where the hazard associated with a substance can be adequately indicated by a single digit, the digit is followed by a zero (i.e., 30, 40, 50)

- A hazard identification number prefixed by the letter "X" indicates that the substance will react dangerously with water (i.e., X88)

The hazard identification numbers listed below have the following meanings:

- 20 Asphyxiant gas or gas with no subsidiary risk

- 22 Refrigerated liquefied gas, asphyxiant

- 223 Refrigerated liquefied gas, flammable

- 225 Refrigerated liquefied gas, oxidizing (fire-intensifying)

- 23 Flammable gas

- 238 Gas, flammable corrosive

- 239 Flammable gas which can spontaneously lead to violent reaction

- 25 Oxidizing (fire-intensifying) gas

- 26 Toxic gas

- 263 Toxic gas, flammable

- 265 Toxic gas, oxidizing (fire-intensifying)

- 268 Toxic gas, corrosive

- 28 Gas, corrosive

- 30 Flammable liquid (flash-point between 23°C and 60°C, inclusive), or flammable liquid or solid in the molten state with a flash point above 60o C, heated to a temperature equal to or above its flash point, or self-heating liquid

- 323 Flammable liquid which reacts with water, emitting flammable gases

- X323 Flammable liquid which reacts dangerously with water, emitting flammable gases

- 33 Highly flammable liquid (flash-point below 23°C)

- 333 Pyrophoric liquid

- X333 Pyrophoric liquid which reacts dangerously with water

- 336 Highly flammable liquid, toxic

- 338 Highly flammable liquid, corrosive

- X338 Highly flammable liquid, corrosive, which reacts dangerously with water

- 339 Highly flammable liquid which can spontaneously lead to violent reaction

- 36 Flammable liquid (flash-point between 23°C and 60°C, inclusive), slightly toxic, or self-heating liquid, toxic

- 362 Flammable liquid, toxic, which reacts with water, emitting flammable gas

- X362 Flammable liquid, toxic, which reacts dangerously with water, emitting flammable gases

- 368 Flammable liquid, toxic, corrosive

- 38 Flammable liquid (flash-point between 23°C and 60°C, inclusive), slightly corrosive or self-heating liquid, corrosive

- 382 Flammable liquid, corrosive, which reacts with water, emitting flammable gases

- X382 Flammable liquid, corrosive, which reacts dangerously with water, emitting flammable gases

- 39 Flammable liquid, which can spontaneously lead to violent reaction

- 40 Flammable solid, or self-reactive substance, or self-heating substance

- 423 Solid which reacts with water, emitting flammable gases, or flammable solid which reacts with water, emitting flammable gases, or self-heating solid which reacts with water, emitting flammable gases

- X423 Solid which reacts dangerously with water, emitting flammable gases, or flammable solid which reacts dangerously with water, emitting flammable gases, or self-heating solid which reacts dangerously with water, emitting flammable gases

- 43 Spontaneously flammable (pyrophoric) solid

- X432 Spontaneously flammable (pyrophoric) solid which reacts dangerously with water, emitting flammable gases

- 44 Flammable solid, in the molten state at an elevated temperature

- 446 Flammable solid, toxic, in the molten state at an elevated temperature

- 46 Flammable or self-heating solid, toxic

- 462 Toxic solid which reacts with water, emitting flammable gases

- X462 Solid which reacts dangerously with water, emitting toxic gases

- 48 Flammable or self-heating solid, corrosive

- 482 Corrosive solid which reacts with water, emitting flammable gases

- X482 Solid which reacts dangerously with water, emitting corrosive gases

- 50 Oxidizing (fire-intensifying) substance

- 539 Flammable organic peroxide

- 55 Strongly oxidizing (fire-intensifying) substance

- 556 Strongly oxidizing (fire-intensifying) substance, toxic

- 558 Strongly oxidizing (fire-intensifying) substance, corrosive

- 559 Strongly oxidizing (fire-intensifying) substance which can spontaneously lead to violent reaction

- 56 Oxidizing substance (fire-intensifying), toxic

- 568 Oxidizing substance (fire-intensifying), toxic, corrosive

- 58 Oxidizing substance (fire-intensifying), corrosive

- 59 Oxidizing substance (fire-intensifying) which can spontaneously lead to violent reaction

- 60 Toxic or slightly toxic substance

- 606 Infectious substance

- 623 Toxic liquid, which reacts with water, emitting flammable gases

- 63 Toxic substance, flammable (flash-point between 23°C and 60°C, inclusive)

- 638 Toxic substance, flammable, (flash-point between 23°C and 60°C, inclusive), corrosive

- 639 Toxic substance, flammable, (flash-point not above 60°C) which can spontaneously lead to violent reaction

- 64 Toxic solid, flammable or self-heating

- 642 Toxic solid which reacts with water, emitting flammable gases

- 65 Toxic substance, oxidizing (fire-intensifying)

- 66 Highly toxic substance 663 Highly toxic substance, flammable (flash-point not above 60°C)

- 664 Highly toxic solid, flammable or self-heating

- 665 Highly toxic substance, oxidizing (fire-intensifying)

- 668 Highly toxic substance, corrosive

- X668 Highly toxic substance, corrosive, which reacts dangerously with water

- 669 Highly toxic substance which can spontaneously lead to violent reaction

- 68 Toxic substance, corrosive

- 69 Toxic or slightly toxic substance which can spontaneously lead to violent reaction

- 70 Radioactive material

- 78 Radioactive material, corrosive

- 80 Corrosive or slightly corrosive substance

- X80 Corrosive or slightly corrosive substance which reacts dangerously with water

- 823 Corrosive liquid which reacts with water, emitting flammable gases

- 83 Corrosive or slightly corrosive substance, flammable (flash-point between 23°C and 60°C, inclusive)

- X83 Corrosive or slightly corrosive substance, flammable (flash-point between 23°C and 60°C, inclusive), which reacts dangerously with water

- 839 Corrosive or slightly corrosive substance, flammable (flash-point between 23°C and 60°C, inclusive), which can spontaneously lead to violent reaction

- X839 Corrosive or slightly corrosive substance, flammable (flash-point between 23°C and 60°C, inclusive), which can spontaneously lead to violent reaction and which reacts dangerously with water

- 84 Corrosive solid, flammable or self-heating

- 842 Corrosive solid which reacts with water, emitting flammable gases

- 85 Corrosive or slightly corrosive substance, oxidizing (fire-intensifying)

- 856 Corrosive or slightly corrosive substance, oxidizing (fire-intensifying) and toxic

- 86 Corrosive or slightly corrosive substance, toxic

- 88 Highly corrosive substance X88 Highly corrosive substance which reacts dangerously with water

- 883 Highly corrosive substance, flammable (flash-point between 23°C and 60°C, inclusive)

- 884 Highly corrosive solid, flammable or self-heating 885 Highly corrosive substance, oxidizing (fire-intensifying)

- 886 Highly corrosive substance, toxic

- X886 Highly corrosive substance, toxic, which reacts dangerously with water

- 89 Corrosive or slightly corrosive substance which can spontaneously lead to violent reaction

- 90 Environmentally hazardous substance; miscellaneous dangerous substances

- 99 Miscellaneous dangerous substance carried at an elevated temperature

Non-Pressure Tank Containers (IM 101 AND IM 102)

Intermodal Tank Containers are non-pressurized vessels of stainless steel surrounded by an insulation and protective layer of usually polyurethane and aluminum. The vessel is in the middle of a steel frame. The frame is made according to ISO standards and is 19.8556 feet (6.05 meters) long, 7.874 feet (2.40 meters) wide and 7.874 feet (2.40 meters) or 8.374 feet (2.55 meters) high. The contents of the tank range from 17,500 to 26,000 liters (3,800 to 5,700 imp gal; 4,600 to 6,900 U.S. gal)

ISO tank containers built to transport hazardous cargo have to meet a variety of regulations including but not limited to IMDG, ADR-RID- US DOT and other. There are a variety of UN Portable tank types, the most common of which is T11 as it is permitted to transport a thousand or more hazardous bulk chemicals.

ISO tank containers come in the following designs:

- Swap body tank - a swap body has a bigger tank which is larger than the frame, usually 23 or 25 feet (7.01 or 7.62 meters) long

- Food-grade tank - a standard tank container which can only be loaded with food-grade products

- Reefer tank - a tank with the ability to cool the product to be transported

- Gas tank - a tank that is suitable for the transport of gases

- Silo tank - a tank for the transport of grains and powders

- T1 ISO tank container (for wine and light liquids)

- T4 ISO tank container (for non-hazardous edible and non-edible oils)

- T11 ISO tank container (for non-hazardous chemicals)

- T14 ISO tank container (for hazardous chemicals and acids like HCl and zinc chloride)

- T50 ISO tank container (for LPG and ammonia gas)

- T75 ISO tank Container (for Cryogenic liquids)

- SWAP tank container (for cargo above 26,000 to 32,000 metric tons or 25,600 to 31,500 long tons or 28,700 to 35,300 short tons)

- Rubber-lined ISO tank container (for acid-based chemicals)

IM 101 and IM 102

IM 101/102 tanks are low pressure tanks (less than 100 psig) and can be either insulated or non-insulated, that have a structural frame for stability. They can hold up to 6,300 USG (24,000 Litres) and are made of stainless steel, steel or aluminum. These tanks are also referred to as International Maritime Organization, IMO, Type 1 & 2.

These tanks are top-loaded tanks that are emptied from the bottom and typically carry flammable liquids, pesticides, corrosives and resins.

2020 Emergency Response Guidebook Guide 117.

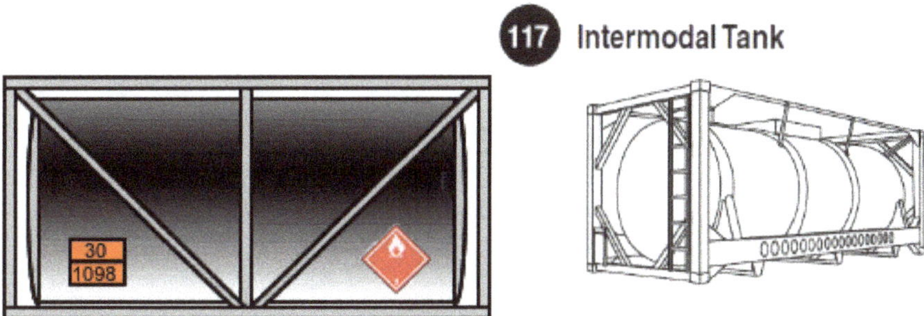

PRESSURE TANK CONTAINERS (DOT SPEC 51 OR IM 5)

DOT Spec 51 (or IMO Type 5) tank containers are high pressure units (500 psig) and can be either insulated or non-insulated, that have a structural frame for stability. They can hold up to 5,500 USG (21,000 Litres) and are made of stainless steel, steel or aluminum.

These tanks are bottom-loaded tanks that are emptied from the bottom and typically carry liquified compressed gases such as propane, high-vapour pressure liquids, and pyrophoric liquids.

2020 Emergency Response Guidebook Guide 117.

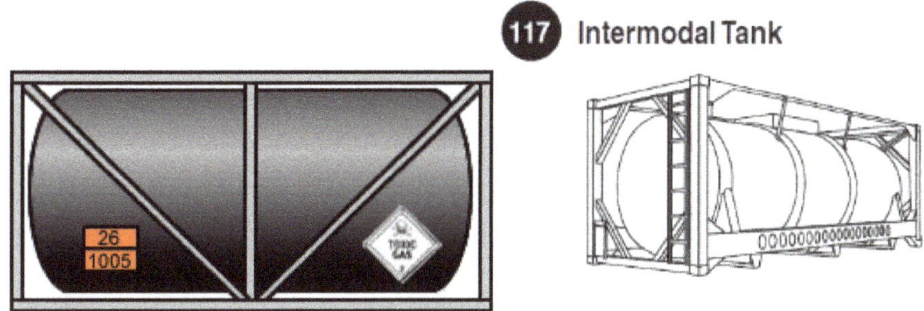

Cryogenic Tank (IMO 7)

IMO 7 tanks are low pressure cryogenic tanks that are insulated, that have a tank-within-a-tank design with the product held in the innermost tank. The unit has a vacuum sealed outer shell with insulation in between the layers and includes a structural frame for stability. They are made of stainless steel or carbon steel.

These tanks are loaded and unloaded from either the top or bottom and carry cryogenic liquids such as nitrogen and oxygen.

2020 Emergency Response Guidebook Guide 117.

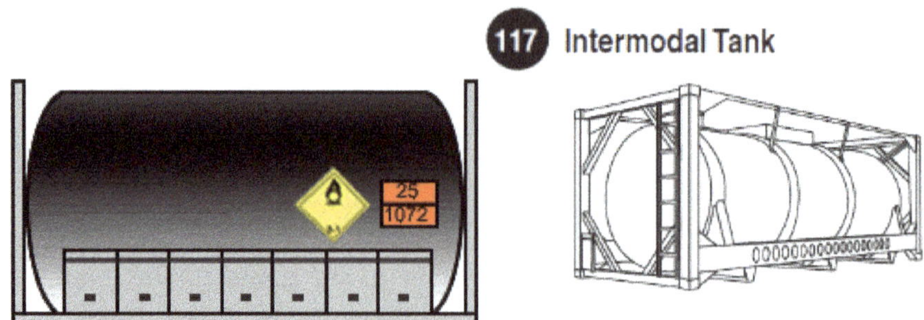

Cargo Tank Trucks

Manufacturer Specification Plates

Each cargo tank truck must have a corrosion resistant metal specification plate attached to it that provides the following information:

- Cargo tank motor vehicle manufacturer and Cargo tank motor vehicle certification date

- Cargo tank manufacturer and Cargo tank date of manufacture

- Maximum payload weight

- Maximum loading rate (per minute) and Maximum unloading rate (per minute)

- Lining material if applicable

- Heating system design pressure if applicable and Heating system design temperature if applicable

Compressed Gas Trailer (MC-331)

MC 331 tankers usually carry a compressed liquified gas at high pressures (100-500psig) such as LPG or anhydrous ammonia. Each tank is specifically designed to meet the physical and chemical specifications of the product being carried.

The tank is tubular in shape with rounded heads and is single compartment without baffles or walls internally. The tanks are made of steel and have no structural frame for support.

2020 Emergency Response Guidebook Guide 117.

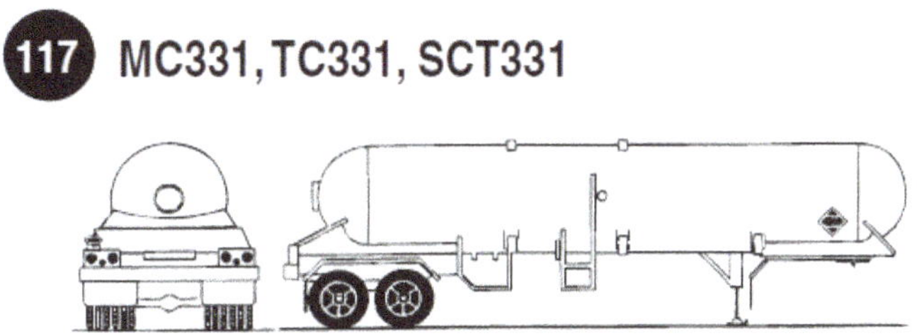

Cryogenic Liquid Tank Truck (MC-338)

MC 338 tankers carry cryogenic liquids at low pressures (25psig) such as liquid oxygen, carbon dioxide and hydrogen. The tank is cylindrical in shape with a box cabinet on the rear for loading and unloading and are a tank-within-a-tank design with the product held in the innermost tank The tanks are made of carbon steel and have no structural frame for support

2020 Emergency Response Guidebook Guide 117.

Flammable Liquids Tank Truck (DOT 406)

DOT 406 tankers generally carry low pressure (4 psig) flammable liquids but may carry items including water and milk. The tank is oval in shape, multi-compartmented and has a roll-over protection for all manways with bottom outlet valves. The tanks are made of aluminum and are generally flat on both ends.

2020 Emergency Response Guidebook Guide 131.

Toxic Tank Truck (DOT 407)

DOT 407 tankers generally carry low pressure (40 psig) mild acids, toxics and some flammable liquids, but may carry items including water and milk. The tank is cylindrical in shape, multi-compartmented and has a roll-over protection for all manways with bottom outlet valves. The tanks are made of stainless steel and are generally flat on both ends.

2020 Emergency Response Guidebook Guide 137.

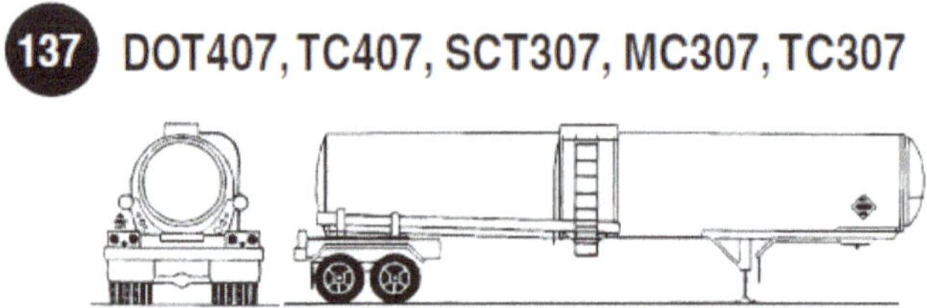

Corrosive Tank Truck (DOT 412)

DOT 412 tankers generally carry low pressure (25 psig) corrosives and high-weight liquids. The tank is cigar in shape, multi-compartmented and has a roll-over protection for all manways with bottom outlet valves. The tanks are made of stainless steel and are generally round on both ends.

2020 Emergency Response Guidebook Guide 137.

Compressed Gas Tube Trailer

Compressed gas tube trailers carry multiple tubes that are each individually contained. Each tube is thermally protected with thermal plugs that are designed to melt during a fire to relieve internal pressure. Generally the trailer holds between 9-12 tubes and carry gases such as helium, nitrogen and argon, all which are off-loaded in a cascade style.

2020 Emergency Response Guidebook Guide 117.

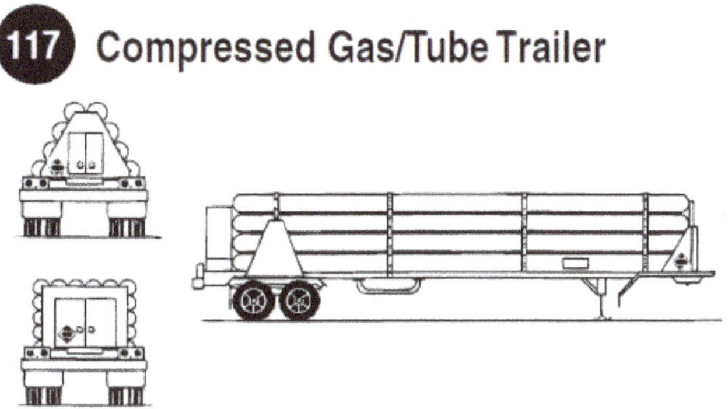

Mixed Cargo Truck

Mixed cargo trucks include cargo trucks that range from 3 tonne units to 53-foot van bodies. The truck can be constructed of various materials ranging from steel to aluminum and may also include soft-shell walls. These units carry both hazardous and non-hazardous materials.

2020 Emergency Response Guidebook Guide 111.

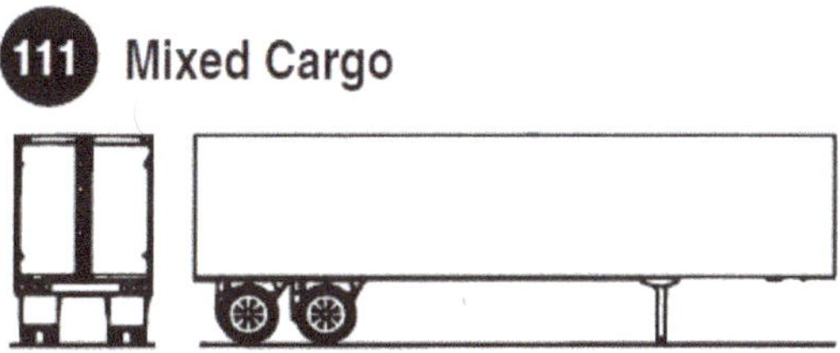

Railroad Tank Cars

Railroad Tank Car Markings

Key markings on the sides and ends of railcars describe the ownership, loading dimensions, and weight characteristics, as well as braking information and other specific equipment on the railcar. Railcars capable of carrying hazardous materials have spaces for standardized hazmat warning placards.

All railcars are identified by reporting marks and car numbers. A reporting mark is an alphabetic code of two to four letters used to identify owners or lessees of rolling stock and other equipment. Combined with the car number, this gives the railcar its unique ID.

The letter codes are assigned to railroads and private railcar owners by the American Association of Railroads' (AAR) subsidiary Railing. Typically, the letter codes are derived from the railroad name; historically, New York Central was NYC, Pennsylvania Railroad was PRR, etc. Private car owners have reporting marks that end in the letter X.

- Dimensional information includes the load limit, indicated by LD LMT, and the railcar's empty tare weight (light weight), indicated by LT WT— both are followed by a total weight figure given in pounds

- The overall dimensions of the car are indicated by a plate figure shown in a black box

- Standard plate dimensions are plates B, C, E, and F, G, H. These dimensions describe a railcar's profile

- EXW describes the extreme width of the car

- EW is the width over the eaves of the railcar

- IL is the interior length

- IW the interior width

- IH is interior height

- Cubic feet, with initials CF (for example: 4750cf), describes overall car volume

- The railcar's original construction date is indicated by BLT followed by numbers reflecting month and year, such as 12-08

- If the car was rebuilt, the initials REBLT are followed by a similar date indication

- Tank cars will have descriptions of maximum capacity in gallons and liters, details on safety valves, and maximum tank pressure in pounds per square inch

- Type of Air Brake Valves On Top – Car Built Date on Bottom:

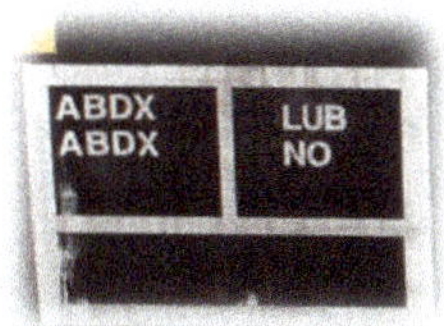

DOT-105-J-500-W

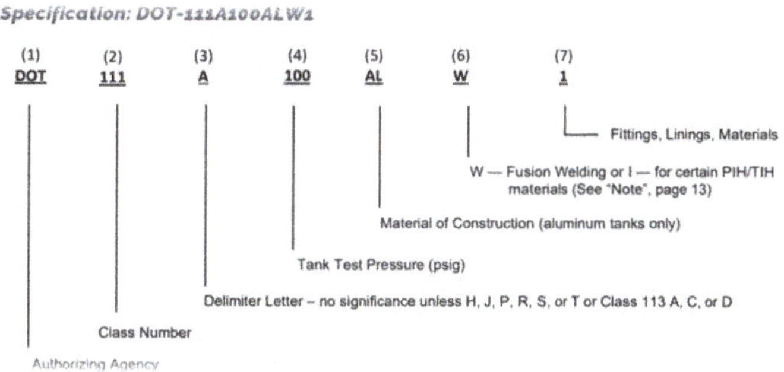

Courtesy of Field Guide to Tank Cars, Fourth Edition, Association of American Railroads

Authorizing Agency

- DOT: Department of Transportation

- CTC: Canadian Transport Commission

- TC: Transport Canada

- AAR: Association of American Railroads

Tank Class Number

- Non-Pressure: 111, 115, 117 (DOT and TC), 206, 211 (AAR)

- Pressure Tank: 105, 109, 112, 114, 120 (DOT and TC), 204 (AAR)

- Cryogenic: 103, 214

Delimiter Letter

- A: No special feature

- S: Equipped with head puncture protection

- T: Thermal protection and head protection

- J: Jacketed with thermal protection and head protection

- R: Car has been retrofitted with safety feature

- H: Tank car authorized for transportation of TIH materials

Cryogenic Liquid Tank Cars

- o A: Authorized for minus 423^0F loading

- o C: Authorized for minus 260^0F loading

- o D: Authorized for minus 155^0F loading

Class – 117 Tank Cars

- o J: Constructed to Class – 117A Specification

- o P: Existing nonpressure tank car that meets performance standards for a Class–117A

- o R: Existing nonpressure tank car retrofitted to conform to retrofit or Class-117A standards

Tank Pressure Test

- The pressure at which the tank was hydrostatically tested at time of construction

Material of Construction

- The letters "AL" after the tank test pressure indicate the tank was constructed of aluminum. If constructed from other materials, no letters or numbers will be shown

Weld Type

- W: Fusion welded tank

- I: Interim standards for TIH car. If tank meets "I" standard, use "H" delimiter letter

Fittings and Lining Materials

SPECIFICATION	INSULATION	BOTTOM OUTLET	BOTTOM WASHOUT	OTHER
W1	Optional	Optional	Optional	
W2	Optional	Prohibited	Optional	
W3	Required	Optional	Optional	
W4	Required	Prohibited	Prohibited	
W5	Optional	Prohibited	Prohibited	Lined
W6	Optional	Optional	Optional	
W7	Optional	Prohibited	Prohibited	

Bottom Washout is used on tank cars when bottom outlet connection is not in use

Pressure Tank Cars

Pressure tank cars are used to transport flammable non-flammable, toxic and liquefied compressed gases and designated by DOT 105 and DOT 112.

2020 Emergency Response Guidebook Guide 117.

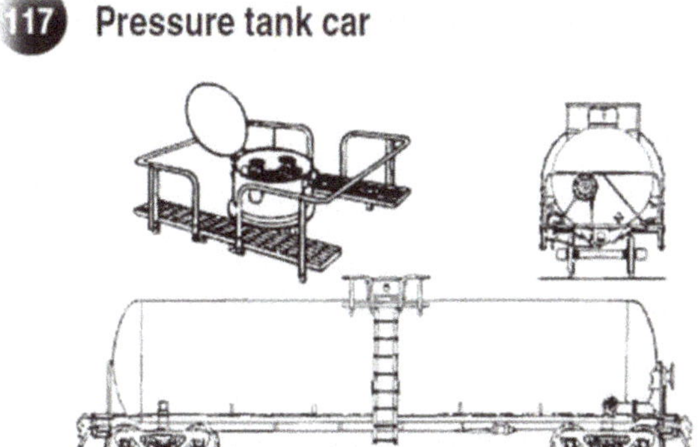

General Service and Low Pressure Tank Cars

General purpose tank cars are non-pressure cars that carry almost any type of material including regulated and non-regulated commodities. These cars are designated by DOT 111 and DOT 117.

2020 Emergency Response Guidebook Guide 131.

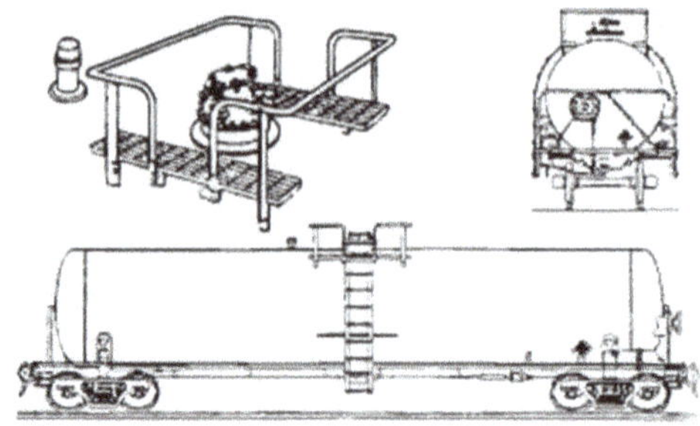

Low pressure tank cars use 2020 Emergency Response Guidebook Guide 128.

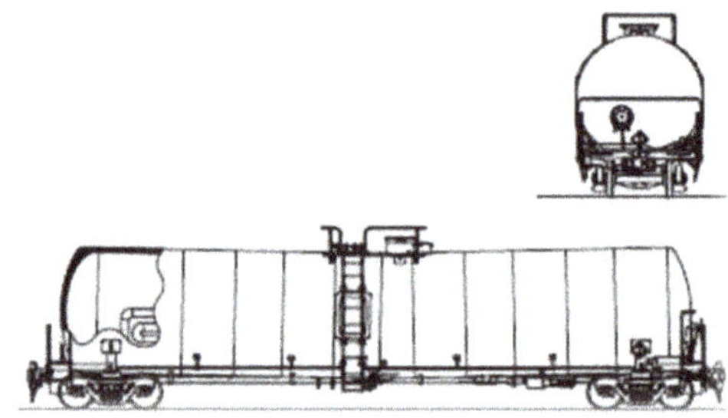

Box Cars

Mixed cargo box cars are used for general freight and may be single or double sided in construction . These units carry both hazardous and non-hazardous materials.

A boxcar is the North American term for a railroad car that is enclosed and generally used to carry freight. The boxcar, while not the simplest freight car design, is probably the most versatile since it can carry most loads. Boxcars have side doors of varying size and operation, and some include end doors and adjustable bulkheads to load very large items.

2020 Emergency Response Guidebook Guide 111.

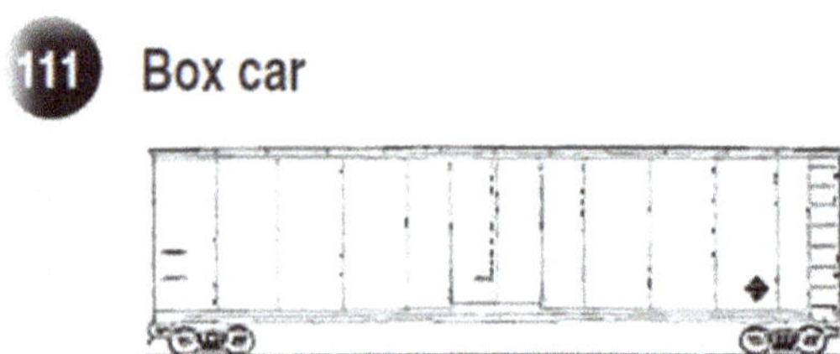

Pneumatically Unloaded Hopper Cars

A hopper car (US) or hopper wagon (UIC) is a type of railroad freight car used to transport loose bulk commodities such as coal, ore, grain, and track ballast. Two main types of hopper car exist: covered hopper cars, which are equipped with a roof, and open hopper cars, which do not have a roof.

This type of car is distinguished from a gondola car in that it has opening doors on the underside or on the sides to discharge its cargo. The development of the hopper car went along with the development of automated handling of such commodities, with automated loading and unloading facilities.

Covered hopper cars are used for bulk cargo such as grain, sugar, and fertilizer that must be protected from exposure to the weather. Open hopper cars are used for commodities such as coal, which can suffer exposure with less detrimental effect.

2020 Emergency Response Guidebook Guide 140.

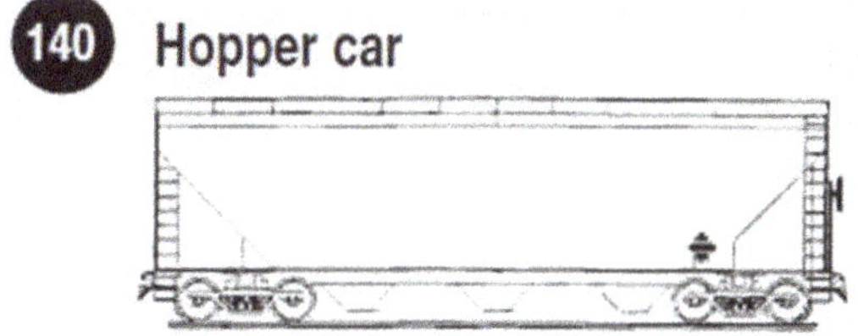

Radioactive Containers

Type A

Type A Packaging is used to transport small quantities of radioactive material with higher concentrations of radioactivity than those shipped in industrial packaging. They are typically constructed of steel, wood, or fiberboard, and have an inner containment vessel made of glass, plastic, or metal surrounded with packing material made of polyethylene, rubber, or vermiculite. Examples of material typically shipped in Type A Packages include nuclear medicines (radiopharmaceuticals), radioactive waste, and radioactive sources used in industrial applications. Type A packaging and its radioactive contents must meet standard testing requirements designed to ensure that the package retains its containment integrity and shielding under normal transport conditions.

Type A Packages must withstand moderate degrees of heat, cold, reduced air pressure, vibration, impact, water spray, drop, penetration, and stacking tests. Type A Packages are not, however, designed to withstand the forces of an accident. The consequences of a release of the material in one of these packages would not be significant since the quantity of material in this package is so limited. Type A packaging are only used to transport non life-endangering amounts of radioactive material.

Type B

Type B Packaging is designed to transport material with the highest levels of radioactivity. Type B packaging range from small hand-held radiography cameras to heavily shielded steel casks that weigh up to 125 tons.

Examples of material transported in Type B packaging include spent nuclear fuel, high-level radioactive waste, and high concentrations of other radioactive material such as cesium and cobalt. These package designs must withstand all Type A tests, and a series of tests that simulate severe or "worst-case" accident conditions. Accident conditions are simulated by performance testing and engineering analysis. Life-endangering amounts of radioactive material are required to be transported in Type B Packages.

Storage Tanks

Atmospheric Non-Pressure Tanks

An atmospheric tank is an enclosed vessel that operates at atmospheric pressure, usually are cylindrical in shape, and are equipped with either a floating or fixed roof and contain non-toxic vapour liquids.

Atmospheric tanks come in several designs as follows:

Horizontal Tank

- Used for flammable and combustible liquids, corrosives and toxic materials

Cone Roof Tank

- Used for flammable and combustible liquids and corrosive liquids

Open Top Floating Roof Tank

- Used for flammable and combustible liquids

Covered Top Floating Roof Tank

- Used for flammable and combustible liquids

Lifter Roof Tank

- Used for flammable and combustible liquids

Vapour Dome Roof Tank

- Used for combustible liquids of medium volatility and non-hazardous materials

Low Pressure Tanks

Low pressure storage tanks deal with pressures less than 15 psig and are used to store light crude oil, naphtha, some volatile chemicals, liquid oxygen and liquid nitrogen.

Low pressure storage tanks come in several designs as follows:

Dome Roof Tank

- Used for flammable and combustible liquids, fertilizers and solvents

Spheroid Tank (Noded and Non-Noded)

- Used for LPG, methane, propane and some flammable liquids such as gasoline

Horizontal Pressure Tank

- Used for LPG, anhydrous ammonia, chlorine, vinyl chloride, hydrogen chloride

Spherical Pressure Tank

- Used for LPG and vinyl chloride

Cryogenic Storage Tank

- Used for liquid carbon dioxide, liquid oxygen, liquid nitrogen

Refrigerated Storage Tank

- Used for liquid propane, butane, ethylene, ammonia and LNG

Pipelines

Types of Pipelines

In North America, hazardous materials are commonly transported through millions of miles of pipelines and related structures. Products transported include natural gas, natural gas liquids, crude oil, gasoline, diesel fuels, anhydrous ammonia, carbon dioxide, jet fuel, and other commodities. Although pipelines are buried, often there are above-ground structures and markers indicating the presence of pipelines. First responders should be aware of the pipelines in their jurisdictions, the products they transport, and the operators responsible for those pipelines. Proactive relationships can be beneficial in the safe and effective management of pipeline emergencies.

Natural Gas Transmission

Natural Gas Transmission Pipelines are large-diameter, steel pipelines that transport flammable natural gas (toxic and non-toxic) at very high pressures ranging from 200 to 1,500 psi*. Natural gas in transmission pipelines is odorless — generally not odorized with mercaptan (the "rotten egg" smell); however, natural gas containing hydrogen sulfide (H_2S) will have a distinct "rotten egg" odor.

Natural Gas Distribution

Natural gas is delivered directly to customers via distribution pipelines. These pipelines are typically smaller-diameter, lower-pressure pipelines constructed of steel, plastic, or cast iron. Natural gas in distribution pipelines is odorized with mercaptan (the "rotten egg" smell).

Natural Gas Gathering and Well Production

Natural gas-gathering/well production pipelines collect "raw" natural gas from wellheads and transport the product to gas-processing and/or gas-treating plants. These gathering pipelines carry natural gas mixed with some quantity of gas liquids, water, and, in some areas, contaminants such as toxic hydrogen sulfide (H2S). Natural gas in these pipelines is not odorized with mercaptan (the "rotten egg" smell); however, natural gas that contains hydrogen sulfide (H2 S) will have a distinct "rotten egg" odor.

Liquid Petroleum and Hazardous Liquids

Crude oil, refined petroleum products, and hazardous liquids often are transported by pipelines and include gasoline, jet fuels, diesel fuel, home heating oils, carbon dioxide, anhydrous ammonia, and other hazardous liquids. Many liquid petroleum pipelines transport different types of liquid petroleum in the same pipeline. To do so, the pipeline operator sends different products in "batches". For example, an operator could send gasoline for several hours, and then switch to jet fuels, before switching to diesel fuel.

Some liquid pipelines transport highly volatile liquids that rapidly change from liquid to gaseous when released from a pressurized pipeline. Examples of these types of liquids include carbon dioxide, anhydrous ammonia, propane, and others.

Pipeline Markers

Since pipelines are usually buried underground, pipeline markers are used to indicate their presence in an area along the pipeline route. Of the three types of pipelines typically buried underground — distribution, gathering, and transmission — only transmission pipelines are marked with the following above-ground markers used to indicate their route.

Markers warn that a transmission pipeline is located in the area, identify the product transported in the line, and provide the name and telephone number of the pipeline operator to call. Markers and warning signs are located at frequent intervals along natural gas and liquid transmission pipeline rights-of-way, and are located at prominent points such as where pipelines intersect streets, highways, railways, or waterways. Pipeline markers only indicate the presence of a pipeline—they do not indicate the exact location of the pipeline. Pipeline locations within a right-of-way may vary along its length and there may be multiple pipelines located in the same right-of-way.

Chapter 6:
Personal Protective Equipment

Protective Clothing

When engineering controls, work practice and administrative controls are not feasible or do not provide sufficient protection to employees, employers are responsible for providing a safe and healthy workplace for their employees. In Canada, the Canadian Council of Occupational Health and Safety, has the requirement for workers to use personal protective equipment, PPE. PPE must be in good repair when being used and there are often requirements instructing workplaces on how to store or clean the equipment, especially respirators.

In the United States, Occupational Health and Safety Administration, OSHA has the role to promote the safety and health of America's working men and women by setting and enforcing standards; providing training, outreach and education; establishing partnerships; and encouraging continual improvement in workplace safety and health.

Flame Retardant Clothing

Flame resistant and flame retardant clothing are commonly referred to as FR. FR clothing is a specific and special type of PPE that is designed to protect you from fire-related hazards. FR clothing is never completely fire-proof however, but will act as an in initial layer of protection to substantially reduce the risk of getting burned. The clothing generally will itself catch fire, but is designed to immediately self-extinguish and not continue to burn once ignited.

It is important to understand the two (2) types of clothing:

Flame Resistant

Flame resistant, also referred to as fire resistant clothing, is made of material that is inherently resistant to flames and embers. The material itself that is used have a chemical structure that is naturally resistant to flame and designed to immediately extinguish themselves and not promote further spread of fire. Flame Resistant is often also referred to as Fire Resistant.

The most common examples of inherent flame resistant material that we are familiar with are:

- Modacrylic fabrics

- Nomex

- Kevlar

Often both Nomex and Kevlar are woven together when used for flame resistant clothing.

Flame Retardant

Flame retardant clothing are comprised of fabrics that have gone through a chemical treatment to make the fabric acquire the same properties of flame resistant clothing. In essence, flame retardant clothing is made of fabrics coated with flame resistant compounds in a similar way that a kitchen frying pan is coated with Teflon.

FR clothing is further broken down into two (2) levels of protection:

- Primary protection – refers to clothing such as firefighter gear that is designed to be worn during activities where the wearer will be continuously exposed to flames, radiant heat or molten substance splashes

- Secondary protection – refers to clothing such as coveralls that is designed to be worn during activities where the wearer will be intermittently exposed to flames, radiant heat of molten substance splashes.

It is important to understand that with flame retardant clothing, the protective coating on the fabric can, and will, eventually wear off over time. It is best practice to avoid washing flame retardant clothing with fabric softeners or bleach since both of these items will increase the rate of decomposition of the flame retardant coating.

Arc Rated Flame Resistant

Arc rated flame resistant (AR/FR) clothing require labels that show the level of protection they provide for arc flash situations. This rating is referred to as the CAT rating, which is short for *CAT*egory rating, and indicates the category of protection the clothing offers against injury in the event of an arc flash. Additionally, the rating must also carry a more precise measurement of protection that is identified in calories/cm^2. Calories are the unit of measure used to identify the force of a particular arc flash and are associated to the CAT rating as follows:

CAT RATING	FR CLOTHING	MINIMUM ARC RATING
1	FR shirt/pants or coveralls (1 layer)	4.0 cal/ cm^2
2	Cotton underwear + FR shirt/pants (2 layer)	8.0 cal/ cm^2
3	Cotton underwear + FR shirt/pants + coveralls Or Cotton underwear + 2 FR coveralls (2-3 layers)	25.0 cal/ cm^2
4	Flash suit (3 or more layers)	40.0 cal/ cm^2

When selecting FR clothing, consideration must be given to the type of fabric being used, and if is either:

- Treated fire retardant fabric

- Inherently flame resistant fabric

The primary difference between the two is durability and the amount of protection the clothing provides. Treated fabrics are generally more economical than inherent fabrics, but the protection can wear off over time through repeated washing of the clothing. Inherent fabrics however have the protection woven into the fabric and therefore the protection cannot be worn away through repeated washing.

Chemical Protective Clothing

Chemical Protective Clothing, CPC, is used to protect an employee from being exposed to the hazards and effects of chemicals. CPC is available in a variety of materials that work with an extensive list of chemicals but need to be evaluated specifically each time based on the chemicals present, the environment which they exist, and the task being performed. Not all materials work adequately for all chemicals. Generally, CPC is referred to in two (2) types:

- Suits

- Gloves

Due to the lack of appropriate standards, choosing the correct CPC can be difficult and is based on the premise of "what is the CPC expected to do and why is it being worn". The National Fire Protection Association, NFPA, uses this practical approach to identify CPC into two (2) primary categories:

- Vapour Protective Ensembles – has the capability to protect against specific chemicals based on permeation data available

- Liquid Splash Protective Ensembles and Clothing – has the capability to protect against specific chemicals based on penetration data.

High Temperature Clothing

High temperature clothing also known as thermal protective clothing, are clothes that are designed to provide protection from hazardous thermal environments by preventing the transfer of thermal energy to the skin.

In many cases the clothing is made from aluminized fabrics which are constructed with a flame resistant base layer, and an aluminium film that is bonded to the surface. With its mirror finish, aluminized clothing is very effective at reflecting radiant heat. The aluminized coating can reflect up to 95 percent of thermal radiation away from the wearer, and some fabrics can withstand temperatures as high as 3000°F for short durations. Aluminized fabrics are often constructed with a flame-resistant base fabric and multiple layers of aluminum, protective films, and heat-stable adhesives so that when one layer of aluminum breaks down, another layer is there to protect. This multi-layer structure improves abrasion resistance and helps ensure that fabrics remain highly reflective even after repeated use and proper care and cleaning. Often commonly referred to as proximity suits, these cloths protect the wearer from flames, molten metal splashes, steam and extreme heat.

Considerations

Permeation

Permeation rate is the rate at which the chemical will move through the material. It is measured in a laboratory and is expressed in units like milligrams per square meter per second. The higher the permeation rate, the faster the chemical will move through the material. Permeation can be thought of as the process by which a chemical dissolves in and moves through protective clothing material on a molecular level.

In warmer temperatures, chemicals may pass through faster. The "permeation breakthrough time" is time it takes a chemical to permeate completely through the material. It is determined by applying the chemical on the glove or suit exterior and measuring the time it takes to detect the chemical on the inside surface. The sensitivity of the analytical instruments used in these measurements influence when a chemical is first detected. The breakthrough time gives some indication of how long a glove or suit can be used before the chemical will permeate through the material.

Degradation

Degradation is the loss of, or change in the fabrics chemical resistance or physical properties due to exposure to chemicals or ambient conditions. The process can be immediate, or it can be slow and unobservable.

Degraded materials may become brittle and stiff in some cases, and soft and sticky in others. Conditions even as simple as exposure to direct sunlight can be a factor in degradation with the worst-case scenario being that the materials actually dissolves in the chemical. It is important to understand that degradation may not always be visible to the naked eye.

Penetration

Unlike permeation, penetration is the bulk flow of a liquid through porous materials, seams, closures, and pinholes or other imperfections in a protective clothing ensemble. Penetration may occur from chemical deterioration of the materials, which leads to a liquid passing through the material.

Durability

Durability of a material pertains to the ability to withstand the physical stress of the task being performed. Durability is based on several factors that need to be considered including but not limited to:

- Task
- Tensile strength
- Seam strength
- Heat
- Size
- Tear points
- Donning and doffing procedures

Flexibility

Flexibility of CPC is determined by how much the CPC interferes with the worker's ability to perform the assigned task. As with durability, the flexibility of the CPC is dependant on several and similar factors, Size plays a large role in flexibility to ensure that the integrity of the CPC is maintained while simultaneously ensuring that it does not increase the ability of the CPC to snag or catch on surrounding obstructions.

Temperature Effects

When using CPC the material needs to be evaluated as to how well it maintains its protective integrity and flexibility under hot and cold exposures. Adverse effects to flexibility, functionality, integrity and comfort need to be evaluated to ensure that the CPC performs adequately in that specific environment.

Decontamination

CPC must be looked at with the question being asked if the materials poses any decontamination problems. The degree of difficulty in decontaminating protective clothing may dictate whether disposable or reusable clothing is used, or a combination of both.

Chemical Compatibility

It is important that protective clothing users realize that no single combination of protective equipment and clothing is capable of protecting against all hazards. Thus protective clothing should be used in conjunction with other protective methods. For example, engineering or administrative controls to limit chemical contact with personnel should always be considered as an alternative measure for preventing chemical exposure.

The use of protective clothing can itself create significant wearer hazards, such as heat stress, physical and psychological stress, in addition to impaired vision, mobility, and communication. In general, the greater the level of chemical protective clothing, the greater the associated risks. For any given situation, equipment and clothing should be selected that provide an adequate level of protection. Overprotection as well as under-protection can be hazardous and should be avoided.

Considerations

Chemical protective clothing must be worn whenever an employee faces potential hazards arising from chemical exposure. OSHA states that the selection of proper CPC involves considering the following:

Chemical Hazards

- o Chemicals present a variety of hazards such as toxicity, corrosiveness, flammability, reactivity, and oxygen deficiency. Depending on the chemicals present, any combination of hazards may exist.

- o Is the hazard vapour, liquid-splash or particulate in nature?

Physical Environment

- o Chemical exposure can happen anywhere: in industrial settings, on the highways, or in residential areas. It may occur either indoors or outdoors; the environment may be extremely hot, cold, or moderate; the exposure site may be relatively uncluttered or rugged, presenting a number of physical hazards; chemical handling activities may involve entering confined spaces, heavy lifting, climbing a ladder, or crawling on the ground. The choice of ensemble components must account for these conditions.

Duration of Exposure

- o The protective qualities of ensemble components may be limited to certain exposure levels (e.g. material chemical resistance, air supply). The decision for ensemble use time must be made assuming the worst case exposure so that safety margins can be applied to increase the protection available to the worker.

Protective Clothing or Equipment Availability

- o Hopefully, an array of different clothing or equipment is available to workers to meet all intended applications. Reliance on one particular clothing or equipment item may severely limit a facility's ability to handle a broad range of chemical exposures. In its acquisition of equipment and clothing, the safety department or other responsible authority should attempt to provide a high degree of flexibility while choosing protective clothing and equipment that is easily integrated and provides protection against each conceivable hazard.

The type of equipment used and the overall level of protection should be re-evaluated periodically as the amount of information about the chemical situation or process increases, and when workers are required to perform different tasks. Personnel should upgrade or downgrade their level of protection only with concurrence with the site supervisor, safety officer, or plant industrial hygienist.

Selection

Vapour, Liquid-Splash, or Particulate Protection

Vapour protective suits also provide liquid splash and particulate protection. Liquid splash protective garments also provide particulate protection. Many garments may be labeled as totally encapsulating but do not provide gas-tight integrity due to inadequate seams or closures. Gas-tight integrity can only be determined by performing a pressure or inflation test and a leak detection test of the respective protective suit. This test involves:

- Closing off suit exhalation valves;

- Inflating the suit to a pre-specified pressure and

- Observing whether the suit holds the above pressure for a designated period.

Splash suits must still cover the entire body when combined with the respirator, gloves, and boots. Applying duct tape to a splash suit does not make it protect against vapours. Particulate protective suits may not need to cover the entire body, depending on the hazards posed by the particulate.

In general, gloves, boots and some form of face protection are required. Clothing items may only be needed to cover a limited area of the body such as gloves on hands. The nature of the hazards and the expected exposure will determine if clothing should provide partial or full body protection.

Chemical Resistance

Manufacturers of vapour protective suits should provide permeation resistance data for their products, while liquid and particulate penetration resistance data should accompany liquid splash and particulate protective garments respectively.

Ideally data should be provided for every primary material in the suit or clothing item. For suits, this includes the garment, visor, gloves, boots, and seams. Permeation data should include the following:

- Chemical name;

- Breakthrough time (shows how soon the chemical permeates);

- Permeation rate (shows the rate that the chemical comes through);

- System sensitivity

Field Selection

Even when end users have gone through a very careful selection process, a number of situations will arise when no information is available to judge whether their protective clothing will provide adequate protection. These situations include:

- Chemicals that have not been tested with the garment materials;

- Mixtures of two or more different chemicals;

- Chemicals that cannot be readily identified;

- Extreme environmental conditions (hot temperatures); and

- Lack of data in all clothing components (e.g. seams, visors).

Testing material specimens using newly developed field test kits may offer one means for making an on-site clothing selection. A portable test kit has been developed by the EPA using a simple weight loss method that allows field qualification of protective clothing materials within one hour. Use of this kit may overcome the absence of data and provide additional criteria for clothing selection. Regardless, selection of chemical protective clothing is a complex task and should be performed by personnel with both extensive training and experience. Under all conditions, clothing should be selected by evaluating its performance characteristics against the requirements and limitations imposed by the application.

Respiratory Protection

Choosing respiratory protection is complicated and requires several sources of information to be evaluated prior to entry. The Canadian Council for Occupational Health and Safety suggests asking the following questions to determine the proper respirator to use:

- Is it to be used in oxygen-deficient atmospheres

- What is the nature of the hazard and is there more than one contaminant present?

- Are the airborne levels below or above the exposure limit, or are they above levels that could be immediately dangerous to life or health?

- What are the health effects of the airborne contaminant?

- What activities will the worker be doing while wearing the respirator

- How long will the worker need to wear the respirator?

- Does the selected respirator fit the worker properly?

Air Purifying Respirators, APR

Air-purifying respirators can remove contaminants in the air that you breathe by filtering out particulates (e.g., dusts, metal fumes, mists, etc.). Other APRs purify air by adsorbing gases or vapours on a sorbent (adsorbing material) in a cartridge or canister. They are tight-fitting and are available in several forms:

- mouth bit respirator (fits in the mouth and comes with a nose clip to hold nostrils closed - for escape purposes only)

- quarter-mask (covering the nose and mouth)

- half-face mask (covering the face from the nose to below the chin)

- full facepiece (covering the face from above the eyes to below the chin)

APR units only protect against specific airborne chemicals and concentration information must be available prior to use. The are not to be used in:

- environments with less than 19.5% oxygen or greater than 23.5% oxygen

- atmospheres that are immediately dangerous to life or health

- atmospheres that are highly toxic at low concentrations

The selection of APR also depends on if oil particles are present. Use the following guide when evaluating:

- N: **N**ot resistant to oil

- R: **R**esistant to oil

- P: **P**roof (Oil Proof)

Supplied Air Respirators, SAR

Supplied-air respirators (SARs) supply clean air from a compressed air tank or through an air line. This air is not from the work room area. The air supplied in tanks or from compressors must meet certain standards for purity and moisture content.

Supplied-air respirators may have either tight-fitting or loose-fitting respiratory inlets. Respirators with tight-fitting respiratory inlets have half or full facepieces. Types with loose-fitting respiratory inlets can be hoods or helmets that cover the head and neck, or loose-fitting facepieces with rubber or fabric side shields. These are supplied with air through airlines.

SAR includes:

- self-contained breathing apparatus (SCBA)

- airline supplied-air respirators

- protective suits that totally encapsulate the wearer's body and incorporate a life-support system

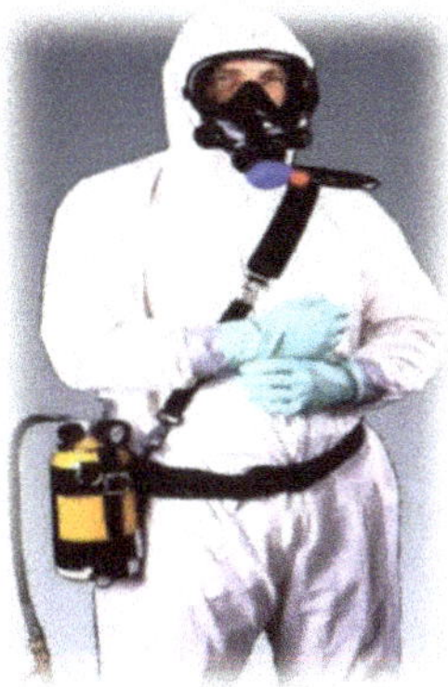

Self Contained Breathing Apparatus, SCBA

A self-contained breathing apparatus, SCBA, is often referred to as a breathing apparatus, BA. SCBA is a device worn that provides breathable air in an immediately dangerous to life or health atmosphere, IDLH, or unknown environment.

An SCBA typically has three main components:

- a high-pressure tank (e.g., 2,216 to 5,500 psi)

- a pressure regulator

- an inhalation connection (mouthpiece, mouth mask or face mask), connected together and mounted to a carrying frame

SCBA utilize a positive pressure system that slightly pressurises the interior of the mask and activates flow when the pressure difference is reduced, but still above ambient. If the mask leaks, there will be continuous flow to maintain the pressure, and no inward leakage is possible. With a good fit this is economical on gas and prevents contamination. If the mask falls off the regulator will continuously expend gas trying to raise the pressure and may consume a significant amount of gas before it is corrected.

Assigned Protection Factor, APF

The Assigned Protection Factor, APF, is an expression of the ratio of the level of contaminant or test agent outside of the respirator compared to the level measured inside the respirator face piece. For example, an APF of 100 means the concentration of contaminant outside of the respirator was 100 times that of the level inside the respirator.

The APF means the workplace level of respiratory protection that a respirator or class of respirators is expected to provide to employees when the employer implements a continuing, effective respiratory protection program as specified by this section. It evaluates the protection in chemical atmospheres as a comparison to the Time Weighted Average values of a compound.

Common APF values are as follows:

Assigned Protection Factors					
Type of respirator	Quarter mask	Half mask	Full facepiece	Helmet/ Hood	Loose-fitting facepiece
SAR					
- Demand mode		10	50		
- Continuous flow mode		50	1,000	25/1,000	25
- Pressure-demand or other positive-pressure mode		50	1,000		
SCBA					
- Demand mode		10	50	50	
- Pressure-demand or other positive-pressure mode			10,000	10,000	

Maximum Use Concentration

Maximum Use Concentration, MUC, means the maximum atmospheric concentration of a hazardous substance from which an employee can be expected to be protected when wearing a respirator, and is determined by the assigned protection factor of the respirator or class of respirators and the exposure limit of the hazardous substance.

The MUC usually can be determined mathematically by multiplying the assigned protection factor specified for a respirator by the permissible exposure limit, PEL. short-term exposure limit, ceiling limit, peak limit, or any other exposure limit used for the hazardous substance.

The MUC for respirators is calculated by multiplying the APF for the respirator by the PEL. The MUC is the upper limit at which the class of respirator is expected to provide protection. Whenever the exposures approach the MUC, then the employer should select the next higher class of respirators for the employees.

When the calculated MUC exceeds the IDLH level for a hazardous substance, or the performance limits of the cartridge or canister, then employers must set the maximum MUC at that lower limit.

Levels of Protection

The individual components of clothing and equipment must be assembled into a full protective ensemble that both protects the worker from the site-specific hazards and minimizes the hazards and drawbacks of the PPE ensemble itself. Personal protective equipment is divided into four categories based on the degree of protection afforded.

Level A

Level A protection should be used when:

- The hazardous substance has been identified and requires the highest level of protection for skin, eyes, and the respiratory system based on either the measured (or potential for) high concentration of atmospheric vapours, gases, or particulates; or the site operations and work functions involve a high potential for splash, immersion, or exposure to unexpected vapours, gases, or particulates of materials that are harmful to skin or capable of being absorbed through the skin,

- Substances with a high degree of hazard to the skin are known or suspected to be present, and skin contact is possible; or

- Operations must be conducted in confined, poorly ventilated areas, and the absence of conditions requiring Level A have not yet been determined.

The following constitute Level A equipment; it may be used as appropriate;

- Positive pressure, full face-piece self-contained breathing apparatus (SCBA), or positive pressure supplied air respirator with escape SCBA, approved by the National Institute for Occupational Safety and Health (NIOSH).

- Totally-encapsulating chemical-protective suit.

- Coveralls.

- Long underwear.

- Gloves, outer, chemical-resistant.

- Gloves, inner, chemical-resistant.

- Boots, chemical-resistant, steel toe and shank.

- Hard hat (under suit).

- Disposable protective suit, gloves and boots (depending on suit construction, may be worn over totally-encapsulating suit).

Level B

Level B protection should be used when:

- The type and atmospheric concentration of substances have been identified and require a high level of respiratory protection, but less skin protection.

- The atmosphere contains less than 19.5 percent oxygen; or

- The presence of incompletely identified vapours or gases is indicated by a direct-reading organic vapour detection instrument, but vapours and gases are not suspected of containing high levels of chemicals harmful to skin or capable of being absorbed through the skin.

Note: This involves atmospheres with IDLH concentrations of specific substances that present severe inhalation hazards and that do not represent a severe skin hazard; or that do not meet the criteria for use of air-purifying respirators.

The following constitute Level B equipment; it may be used as appropriate.

- Positive pressure, full-facepiece self-contained breathing apparatus (SCBA), or positive pressure supplied air respirator with escape SCBA (NIOSH approved).

- Hooded chemical-resistant clothing (overalls and long-sleeved jacket; coveralls; one or two-piece chemical-splash suit; disposable chemical-resistant overalls).

- Coveralls.

- Gloves, outer, chemical-resistant.

- Gloves, inner, chemical-resistant.

- Boots, outer, chemical-resistant steel toe and shank.

- Boot-covers, outer, chemical-resistant (disposable).

- Hard hat.

- Face shield.

Level C

Level C protection should be used when:

- The atmospheric contaminants, liquid splashes, or other direct contact will not adversely affect or be absorbed through any exposed skin;

- The types of air contaminants have been identified, concentrations measured, and an air-purifying respirator is available that can remove the contaminants; and

- All criteria for the use of air-purifying respirators are met.

The following constitute Level C equipment; it may be used as appropriate.

- Full-face or half-mask, air purifying respirators (NIOSH approved).

- Hooded chemical-resistant clothing (overalls; two-piece chemical-splash suit; disposable chemical-resistant overalls).

- Coveralls.

- Gloves, outer, chemical-resistant.

- Gloves, inner, chemical-resistant.

- Boots (outer), chemical-resistant steel toe and shank.

- Boot-covers, outer, chemical-resistant (disposable).

- Hard hat.

- Escape mask.

- Face shield.

Level D

Level D protection should be used when:

- The atmosphere contains no known hazard; and

- Work functions preclude splashes, immersion, or the potential for unexpected inhalation of or contact with hazardous levels of any chemicals.

The following constitute Level D equipment; it may be used as appropriate:

- Coveralls.

- Gloves.

- Boots/shoes, chemical-resistant steel toe and shank.

- Boots, outer, chemical-resistant (disposable).

- Safety glasses or chemical splash goggles.

- Hard hat.

- Escape mask.

- Face shield.

Support

Donning Procedures

Donning is the act of putting something on. The Centre for Disease Control, CDC recommends the following basic guidelines at all times:

- Keep hands away from face.

- Work from clean to dirty.

- Limit surfaces touched.

- Change PPE when torn or heavily contaminated.

The following is an example of the donning procedure for a Level B ensemble:

- Verify that all PPE is ready and in the dress out area

- Perform an operational check of the SCBA

- Remove watches, jewelry, leather shoes and other personal items

- Don inner suit

- Inspect suit

- Don Level B suit to waist

- Don chemical resistant boots with boot covers

- Conduct entry briefing
  - Describe Incident
  - Identify Hazards
  - Assign Duties/Jobs
  - Confirm Equipment and Decon Readiness
  - Confirm Primary, Secondary and Emergency Communications
  - Identify Emergency Showers/Decon

- Don inner glove

- Don middle glove

- Insert arms into the sleeves of the suit and pulling it over shoulders

- Gloves will be turned inside out over the thumb and palm of hand, then carefully taped making sure to stretch the elastic as far as possible and folded back over suit

- Don chemical resistant outer gloves, and tape seam between glove and suit leaving a tab

- Don facepiece

- Don attached hood of suit, zip up front zipper, attach zipper flap and tape flap leaving a tab

- Don SCBA

- Conduct a positive and negative pressure check of respirator facepiece

- Don hardhat, if required (tape if needed)

- Assign suit number

- Rapid Intervention Team/Decon people to decon line

- Entrant connects regulator to face piece and enters Hot Zone after Decon line is ready and IC approves

- Ensure wearer is breathing air and indicates readiness with a thumbs-up sign

Doffing Procedures

Doffing is the act of taking something off. The following is an example of the doffing procedure for a Level B ensemble:

- Step onto disposable mat or into decontamination pool

- Air Supply

  - First Responder loosens the shoulder straps and waist belt

  - Decon Team Member removes harness from back protecting the facepiece, regulator and hose line

- Sit

  - Use "Pull Tab" to remove tape

- o Place tape in trash

- Boots

  - o Use heel-toe release – Limit external exposure when possible – Boots may be too tight

  - o Step to next decon pool to begin removing suit

- Facepiece

  - o Decon Team Member will indicate where pull tabs are located

  - o Use "Pull Tab"

  - o Pull gently

  - o Place tape in trash

- Unzip Suit

  - o Pull back overlap

  - o Pull gently on zipper extension

- Remove Hood and Peel Suit

  - o Remove hood

  - o Use gloved hands to remove suit from shoulders (peel)

  - o Gently shake from the shoulders to release suit

  - o Keep outer gloves on the outside of suit

  - o Remove hand from glove

  - o Gently shake hand away from glove into the sleeve

  - o Gently shake suit from shoulders

  - o Use inner gloved hand on inside to assist with other hand

  - o Peel down like a banana

  - o Use inner gloved hands

- o Peel from the inside away from torso to lower legs

- Peel Level "B" Suit using the inner gloved hands on the inside of the suit

- Remove legs and fee

- Move towards the Cold Zone

- Air Flow

  - o With the gloved hand loosen the facepiece straps and gently push the facepiece away from the face with activated donning switch (open or on)

- Inner Glove

  - o Remove the inner glove by rolling or peeling the glove from the wrist to the fingertip

Inspection and Maintenance

The end user in donning protective clothing and equipment must take all necessary steps to ensure that the protective ensemble will perform as expected. During emergencies is not the right time to discover discrepancies in the protective clothing.

Teach end user care for his clothing and other protective equipment in the same manner as parachutists care for parachutes. Following a standard program for inspection, proper storage, and maintenance along with realizing protective clothing/equipment limitations is the best way to avoid chemical exposure during emergency response. OSHA recommends the following mechanisms:

Inspection

- An effective chemical protective clothing inspection program should feature five different inspections:

  - o Inspection and operational testing of equipment received as new from the factory or distributor

- o   Inspection of equipment as it is selected for a particular chemical operation

- o   Inspection of equipment after use or training and prior to maintenance

- o   Periodic inspection of stored equipment

- o   Periodic inspection when a question arises concerning the appropriateness of selected equipment, or when problems with similar equipment are discovered.

- Each inspection will cover different areas with varying degrees of depth. Those personnel responsible for clothing inspection should follow manufacturer directions; many vendors provide detailed inspection procedures.

- Records must be kept of all inspection procedures. Individual identification numbers should be assigned to all reusable pieces of equipment (many clothing and equipment items may already have serial numbers), and records should be maintained by that number. At a minimum, each inspection should record:

- o   Clothing/equipment item ID number;

- o   Date of the inspection;

- o   Person making the inspection;

- o   Results of the inspection; and

- o   Any unusual conditions noted.

Periodic review of these records can provide an indication of protective clothing which requires excessive maintenance and can also serve to identify clothing that is susceptible to failure.

Maintenance

- Manufacturers frequently restrict the sale of certain protective suit parts to individuals or groups who are specially trained, equipped, or authorized by the manufacturer to purchase them. Explicit procedures should be adopted to ensure that the appropriate level of maintenance is performed only by those individuals who have this specialized training and equipment. In no case should you attempt to repair equipment without checking with the person in your facility who is responsible for chemical protective clothing maintenance.

- The following classification scheme is recommended to divide the types of permissible or non-permissible repairs:

- o **Level 1:** User or wearer maintenance, requiring a few common tools or no tools at all.

- o **Level 2:** Maintenance that can be performed by the response team's maintenance shop, if adequately equipped and trained.

- o **Level 3:** Specialized maintenance that can be performed only by the factory or an authorized repair person.

- Each facility should adopt the above scheme and list which repairs fall into each category for each type of protective clothing and equipment. Many manufacturers will also indicate which repairs, if performed in the field, void the warranty of their products. All repairs made must be recorded on the records for the specific clothing along with appropriate inspection results.

Training

Training in the use of protective clothing:

- Allows the user to become familiar with the equipment in a nonhazardous, nonemergency condition.

- Instills confidence of the user in his/her equipment.

- Makes the user aware of the limitations and capabilities of the equipment.

- Increases worker efficiency in performing various tasks.

- Reduces the likelihood of accidents during chemical operations.

Training should be completed prior to actual clothing use in a non-hazardous environment and should be repeated at the frequency required by legislation. As a minimum the training should point out the user's responsibilities and explain the following, using both classroom and field training when necessary, as follows:

- The proper use and maintenance of selected protective clothing, including capabilities and limitations

- The nature of the hazards and the consequences of not using the protective clothing

- The human factors influencing protective clothing performance

- Instructions in inspecting, donning, checking, fitting, and using protective clothing

- Use of protective clothing in normal air for a long familiarity period

- The user's responsibility (if any) for decontamination, cleaning, maintenance, and repair of protective clothing

- Emergency procedures and self-rescue in the event of protective clothing/ equipment failure

- The buddy system.

The discomfort and inconvenience of wearing chemical protective clothing and equipment can create a resistance to its conscientious use. One essential aspect of training is to make the user aware of the need for protective clothing and to instill motivation for the proper use and maintenance of that protective clothing.

Emergency Procedures

SCBA Failure

In situations that the SCBA experiences a failure while working in IDLH environments, it is important to remember that air conservation is the priority. Conserve air as much as possible and immediately leave the area. To do this follow the following steps:

- Remain calm. Control your breathing to minimize use. Alert your team/buddy member.

- Immediately evacuate from the area. Ensure that you leave with your team members as part of the buddy system and move to the nearest exit point. If available exits are not an option, create an exit as necessary.

- Declare an emergency over your radio by vocalizing "Mayday – Mayday – Mayday".

- If separated from your team:

  o Describe your surroundings

  o Control your environment as best as you can in the situation

  o Maintain breathing control

Mask Failure

SCBA polycarbonate masks will fail due to heat exposure when approaching the $230^{\circ}C$, with the lens portion melting near the $290^{\circ}C$ range. Additional concerns other than heat may become an issue with mask failure so it is important to remember that the positive pressure in your mask will help with breathing during a mask failure.

- If you mask is knocked off, immediately hold your breath and quickly get it back on and avoid inhalation until the mask is secure

- If the lens becomes compromised from a break or from melting, it is important to cover the hole with your gloves as best as possible and immediately leave the area. If the hole is large, control your breathing to minimize air use as well as potential exposure to the environment

Breathing from a Low Pressure Hose

- If the mask is completely compromised, the older style chest mounted regulators can still provide a source of air in the event of an emergency

  o Disconnect the hose from the mask, cutting it off if necessary, and place hose in your mouth. Use your other hand to plug your nose. Inhale through the hose in your mouth and exhale through your nose.

- If your face piece is knocked off, melts or is damaged in way that it is no longer useful or hampers your ability to get out you should discard it.

Regulator Breathing

- If the mask is completely compromised, the regulator can still provide a source of air in the event of an emergency

  o Disconnect the regulator from the mask and purge.

  o Hold the regulator in a cupped position over your mouth. Use your other hand to plug your nose. Inhale through the air that is flowing from the regulator into your mouth and exhale through your nose.

Loss of Suit Integrity

At any time, if the PPE being used fails or is compromised by tearing, breakthrough or any related alteration, the wearer and associated partner (buddy system) shall immediately exit the hot zone. Re-entry into the hot zone is not permitted until the PPE is repaired or replaced. In all situations, the buddy system will be adhered to.

Ina ll cases, the Incident Commander and the Safety Officer need to be notified so that determination can be made on the effect this may have on continuing operations. If it is determined that failure of PPE is affecting or has the potential to affect safety, all personnel are required to leave the hot zone until further steps and actions can be taken to rectify the situation.

Loss of Communications

All personnel involved in entry team activities shall remain in constant communication, via radio, visual, or verbal methods with the incident commander assigned designee. Failure of communication requires the entry team to exit the hot zone.

The following universal hand signals shall be used in by responders in case of radio failure:

- Hands gripping throat: Out of air/Breathing difficulty

- Grip partner's wrist: Leave area immediately

- Hands-on top of head: Need assistance

- Thumbs up: I'm OK/I understand

- Thumbs down: I'm not OK

- Both thumbs outward: Doff suit

- Clenched fist arm out: Point to the direction of danger

Man Down and Recovery

Rescuer safety requires that all risks placed on rescuers are evaluated to ensure that rescuer safety comes first. As well as addressing rescue concerns, First Aid capabilities must also be assessed. Before attempting any rescue, ensure that all hazards are identified and addressed to ensure the protection of yourself. Review and assess the rescue plan against immediate and existing conditions.

Communicate the plan requirements to the response team and have team acknowledge understanding. Don all appropriate personal protective equipment necessary to safely perform any rescue efforts and execute the plan as best as reasonably acceptable.

Finally, manage the response with planned controls: Monitor and continuously evaluate response. Stop and re-evaluate if conditions change.

Man Down Recovery

Four (4) primary techniques are used in recovery and rescue of a downed individual:

Collar Drag

This is a technique used when it is a one-on-one rescue

- Place the downed individual on their back

- Unzip the individuals coveralls or parka to allow for grab points

- Roll the collar into a large enough area that can be grabbed with both hands.

- Grab the collar with both hands and lift the individual into a semi-sitting upright position with the individuals head resting on your forearm

- Drag the individual head first away from the scene to safety

Two-Arm Drag

This technique works well on uneven surfaces for one-on-one rescues.

- Place the downed individual on their back

- Lift the individual into a semi-sitting upright position while supporting the individuals head and neck

- Use your knee to support the individuals back

- Place your arms under the individuals armpits, cross their arms, and firmly grab their wrists while holding them against the individuals chest

- Lift with your legs, and raise the individual against your chest as you stand

- Drag the individual away from the scene to safety

Two-Rescuer Drag

- Place the downed individual on their back

- Unzip the individuals coveralls or parka to allow for "grab points"

- Stand on opposite sides of the individual and face away from the individuals feet

- Grab the collar (each person on each side) and lift the individual

- Drag the individual away from the scene to safety

Two -Rescuer Carry

- Place the downed individual on their back

- Rescuer 1 will support the individuals head and neck

- Rescuer 2 will sit at individuals feet, grip the individuals wrists and slowly pull the individual into a sitting position

- Rescuer 1 Place your arms under the individuals armpits, cross their arms, and firmly grab their wrists while holding them against the individuals chest

- Rescuer 2 crosses the individuals legs at the ankles, and lifts the legs with one hand, leaving the other hand available to open doors and move obstacles.

- Carry the individual away from the scene to safety.

Chapter 7: Handling

Container Handling

Industrial containers that are handled incorrectly can lead to serious injury, exposure to occupational diseases and in the worst case, death. Methods and protocols to properly handle all containers that pose a potential threat is essential to all employees, and each employee is responsible to familiarize themselves with both the procedures and required equipment. Employers are required to provide proper supervision, instruction and training to all employees that are specific to the work environment the worker is in.

General container handling guidelines recommend that when handling containers:

- All necessary personal protective equipment must be worn to protect against physical, chemical and health hazards

- All containers must be clearly labelled at all times from both a regulatory perspective as well as a workplace hazard perspective

- High volume areas such as transfer stations must have a supply of spill cleanup materials readily available in the areas where containers are handled. Personnel working in these areas must be familiar with the application of these cleanup products, the limitations of these products, and the internal procedures for notification of all spills. Spill kits should be periodically assessed to ensure that all supplies are available and adequate for that area

- Incompatible chemicals should not be handled together in an effort to prevent against reactions during handling or accidental release

- All volumes of containers handled require the proper level of contain-and-carry equipment to provide a secure and contained method.

Small Bottles and Containers

- Single containers should use the appropriate chemical bottle contain-and-carry equipment. The container should be supported with one hand at the top of the container with the other hand supporting the bottom of the container

- Multiple small contains of similar size can be carried in an approved chemical contain-and-carry item provided they are not incompatible

- Full or empty containers are to be transported in the upright position with the appropriate cap or cover firmly fastened

- Multiple containers that exceed 4 litres (I gallon) should be transported by means of a cart which is constructed with a chemical resistant material when possible. The cart should be equipped sufficiently to prevent the movement and dislodging of any and all containers, and be large enough to contain the volume of the largest item in the event that it breaks

- Stacking of chemicals when handling is not recommended.

Pails

- Pails exceeding 25 litres (5 gallons)should be transported in the upright position by means of a cart or some form of hand truck

- Pails should not be stacked during transport

- Pails that have had the lock-tight lids removed should have a suitable cover over the opening prior to handling. Pails that have had the pull-tab bungs opened should also be sealed prior to handling.

Drums

- 205 Litre (55 gallon) drums require the use of a drum-cart for movement. Movement by tipping and balancing the drum on the bottom edge of the drum and "rolling" the unit should not be used

- Drums must be moved withal openings and bungs in the upright position

- Drums should not be manually lifted onto pallets

- Avoid steep and uneven surfaces when handling drums

Bulk Chemicals

- When using powered equipment to handle bulk packages, only trained and authorized personnel are allowed to operate equipment

- Bulk containers such as pallets, bins or totes must only contain chemically compatible items and secured during movement at all times

- Open bulk units must be suitable lined to ensure the containment of any free liquids.

Lab Pack

Laboratory chemical packing, or lab pack, is a term defined under the United States EPA Code of Federal Regulations, 40 CFR 264.316. Lab packing is used to describe the process of consolidation of smaller containers, generally 10 litres (2.6 gallons) or less, in a secondary open head drum for transportation. Often referred to as overpack drums, the secondary drum is a U.N. approved 205 litre (55 gallon) drum lined with sufficient non-biodegradable sorbent material that is not capable of reacting with, being decomposed by, or being ignited by the contents of the inside containers.

The volume of the sorbent, generally vermiculite or a diatomaceous earth material such as floor dry, must be sufficient enough in volume to absorb all the liquid content inside the individual containers. Therefore, the maximum volume for packing into lab packs is 66 litres (18 gallons). At this volume when covered with sorbent, a 3:1 ratio of absorbent to chemical is maintained in the event of breakage inside the drum.

Lab packing is more involved than simply packing by the 9 Classes identified by Transport Canada, TDG, or Department of Transport, DOT, and involves the specific chemistry and nature of a compound when considering other compatibilities. TDG and DOT generally deals with dangerous goods that are in their original state and doesn't easily accommodate for the biproducts and decomposition products of mixed and old chemicals. This is where the differences come in from both TDG and DOT to the field chemist system which is based on the actual behaviour and nature of a product instead of the original labeling it was identified under.

Segregation

As discussed earlier in Section 3 Hazardous Materials Chemistry and Section 6 Hazard Assessment, the segregation of chemicals by compatibility, nature, class and behaviour of biproducts is both essential and critical in handling hazardous materials. Often chemicals are incorrectly simplified simply by the TDG or DOT classification which as previously noted, does not address the interactions that chemicals can have when exposed to a several variables. Therefore, segregation must be clearly understood and a learned practice that every employee who handles hazardous materials needs to learn.

Compatibility

The first and primary categorization of materials is based on compatibility. Recognizing the inherent nature of the product as well as the biproducts that result during heating or mixing is essential not only for personal safety, but from a disposal and destruction perspective.

The definition of compatible and incompatible are as follows:

- Compatible – capable of existing or performing in harmonious, agreeable, or congenial combination with another or others and/or capable of forming a chemically or biochemically stable system

- Incompatible – capable of producing an undesirable effect when used in combination with a particular substance and/or incapable of associating or blending with each other resulting in a hazardous condition or state.

Lab Packing incompatible waste streams may cause unwanted reactions to occur that may result in any number of risks.

Characteristics

Segregation is also very dependent on the four characteristics of hazardous materials identification:

- Ignitability - ignitable materials can create fires under certain conditions, are spontaneously combustible, or have a flash point less than 60.0°C (140 °F).

    o include solids that are spontaneously combustible

    o most oxidizers

    o some compressed gases

- Reactivity – reactive materials are evaluated by the rate at which a chemical substance tends to undergo a chemical reaction. It is very difficult to identify all situations that would deem a material as reactive simply due to conditions and situations, but generally these include

- o unstable materials that undergo a violent change that are below the classification of detonation

- o water reactive materials

- o Toxic by Inhalation, TIH materials

- Corrosivity - corrosive materials are generalized as acids or bases with a pH value that is less than or equal to 2, or greater than or equal to 12.5. These materials are capable of corroding metal containers, such as storage tanks, drums, and barrels

- Toxicity - the degree to which a substance can damage an exposed organism, either from short term acute exposure or long-term chronic exposure.

Each of these characteristics can be easily determined and evaluated in the field with the exception of toxicity as discussed in Section 6, Hazard Assessment. Toxicity information will need to be evaluated for each chemical of concern with the understanding that various products when reacted, will create an environment that is substantially more toxic than the sum of the individual chemicals involved. Additionally, unknown environments pose a much higher risk due to the lack of information that the responder has at their disposal for that particular chemical or mixtures.

General rules for segregation include:

- segregate compatible and incompatible chemicals

- segregate acidic and basic materials

- segregate organic materials from inorganic materials

- segregate flammable and ignitable materials from non-flammable materials

- segregate halogenated compounds from non-halogenated materials

- segregate liquids and solids

- segregate thio based compounds from isothio materials

- segregate heavy metal impacted materials

- segregate high hazard materials

- segregate reactive materials from non-reactive materials

- segregate polychlorinated biphenyls, PCB, from all other items.

Lab Pack Segregation Categories

Household Hazardous Waste and Commercial Waste:

Automotive

> ➢ Gas, diesel, glycols, oil filters, & oils
>
> ➢ Windshield fluid, lubricants & greases
>
> ➢ Auto-body resins, auto paints, solder

Agricultural

> ➢ Pesticides, herbicides, insecticides, fungicides
>
> ➢ Fertilizers, plant foods, lawn foods

Batteries

> ➢ Cell phones, rechargeable, portable 2-way radios
>
> ➢ NiCad, lithium Alkaline, lead acid,
>
> ➢ Watch, hearing-aid, flashlight

Cylinders

> ➢ Propane, acetylene torches, carbon dioxide, compressed air
>
> ➢ BBQ tanks

Household, Janitorial, Maintenance

> ➢ Cleaners, disinfectants, pool chemicals, water treatment
>
> ➢ Glues, epoxy, silicon, caulking
>
> ➢ Fluorescent tubes, fire extinguishers
>
> ➢ Off, Raid, Rat Poison, Ant Traps, Spider Killer, CLR, Mr. Clean, Bleach, Borax, Ajax

Paint

- Paints, thinners, spray paints

- Stains, shellac, varnish

- Varsol, latex paint, oil-based paint(s), aerosol cans

Specialty

- Explosive, radioactive sources, gun powders,

- PCB Ballasts,

- Mercury,

- Thermostat switches, ammunition, blasting caps, light ballasts

Pharmaceuticals

- Medicines – Warfarin, Insulin

- Topical creams, ointments

- Heart medication

- Anti-depressants

- Prescriptions:

    - Morphine, Codeine, Demerol, Valium, OxyContin/Oxycodone, Prozac, Ritalin, Cocaine packs, legalized marihuana

Controlled Materials

- Controlled Substance compounds

    - Schedule I, Controlled Drugs and Substances Act

    - Schedule II Cannabis Derivatives,

    - Schedule III Amphetamines/Barbiturates,

    - Schedule IV Steroids and Phenobarbitals,

    - Schedule V Propylhexedrine,

> - Schedule VI Precursors,
>
> - Schedule VII - 3kg Hashish or Cannabis,
>
> - Schedule VIII - 1g Hashish and 30 grams Cannabis
>
> - Smoke Detectors – Americium radioactive source
>
> - Bio-hazardous Materials
>
>> - Body fluids (human or animal) – urine, feces, blood, serum
>>
>> - Sharps – needles, scalpels, surgical items
>>
>> - Animal remains
>>
>> - Laboratory cultures
>>
>> - Septic waste

Chemical Hazardous Materials Waste – Lab Pack:

<u>Group A</u>

> - Inorganic acids that do not liberate poisonous gases
>
> - Examples include sulphuric, hydrochloric acid
>
> - TDG Class 8

<u>Group B</u>

> - Inorganic bases that do not liberate poisonous gases
>
> - Examples include sodium hydroxide, potassium hydroxide
>
> - TDG Class 8

<u>Group C</u>

> - Organic Solids
>
> - Examples include dry citric acid, sodium bicarbonate
>
> - TDG Class 6.1 with possible subgroups of 3, 8

Group D

- Organic Liquids
- Examples include acetone, methanol
- TDG Class 6.1 with possible subgroups of 3, 8

Group E

- Oxidizing Compounds
- Examples include Bleach, nitric acid, hydrogen peroxide, organic peroxides
- TDG Class 5.1, 5.2

Group F

- Pesticides (F1) and Herbicides (F2)
- Examples include 2,4-D, Roundup, Weedex, Mouse poison, ant/spider powder
- TDG Class 6.1 with possible subgroups of 3, 8

Group G

- Scintillation Vials (Solvent Based, non radioactive)
- TDG Class 3.1 with possible subgroups of 6.1

Group H

- Air and Water Reactive, Pyrophoric
- Examples include sodium metal, magnesium, lithium, phosphorous
- TDG Class 4

Group I

- Cyanide, Isocyanide (nitrogen-based)
- TDG Class 6.1 with possible subgroups of 8

Group J

- Thiocyanate (sulphur based)

- ➢ TDG Class 6.1 with possible subgroups of 8

Group K

- ➢ Arsenic Compounds
- ➢ Non Pesticide/Herbicide, Arsenic Trioxide, Arsenic Pentafluoride
- ➢ TDG Class 3.1 with possible subgroups of 3, 8

Group L

- ➢ Lecture Bottles and Cylinders
- ➢ Lab cylinders, small compressed cylinders
- ➢ TDG Class 3.1 with possible subgroups of 3, 8

Group M

- ➢ Over the Counter (OTC) medicines
- ➢ No Schedule I – VIII narcotics or controlled products
- ➢ TDG Class 6.1

Group P

- ➢ Paint Related Materials
- ➢ Oil-based paint, Latex, Varnish, Stain
- ➢ TDG Class 3, 6

Group X

- ➢ Polychlorinated biphenyls - PCB
- ➢ PCB Ballasts, PCB Liquid
- ➢ TDG Class 9

Group AE

- ➢ Aerosol Cans
- ➢ No lecture bottles, cylinders

➢ TDG Class 2

Chemical Hazardous Materials Waste – Bulk:

<u>Bulk Group AA1</u>

➢ Flammable Non-Halogenated Liquids, Less than 1% Solids

➢ Methanol, Toluene, Xylene, Flammable fuels

➢ TDG Class 3.1 with possible subgroups of 6.1

<u>Bulk Group AA2</u>

➢ Non-Flammable Non-Halogenated Liquids, Less than 1% Solids

➢ Formalin, Developing Fluids, Fixer, Dyes

➢ TDG Class 6.1 with possible subgroups of 8

<u>Bulk Group BB1</u>

➢ Flammable Halogenated Liquids, Less than 1% Solids

➢ Dichloromethane, Dibromomethane, Ethylene chloride

➢ TDG Class 3.1 with possible subgroups of 6.1

<u>Bulk Group BB2</u>

➢ Non-Flammable Halogenated Liquids, Less than 1% Solids

➢ Disinfectants, Pool Chemicals, Chloramine, Nitrogen Trichloride

➢ TDG Class 6.1 with possible subgroups of 6.1 and 8

Lab Pack Procedures

The general procedure for lab packing involves the following steps:

- Open-top drums should be set up on pallets in the designated lab packing area, with one drum for each category of materials that will be handled.

  - A 4 mil low density polyethylene drum liner should be put in drums that will hold oxidizers, acids, bases, picric acid, and other reactive materials that could damage the drum if released.

  - The drums need to be labeled with a shipping name and TDG/DOT information

  - A supply of sorbent will be required for the packing procedure. Additional spill response supplies (pads, absorbent, neutralization kits, fire extinguisher) should be immediately available as well.

  - Ensure the area is well-ventilated.

- Place a layer of about two - three inches of sorbent on the bottom of each drum.

  - Identify the chemical to be lab packed by identifying the chemical composition of the individual item or mixture from the manufacturer label, workplace label or any dangerous goods markings. Unknown materials are discussed in Section 6 Hazard Assessment.

- Placer the container into the appropriate lab pack drum based on categorization.

  o Place containers in an upright position in the drum. After the first layer is full, fill in empty spaces between containers with sorbent and start a second level.

  o Continue this process until the drum is full. Top off the drum with sorbent so that the containers will not move around while the drum is being transported. Fold the drum liner in (if applicable) and seal the drum.

- Ongoing documentation is needed to record each container that goes into the drum that has the chemical name, volume of container, and chemical state. This packing list is to be left with the drum at all times during packing. Lids on drums should be closed at all times when not being used.

- Once closed, the packing list is to be attached to the outside of the drum at all times to provide response personnel and employees to accurately identify the hazards of that drum.

- All closed drums that have been completed are to be stored and segregated accordingly.

Precautions

- Do not assume the label is correct. Generally, lab pack drums are for waste products so any labels, safety data sheets or workplace labels are subject to scrutiny. Assume the worst.

- Employees who lab pack are expected to have a comprehensive knowledge of chemicals and their properties both as a product and as a biproduct. If unsure of a compound, do not proceed until further information is obtained and confirmed by a person of senior competency.

- Unknown compounds require a great deal of caution and respect. If in doubt, secure the unknown container in a safe location and immediately contact your supervisor for additional help. Slow and easy is always the best choice.

- Personal protective equipment is mandatory. Understanding the hazard and the environment will help you choose the proper level of protection. Additional PPE may be required to accommodate for specific hazards associated with specific chemicals. In addition to standard PPE, respiratory protection, nitrile gloves, and face shields may be necessary.

Small Means of Containment Bulking

Chemicals which exist at ambient temperatures in a liquid form with sufficient vapour pressure to ignite in the presence of an ignition source are called flammable or combustible liquids (note that the flammable/combustible liquid itself does not burn; it is the vapor from the liquid that burns). Flammable Liquids are defined by several agencies such as NFPA, OSHA and the Global Harmonized System (GHS) at different Flashpoint values.

Frequently small containers of flammable liquids are consolidated into larger containment vessels through the process referred to as bulking. Depending on facility license and permits as well as workplace health and safety protocols, other liquids such as non-flammable liquids and corrosive liquids are often also bulked into larger containers. Each category of material being bulked will required specific precautions that are unique to the properties of that liquid, with flammable liquid bulking requiring particular attention to specific steps.

Flammable liquids possess a range of physical, ignition, combustion and reactivity properties that can affect the ability to control or extinguish fires. These hazards can be substantially magnified when these liquids are subjected to elevated ambient temperatures and/or pressure.

The general procedure for bulking flammable liquids involves the following steps:

- The liquid to be bulked needs to have less than 1% solid material since solids create issues for incineration during the disposal phase. It may be prudent to utilize a screen within the funnel that is used to pour the liquid into the drum.

- The receiving Drum needs to be grounded to ensure that no static electricity causes a spark during consolidation. Equally important, the effluent container holding the waste that will be poured into the receiving drum should be bonded to the funnel to also remove any possibility of static electricity. It is important to note that when using plastic 205 Litre (55 gallon) drums as the receiving drum, static electricity can build between the funnel and the effluent container and grounding is still required. Friction with concrete floors can also create static electricity and proper moving equipment is required to avoid this.

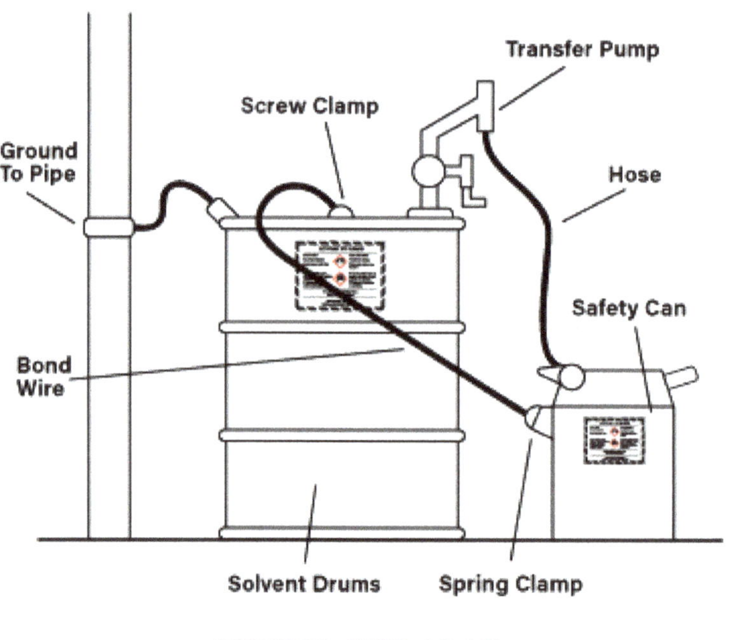

(CCOHS, 2023-08-15)

- Ensure the area is well ventilated and isolated from flammability sources.

- Open the receiving drum utilizing a spark proof wrench which is made of bronze alloy. It is important to open both bungs on the closed top drum during bulking to allow for air and pressure to be evacuated from the small bung during bulking.

- Carefully and slowly pour a small amount of the liquid into the receiving drum. If there is no reaction, continue with bulking. Set the empty originating containers to the side, for proper disposal.

- Fill the receiving drum allowing for a minimum 2 inches of expansion space at the top of the drum. Secure the bungs. And properly tighten it, with the bung wrench. Set aside for proper disposal and set up another plastic drum as needed.

Precautions

- It is important to know the chemical compatibility of the chemicals before you start bulking, to avoid possible dangerous chemical reactions.

- Regularly feel the side of the receiving drum to ensure there is no heat from a possible chemical reaction. Visually monitor the process for any smoke or reaction coming from the plastic drum. If either occurs, stop the procedure immediately and contact the supervisor.

- Flame retardant clothing is mandatory for flammable liquid bulking. Additional PPE may be required to accommodate for specific hazards associated with specific chemicals. In addition to standard PPE, respiratory protection, nitrile gloves, and face shields are frequently necessary.

Bonding and Grounding

Overview

The terms bonding and grounding are often used interchangeably within the industry but in fact have completely different meanings and methods which will be discussed in this section.

Bonding and grounding are both important and often required safeguards to be implemented by employees but alone do not provide adequate fire safety for operations such as flammable liquid transfers. Bonding and grounding techniques do provide some mitigation of static electrical hazards that are associated with flammable and explosive atmospheres but also required the use of proper containers and dispensing devices to assist with all other potential concerns.

Static electricity is very common, with lightning being one of the most observable examples of static discharge. Other common examples where static electricity builds are:

- Loading and unloading flammable materials

- Transferring flammable materials between containers

- Using vacuum trucks

- Using pressure/steam washers for tank cleaning

- Sandblasting

- Using centrifuges on drilling rigs

Static electricity essentially an imbalance of electrical charges within or on the surface of the material that remains on the material until it finds a pathway to move away. Static electricity can be created when two surfaces contact or separate, especially when one of the surfaces is an insulator and is highly resistant to electrical current. When this charge is released, it is referred to as static shock and can be enough to ignite environments that are dealing with flammable substances and vapours. Static electricity can be conducted through materials that have low electrical resistance via contact since there are some free electrons that are able to freely move within the material. Static can also be transferred by induction which is the transfer of these electrons across a gap that occurs due to unbalanced charges.

It should also be noted early on that people can also accumulate static electricity charges on their body which requires specific procedures to be implemented to discharge this static charge prior to entering suspect environments or working on electrostatic sensitive equipment that are susceptible to damage due to slight static discharge. Addition concerns with finely ground particles of dust also need to be noted since static electricity can become the ignition source for these environments.

Bonding

Bonding is the term used when all electrically conductive metallic surfaces of the equipment are interconnected to prevent any appreciable difference in conductivity between any individual points. The surfaces are generally not intended to be energized, such as the steel used in a 205 litre (55 gallon) drum.

Unlike grounding, bonding creates a low impedance pathway between structures and are not in any way related to the contact or connection with the Earth. A clear example of this is evident when we look at aircraft. Planes and jets themselves do not have contact with the ground but need to have all metallic surfaces bonded together to prevent unwanted reactions due to lightning strikes on the craft or even the static that builds up due to windspeed on the surface of the airplane. Common bonding equipment includes copper conductive wires that are fastened between the various metallic structures that can potentially incur static charges.

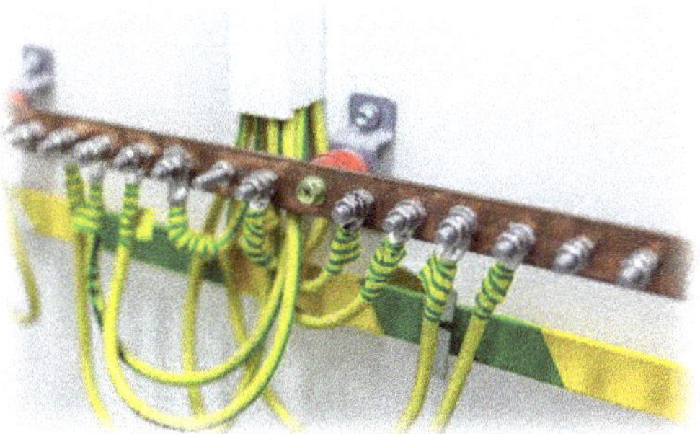

Grounding

Grounding as suggested by the term itself is the process of connecting all electrically conductive metallic surfaces of the equipment to the planet itself or to some conducting body that serves in place of the Earth. The term grounding is used primarily in North America, and is referred to as Earthing throughout much of Europe.

Grounding is accomplished by implementing a dedicated line commonly referred to as an electrode that ensures a direct electrical connection to the Earth. Grounding provides several protection mechanisms such as helping trigger fuses and circuit breakers if the internal insulation fails, ensuring that exposed metal surfaces do not have dangerous voltages with respect to the ground itself and preventing electric shock. As well, grounding limits the buildup of static electricity as earlier discussed.

Grounding electrodes are not only metal rods that go into the ground as depicted above and can include several alternate mechanisms including:

- Underground water lines

- Steel columns inherent in building design

- Rebar that is encased in concrete

- Copper tubing

- Some neoprene rubber blankets that are semi-conductive

Limitations

Bonding and grounding alone do not provide adequate fire safety for operations as mentioned earlier. In both cases, risks and limitations exist that need to be identified and understood.

- Grounding does not always reduce the dangers of touch potential. The electrode to Earth contact resistance is very high which in turn means that very little fault current will return to the power supply. In turn, the internal circuit overcurrent switch will therefore not open and clear the ground fault circuit which will make the metal parts associated with the equipment remain energized. Touching the equipment will then result in electric shock.

- Paint, rust and other residues that exist on bonding and grounding contact points can significantly affect the ability to dissipate static electricity. Ensuring a clean and strong contact point that is secure is critical for effective results.

- Weather conditions that have low humidity increase the rate at which static electricity builds. Work in dry and cold winter situations increases the amount of static electricity that needs to be dissipated.

- Addition of components to equipment such as stingers and hoses need to be bonded even if all other equipment is already bonded.

- The amount of current created by friction is dependent on several factors including the connection of two materials that have substantially different electrical potentials.

Grounding sites need to have adequate soil to provide proper results. Sandy soils and frozen grounds provide poor grounding since sand is a poor conductor and frozen ground has a higher resistance to electricity. Dry soil is also a poor conductor and has higher resistance as well where salty (alkaline) soil has a lower resistance and is a better conductor.

Chapter 8:

Spill Response

Emergency management and response plan

An emergency can be defined as an unplanned event that causes or creates the potential for fatalities, serious injuries, major loss or damage to property, significant environmental impacts or danger to the public. The occurrence of one or more of these events requires the prompt coordination of resources to protect the health, safety, and welfare of people and to limit damage to property and the environment.

The primary objective of any Emergency Management and Response Plan is to clearly define the framework and process that will facilitate the competency of any company to manage emergency situations throughout all multi-jurisdictional regions that a company may operate within. In the event of an emergency, these plans provide general guidance, organizational structure and specific direction on preparedness and response activities intended to preserve and protect life, property and the environment.

All emergency plans should be progressive documents designed to follow traditional format of emergency management and compartmentalize sections for ease of use before, during, and after the incident. As well as having plans developed for emergencies, the ongoing growth of the plan will often allow for the discovery of unacknowledged or unrecognized hazardous environments that may impinge on a response, and allow for proactive elimination and control. By preplanning and ongoing training, deficiencies and potential lack of resources become evident, allowing for action before the emergency arises. Often regular channels of authority, communication and resources cannot be relied on to function normally, and having a plan in place can prevent health and safety as well as financial impacts.

Emergency plans are continuous cycles that hinge on 4 core principles:

- **Preparation**: the planning, training and preparation of frontline and support staff for emergencies through a continuous training program

- **Response**: the implementation of the plan by responding in a safe and planned manner with preservation of life as the highest priority

- **Recovery**: providing restoration efforts and continuously improving to reduce future vulnerability

- **Mitigation:** Utilize the learnings to improve the plan and prevent future events

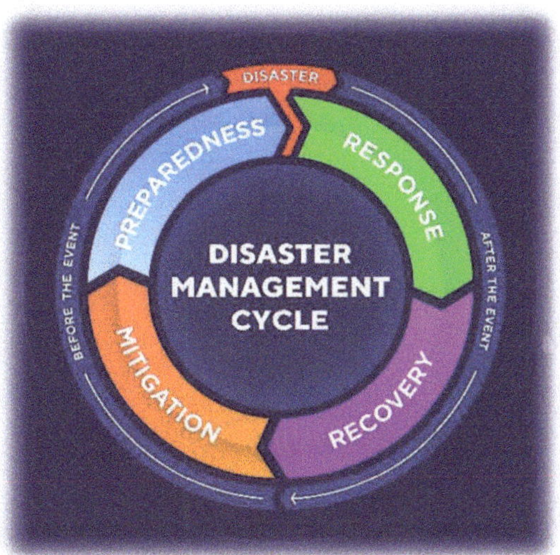

Incident Command System

The Incident Command System, ICS, is a standardized management system that approaches the command, control and coordination of a response by integrating a system of personnel, equipment, procedures and communications within a common organization structure. ICS is designed to:

- ensure the safety of all personnel

- successfully achieve the objectives of the response

- efficiently utilize all resources required

Emergency planning establishes an emergency organizational structure within the Incident Command System to integrate the resources of a company and coordinate external resources and agencies to ensure provision of the most effective and recognized protocols for response and recovery during an event. ICS is an international on-scene and All-Hazard emergency management standardized system adopted by both provincial and federal agencies to represent organizational best practices. An emergency plan facilitates mutual alignment through facility leadership training, staff orientation, emergency management practice and mock exercises, evaluation of actual emergency events and continuous improvement efforts driven by the stakeholders. ICS can be used to manager:

- Fires

- Hazmat spills

- Multiple casualties

- Derailments

- Facility releases

- Natural disasters

ICS is based on five core values:

- Standardization

    o The use of common terminology

- Command

    o Establishment and transfer of Command

    o Chain of Command and unity of Command

- Planning and Organization

    o Management by objectives

    o Incident Action Plan (IAP)

    o Modular organization

    o Manageable span of control

- Facilities and Resources

    o Comprehensive resource management

    o Incident locations and facilities

- Professionalism

    o **Accountability:** Effective accountability at all jurisdictional levels and within individual functional areas during incident operations is essential. To that end, the following principles must be adhered to:

- o **Check-In:** All responders, regardless of agency affiliation, must report in to receive an assignment in accordance with the procedures established by the Incident Commander.

- o **Incident Action Plan:** Response operations must be directed and coordinated as outlined in the IAP.

- o **Unity of Command:** Each individual involved in incident operations will be assigned to only one supervisor.

- o **Span of Control:** Supervisors must be able to adequately supervise and control their subordinates, as well as communicate with and manage all resources under their supervision.

- o **Resource Tracking:** Supervisors must record and report resource status changes as they occur. (This topic is covered in a later unit.)

- o **Dispatch/Deployment:** Personnel and equipment should respond only when requested or when dispatched by an appropriate authority.

ICS consists of 5 functional components which fall under the span of control of one delegated Incident Commander who is responsible to manage the incident unless that incident requires a multi-discipline response system referred to as Unified Command. These components are:

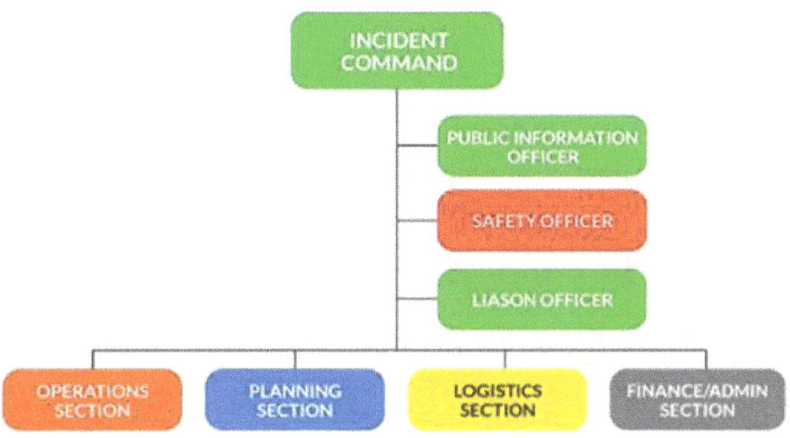

Command: (Green)

- Consists of Incident Commander and Command Staff positions who report to the Incident Commander

- Sets the objectives and priorities of the plan and has overall responsibility at the event

Operations: (Orange)

- Responsible for all tactical activities with a focus on reducing the immediate hazard, saving lives and property

- develops objectives and directs all resources to conduct operations to establish control and accomplish objectives

Planning: (Blue)

- Develops action plan to accomplish the objectives and collects/maintains information to maintain resources

Logistics: (Yellow)

- Provides support, resources and related services needed to support the incident objectives

- Provides facilities, security, transportation, supplies, maintenance, fuel, food, medical services and communications

Finance/Admin: (Grey)

- Provides accounting services and procurement, time recording and cost analyses

- Established when activities require on-scene or incident specific finance and administrative support services

Concept Of Operations

The plan is based upon the concept that emergency operations will be initiated and handled with internal response and resources until such time that external assistance is required or requested when a situation exceeds internal capabilities. All incidents will begin with an Alert Level of response and escalate as required.

Emergency incidents are managed by the Incident Commander, which is initially the person who witnesses the event. This individual manages the incident until such time that command can be transferred to a trained employee. The Incident Commander utilizes the basics of the ICS system to manage the incident. This effort is supported by facility and corporate emergency operations groups as well as local emergency measures organizations and identified sub-contractors and cooperative agencies.

ICS is a field-driven system that builds from the ground up with the capacity to expand as the situation and resources required grow. The larger the event, the greater the need to have clearly identified and defined roles assigned to individuals to allow for continued expansion. With smaller and less complex events, one individual may frequently be required to act in various roles provided they can maintain a proper span of control on the responsibilities that are required for each identified role. The following summarizes the typical essential positions that will be assigned for events:

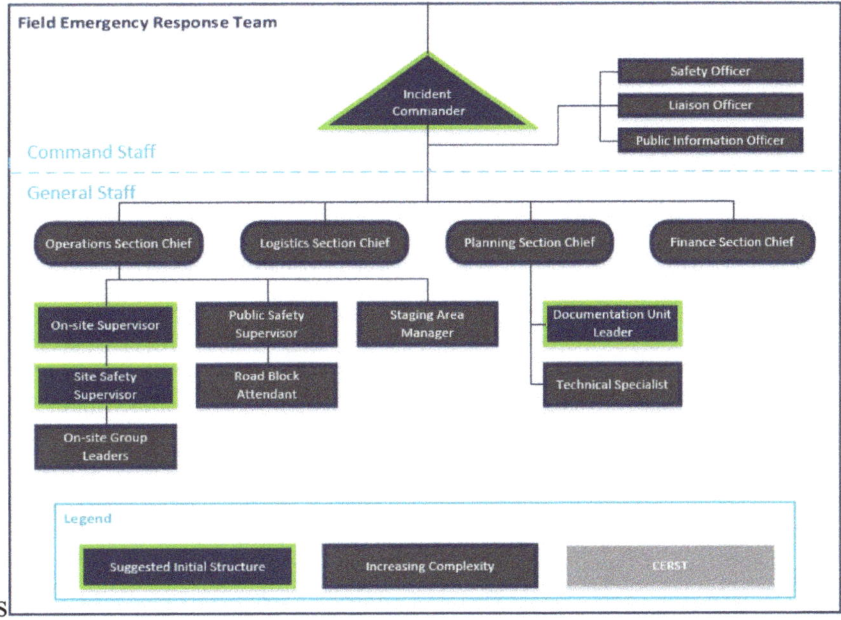

The Plan addresses the need for coordinated responses to all incidents and has been developed with the following priorities:

1.   To preserve the health and safety of people;

2.   To protect and minimize impact to the property;

3.   To protect and minimize impact to the environment.

Upon discovery of an emergency, the individual who initially discovers the scene will assume the role of Interim Incident Commander with the primary function to keep people safe and secure the scene. The Interim Incident Commander will immediately contact their supervisor and will remain in the role of Interim Incident Commander until such time that a more qualified or experienced individual is present and capable of assuming command.

Response to all emergencies follows the Seven-Step Response Strategy:

1. Evacuate

2. Alarm

3. Assess

4. Protect/Plan

5. Execute/Rescue

6. Aid

7. Stand-down

Incident Classification

An incident is classified by evaluating two factors:

- Consequence of the incident

- Likelihood of the Incident Escalating

To use the matrix first determine the consequence rating of the incident by using table 1. Select the most applicable category based on the description. Then apply the same to process to table 2 "Likelihood." Add the corresponding numbers to the two most applicable category's (Consequence & Likelihood) to calculate the risk level and corresponding emergency level in Tables 3 & 4.

Table 1 - Consequences of Incident

Rank	Category	Example of consequence in category
1	Minor	• No worker injuries. • Nil or low media interest. • Liquid release contained on-lease. • Gas release impact on-lease only.
2	Moderate	• First aid treatment required for on-lease worker(s). • Local and possible regional media interest. • Liquid release not contained on-lease. • Gas release impact has potential to extend beyond lease.
3	Major	• Worker(s) require hospitalization. • Regional and national media interest. • Liquid release extends beyond lease - not contained. • Gas release impact extends beyond lease - public health/safety could be jeopardized.
4	Catastrophic	• Fatality. • National and international media interest. • Liquid release off-lease not contained - potential for, or is impacting water or sensitive terrain. • Gas release impact extends beyond lease - public health/safety jeopardized.

Table 2 – Likelihood of Incident Escalating

Rank	Descriptor	Description
1	Unlikely	The incident is contained or controlled and it is unlikely that the incident will escalate. There is no chance of additional hazards. Ongoing monitoring required.
2	Moderate	Control of the incident may have deteriorated but imminent control of the hazard by the licensee is probable. In either case it is unlikely that the incident will further escalate.
3	Likely	Imminent and/or intermittent control of the incident is possible. The licensee has the capability of using internal and/or external resources to manage and bring the hazard under control in the near term.
4	Almost certain or currently occurring	The incident is uncontrolled and there is little chance that the licensee will be able to bring the hazard under control in the near term. The licensee will require assistance from outside parties to remedy the situation.

What is the likelihood that the incident will escalate, resulting in an increased exposure to public health, safety, or the environment?

Table 3 - Risk Levels based on Likelihood and Consequences

Consequence Rank		Likelihood Rank			
Minor (1)		2	3	4	5
Moderate (2)		3	4	5	6
Major (3)		4	5	6	7
Catastrophic (4)		5	6	7	8
		Unlikely (1)	Moderate (2)	Likely (3)	Almost Certain (4)

Table 4 – Incident Classification

Risk Level	Assessment Results
Very Low 2-3	Alert (Level 0)
Low 4-5	Level 1 Emergency
Medium 6	Level 2 Emergency
High 7-8	Level 3 Emergency

(Courtesy of Manitoba Conservation and Water Stewardship)

Site Control

Site Map

A site map should be prepared prior to site entry and updated throughout the course of site operations. The map should show:

- Topographic features

- Prevailing wind direction

- Water drainage and site directional flow

- Location of key locations

    o Buildings

    o Ponds

    o Incident Command Post

    o Incident Location

    o Staging Areas

    o Muster Points

Site Work Zones

Work zones are established to control the flow of personnel and avoid the spread of hazardous materials from the contaminated zone to other areas. Defined delineation of each work area is essential and are broken down into three primary zones:

- Hot Zone

    o Referred to as the Exclusion Zone

    o The area where contamination exists

    o Includes the Hot Line which is the outer boundary of where the exclusion zone stops

- Warm Zone

    o Referred to as the Contamination Reduction Zone

    o The area that transitions between the Hot Zone and Cold Zone

    o Includes the Contamination Reduction Corridor often referred to as the Decontamination Zone

- Cold Zone

    o Referred to as the Support Zone

    o The location of administrative and other support personnel

Decontamination

A decontamination plan should be developed and set up before any personnel or equipment may enter areas where the potential for exposure to hazardous substances exists. The decontamination plan should determine:

- The number of stations needed and the layout of the route

- The equipment needed at each station

- The methods to be used at each station

- The procedures to prevent contamination of clean areas

- The methods needed to minimize all worker contact

- The disposal methods and requirements needed for clothing and equipment

Decontamination should occur in the Warm Zone. It is important to understand that decontamination is not optional – the level and depth of what is needed will vary for each job, and may be very simple (wiping your boots) to extremely detailed (several stages of decon).

Spill Containment And Control

Source Control

Stopping the source of any release will be case-by-case and specifically dependent on the situation, material, area, and availability of equipment. Many hazardous material events involve a breach of a specified volume of product that will eventually stop releasing once the material is exhausted. The concern becomes great when dealing with extremely hazardous materials including Toxic by Inhalation Hazard (TIH) materials, biological threats, and materials that exhibit explosive properties. In each case, various pieces of equipment can be utilized that range from market patch kits, wood plugs and blocks, and a variety of tarps and drip trays.

When dealing with compressed cylinders, especially at larger volumes, the units become more difficult to deal with and require the use of specialized "capping kits". These kits specifically deal with three types of compressed units:

- A Kit: used for capping and sealing the valves on a variety of 100/150 pound cylinders

- B Kit: used for capping and sealing the vales on the tonne sized cylinders

- C Kit: used for capping and sealing the valves on rail tank cars

Sorbents

Sorbents are insoluble materials or mixtures of materials used to recover liquids through the mechanism of absorption, or adsorption, or both. There are two categories of sorbents:

- **Absorbents** are materials that pick up and retain liquid causing the material to swell (50 percent or more).

- **Adsorbents** are insoluble materials that are coated by a liquid on its surface. To be useful in combating oil spills, sorbents need to be both oleophilic (oil-attracting) and hydrophobic (water-repellent).

As per the EPA, sorbents can be divided into three basic categories:

- **Natural organic sorbents:**

  - peat moss,

  - straw,

  - sawdust,

  - Organic sorbents can adsorb between 3 and 15 times their weight in oil.

  - **Natural inorganic sorbents:**

  - clay,

  - vermiculite,

  - sand

  - can adsorb from 4 to 20 times their weight in oil.

  - **Synthetic sorbents:**

    - include man-made materials that are similar to plastics, such as polyurethane, polyethylene, and polypropylene

- o designed to adsorb liquids onto their surfaces

- o synthetic sorbents can absorb up 70 times their own weight in oil.

SOCKS

Temporary placement to collect various products

- Hydrophilic (attracts oil) polypropylene that is hydrophobic (rejects water) and allows water to pass through

- Light and cost effective with overlapping carabiner-type connections to create a secure containment

- Must be compatible with product

BOOMS

Floating Containment barrier

- NOT the same as Socks which absorb/adsorb

- Consists of:

  - o Containment partition that floats and extends above the surface of the water

  - o Curtain that sinks into the water and extends below the surface of the water

  - o Inter-lockable metal ends to allow secure extension of booms

- General Purpose Booms

  - o Cost effective and re-usable

- o Inter-lockable sections that range in sizes from 6" (15cm) to 36" (90cm)

- o PVC that will not absorb oil but floats on surface to act as a containment

- o Sturdy but not suitable for high current situations

- o Temporary applications

- River Booms

  - o More expensive than general boom and re-usable

  - o Inter-lockable sections that range in sizes from 6" (15cm) to 36" (90cm) – usually custom order

  - o PVC that will not absorb oil but floats on surface to act as a containment. Tension units on top and bottom make them sturdy and rigid make them sturdy and very suitable for high current situations

  - o Temporary applications

- Ocean Booms

- Permanent Barrier Booms

  o Permanent installation applications up to 20 years

  o Debris and containment

  o Polyurathane foam buoyancy that are abrasion and UV resistant

Skimmers

A skimmer is a device for recovering spilled oil from the water's surface and can either be placed statically downstream of current or pulled behind boat to create a flow through skimmer. There are three types of skimmers:

Weir skimmers:

  o Use a dam or enclosure positioned at the oil/water interface.

Oleophilic ("oil-attracting") skimmers:

- o Use belts, disks, or continuous mop chains of oleophilic materials to blot the oil from the water surface. The oil is then squeezed out or scraped off into a recovery tank.

- o Includes chain or "rope-mop" skimmer.

Suction skimmers:

- o Oil is sucked up through wide floating heads and pumped into storage tanks.

Pumps

Centrifugal Pump:

- o Used to transport fluids by accelerating the fluid with an impeller and sending it to the discharge.

Diaphragm Pump:

- o Also referred to a s a membrane pump

- o Uses the reciprocating or "pumping" action of the vales on either side of the diaphragm

Lobe Pump:

- o Often referred to as a rotary pump.

- o Good for solids and viscous materials

Peristaltic Pump:

- o Often referred to as a roller pump.

- o Good for running dry and creating suction

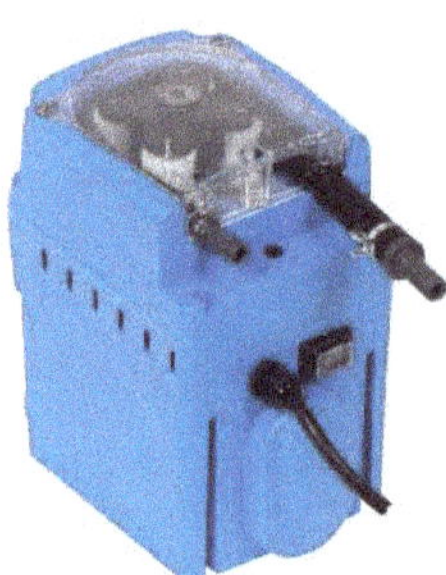

Response To A Small Spill (Less Than 450 Litres)

- **Notify other people** in the area that a spill has occurred. Prevent others from coming in contact with the spill (i.e. walking through the spilled chemical). The first priority is to always protect yourself and others.

- **Don the appropriate PPE/CPC** before beginning cleanup. Do not unnecessarily expose yourself to the chemical.

- **Stop the source** of the spill if possible, and if safe to do so.

- **Prevent spilled chemicals** from moving from location by building a dike with absorbent material if you can safely do so.

- **Add absorbent** material on and around the spill and allow the chemical to absorb. Apply enough absorbent to completely cover the spilled liquid.

- **Shovel** up the absorbed spill from the outside towards the middle.

- **Collect and contain** spilled material in a leak-proof container.

- **Label** the container accordingly.

- **Report** the spill to your supervisor.

- **Restock** any supplies used from any spill kits.

Response To A Large Spill (Greater Than 450 Litres)

- **Evacuate**

  o Stay calm.

  o Shut down the Facility

  o Get to the nearest safe area.

  o Move Upwind if release is downwind of you. Move Crosswind if release is upwind of you

  o Physically check into identified Muster Point locations

  o Alarm

  o Recognize the problem and try to identify the cause that must be controlled.

  o Call for onsite help. Notify your supervisor and activate the alarm system.

  o If immediately apparent, request regional off-site agency support as necessary

- **Assess**

  o Perform an immediate head count. Locate unaccounted personnel. Identify any casualties/potential casualties

  o Obtain situational awareness by gathering information from as many sources as possible, as quickly as possible

- o Assess and identify hazards, for example: trapped personnel, chemical release, fire.

- o Determine what happened, where it happened, and who saw it

- o Initiate the EMP Hazard Assessment to determine Level of situation using the risk assessment framework (matrix). Assess and initiate the Primary Internal Notification

- **Protect and Plan**

- o Protect people, environment, and property

- o Eliminate further losses and safeguard the area. Do not accept unnecessary risk

- o Remove all non-essential personnel from the area

- o Make a plan to identify and manage risks with logical steps to follow

- o Discuss the plan as a group to determine feasibility and effectiveness versus potential consequence

- o Establish a *Go/No Go* decision based on the acceptability of remaining risk(s)

- o Validate the action plan with the Station Manager who acts as Incident Operations Manager (IOM)

- o Initiate external notification assessment

- o Establish Incident Command Post

- o Assign roles

- o Begin documentation

- **Execute and Rescue**

- o Review and assess the rescue plan against immediate and existing conditions

- o Communicate the plan requirements to the response team and have team acknowledge understanding

- o Don all appropriate personal protective equipment necessary to safely perform any rescue efforts

- o Execute the plan as best as reasonably acceptable.

- o Manage the response with planned controls: Monitor and continuously evaluate response. <u>Stop</u> and re-evaluate if conditions change.

- **Aid**

- o Perform standard First Aid or help those already doing so

- o Arrange for transport to medical aid

- o Provide information to Emergency Medical Services

- **Stand-down**

- o Down-grade emergency by gaining approval from all necessary internal and external authorities

- o Demobilize emergency response teams and equipment

- o Undertake comprehensive debrief with Response Team

GLOSSARY

Absorption: A route of exposure. It occurs when a toxic material contacts the skin and enters the bloodstream by passing through the skin.

Accidental explosion: An unplanned or premature detonation/ignition of explosive/ incendiary material or material possessing explosive properties. The activity lead- ing to the detonation/ignition has no criminal intent and is primarily associated with legal, industrial, or commercial activities.

Accidental release measures – the steps to be taken in response to spills, leaks, or releases of a hazardous product to prevent or minimize adverse effects on people and property.

ACGIH® – see American Conference of Governmental Industrial Hygienists.

Acid: (1) Any of a class of chemical compounds whose aqueous solutions turn litmus paper red (has a pH less than 7) or react with and dissolve certain metals or react with bases to form salts. (2) A compound capable of transferring a hydrogen ion in solution. (3) A molecule or ion that combines with another molecule or ion by forming a covalent bond with two electrons from other species.

Acid, corrosive: A material that usually contains an H+ ion and is capable of dehydrating other materials.

Acute – sudden or brief. "Acute" can describe either the duration (length) of an exposure or a health effect. An acute exposure is a short-term exposure (lasting for minutes, hours or days-less than 14 days). An acute health effect is an effect that develops immediately or

Acute Toxicity - hazardous products classified in this hazard class cause serious health effects, including death, if swallowed, in contact with skin and/or if inhaled. Acute toxicity refers to adverse effects following:

- oral (swallowing) or dermal (skin) administration of a single dose, or multiple doses given within 24 hours, or

- an inhalation exposure of 4 hours or of a duration that is converted to four hours.

Acute inhalation toxicity could result from exposure to the hazardous product itself, or to a product that, upon contact with water, releases a gaseous substance that is able to cause acute toxicity. (See also "LC50" and "LD50".)

Acute toxicity estimate (ATE) – a numerical value that is used to evaluate acute toxicity. For a substance, the ATE is the LC50 or the LD50, if available, or a converted acute toxicity point estimate that is based on an experimentally obtained range or the classification category. For a mixture, the ATE is calculated for oral, dermal and inhalation toxicity based on the ATE values for all relevant ingredients and the percentage concentration in the product.

Administrative controls – controls that alter the way the work is done, including the timing of work, policies and other rules, and work practices such as standards and operating procedures (including training, housekeeping and equipment maintenance).

Aerosol: The dispersion of very fine particles of a solid or liquid in a gas, fog, foam, or mist.

Agent dosage: The concentration of a toxic vapor in the air multiplied by the time that the concentration is present or the time that an individual is exposed (mg-min/m3).

Alkaline: Any compound having the qualities of a base. Simplified, a substance that readily ionizes in aqueous solution to yield hydroxyl (OH−) anions. Alkalis have a pH greater than 7 and turn litmus paper blue.

Alpha particle: A form of ionizing radiation that consists of two protons and neutrons.

Ambient temperature: The normal temperature of the environment.

American Conference of Governmental Industrial Hygienists (ACGIH®) – an international association of occupational hygienists that develops guidelines for the practice of occupational hygiene, including Threshold Limit Values (TLVs®) and Biological Exposure Indices (BEIs®). This publication serves as the basis for occupational exposure limits in many jurisdictions around the world.

ANFO: An ammonium nitrate and fuel oil mixture, commonly used as a blasting agent. The proportions are determined by the manufacturer or user. It is commonly mixed with the addition of an "enhancer," such as magnesium or aluminum, to increase the rate of burn.

Anhydrous: Describes a material that contains no water (water-free).

Anion: A negatively charged ion that moves toward the anode (+ terminal) during electrolysis.

Oxidation occurs at the anode.

ANSI – ANSI stands for the American National Standards Institute.

Antidote: A material administered to an individual who has been exposed to a poison in order to counteract its toxic effects.

APF: Assigned protection factor. An expression of the ratio of the level of contaminant or test agent outside the respirator compared to the level measured inside the respirator face piece.

Asphyxia: Lack of oxygen and interference with oxygenation of the blood. Can lead to unconsciousness.

Asphyxiant: A vapor or gas that can cause unconsciousness or death by suffocation (lack of oxygen). Most simple asphyxiants are harmful to the body when they become so concentrated that they reduce (displace) the available oxygen in air (normally about 21%) to dangerous levels (18% or lower). Chemical asphyxiants, like carbon monoxide (CO), reduce the blood's ability to carry oxygen or, like cyanide, interfere with the body's utilization of oxygen

Asphyxiation: Asphyxia or suffocation. Asphyxiation is one of the principal potential hazards of working in confined spaces.

Aspiration hazards –liquids or solid products classified in this hazard class may be fatal if they enter directly through the mouth or nose, or indirectly from vomiting, into the trachea and lower respiratory system.

Aspiration toxicity includes severe acute effects, such as chemical pneumonia and varying degrees of pulmonary injury or death.

Atmospheric container: A type of container that holds products at atmospheric pressure (760 mm).

Atom: The smallest unit into which a material may be broken by chemical means. In order to be broken into any smaller units, a material must be subjected to a nuclear reaction.

Atomic weight (at. wt.): The relative mass of an atom. Basically, it equals the number of protons plus neutrons.

Autoignition: A process in which a material ignites without any apparent outside ignition source. In the process, the temperature of the material is raised to its ignition temperature by the heat transferred by radiation, convection, combustion, or some combination of all three.

Autoignition temperature: See Ignition temperature.

Bacteria: Single-celled organisms that multiply by cell division and can cause disease in humans, plants, or animals. Examples include anthrax, cholera, plague, tularemia, and Q fever.

Base: A chemical compound that reacts with an acid to form a salt. The term is applied to the hydroxides of the metals, to certain metallic oxides, and to groups of atoms containing one or more hydroxyl groups (OH−) in which hydrogen is replaceable by an acid radical. See Alkaline.

Beta particle: A form of ionizing radiation that consists of either electrons or positrons.

Bioaccumulative potential - describes the potential for the substance or certain components of a mixture to accumulate in animal or plant life, and possibly pass through the food chain.

Biohazard: Those organisms that have a pathogenic effect on life and the environment, and can exist in normal ambient environments. These hazards can represent themselves as disease germs and viruses.

Biological agent: Living organism, or the materials derived from it, that cause disease in or harm humans, animals, or plants, or cause deterioration of material. Biological agents may be found as liquid droplets, aerosols, or dry powders. A biological agent can be adapted and used as a terrorist weapon, such as anthrax, tularemia, cholera, encephalitis, plague, and botulism. There are three different types of bio- logical agents: bacteria, viruses, and toxins.

Biological Exposure Indices (BEIs®) - guidance values developed by ACGIH to assess biological monitoring results. Biological monitoring involves the measurement of the concentration of a chemical indicator (such as the substance itself or a chemical formed from the substance by the body) in body components (e.g., blood, urine) of people who have been exposed to the substance. Biological monitoring is used to indicate how much of the substance has been absorbed into the body. The BEI generally identifies a concentration below which nearly all workers should not experience adverse health effects.

Biohazardous infectious materials – hazardous products that are classified in this hazard class are products that contain microorganisms, nucleic acids or proteins that cause or are a probable cause of infection, with or without toxicity, in humans or animals.

Blasting agent: A material designed for blasting that has been tested in accordance with Sec. 173.114a (49 CFR). It must be so insensitive that there is little probability of accidental explosion or going from burning to detonation.

BLEVE: See Boiling liquid, expanding vapor, and explosion.

Blister agent: A chemical agent, also called a vesicant that causes severe blistering and burns to eyes, skin, and tissues of the respiratory tract. Exposure is through liquid or vapor contact. Also referred to as mustard agent. Examples include mustard and lewisite.

Blood agent: A chemical agent that interferes with the ability of blood to transport oxygen and causes asphyxiation. These substances injure a person by interfering with cell respiration (the exchange of oxygen and carbon dioxide between blood and tis- sues). Common examples are hydrogen cyanide and cyanogen chloride.

Blood asphyxiant: A chemical that is absorbed by the blood and changes or prevents the blood from flowing or carrying oxygen to cells. An example is carbon monoxide poisoning.

Boiling liquid, expanding vapor, explosion (BLEVE): The explosion and rupture of a container caused by the expanding vapor pressure as liquids in the container become overheated.

Boiling point: At this temperature, vapor pressure of a liquid now equals the surrounding atmospheric pressure (14.7 psi at sea level).

BTU (British Thermal Unit): Amount of heat required to raise 1 lb of H2O $-1°F$ at sea level.

Bulk shipment - a shipment of a hazardous product that is contained in any of the following, without intermediate containment or intermediate packaging,

- a vessel that has a water capacity equal to or greater than 450 l,

- a freight container, road vehicle, railway vehicle or portable tank,

- the hold of a ship, or

- a pipeline.

Canadian Centre for Occupational Health and Safety (CCOHS) – an occupational health and safety information service with the mandate to promote workplace health and safety, and encourage attitudes and methods that will lead to improved worker physical and mental health.

CCOHS provides a wide range of products and services, including free access to a large collection of factsheets on occupational health and safety topics.

CANUTEC: Canadian Transport Emergency Centre operated by the Transportation of Dangerous Goods (TDG) Directorate of Transport Canada. The Directorate's overall mandate is to promote public safety in the transportation of dangerous goods by all modes. CANUTEC was established in 1979 and is one of the major safety programs Transport Canada delivers to promote the safe movement of people and goods throughout Canada. Can be reached 24 h a day by calling 1-888-CAN-UTEC (226-8832), or *666 on a cellular phone.

Carcinogen: A material that either causes cancer in humans or, because it causes cancer in animals, is considered capable of causing cancer in humans.

Carcinogenicity – hazardous products classified in this hazard class may cause cancer or are suspected of causing cancer. Carcinogenicity means the production of cancer or an increase in the incidence of cancer occurring after exposure to a mixture or substance.

CAS Registry Number –the Chemical Abstracts Service Registry Number. This identification number that contains up to 10 digits is assigned to a chemical by the Chemical Abstracts Service, a division of the American Chemical Society. The CAS number is a unique identifier that designates only one substance.

Cation: A positively charged ion that moves toward the cathode during electrolysis. Reduction occurs at the cathode.

Caustic: (1) Burning or corrosive. (2) A hydroxide of a light metal. Broadly, any compound having highly basic properties. A compound that readily ionizes in aqueous solution to yield OH− anions, with a pH above 7, and turns litmus paper blue. See Alkaline; Base.

Cellular asphyxiant: A material that, upon entering the body, inhibits the normal function of cells. Examples are CO, hydrogen cyanide, or hydrogen sulfide poisoning.

Central nervous system (CNS): In humans, the brain and spinal cord, as opposed to the peripheral nerves found in the fingers, etc.

Chemical agent: There are five classes of chemical agents, all of which produce incapacitation, serious injury, or death: nerve agents, blister agents, blood agents, choking agents, and irritating agents. A chemical substance used in military operations intended to kill, seriously injure, or incapacitate people through its physiological effects.

Chemical burn: A burn that occurs when the skin comes into contact with strong acids, strong alkalis, or other corrosive materials. These agents literally eat through the skin and, in many cases, continue to do damage as long as they remain in contact with the skin.

Chemical name – a scientific designation of a material or substance:

- that is made according to the naming rules of either the Chemical Abstracts Service, a division of the American Chemical Society, or the International Union of Pure and Applied Chemistry, or

- that is internationally recognized and that clearly identifies the material or substance.

Chemical properties: A property of matter that describes how it reacts with other substances.

Chemical reaction: A process that involves the bonding, unbonding, or rebonding of atoms. A chemical change takes place that actually changes substances into other substances.

Chemical reactivity: The process whereby substances are changed into other substances by the rearrangement, or recombination, of atoms.

Chemical stability – the ability of a product to remain unchanged under normal ambient and anticipated storage and handling conditions of temperature and pressure. An unstable product may decompose, burn or explode under normal environmental conditions. Any indication that the product is unstable gives a warning that special handling and storage precautions may be necessary.

Chemically unstable gas – a flammable gas that is liable to react explosively even in the absence of air or oxygen.

Chemicals under pressure – relates to hazardous products that are liquids or solids that are packaged in a receptacle (other than an aerosol dispenser) and that are pressurized with a gas at a gauge pressure of 200 kPa or more at 20°C. This hazard class excludes any gas under pressure as defined by the *Hazardous Products Act* and regulations.

Chronic– long-term or prolonged. "Chronic" can describe either the length (duration) of an exposure or a health effect. A chronic exposure is a long-term exposure (lasting for months or years). A chronic health effect is an adverse health effect resulting from long-term exposure or a persistent adverse health effect resulting from a short-term exposure.

CHEMTREC: Chemical Transportation Emergency Center operated by the Chemical Manufacturers Association. Provides information or assistance to emergency responders. CHEMTREC contacts the shipper or producer of the material for more detailed information, including on-scene assistance when feasible. Can be reached 24 h a day by calling 1-800-424-9300.

CHLOREP: Chlorine Emergency Plan operated by the Chlorine Institute. A 24-h mutual- aid program. Response is activated by a CHEMTREC call to the designated CHLOREP's geographical-sector assignments for teams.

Choking agents: These agents exert their effects solely on the lungs and result in the irritation of the alveoli of the lungs. Agents cause the alveoli to constantly secrete watery fluid into the air sacs, which is called pulmonary edema. When a lethal amount of a choking agent is received, the air sacs become so flooded that the air cannot enter and the victim dies of anoxia (oxygen deficiency); also known as dry drowning.

Chronic: Applies to long periods of action, such as weeks, months, or years.

Chronic effects: An adverse health effect on a human or animal body with symptoms that develop slowly or that recur frequently due to the exposure of hazardous chemicals.

Chronic exposure: Repeated doses or exposure to a material over a relatively prolonged period of time.

Closed-cup tester: A device for determining flash points of flammable and combustible liquids, utilizing an enclosed cup or container for the liquid. Recognized types are the Tagliabue (Tag) Closed Tester, the Pensky–Martens Closed Tester, and the Setaflash Closed-Cup Tester.

CNS: See Central nervous system.

Coefficient of water/oil distribution – the ratio of a product's distribution between the water and oil portions of a mixture of water and oil. A value of less than 1 indicates that the product is more soluble in oils. A value of greater than 1 indicates that the product is more soluble in water.

Combustibility: The ability of a substance to undergo rapid chemical combination with oxygen, with the evolution of heat.

Combustible dust: Particulate material that, when mixed in air, will burn or explode.

Combustible liquid: The term commonly used for liquids that emit burnable vapors or mists. Technically, a liquid whose vapors will ignite at a temperature of 100°F or above.

Compound: A substance composed of two or more elements that have chemically reacted. The compound that results from the chemical reaction is unique in its chemical and physical properties.

Complex mixture – a mixture that has a commonly known generic name and that is:

- naturally occurring,

- a fraction of a naturally occurring mixture that results from a separation process, or

- a modification of a naturally occurring mixture or a modification of a fraction of a naturally occurring mixture that results from a chemical modification process.

Compressed gas: Any material or mixture having in the container an absolute pressure exceeding 40 psi at 70°F or, regardless of the pressure at 70°F, having an absolute pressure exceeding 104 psi at 130°F; or any liquid flammable material having a vapor pressure exceeding 40 psi absolute at 100°F as determined by testing. Also includes cryogenic or "refrigerated liquids" (DOT) with boiling points lower than −130°F at 1 atm.

Concentration: The amount of a material that is mixed with another material.

Concentration (corrosives): In corrosives, the amount of acid or base compared to the amount of water present. Corrosives have "strength" and "concentration." See Strength.

Container – includes a bag, barrel, bottle, box, can, cylinder, drum or similar package or receptacle but does not include a storage tank. (See also "Outer container".)

Control parameters– include occupational exposure limits and biological limit values. Depending on their source, occupational exposure limit values have different names and often have different numerical values. (See also "Occupational exposure limit values".)

Controls– measures used to protect workers from exposure to a hazardous product. Control measures include engineering controls (e.g., ventilation), administrative controls (e.g., scheduling, training) or personal protective equipment.

Consignee: The person or organization to whom the consignment is to be delivered.

Consigner: The person or organization who acts as the shipper.

Contaminant: (1) A toxic substance that is potentially harmful to people, animals, and the environment. (2) A substance not in pure form.

Corrosive: A chemical that causes visible destruction of or irreversible alterations in living tissue by chemical action at the site of contact; a liquid that causes a severe corrosion rate in steel. A corrosive is either an acid or a caustic (a material that reads at either end of the pH scale).

Corrosive material (DOT): A material that causes the destruction of living tissue and metals.

Covalent bond: A chemical bond in which atoms share electrons in order to form a molecule.

Critical pressure: The pressure required to liquefy a gas at its critical temperature.

Critical temperature: The temperature above which a gas cannot be liquefied by pressure.

Cryogenic burn: Frostbite; damage to tissues as a result of exposure to low temperatures. It may involve only the skin, extend to the tissue immediately beneath it, or lead to gangrene and loss of affected parts.

Cryogenic cylinder: An insulated metal cylinder contained within an outer protective metal jacket. The area between the cylinder and the jacket is normally under vacuum. The cylinders range in size from a Dewier (similar to a small thermos) up to 24 in. in diameter and 5 ft in length. Examples of materials found in these types of cylinders are argon, helium, nitrogen, and oxygen.

Cryogenic liquid: A liquid with a boiling point below −130°F.

Cylinder: A container for liquids, gases, or solids under pressure. Ranges in size from aerosol containers found at home, such as spray deodorant, to the cryogenic (insulated) cylinders for nitrogen that can be approximately 24 in. in diameter and 5 ft in length. Pressure ranges from a few pounds to 6000 lb per in.2

Dangerous when wet: Materials that when exposed to water allow a chemical reaction to take place and often produce flammable or poisonous gases, heat, and a caustic solution. An example is sodium.

Decomposition: Separation of larger molecules into separate constituent and smaller parts.

Decomposition (chemical): A reaction in which the molecules of a chemical break down to its basic elements, such as carbon, hydrogen, or nitrogen, or to more simple com- pounds. This often occurs spontaneously, liberating considerable heat and often large volumes of gas.

Decomposition temperature – the temperature at which the product chemically decomposes.

Decontamination: The physical or chemical process of reducing and preventing the spread of contamination from persons and equipment used at a hazardous materials incident.

Deflagration: Explosion, with rapid combustion, up to 1250 ft/s.

Density – the weight of a product for a given volume. Density is usually given in units of grams per millilitre (g/mL) or grams per cubic centimetre (g/cc). The volume of a product in a container can be calculated from its density and weight.

Detonating cord: A flexible cord containing a center cord of high explosives used to detonate other explosives with which it comes in contact.

Detonation: An explosion at speeds above 1250 ft/s and many times over 3300 ft/s.

Detonator: Any device containing a detonating charge that is used for initiating detonation in an explosive. This term includes, but is not limited to, electric and nonelectric detonators (either instantaneous or delayed) and detonating connectors.

Dewer container: Small (less than 25 gal) container used for temporary storage or handling of cryogenic liquids.

Dilution: The application of water to water-miscible hazardous materials. The goal is to reduce the hazard of a material to safe levels by reducing its concentration.

Dose: The accumulated amount of a chemical to which a person is exposed.

DOT: U.S. Department of Transportation. Regulates transportation of materials to protect the public as well as fire, law, and other emergency response personnel.

Element: A substance that cannot be broken down into any other substance by chemical means.

Empirical formula: Describes the ratio of the number of each element in the molecule, but not the exact number of atoms in the molecule.

Emulsification: The process of dispersing one liquid in a second immiscible liquid. The largest group of emulsifying agents are soaps, detergents, and other compounds whose basic structure is a paraffin chain terminating in a polar group.

Endothermic: A process or chemical reaction that is accompanied by absorption of heat.

Engineering controls – controls used to remove the hazardous conditions or separate a worker from a hazard. These controls include design of or modifications to plants, equipment, or processes to reduce or eliminate hazards (e.g., process enclosure, isolation of an emission source, or ventilation).

Etiologic agent: Those living organisms or their toxins that contribute to the cause of infection, disease, or other abnormal condition.

Evaporation: The process in which liquid becomes vapor as more molecules leave the vapor than return.

Evaporation rate – a term that indicates how quickly a product evaporates compared to n-butyl acetate. The evaporation rate of butyl acetate is 1. A value greater than 1 means the product has a high evaporation rate and will mix with air very quickly.

Exothermic reaction: A chemical reaction that liberates heat during the reaction.

Expansion ratio: The amount of gas produced from a given volume of liquid escaping from a container at a given temperature.

Explosion: The sudden and rapid production of gas, heat, noise, and many times a shock wave, within a confined space.

Explosive(DOT): Any chemical compound or mixture whose primary function is to produce an explosion.

Explosives, high: Explosive materials that can be used to detonate by means of a detonator when unconfined (e.g., dynamite).

Explosives, low: Explosive materials that deflagrate rather than detonate (e.g., black pow- der, safety fuses, and "special fireworks" as defined by Class 1.3 Explosives).

Explosive limits – see Lower explosive limit (LEL) or Lower flammability limit (LFL) and Upper explosive limit (UEL) or Upper flammability limit (UFL).

Extinguishing media – agents which can put out fires. Common extinguishing agents are water, carbon dioxide, dry chemical, and "alcohol" foam. It is important to know which extinguishers can be used on fires caused by the hazardous products in the workplace (suitable extinguishing media) so they can be made available at the worksite. It is also important to know which agents cannot be used (unsuitable extinguishing media) since an incorrect extinguisher may not work or may create a more hazardous situation. If several products are involved in a fire, an extinguisher effective for all of the products should be used.

Eye irritation – hazardous products classified for Eye irritation, as part of the Serious eye damage/eye irritation hazard class, produce changes in the eye after exposure of the eye to a substance or mixture which are fully reversible within an observation period of 21 days after exposure. Effects could include redness, itching or swelling.

Fire point: The lowest temperature at which the vapor above the liquid will ignite and continue to burn, usually a few degrees above the flash point.

First-aid measures – emergency care given immediately to a person who is experiencing symptoms of exposure to the product.

Flammable gas: A gas that at ambient temperature and pressure forms a flammable mixture with air at a concentration of 13% by volume or less; or a gas that at ambient temperature and pressure forms a range of flammable mixtures with air greater than 12% by volume, regardless of the lower explosive limit.

Flammable limits: The range of the percentages of vapor mixed with air that are capable of ignition, as opposed to those mixtures that have too much or too little vapor to be ignited. Also called explosive limits.

Flammable gases – hazardous products classified in this hazard class are gases that have a flammable range when mixed with air (at 20° C and 101.3 kPa).

Flammable liquid: A liquid that gives off readily ignitable vapors. Defined by the NFPA and DOT as a liquid with a flash point below 100°F (38°C).

Flammable range: The percentage of fuel vapors in air where ignition can occur. Flammable range has an upper and lower limit.

Flammable solid: A solid (other than an explosive) that ignites readily and continues to burn. It is liable to cause fires under ordinary conditions or during transportation through friction or retained heat from manufacturing or processing. It burns so vigorously and persistently as to create a serious transportation hazard. Included in this class are spontaneously combustible and water-reactive materials. An example is white phosphorus.

Flash point: The minimum temperature at which a liquid gives off vapor within a test vessel in sufficient concentration to form an ignitable mixture with air near the surface of the liquid.

Formula: A combination of the symbols for atoms or ions that are held together chemically.

Freezing point: The temperature at which a material changes its physical state from a liquid to a solid.

Fugitive emission – a gas, liquid or solid, vapour, fume, mist, fog or dust that escapes from process equipment or from emission control equipment or form a product where workers may be readily exposed to it.

Fumes – very small, airborne, solid particles formed by the cooling of a hot vapour. For example, a hot zinc vapour may form when zinc-coated steel is welded. The vapour then condenses to form fine zinc fume as soon as it contacts the cool surrounding air. Fumes are smaller than dusts and are more easily breathed into the lungs.

Gas: A formless fluid that occupies the space of its enclosure. It can settle to the bottom or top of an enclosure when mixed with other chemicals. It can be changed to its liquid or solid state only by increased pressure and decreased temperature.

Germ cell mutagenicity – hazardous products classified in this hazard class cause or may cause an increased occurrence of heritable gene mutations, including heritable structural and numerical chromosome aberrations in germ cells, occurring after exposure to a mixture or substance.

GHS: Global Harmonized System

Globally Harmonized System of Classification and Labelling of Chemicals (GHS) –an international system that defines and classifies the hazards of chemical products, and communicates health and safety information on labels and SDSs in a standardized way. The GHS is developed through consensus at the United Nations. The GHS "purple book" is a guidance document. Only the elements of GHS that have been explicitly adopted in legislation (e.g., in the HPR) are enforceable.

Half Life: The time required for a quantity to reduce to half its initial value.

Halogens: A chemical family that includes fluorine, chlorine, bromine, and iodine.

Halon: Halogenated hydrocarbons (containing the elements F, Cl, Br, or I) used to sup- press or prevent combustion.

Handling and storage – the basic precautions to be followed when handling and for storing a hazardous product, or the basic equipment to be used during handling and storing.

Hazard – the potential for harmful effects. The hazards of a product are evaluated by examining the properties of the product, such as toxicity, flammability and chemical reactivity.

Hazard class – a way of grouping products together that have similar hazards or properties.

Hazard category – the subdivision within a hazard class that tells you about how hazardous the product is (the severity of hazard). Category 1 is always the greatest level of hazard (it is the most hazardous within that class). If Category 1 is further divided, Category 1A within the same hazard class is a greater hazard than category 1B. Category 2 within the same hazard class is more hazardous than category 3, and so on.

Hazard classification – the hazard class and category assigned to a hazardous product based on the comparison of the properties of the hazardous product with the criteria for each hazard class in the HPR.

Hazardous combustion product – hazardous substance(s) formed when the product burns. These substances may be flammable, toxic, reactive and/or have other hazards.

Hazard statement – a required phrase assigned to a category or subcategory of a hazard class that describes the nature of the hazard presented by a hazardous product.

Hazardous decomposition product –hazardous substance(s) that may be released when a product breaks down, as a result of aging, exposure to oxygen, moisture, or heat, light, or electricity.

Hazardous ingredient – an ingredient in a mixture that, when evaluated as an individual substance according to the HPR, is classified in a category or subcategory of a health hazard class.

Hazardous product – a product, mixture, material or substance that meets the criteria to be classified in one or more of the hazard classes of the HPR.

Hazardous Products Act / Hazardous Products Regulations – The *Hazardous Products Regulations* (HPR) are Canadian federal regulations enabled by the *Hazardous Products Act* (HPA). They are part of the national Workplace Hazardous Materials Information System (WHMIS 2015), and replace the Controlled Products Regulations (CPR). The HPR applies to all Canadian suppliers (importers or sellers) of hazardous products intended for use, handling or storage in Canadian workplaces. The regulations specify the criteria for classification of hazardous products. They also specify what information must be included on labels and Safety Data Sheets (SDSs).

HAZWOPER: Hazardous Waste Operations and Emergency Response

Health hazards not otherwise classified (HHNOC) – hazardous products classified in this hazard class have a health hazard that is different from any other health hazard addressed in the HPR. These hazards must have the characteristic of occurring following acute or repeated exposure and having an adverse effect on the health of a person exposed to it, including an injury, or resulting in the death of that person. If a product is classified in this hazard class, the hazard statement on the label and SDS will describe the nature of the hazard.

Health professional – as defined by the *Hazardous Products Regulations*, are

1. physicians who are registered and entitled under the laws of a province to practice medicine and who are practicing medicine under those laws in that province; and

2. nurses who are registered or licensed under the laws of a province to practice nursing and who are practicing nursing under those laws in that province.

HPA – the *Hazardous Products Act*. See *"Hazardous Products Act / Hazardous Products Regulations"*.

HPR – the *Hazardous Products Regulations.* See *"Hazardous Products Act / Hazardous Products Regulations"*.

IARC – IARC stands for the International Agency for Research on Cancer. IARC is an agency of the World Health Organization. IARC evaluates information to identify environmental factors that can increase the risk of human cancer. These factors include chemicals, complex mixtures, occupational exposures, physical agents, biological agents and lifestyle factors. IARC publishes lists of agents which are classified as carcinogenic to humans (Group 1), probably carcinogenic to humans (Group 2A), possibly carcinogenic to humans (Group 2B), or not classifiable as to its carcinogenicity to humans (Group 3).

IDLH (Immediately Dangerous to Life and Health): The maximum levels to which a healthy worker can be exposed for 30 min to a chemical and escape without suffering irreversible health effects or escape impairing symptoms.

Ignition temperature: The minimum temperature at which a material will ignite without a spark or flame present. This is also the temperature the ignition source must be.

Immiscible: Matter that cannot be mixed. For example, water and gasoline are immiscible.

Incapacitating agent: An agent that produces physiological or mental effects or both that may persist for hours or days after exposure, rendering an individual incapable of performing his or her assigned duties.

Impervious –is a term used to describe protective gloves and other protective clothing. If a protective material is impervious to a substance, then that substance cannot readily penetrate through the material or damage the material. Different materials are impervious (resistant) to different substances. No single material is impervious to all substances. If a SDS recommends wearing impervious gloves, you need to know the specific type of material from which the gloves should be made.

Incompatibility: The inability to function or exist in the presence of something else, such as when a chemical will destroy the container.

Inert: A material that under normal temperatures and pressures does not react with other materials.

Inhibited: A substance that has had another substance added to prevent or deter its reaction either with other materials or itself (polymerization). This is usually used to deter polymerization.

Inhibitor: A substance that is capable of stopping or retarding a chemical reaction. To be technically useful, it must be effective in low concentration (i.e., to stop polymerization).

Initiator: The substance or molecule (other than reactant) that initiates a chain reaction, as in polymerization.

Inorganic: Pertaining to or composed of chemical compounds that do not contain carbon as the principal element (except carbonates, cyanides, and cyanates). Matter other than plant or animal.

Inorganic peroxides: Inorganic compounds containing an element at its highest state of oxidation (such as sodium peroxide), or having the peroxy group $-O-O-$ (such as perchloric acid).

Ion: An atom that possesses an electrical charge, either $(+)$ positive or $(-)$ negative.

Ionic bond: A chemical bond in which atoms of different elements transfer(exchange)electrons. As the electrons are exchanged, charged particles known as ions are formed.

Ionizing radiation: High-energy radiation, such as an x-ray, that causes the formation of ions in substances through which it passes (gamma rays). Excessive amounts of ionizing radiation will cause permanent genetic or bodily damage.

Irritant: A noncorrosive material that causes a reversible inflammatory effect on living tissue by chemical action at the site of contact.

Label – a group of written, printed or graphic information elements that relate to a hazardous product. The label is to be affixed to, printed on or attached to the hazardous product or the container in which the hazardous product is packaged.

Lacrimation: Secretion and discharge of tears.

LC50: Lethal concentration 50, median lethal concentration. The concentration of a material in air that on the basis of laboratory tests (respiratory route) is expected to kill 50% of a group of test animals when administered as a single exposure in a specific time period.

LD50: Lethal dose 50. The single dose of a substance that causes death of 50% of an animal population from exposure to the substance by any route other than inhalation.

Lethal chemical agent: An agent that may be used effectively in a field concentration to produce death.

Leachable: capable of being removed from a substance by a percolating

Liquid: A substance that is neither a solid nor a gas; a substance that flows freely, like water.

Lower explosive limit: The lowest concentration of gas or vapor (% by volume in air) that burns or explodes if an ignition source is present at ambient temperatures.

Low-order explosion: Materials that require excessive heat and reducing agents to initiate combustion.

Low-pressure container: A container designed to withstand pressures from 5 to 100 psi.

Maximum Use Concentration: MUC. The maximum concentration under which use of a respirator is permitted.

Median incapacitating dosage (ICT50): The volume of a chemical agent vapor or aerosol inhaled that is sufficient to disable 50% of exposed, unprotected people (expressed as mg-min/m3).

Median incapacitating dosage (LD50): The volume of a liquid chemical agent expected to incapacitate 50% of a group of exposed, unprotected individuals.

Median lethal dosage (LCT50): The dosage of a chemical-agent vapor or aerosol inhaled that is lethal to 50% of exposed, unprotected people (expressed as mg-min/m3).

Median lethal dosage (LD50): The amount of liquid chemical agent expected to kill 50% of a group of exposed, unprotected individuals.

Melting point: The degree of temperature at which a solid substance becomes a liquid, especially under the pressure of one atmosphere.

Miscible: Mixable in any and all proportions to form a uniform mixture. Water and alcohol are miscible; water and oil are not.

Mixture – a combination of, or a solution that is composed of, two or more ingredients that, when they are combined, do not react with each other. (This definition does not include any such combination or solution that is a substance. (See also "Substance")

Molecular formula: Shows the exact number of each atom in the molecule.

Molecular weight: The sum of the atomic weights of all the atoms in a molecule.

Molecule: The smallest possible particle of a chemical compound that can exist in the free state and still retain the characteristics of the substance. Molecules are made up of atoms of various elements that form the compound.

Monomer: A simple molecule capable of combining with a number of like or unlike molecules to form a polymer. It is a repeating structure unit within a polymer.

Mutagen: A material that induces genetic changes (mutations) in the DNA of chromosomes. Chromosomes are the "blueprints" of life within individual cells.

Mutagenicity – see Germ cell mutagenicity.

Narcosis: General and nonspecific reversible depression of neuronal excitability, produced by a number of physical and chemical agents, usually resulting in stupor rather than in anesthesia.

Necrosis: Cell or tissue death due to disease or injury.

Nerve agent: A substance that interferes with the central nervous system. Exposure is primarily through contact with the liquid (skin and eyes) and secondarily through inhalation of the vapor.

Neutralization: A chemical reaction used to remove H+ ions from acidic solutions and OH− ions from basic solutions. The reaction can be violent and usually produces water, a salt, heat, and many times, a gas.

NIOSH – NIOSH stands for National Institute for Occupational Safety and Health. NIOSH is a branch of the United States government. It is the mission of NIOSH to develop new knowledge in the field of occupational safety and health, and to transfer that knowledge into practice.

NOEL – NOEL stands for No Observable Effect Level.

Non persistent agent: An agent that remains in the target areas for a relatively short period of time. The hazard, predominantly vapor, will exist for minutes or, in exceptional cases, hours after dissemination of the agent. As a general rule, nonpersistent agent duration will be less than 12 h.

Normal: A solution that contains one equivalent of solute per liter of solution.

NOS – NOS stands for Not Otherwise Specified.

NTP – NTP stands for National Toxicology Program. This program is part of the United States Department of Health and Human Services. The NTP has a program for testing the potential short-term and long-term health effects, including the carcinogenicity, of chemicals.

Occupational exposure limit values or exposure limits – the airborne concentration of a substance that must not be exceeded in workplace air. Exposure limits have various names and often have different numerical values in different jurisdictions. In most Canadian provinces and territories, the exposure limits are called Occupational Exposure Limits (OELs). (See also "Control parameters" and "Threshold limit values (TLV®s)".)

There are three different types of exposure limits in common use:

- **Time-weighted average (TWA)** exposure limit is the time-weighted average concentration of a chemical in air for a conventional 8-hour workday, 40 hours a week, to which nearly all workers may be exposed day after day without harmful effects. "Time-weighted average" means that the average concentration has been calculated using the duration of exposure to different concentrations of the chemical during a specific time period (usually 8 hours). In this way, higher and lower exposures are averaged over the day or week.

- **Short-term exposure limit (STEL)** is the average concentration to which workers can be exposed for a short period (usually 15 minutes) without harmful effects. ACGIH specifically defines the harmful effects as irritation, long-term or irreversible tissue damage, reduced alertness or other toxic effects. The number of times the concentration reaches the STEL and the amount of time between these occurrences can also be restricted.

- **Ceiling (C)** is the concentration which should not be exceeded at any time.

Odour: A quality of something that affects the sense of smell; fragrance.

Odour threshold: The greatest dilution of a sample with odor-free water to yield the least definitely perceptible odor.

Organic: A material that comes from living plants or animals, such as waste or decay products. Distinguished from mineral matter. Organic chemistry deals with materials that contain the element carbon (C).

Organic peroxides: Any organic compound containing oxygen (O) in the bivalent –O–O–

structure and that may be considered a derivative of hydrogen peroxide, where one or more of the hydrogen atoms have been replaced by organic radicals.

OSHA – OSHA stands for Occupational Safety and Health Administration. It is the branch of the United States government which sets and enforces occupational health and safety legislation.

Over pack: An enclosure used by a single shipper to contain one or more packages which then forms one handling unit.

Oxidizer: A material that gives up oxygen easily, removes hydrogen from another com- pound, or attracts negative electrons (such as chlorine or fluorine), thus enhancing the combustion of other materials.

Oxidizing agent: A material that gains electrons from the fuel during combustion.

Oxygen deficient: Defined by OSHA as ambient air containing less than 19.5% oxygen concentration.

Oxygen enriched: Defined by OSHA as ambient air containing above 24% oxygen concentration.

PEL (permissible exposure limit): Term used by OSHA for its health standards covering exposures to hazardous chemicals. PEL generally relates to legally enforceable TLV limits.

Permissible Exposure Limit (PELs) are the legal occupational exposure limits in the United States set by the U.S. OSHA.

Persistency: An expression of the duration of effectiveness of a chemical agent, dependent on physical and chemical properties of the agent, weather, method of dissemination, and terrain conditions.

Persistent agent: An agent that remains in the target area for longer periods of time. Hazards from both vapor and liquids may exist for hours, days, or in exceptional cases, weeks or months after dissemination of the agent. As a general rule, persistent-agent duration will be greater than 12 h.

pH: The "power of hydrogen." A measure of the acidity or basicity of a solution, that is, of the concentration of H+ or OH− ions in solution. Scale ranges from 0 to 14, where a reading of 7 is neutral.

Physical properties: A property of matter that describes only its condition, not the way it reacts with other substances. Examples are size, density, color, and electrical conductivity.

Physical state – indicates whether a product is a solid, liquid or gas.

Pictogram – a graphical composition that includes a symbol along with other graphical elements, such as a border or background colour.

Poison: Any substance (solid, liquid, or gas) that, by reason of an inherent deleterious property, tends to destroy life or impair health.

Polar-solvent liquids: Those liquids that mix (are miscible with water).

Polymer: A long chain of molecules having extremely high molecular weights made up of many repeating smaller units called monomers or comonomers.

Polymerization: A chemical reaction in which small molecules combine to form larger molecules. A hazardous polymerization is a reaction that takes place at a rate that releases large amounts of energy that can cause fires or explosions or burst containers. Materials that can polymerize usually contain inhibitors that can delay the reaction.

Powder: A solid reduced to dust by pounding, crushing, or grinding.

ppm (parts per million): Parts of vapor or gas per million parts of contaminated air by volume at 25°C and 1 torr pressure.

Precautionary statement – a phrase that describes the recommended measures to take in order to minimize or prevent adverse effects resulting from exposure to a hazardous product or resulting from improper storage or handling of a hazardous product.

Pressure vessel: A tank or other container constructed so as to withstand interior pressure greater than that of the atmosphere.

psi: Pounds per square inch.

Pyrolysis: A chemical decomposition or breaking apart of molecules produced by heating in the absence of air.

Pyrophoric: Material that ignites spontaneously in air below 130°F (54°C). Occasionally caused by friction.

Pyrophoric gas: Gaseous materials that spontaneously ignite when exposed to air under ambient conditions. An example is trimethyl aluminum.

Pyrophoric liquid: Liquid materials that spontaneously ignite when exposed to air under ambient conditions.

Pyrophoric solid: Solid materials that spontaneously ignite when exposed to air under ambient conditions. An example is phosphorus.

RAD: Radiation-absorbed dose.

Radiation: Ionizing energy, either particulate or wave, that is spontaneously emitted by a material or combination of materials.

Radioactive material (DOT): Materials that emit ionizing radiation.

Radioactivity: Any process by which unstable nuclei increase their stability by emitting particles (alpha or beta) or gamma rays.

RCRA: Resource Conservation and Recovery Act (of 1976), which established a frame- work for the proper management and disposal of all wastes.

Reactivity: The force of which a chemical undergoes a reaction with an overall release of energy.

Reactivity –Describes the intrinsic ability of a product to undergo a hazardous chemical change (e.g., organic peroxide, oxidizer, self-reactive, pyrophoric, self-heating have the intrinsic ability to undergo a chemical change).

Readily combustible solid - powdered, granular, or pasty hazardous product that can be easily ignited by brief contact with an ignition source and, when ignited, has a flame that spread rapidly.

Recommended Exposure Limits (RELs) are the occupational exposure limits set by the U.S. NIOSH.

Reducing agent: A substance that gives electrons to (and thereby reduces) another substance.

Relative density –the ratio of the density of a substance to the density of a standard substance (usually water). This translates into the ratio of the weight of a product to the weight of an equal volume of water. Products with a relative density greater than 1 are heavier than water. Products with a relative density less than 1 are lighter than water.

Reproductive toxicity – hazardous products classified in this hazard class may damage or are suspected of damaging fertility and/or the unborn child (baby) after exposure to a mixture or substance. This hazard class has an additional category for products that may cause harm to breast-fed children. Reproductive toxicity refers to:

- adverse effects on sexual function and fertility

- adverse effects on the development of the embryo, fetus, or offspring, or

- effects on or via lactation

Respiratory asphyxiant: A material that prevents or reduces the available oxygen necessary for normal breathing. Divided into simple and chemical asphyxiants.

Respiratory dosage: This is equal to the time in minutes an individual is unmasked in an agent cloud multiplied by the concentration of the cloud.

Respiratory sensitizers – hazardous products classified as Respiratory sensitizers, as part of the Respiratory or Skin Sensitization hazard class, are liable (likely) to lead to hypersensitivity (increased sensitivity) of the airways following inhalation of a mixture or substance.

Roentgen: The amount of ionization that occurs per cubic centimeter of air.

Routes of exposure: Ways in which chemicals get in contact with or enter the body. These are inhalation, absorption, ingestion, or injection.

RTECS® – RTECS® stands for Registry of Toxic Effects of Chemical Substances.

SADT: See Self-accelerating decomposition temperature.

SARA: The Superfund Amendments and Reauthorization Act of 1986. Title III of SARA includes detailed provisions for community planning.

Safety Data Sheet (SDS) – a document that contains specified, required information about a hazardous product, including information related to the hazards associated with any use, handling, or storage of the hazardous product in a workplace.

SDS: Safety Data Sheet

Self-accelerating decomposition temperature (SADT): Organic peroxides or other synthetic chemicals that decompose at ambient temperature, or react to light or heat, resulting in a chemical breakdown. This releases oxygen, energy, and fuel in the form of rapid fire or explosion. To ensure stabilization, these materials must be kept in a dark or refrigerated environment.

Self-heating substances and mixtures –hazardous products classified in this hazard class are solid or liquid products that self-heat and consequently may catch fire, or that may catch fire when in large quantities. These products are liable to self-heat by reaction with air and without energy supply. They differ from pyrophoric substances in that they will ignite only after a longer period of time or when in large amounts.

Self-reactive substances and mixtures – hazardous products classified in this hazard class may cause a fire or explosion if heated. These products are liable to undergo a strongly exothermic (producing heat and energy) decomposition, having a heat of decomposition equal to or greater than 300 J/g, even without participation of oxygen.

Sensitizer: A substance that on first exposure causes little or no reaction in humans or test animals, but that on repeated exposure may cause a marked response not necessarily limited to the contact site.

Serious eye damage/eye irritation – see "Serious eye damage" and/or "Eye irritation".

Serious eye damage – hazardous products classified for Serious eye damage, as part of the Serious Eye Damage/Eye Irritation hazard class, can produce tissue damage in the eye or serious physical decay of vision occurring after exposure of the eye to a mixture or substance that is irreversible or not fully reversed within 21 days. Effects could include permanently impaired vision or blindness.

Simple asphyxiant: A material that replaces the amount of oxygen admitted into the body without further damage to tissue or poisoning. Examples are nitrogen and carbon dioxide.

Slurry: A pourable mixture of solid and liquid.

Skin irritation – hazardous products that classify for Skin irritation, as part of the Skin Corrosion/Irritation hazard class, are liable (likely) to produce reversible damage to the skin occurring after exposure to a mixture or substance. Effects could include redness, itching, or swelling.

Skin sensitizers – hazardous products that classify as Skin sensitizers, as part of the Respiratory or Skin Sensitization hazard class, may cause an allergic response after skin contact with a mixture or substance.

Solid: The state of matter having definite volume and rigid shapes. Its atoms or molecules are restricted to vibration only.

Solubility: The ability of a substance to form a solution with another substance.

Solution: Theevendispersion(mixing)ofmoleculesoftwoormoresubstances.Themost commonly encountered solutions involve mixing of liquids and liquids or solids and liquids.

Solvent: A substance, usually a liquid, capable of absorbing another liquid, gas, or solid to form a homogeneous mixture.

Specific gravity: The weight of a solid or liquid substance as compared to the weight of an equal volume of water; specific gravity of water equals 1.

Specific target organ toxicity (STOT) – Repeated exposure – hazardous products classified in this hazard class cause or may cause damage to organs (e.g., liver, kidneys or blood) following prolonged or repeated exposure to the product.

Specific target organ toxicity (STOT) – Single exposure – hazardous products classified in this hazard class cause or may cause damage to organs (e.g., liver, kidneys, or blood) following a single exposure to the product. This hazard class also includes a category for products that cause transient (temporary) respiratory irritation, or transient (temporary) drowsiness or dizziness.

Specific target organ toxicity arising from a single exposure to a hazardous product means specific, non-lethal toxic effects on target organs that arise from a single exposure to a hazardous product including all health effects liable to impair function of the body or any of its parts, whether reversible or irreversible, immediate or delayed. This hazard class excludes health hazards addressed by the Acute toxicity, Skin corrosion/irritation, Serious eye damage/eye irritation, Respiratory or skin sensitization, Germ cell mutagenicity, Carcinogenicity, Reproductive toxicity or Aspiration hazard classes.

Spontaneous combustion: A process by which heat is generated within material by either a slow oxidation reaction or by microorganisms.

Spontaneous ignition: Ignition that can occur when certain materials, such as tung oil, are stored in bulk, resulting from the generation of heat, which cannot be readily dissipated; often heat is generated by microbial action.

Spontaneous ignition temperature: See Ignition temperature.

States of matter: Any of three physical forms of matter: solid, liquid, or gas.

STEL - STEL stands for Short-Term Exposure Limit. (See Occupational exposure limit values.)

Strength (acid/base): The amount of ionization that occurs when an acid or a base is dis- solved in a liquid.

Sublimation: The direct change of state from solid to vapor.

Substances and mixtures which, in contact with water, emit flammable gases – hazardous products classified in this hazard class react with water to release flammable gases. In some cases, the flammable gases may ignite spontaneously (very quickly). These products are liquids and solids that, by interaction with water, are liable to become spontaneously flammable or give off flammable gases in dangerous quantities.

Symbol: Letters used to identify each element. The symbol for an element represents a definite weight (1 atomic weight) of that element.

Systemic toxicity: Poisoning of the whole system or organism, rather than poisoning that affects, for example, a single organ.

Target organ: The primary organ to which specific chemicals cause harm. Examples are the lungs, liver, or kidneys.

TDG: Transportation of Dangerous Goods

Temperature: Measure of the vibratory rate of a molecule.

Teratogen: Material that affects the offspring when a developing embryo or fetus is exposed to that material.

Threshold limit values (TLV®s) – airborne concentrations of substances to which it is believed that nearly all workers may be exposed day after day without experiencing adverse effects. ACGIH® develops these values.

TLV: Threshold limit value, estimated exposure value, below which no ill health effects should occur to the individual.

Toxic: Harmful, poisonous.

Toxicity: The ability of a substance to cause damage to living tissue, impairment of the central nervous system, severe illness, or death when ingested, inhaled, or absorbed by the skin.

Toxins: Toxic substance of natural origin produced by an animal, plant, or microbe. They differ from chemical substances in that they are not manmade. Toxins may include botulism, ricin, and mycotoxins.

Transportation of Dangerous Goods **(TDG)** – federal legislation that controls the conditions under which dangerous goods may be transported on public roads, in the air, by rail or by ship. Its purpose is to protect the health and safety of persons in the vicinity of transport accidents involving those goods.

TWA – TWA stands for Time-Weighted Average. (See "Occupational exposure limit values".)

UN number – the four-digit identification number issued in accordance with the United Nations Model Regulations.

Upper explosive limit: The maximum fuel-to-air mixture in which combustion can occur.

Upper explosive limit (UEL) or Upper flammability limit (UFL) – the maximum concentration of a product in air that will burn or explode when it is exposed to a source of ignition. At concentrations greater than the UEL, the mixture is "too rich" to burn or explode. The UEL is the same as the UFL. (See also "Lower explosive limit (LEL) or Lower flammability limit (LFL)".)

Urticant: A chemical agent that produces irritation at the point of contact, resembling a stinging sensation, such as a bee sting. For example, the initial physiological effects of phosgene oxime (CX) upon contact with a person's skin.

Vapour – the gaseous form of a mixture or substance released from its liquid or solid state.

Vapour density: The weight of a vapor or gas compared to the weight of an equal volume of air; an expression of the density of the vapor or gas calculated as the ratio of the molecule weight of the gas to the average molecule weight of air, which is 29. Materials lighter than air have vapor densities less than 1.

Vapour pressure: The pressure exerted by a saturated vapor above its own liquid in a closed container. Vapor pressure reported on MSDS is in millimeters of mercury at 68°F (20°C), unless stated otherwise.

Vapours: Molecules of liquid in air; moisture, such as steam, fog, mist, etc., often forming a cloud suspended or floating in the air, usually due to the effect of heat upon a liquid.

Ventilation – the movement of air, which is intended to remove contaminated air from the work place. There are several different kinds of ventilation.

Vesicant: Chemical agents also called blister agents, that cause severe burns to eyes, skin, and tissues of the respiratory tract. Also referred to as mustard agents, examples include mustard and lewisite.

Violent reaction: The action by which a chemical changes its composition near or exceeding the speed of sound, often releasing heat and gases.

Virus: The simplest type of microorganism, lacking a system for its own metabolism. It depends on living cells to multiply and cannot live long outside of a host. Types of viruses are smallpox, Ebola, Marburg, and Lassa fever.

Viscosity: The measurement of the flow properties of a material expressed as its resistance to flow. Unit of measurement and temperature are included.

VOC – VOC stands for Volatile Organic Compound.

Volatility: The ease by which a chemical evaporates at normal temperature. High vapour pressure at normal temperatures is referred to as volatile.

Vomiting agent: Compounds that cause irritation of the upper respiratory tract and involuntary vomiting.

Water-reactive material: A material that will decompose or react when exposed to moisture or water.

Water solubility: The ability of a substance to mix with water.

WHMIS – WHMIS stands for Workplace Hazardous Materials Information System. WHMIS is Canada's national hazard communication system for hazardous products in the work place. It applies to suppliers, importers, and distributors of hazardous products that are sold in or imported into Canada and intended for use, handling or storage in Canadian work places. WHMIS applies - as well to the employers and workers who use those products.

WHMIS 1988 – The original WHMIS system enacted in 1988 through the *Hazardous Products* Act and the *Controlled Products Regulations* is now referred to as "WHMIS 1988".

WHMIS 2015 – On February 11, 2015, the Government of Canada published the *Hazardous Products Regulations* (HPR), which, in addition to the amendments made to the *Hazardous*

Products Act (HPA), modified WHMIS 1988 to incorporate the GHS for workplace chemicals. This modified WHMIS was referred to as WHMIS 2015 until December 15, 2022, when WHMIS was again amended. The current terminology is WHMIS.

About The Author

Bart Taylor worked as a hazardous materials specialist throughout Canada and the United States for over 30 years. He earned his Bachelors degree in Chemistry while working full time and has spent his entire career creating and delivering industry based training videos and seminars that are easily understood and digestible for any audience. Bart grew up in Moosomin Saskatchewan and now resides in beautiful Calgary Alberta. He loves spending his time with family and his dogs, great coffee, riding motorcycles, and playing his beloved drums.